NEUES MUSEUM NÜ

BORIS LURIE

ANTI-POP

VERLAG FÜR MODERNE KUNST

Inhalt

4 Grußwort
Gertrude Stein

6 Vorwort
Eva Kraus

16 Boris Lurie: Our only master is truth
Eckhart Gillen

30 Abbildungen
mit Texten von Claudia Marquardt
und Thomas Heyden

130 Boris Lurie: Um im Angesicht
des Negativen zu verweilen.
Der Holocaust und das Problem
der visuellen Repräsentation
Peter Weibel

170 Around Lurie
Thomas Heyden

202 Liste der ausgestellten Werke

208 Biografie

210 Dank

214 Impressum

Content

5 Foreword
Gertrude Stein

7 Preface
Eva Kraus

17 Boris Lurie: Our only master is truth
Eckhart Gillen

31 Illustrations
with texts by Claudia Marquardt and Thomas Heyden

131 Boris Lurie: Tarrying with the Negative. The Holocaust and the Problem of Visual Representation
Peter Weibel

171 Around Lurie
Thomas Heyden

202 List of exhibited works

207 Biography

211 Acknowledgement

214 Imprint

Grußwort

Gertrude Stein

Das Gestern ist Geschichte.
Das Morgen ist ein Mysterium.
Die Gegenwart ist ein Geschenk.

Das war das Leben von Boris.

Die Geschichte war der erste und schwierige Teil seines Lebens. Er hat es geschafft, mit dem schwierigen Teil seines Lebens klarzukommen und konnte ihn überwinden.

Das Morgen ist ein Mysterium. Der Traum von Boris war die Zukunft, um Kunstwerke zu hinterlassen, die Einfluss auf eine bessere und freundlichere Welt haben.

Das Heute ist ein Geschenk. Die Ausstellung, die Sie sehen, ist ein wunderbares Geschenk für Boris, deshalb würde er es als Gegenwart bezeichnen.

Danke für Ihr Kommen und dass Sie an dieser großartigen Ausstellung in diesem großartigen Museum teilnehmen.

Schumann hatte Clara.
Van Gogh hatte Theo.
Lurie hat Gertrude.

Foreword

Gertrude Stein

Yesterday is history.
Tomorrow is mystery.
The present is a gift.

This is what Boris' life was about.

Yesterday was the early and difficult part of his life. He was able to deal with the difficulties and overcome them.

Tomorrow is a mystery. Tomorrow was the dream of Boris to have left behind works of art that would be influential in having a better and gentler world.

Today is a gift. The show that you are seeing is a great gift to Boris that is why it is called the present.

Thanks for your being here to share in this magnificent exhibit at this magnificent museum.

Schumann had Clara.
Van Gogh had Theo.
Lurie has Gertrude.

Boris Lurie Anti-Pop

Vorwort

Eva Kraus

„Dennoch – und tief in uns drin wissen wir das alle, egal was die Zyniker sagen – wird große Kunst nicht durch Gehorsam, Coolsein, Distanziertheit, Apathie oder Langeweile erzeugt. Das Erfolgsgeheimnis aller Kunst ist das, was am schwersten zu lernen ist: nämlich Mut.“[1]

Boris Lurie sagte Nein. Dieses NO visualisiert sich bei ihm auf medial unterschiedliche Weise und steht symbolisch für ein radikales Werk, das er hinterlassen hat, ein Werk, das sich dem bürgerlichen Kunstbegriff entgegensetzte, ein Werk, das sich formalästhetischen Konventionen entzog. Es ist eine klare Negation, als Mahnmal gegen die Verdrängung der historischen Ereignisse zu verstehen, die Boris Lurie selbst als junger Mensch erleben musste. Das NO diente als bildliches Signal seines Protests gegen jegliche Form von Unterdrückung. Luries Ablehnung galt auch der Ästhetisierung, der Affirmation im Kunstbetrieb, der Kommerzialisierung in seiner neuen „Heimat“, den Vereinigten Staaten von Amerika. Er richte sich gegen die „scheinheilige Intelligenz, die kapitalistische Manipulation der Kultur, die Konsumgesellschaft und andere Moloche“,[2] meinte Lurie selbst. Seine Kunst war eine „satirische Unabhängigkeitserklärung von allem oberflächlich Alltäglichen.“[3]

Lurie bezeichnete sich mitunter als „Judenhund“, als „Lumpenproletariat“. Seine Kunst nannte er ironischerweise selbst „Jew Art“, auch wenn seine Familie (oder das, was davon noch übrig geblieben war) säkulare Juden waren. „Man betrachtete uns in der Kunstwelt als Zyniker“, sagte er einst, „als einen Haufen wildgewordener Straßenkehrer, der sich an jeder Hässlichkeit berauschte.“[4] Unerbittlich hatte er sich gegen das zur Wehr gesetzt, was ihm unehrlich erschien. Kein Geringerer als der Künstler George Grosz war es, der ihn darin beeinflusste, seinen traumatischen Erfahrungen künstlerischen Ausdruck zu verleihen. Diese waren durch den Holocaust bestimmt. Als Kind russischer Eltern wurde Boris 1924 in Leningrad[5] geboren, in Riga war er aufgewachsen. Seine Mutter, seine Großmutter, eine der Schwestern und seine Jugendliebe wurden am 8. Dezember 1941 im lettischen Rumbula bei einer der größten Vernichtungsaktionen durch die Nazis getötet. Als Überlebender des Rigaer Ghettos und mehrerer Konzentrationslager – u. a. Kaiserwald, Stutthof und zuletzt Buchenwald – wurde er 1945 befreit.

Lurie war weitestgehend Autodidakt. Die Grundlagen seiner bildnerischen Erziehung erwarb er in seinen Jahren in den deutschen Konzentrationslagern. Als 22-Jähriger wanderte er 1946 mit seinem Vater nach New York aus, wo er trotz seiner Aversionen der amerikanischen Gesellschaft gegenüber bis zu seinem Tod im Jahr 2008 bleiben sollte. Seine erste Einzelausstellung fand 1950 in der Creative Gallery statt, *Dismembered Women* stellte er 1951 in der Barbizon Plaza Gallery aus, Ende der 1950er Jahre gründete er gemeinsam mit Sam Goodman und Stanley Fisher die March Group in der gleichnamigen Galerie in der 10th Street in Manhattan – die für „Andersdenkende aller Schattierungen war. Andersdenkende unter dem herrschenden politischen Druck.“[6] Aus diesen Aktivitäten ist bald die NO!art entstanden, ein loses Kollektiv der zumeist jüdischen Künstlerschaft in New York, das von 1959 bis 1964 aktiv war und alsbald schon mit Ausstellungen uptown in der Galerie von Gertrude Stein gastierte. Die NO!art-Künstler forderten einen politischen Anspruch der Kunst in einer Zeit, die noch immer geprägt durch die McCarthy-Ära, getrieben vom Kapitalismus, den American Way of Life zelebrierte, eine heile Welt

Boris Lurie Anti-Pop

Preface

Eva Kraus

"But, as we all know deep down, it is not by submission, coolness, remoteness, apathy, and boredom that great art is created, no matter what the cynics might tell us. The secret ingredient of all art is what is most difficult to learn, it is courage."[1]

Boris Lurie said NO. In his work, this NO is visualized in different media, symbolizing the radical oeuvre he left behind, an oeuvre that opposed the bourgeois definition of art and eschewed formal aesthetic conventions. It is a clear negation, to be understood as a warning against repression of the historical events which Boris Lurie himself had to experience as a young person. The NO served as a pictorial signal of his protest against every form of oppression. Lurie also rejected aestheticization, the affirmation of the art business, the commercialism of his new "home," the United States of America. In Lurie's own words, he was fighting against "the hypocritical intelligentsia, capitalist culture manipulation, consumerism, American and other molochs."[2] His art was a "satirical declaration of independence against the shallow common place."[3]

Lurie sometimes referred to himself as "Jew dog," as "lumpen proletariat." He ironically called his own art "Jew Art," even though his family (or what was left of it) were secular Jews. "The cognoscenti considered us cynics about art," he wrote, "feasting on all ugliness like a bunch of savage scavengers."[4] He ruthlessly opposed what he perceived as dishonest. In giving artistic expression to his traumatic experiences during the Holocaust, he was influenced by none other than George Grosz.

Born to Russian parents in 1924 in Leningrad,[5] Lurie grew up in Riga. His mother, his grandmother, one of his sisters, and his teenage girlfriend were murdered by the Nazis on December 8, 1941, in Rumbula, Latvia, during a large-scale extermination campaign. As a survivor of the Riga ghetto and several concentration camps – including Kaiserwald, Stutthof, and finally Buchenwald – he was liberated in 1945.

Lurie was largely an autodidact. His basic artistic training was acquired during his years in the camps. In 1946, aged 22, he emigrated with his father to New York where, in spite of his aversion to American society, he was to remain until his death in 2008. His first exhibition took place in 1950 at Creative Gallery. In 1951 he showed his *Dismembered Women* at Barbizon Plaza Gallery. At the end of the 1950s, with Sam Goodman and Stanley Fisher, he founded the March Group in the gallery of the same name on 10th Street in Manhattan – for "social dissidents of varying stripes" under "the obvious political pressures" of the time.[6] These activities soon gave rise to NO!art, a loose-knit collective of mostly Jewish artists in New York that was active from 1959 through 1964, and which had exhibitions uptown at Gallery Gertrude Stein. The NO!artists made political art in a time that was still marked by the McCarthy era and driven by capitalism, that celebrated the American way of life and projected an idyllic world, and that relentlessly combatted communism in the Cold War. The politicization of society had not yet taken place. Under these conditions, Lurie became an artistic personality with chutzpah who made bold public statements. In a way, NO!art prefigured the concerns of the counterculture of the late 1960s. It adopted a critical position with regard to Abstract Expressionism. One might describe it as a politically committed version of Pop Art. From

vorgaukelte und im Kalten Krieg unnachgiebig den Kommunismus bekämpfte. Die gesellschaftliche Politisierung war noch nicht vollzogen. Unter diesen Voraussetzungen formierte sich in Boris Lurie eine Künstlerpersönlichkeit, die „Chuzpe“ hatte, sich öffentlich kontrovers äußerte. Gewissermaßen nahm die NO!art die Anliegen der Gegenkultur der späteren sechziger Jahre vorweg. Sie positionierte sich kritisch gegenüber dem Abstrakten Expressionismus. Man könnte sie als engagierte, politisierte Version der Pop-Art einordnen. Ab 1962 kam der Begriff „Anti-Pop“ auf, und es wurde gegen die bildinhaltlichen Konventionen der Pop-Art gearbeitet, selbst wenn deren wachsender Einfluss auch bei Lurie ästhetische Spuren hinterließ.

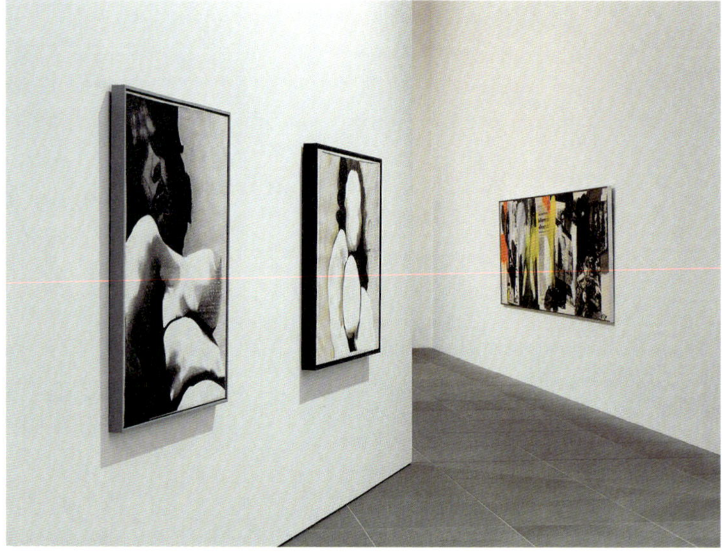

Boris Lurie. Anti-Pop,
Neues Museum Nürnberg

Im Lichte des vorherrschenden „Formalismus“ erschien die Kunst Luries jedoch als unanständig, schmuddelig und ekelhaft. Er prahlte damit, dass seine Kunst von „Pin-ups zu Exkrementen“ reichen würde. Seine Collagen bestanden aus unzähligen Girls, deren Vorlagen aus Sex-Illustrierten-Geschäften von der 42. Straße kamen. Zunächst umgaben sie ihn in seinem Studio, bevor sie auf die Leinwände wanderten – „was an den Wänden hing, wurde zu Bildern“[7] –, und entwickelten sich zum doppeldeutigen Sinnbild für die ihm so verhasste, heuchlerische Prüderie wie auch für seine Frustration darüber, dass selbst Sexualität und Liebe in seiner neuen Lebensrealität durch merkantile Interessen gesteuert wurden. „American-Reality-Sandwiches“ nannte Jean-Jacques Lebel, ein Freund und europäischer Mitstreiter, treffend die Pin-up-Collagen von Lurie.[8] Die Exkremente manifestierten sich in plastischer Form als Scheißehaufen, die in der NO Sculpture Show (1964), später in Shit Show umbenannt, ihren Höhepunkt fanden. Luries Kunst war nicht nur Anti-Pop, sondern auch Anti-Kunst im Sinne der Verweigerung, dass nicht Nichts gemacht werden sollte, aber eine klare Übereinkunft darin bestand, dass jegliche Ablehnung der konventionellen Vorstellungen von Kunst zum Ausdruck kam. „Meine Kunst ist eine Art von Extremer Expressionismus, Selfexpressionism, kombiniert mit sozialen und politischen Ideen – und ein wenig Neo-Dada“, meinte Lurie.[9] Anfügen könnte man hier noch seine Nähe zur Fluxus-Bewegung, mit der ihn jenseits stilistischer Parallelen seine lebenslange Freundschaft zu Wolf Vostell verband.

Luries größtes Vermächtnis war seine Auseinandersetzung mit dem Holocaust in der visuellen Kultur. Die Ästhetisierung der Bilder des Grauens schien lange ausgeschlossen, und doch hat Lurie einen Ansatz gewagt und insbesondere mit den *Saturation Paintings* das unlösbare Problem gelöst, Kunst „nach Auschwitz“ (Theodor W. Adorno) zu machen. Zu den schockierendsten und gleichzeitig auch schärfsten Beiträgen zählen jene Collagen, in denen er pornografische Abbildungen mit Aufnahmen der Vernichtungsaktionen kombinierte. Ein Moment der (negativen) Inspiration dabei war die Vereinigung der Bildwelten des Holocausts in den auflagenstärksten Magazinen wie u. a. *Time*, *Newsweek* und *Life*[10] mit den direkt in Nachbarschaft stehenden Werbeanzeigen für Konsumprodukte, Anzeigen für Kosmetik, Unterwäsche etc. – das war für ihn wahre Pornografie, der Exhibitionismus des Lebens. Lurie sezierte den Begriff des Obszönen. Hintergrund dafür ist sicherlich die tief greifende Erfahrung der Verbindung von Macht und sexueller Erniedrigung, die in der Praxis der Nazis auf Demüti-

1962, the term "Anti-Pop" came into use and the pictorial conventions of Pop Art were combatted, even if its growing influence also affected Lurie in aesthetic terms.

In the context of the prevailing "formalism" of the time, however, Lurie's art appeared obscene, filthy, and revolting. He boasted that it ranged from "pin-ups to excrement." His collages consist of countless "girlies" from magazines purchased in sex shops on 42nd Street. At first they surrounded him in his studio, before moving onto his canvases – "paintings started coming off the walls"[7] – where they became an ambiguous symbol of the hypocritical prudishness he so hated and of his frustration over the fact that in his new environment, commercial interests influenced even love and sexuality. Jean-Jacques Lebel, a friend and European collaborator of Lurie's, called his pin-up collages "American reality sandwiches."[8] The excrement manifested itself in sculptural form as piles of shit, culminating in the NO Sculpture Show (1964), later renamed Shit Show. Lurie's art was not just anti-Pop, but also anti-art – in a spirit of refusal, not that nothing at all should be created, but with a clear understanding that rejection of all conventional notions of art would be expressed. "My art is a kind of extreme expressionism, self-expressionism," he said, "combined with social and political ideas – plus a bit of neo-dada."[9] One could also mention his affinity to the Fluxus movement, to which he was connected beyond stylistic parallels through his life-long friendship with Wolf Vostell.

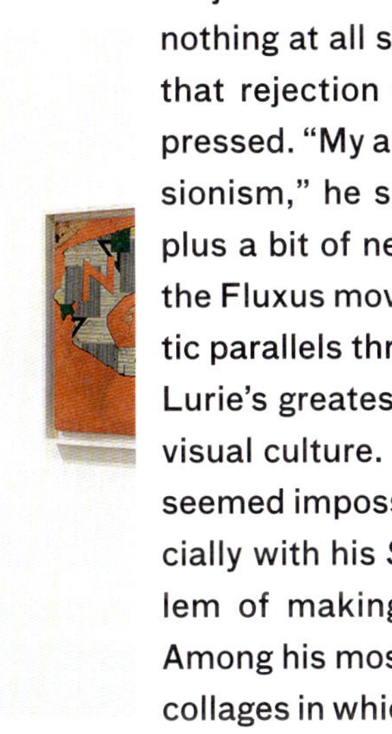

Boris Lurie. Anti-Pop,
Neues Museum Nürnberg

Lurie's greatest legacy is his engagement with the Holocaust in visual culture. For a long time, aestheticizing images of atrocity seemed impossible, but Lurie forged a bold approach and, especially with his *Saturation Paintings,* solved the unsolvable problem of making art "after Auschwitz" (Theodor W. Adorno). Among his most shocking but also most trenchant works are the collages in which he combines pornographic imagery with photographs of Holocaust victims. One source of (negative) inspiration for this came from the way high-circulation magazines like *Time, Newsweek,* and *Life*[10] printed images of the concentration camps alongside adverts for consumer goods, cosmetics, lingerie, etc., which he saw as the true pornography, the exhibitionism of life. Lurie dissected the concept of the obscene, based on his profound experience of the combination of power and sexual degradation practiced by the Nazis in order to humiliate – as in the unimaginable scenes with naked victims on their way to their deaths. In this light, Lurie's accumulations of female bodies can also be read as mass graves. In collages using sadomasochist imagery, the "bootlickers" also create a double echo. "We meant to show, draw attention to, underline the vulgarity within us quite as much as the vulgarity around us."[11] The outrageous parallelism with which images of atrocities coexist with the everyday, and in Lurie's case even with casual sexuality, could be understood in terms of the "banality of evil" (Hannah Arendt). After the initial shock, however, even images of horror are subject to the "saturation effect" (Susan Sontag), as revulsion over and memory of what one has seen soon fade. "Can it happen again?" is written on one collage in which a photograph from Buchenwald is encircled by pin-ups. The piercing gazes of the concentration camp prisoners are directed at us as viewers, but also at society in general. This question captures Lurie's life-long endeavor against forgetting – and thus against any repetition of history.

gung abzielte. In diese Kerbe schlagen die unvorstellbaren Bilder der entblößten, dem Tode geweihten Opfer vor der Hinrichtung, auf dem Weg in die Gaskammer. So sind seine Akkumulationen von Frauenleibern auch als Massengräber zu verstehen. Die „Stiefellecker" sind es darüber hinaus, die in Luries Werken mit sadomasochistischen Bildinhalten ein doppeltes Echo erzeugen. „Wir wollten das Vulgäre in uns genauso anprangern, wie das Vulgäre um uns herum."[11] Im Sinne der „Banalität des Bösen" (Hannah Arendt) kann vielleicht die schier unfassbare Parallelität verstanden werden, mit der die Bildwelten des Grauens gleichzeitig auf größte „Alltäglichkeit", bei Lurie sogar auf sexuelle Unbekümmertheit, stoßen. Jedoch unterliegen die Darstellungen von Grausamkeit nach anfänglichem Schock auch dem „Sättigungseffekt" (Susan Sontag), die Übelkeit und die Erinnerung an das Gesehene fällt rapide schnell. „Can it happen again?" liest man auf einer Collage, bei der Lurie eine Abbildung aus Buchenwald mit Pin-ups umringt. Die bohrenden Blicke der KZ-Häftlinge sind auf uns als Betrachter, aber auch auf die Gesellschaft an sich gerichtet. Mit dieser Frage formuliert sich Luries lebenslanges Bemühen, dem Vergessen – und damit der Wiederholung – entgegenzuwirken.

Eine Würdigung seiner Kunst, aber auch seines Engagements durch die Kunst hatte Lurie zu Lebzeiten kaum erfahren – auch wenn man annehmen könnte, dass der künstlerische Durchbruch längst mit Ausstellungen der zwei damals wichtigsten europäischen Galeristen, Arturo Schwarz 1962 und René Block 1973, hätte erfolgen können. Die unbeugsame Art von Lurie und seinen Mitstreitern stand einer stringenten Karriere auf dem Kunstmarkt entgegen, und so wurde diese besser abgelehnt: „Ich scheiß darauf", war der unmissverständliche Refrain der Shit Show (1964). Die „Unmodernen" betitelte der Kritiker Seymour Krim die Beteiligten der NO!art.[12] Die Ästhetik der sozialen Kritik war Anfang der 1960er Jahre wenig populär, politischer Aktivismus damals noch nicht in Mode. Als „Künstler-Künstler" bezeichnete ihn der Künstler und Kunsttheoretiker Peter Weibel viel später – von seinen Kollegen anerkannt, wenn auch vom Kunstmarkt ignoriert. Der Happening-Künstler Allan Kaprow meinte: „Boris Lurie erweist sich (wieder) als der wichtige Pionier, der uns über unser kollektives Bewußtsein aufklärte."[13]

Mit der Ausstellung im Neuen Museum möchten wir eine Rezeptionslücke schließen, da Luries Werk bis heute unterrepräsentiert geblieben ist (wenn auch zugleich ein starker Aufschwung dank der wachsenden Aktivitäten der posthum gegründeten Boris Lurie Art Foundation verzeichnet wird). In den vergangenen Jahrzehnten stand – bis auf seine Einladung 1995 in die Neue Gesellschaft für Bildende Kunst nach Berlin – Luries Schicksal im Vordergrund der Ausstellungen: 1999 wurde er ins Kölner NS-Dokumentationszentrum noch persönlich eingeladen. In der Gedenkstätte Buchenwald zeigte man ihn 2014, im Jüdischen Museum Berlin war er 2016 zu Gast. Bei uns wird er als bildender Künstler präsentiert, der durch seinen zentralen Beitrag zur Suche nach adäquaten künstlerischen Ausdrucksmitteln für virulente Themen in einer Institution für zeitgenössische Kunst große Aufmerksamkeit verdient. Um seine Leistungen vor dem Hintergrund des kunsthistorischen Kontexts in Erinnerung zu bringen, zeigen wir Luries Werk gemeinsam mit seinen Wegbegleitern und Zeitgenossen.

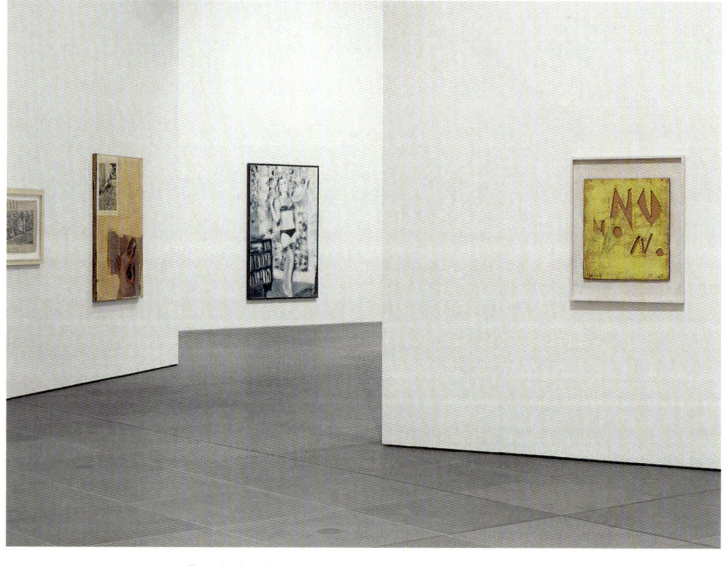

Boris Lurie. Anti-Pop,
Neues Museum Nürnberg

Lurie's art received little recognition during his lifetime, and the same applies to his engagement through art – even if shows with two of Europe's most important gallerists at the time, Arturo Schwarz in 1962 and René Block in 1973, could, one might think, have led to a breakthrough. The unrelenting stance of Lurie and his colleagues was at odds with a straightforward career in the art market, so it made more sense to reject that market: "I couldn't care less" was the unmistakable refrain of the Shit Show (1964). Critic Seymour Krim referred to the NO!-artists as a "group of unfashionables."[12] In the early 1960s, the aesthetic of social critique was not popular, political activism not yet in vogue. Much later, artist and art theorist Peter Weibel called him an "artist's artist" – acknowledged by his fellow artists but ignored by the market. And for Happening artist Allan Kaprow: "Boris Lurie proves himself (once again) to be the key pioneer who explained our collective consciousness to us."[13]

With this exhibition at Neues Museum, we aim to fill a gap in reception, as Lurie's oeuvre has remained underrepresented to this day (in spite of a sharp upturn thanks to the activities of the posthumously established Boris Lurie Art Foundation). In recent years, apart from an invitation to the Neue Gesellschaft für Bildende Kunst in Berlin in 1995, the focus in terms of exhibitions has been on Lurie's biography: in 1999, he was invited to appear in person at the NS-Documentation Center of the City of Cologne. His work was shown at the Buchenwald Memorial in 2014, and at Berlin's Jewish Museum in 2016. In our exhibition, he is presented as a fine artist whose key contribution to the search for adequate artistic means of expression for pressing themes fully merits the attention of an institution of contemporary art. In order to highlight his achievements against the backdrop of the art historical context, Lurie is being shown together with his companions and contemporaries.

In spite of this focus on Lurie's art, Nuremberg is also the right place to pay homage to him as a person. In the city of the Nazi Party Rallies – but also the city of the Nuremberg Trials and the City of Human Rights – we bear a special responsibility in dealing with our own history. For Neues Museum, the request from the Boris Lurie Art Foundation to cooperate on an exhibition was a welcome opportunity to present a life's work that deals like no other with the dark legacy of the Holocaust in fine art.

Were art not to deal with the greatest crime in human history, then in Lurie's view this would have left a vacuum in art history, and to him personally it would have felt like self-deception. The ignorance of (American) society concerning the Holocaust was what prompted him to devote his entire creative output to this theme. This probably also served to process a long-lasting trauma, even if his cynicism actually caused him to appear unbroken. In New York, Lurie created his own ghetto where even in later years, free of financial worries, he would still hoard food, living simply and rejecting wasteful consumerism. He was a nonconformist and made a point of defying each and every aesthetic expectation. By nature he was radical and courageous, authentic and thus credible. He was not like the others – which defines the concept of "degenerate art."[14] Ultimately, he was vilified throughout his working life as an artist and he celebrated his role as an outsider. As a witness to the inconceivable, he tried to do justice to his memories – in order to create images of the unimaginable. In his own way.

Trotz des Fokus auf die Kunst Luries, ist Nürnberg der richtige Ort, ihn auch als Person zu würdigen. In der Stadt der Reichsparteitage – aber auch in der Stadt der Nürnberger Prozesse und der Menschenrechte – tragen wir eine besondere Verantwortung in der Auseinandersetzung mit der eigenen Geschichte. Für das Neue Museum bot sich mit der Kooperationsanfrage der Boris Lurie Art Foundation eine willkommene Möglichkeit, ein Lebenswerk zu präsentieren, das sich wie kein anderes dem dunklen Erbe des Holocausts in der bildenden Kunst gewidmet hat.
Würde die Kunst das größte Verbrechen der Menschheitsgeschichte nicht behandeln, hätte dies laut Lurie ein Vakuum in der Kunstgeschichte hinterlassen, ihm persönlich wäre es wie Selbsttäuschung vorgekommen. Die Ignoranz der (amerikanischen) Gesellschaft dem Holocaust gegenüber war wohl ausschlaggebend, sein gesamtes schöpferisches Werk diesem Thema zu widmen. Wahrscheinlich diente es auch der Verarbeitung eines anhaltenden Traumas, auch wenn er durch seinen Zynismus selbst eher ungebrochen erschien. Lurie schuf sich in New York sein eigenes Ghetto, wo er auch ohne finanzielle Not in späteren Jahren noch Lebensmittel hortete, er lebte genügsam und verweigerte den verschwenderischen Konsum. Er war nonkonform und legte es darauf an, jegliche ästhetische Erwartungen zu verletzen. In seiner Art war er radikal und mutig, authentisch und daher glaubwürdig. Er schlug aus der Art – was den Begriff „entartete Kunst" definiert.[14] Im Endeffekt produzierte er sich lebenslang als diffamierter Künstler und zelebrierte seine Außenseiterrolle. Als Zeuge des Unvorstellbaren versuchte er seiner Erinnerung Rechnung zu tragen – um das Undarstellbare darzustellen. Auf seine Art.

Der vorliegende Katalog beinhaltet neben einem umfangreichen Bildteil zur Ausstellung und ausführlichen Beschreibungen zu den Werkgruppen von Claudia Marquardt verschiedene Essays, die rund um Lurie kreisen. Ausführliche biografische Abhandlungen gibt es andernorts – wie auch einige schriftliche Hinterlassenschaften von ihm selbst: die nicht veröffentlichten Lebenserinnerungen *In Riga*, einen umfangreichen Gedichtband oder seine traumatischen Erfahrungen in Form des SM-Romans *House of Anita*.
Der Kunsthistoriker Eckhart Gillen hat jüngst einen lesenswerten Artikel zu Luries Position für das Magazin *Art in America* verfasst, den wir unbedingt hier reproduziert wissen wollten. Auf unsere Einladung hin hat der Künstler und Kunsttheoretiker Peter Weibel seinen Beitrag „Der Holocaust und das Problem der visuellen Repräsentation", dessen Initiative auf einen Vortrag im Jüdischen Museum Berlin 2016 zurückgeht, für uns in dem vorliegenden, äußerst bemerkenswerten Text ausgeführt. Er nähert sich darin dem Werk von Boris Lurie über die Geschichte der modernen Kunst als Krise der visuellen Repräsentation – und stellt die Frage, wie man mit den Mitteln der Kunst adäquat auf den Holocaust reagieren kann.
Thomas Heyden, Kurator am Neuen Museum, blickt von außen auf Boris Lurie und umkreist sein Werk mit Arbeiten seines direkten Umfelds in New York bis hin zu seinen Kollegen im Geiste, die wir in der Ausstellung mit einigen Sammlungsstücken und Leihgaben in Referenz zu Boris Lurie gesetzt haben. Diesen

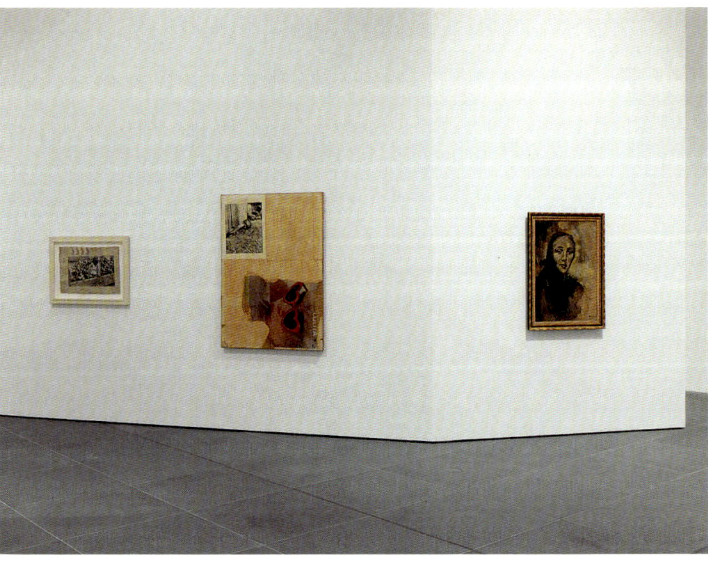
Boris Lurie. Anti-Pop,
Neues Museum Nürnberg

As well as extensive illustrations and descriptions of the works in the exhibition by Claudia Marquardt, this catalogue contains various essays on Boris Lurie. Comprehensive biographies are available elsewhere – as are several written works of his own: his unpublished memoirs *In Riga*, a large volume of poems, and his traumatic experiences in the form of the sadomasochist novel *House of Anita*.

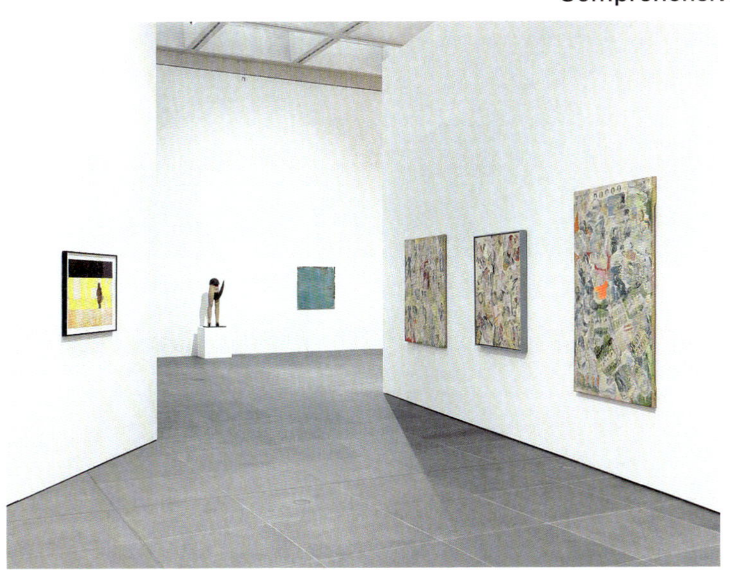

Boris Lurie. Anti-Pop, Neues Museum Nürnberg

Art historian Eckhart Gillen recently wrote an interesting article on Lurie for *Art in America* that we wanted to reprint here. At our invitation, artist and art theorist Peter Weibel wrote his essay on "The Holocaust and the Problem of Visual Representation," based on a lecture he gave at Berlin's Jewish Museum in 2016. In this remarkable text, he approaches Boris Lurie's oeuvre via the history of modern art as a crisis of visual representation – and asks how the means of art can be used to respond adequately to the Holocaust.

Thomas Heyden, curator at Neues Museum, looks at Boris Lurie from outside and situates his oeuvre among works by kindred spirits and artists from his immediate milieu in New York, some of which, drawn from the museum's collection or on loan, are presented in dialogue with Lurie in the exhibition. This context is divided into "three concentric circles: the first includes Lurie's closest associates in the March Group (Sam Goodman and Stanley Fisher); the second consists of other artists linked to the NO!art movement (Jean-Jacques Lebel here represents many others) as well as friends (Wolf Vostell); and the third, outer circle is made up of artists whose work in one way or another provides an interesting comparison to Lurie's (H. P. Alvermann, Piero Manzoni, Gustav Metzger, and Gerhard Richter)."

For us, it was important to honor an oeuvre that has been undeservedly ignored and forgotten. With the exhibition at Neues Museum Nürnberg and with this catalog, we are glad to contribute to the (re-)discovery of Boris Lurie.

1 Boris Lurie, "Introduction to Sam Goodman 'NO-sculptures' (1964)". http://text.no-art.info/en/lurie_no-sculpt.html (retrieved May 11, 2017)
2 Boris Lurie, "Preface" in Boris Lurie, Seymour Krim: *NO!art. Pin-ups, Excrements, Protest, Jew-Art* (Cologne/Berlin 1988), p. 13.
3 Stanley Fisher, "Involvement-Show Statement (1961)" in: ibid., p. 37.
4 Boris Lurie, "Shit No! (1970)" in: ibid., p. 60.
5 Today's St. Petersburg. In 1924, Petrograd was renamed Leningrad.
6 Dore Ashton, "Merde, alors! (1969)" in: *NO!art* (Cologne/Berlin 1988), p. 55.
7 Boris Lurie, "Les Lions show Introduction (1960)" in: ibid., p. 21.
8 Jean-Jacques Lebel, "Die finsteren Zeiten sind wieder da" in: *NO!art*, exhibition catalogue, Neue Gesellschaft für Bildende Kunst (Berlin 1995), p. 156.
9 Boris Lurie interviewed by Estera Milman, https://vimeo.com/23023159 (retrieved May 11, 2017).
10 NO!art (Berlin 1995), p. 14.
11 Boris Lurie, "Shit No! (1970)" in: *NO!art* (Cologne/Berlin 1988), p. 58.
12 Seymour Krim, "NO!Show (1963)" in: ibid., p. 24.
13 Allan Kaprow, in: *NO!art* (Berlin 1995), p. 166.
14 "I suspect that many [German] citizens would like to return to using the term 'degenerate art' for whatever is not to their taste, if only this quotation did not expose their views." Wolf Vostell, "Brief an Boris Lurie," May 1995, in: ibid., p. 163.

Kontext gliedert er in „drei konzentrische gedankliche Kreise: die engsten Weggefährten der March Group (Sam Goodman, Stanley Fisher), die NO!art-Mitstreiter (stellvertretend für viele andere Jean-Jacques Lebel) bzw. Freunde (Wolf Vostell) und schließlich als äußerster Kreis jene Künstler, die in bestimmten Aspekten aufschlussreiche Vergleiche ermöglichen (H.P. Alvermann, Piero Manzoni, Gustav Metzger und Gerhard Richter)."
Es war uns ein Anliegen, ein künstlerisches Werk zu würdigen, das wohl zu Unrecht ignoriert bzw. in Vergessenheit geraten ist. Es freut uns, mit der Ausstellung im Neuen Museum Nürnberg und dem vorliegenden Katalog einen Beitrag leisten zu dürfen, damit Boris Lurie (wieder-)entdeckt werden kann.

1 Boris Lurie: Introduction to Sam Goodman „NO-sculptures" (1964). http://text.no-art.info/en/lurie_no-sculpt.html (Zugriff vom 11.5.2017).
2 Boris Lurie: „Vorwort", in: Boris Lurie und Seymour Krim: *NO!art. Pin-ups, Excrements, Protest, Jew-Art,* Köln/Berlin, 1988, S. 13.
3 Stanley Fisher: Statement zur Involvement Show (1961), in: ebd.
4 Boris Lurie: „Scheiss Nein! (1970)", in: ebd., S. 68.
5 Heute St. Petersburg, 1924 wurde Petrograd in Leningrad umbenannt.
6 Dore Ashton: „Merdre [sic] alors" in: Lurie und Krim 1988, vgl. Anm. 2, S. 61.
7 Boris Lurie: „Anmerkungen zur Ausstellung ‚Les Lions' (1960)", in: ebd., S. 21.
8 Jean-Jacques Lebel: „Die finsteren Zeiten sind wieder da", in: *NO!art,* Ausstellungskatalog, Neue Gesellschaft für Bildende Kunst, Berlin, 1995, S. 156.
9 https://vimeo.com/23023159 (Zugriff vom 11.5.2017).
10 *NO!art,* 1995, vgl. Anm. 8, S. 14.
11 Boris Lurie: „Scheiss Nein! (1970)", in: Lurie und Krim 1988, vgl. Anm. 2, S. 66.
12 Seymour Krim, zur „NO!Show" (1963) in: ebd., S. 25.
13 Allan Kaprow in: *NO!art,* 1995, vgl. Anm. 8., S. 166.
14 Vgl. „Ich habe den Verdacht, dass viele [deutsche] Bürger gerne den Begriff „entartete Kunst" für das, was ihnen nicht schmeckt, wieder benützen würden; würde dieses Zitat sie nicht in ihren Ansichten decouvrieren." Wolf Vostell, „Brief an Boris Lurie", Mai 1995, in: ebd., S. 163.

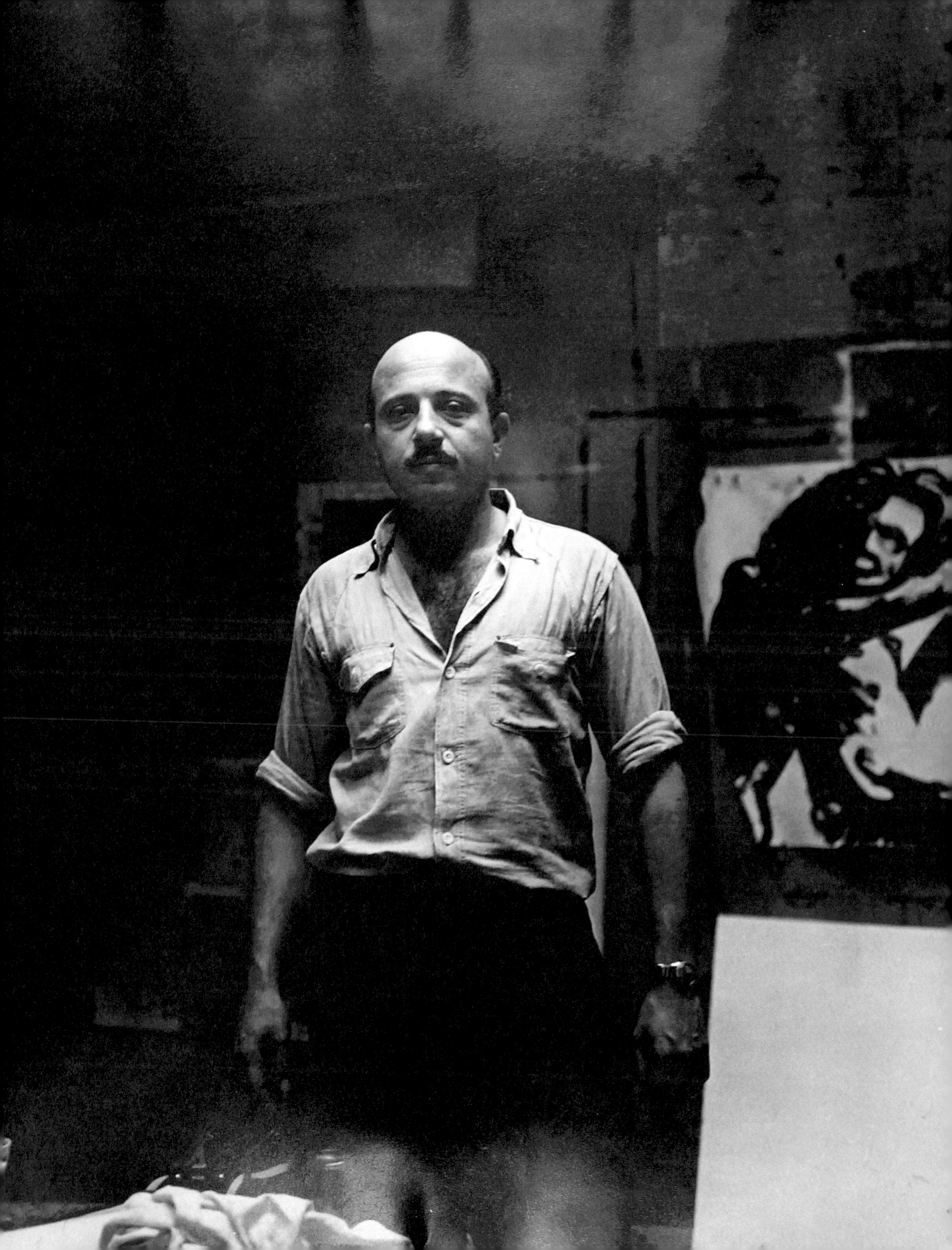

Eckhart Gillen

Boris Lurie: Our only master is truth

Der Blick auf das künstlerische Lebenswerk von Boris Lurie ist mehrfach verstellt durch übergroße, einschüchternde Labels wie Holocaust-Kunst, Antikunst, NO!art. Jeder Wunsch, sich der Kunst von Boris Lurie unbefangen anzunähern, muss scheitern angesichts der Einmaligkeit der Konstellation, in der diese Werke entstanden sind.

1924 in Leningrad geboren als jüngstes Kind von Shaina und Ilja Lurie, muss Boris Lurie im Teenageralter von 17 Jahren erleben, wie die 1925 aus der Sowjetunion in das unabhängig gewordene Lettland nach Riga übersiedelte Familie brutal auseinandergerissen wird. Seine Mutter Shaina, seine Großmutter und die jüngere seiner beiden Schwestern, Jeanne, warteten im „Großen Ghetto" des lettischen Riga auf ihre „Evakuierung", die in Wirklichkeit eine Deportation in den Wald von Rumbula war, acht Kilometer von Riga entfernt, wo sie am 8. Dezember 1941 sich mitten im Winter nackt ausziehen mussten und erschossen wurden. Unter ihnen fand auch Ljuba Treskunova, seine Jugendliebe, den Tod. Es war nach dem 30. November die zweite „Aktion", die zur Ermordung von insgesamt mehr als 30 000 Juden geführt hat, noch bevor die Tötungsfabriken in Auschwitz, Belzec, Sobibor und Treblinka im Frühjahr 1942 ihre „Arbeit" aufgenommen hatten.

Gegen alle Wahrscheinlichkeit gelang es Boris Lurie, mit seinem Vater Ilja die nächsten vier Jahre in Lagern zu überleben. Zunächst in den Arbeitslagern Lenta und Salaspils, dann in dem Konzentrationslager Stutthof und einem Außenlager von Buchenwald in Magdeburg, wo die Zwangsarbeiter für die Polte Munitionsfabrik untergebracht waren.

Vierzehn Jahre nach Kriegsende lagern sich diese traumatischen Ereignisse erstmals ab auf seinem Bild *Liberty or Lice* von 1959/60 (Öl und Collage auf Leinwand, 166 × 212 cm, heute im Israel Museum, Jerusalem). Der Bildtitel „Freiheit oder Läuse" kann als sarkastische Zerrissenheit zwischen den Läusen als tödliche Bedrohung im Lager und der versprochenen „Freiheit" in der neuen, doch fremden Heimat Amerika verstanden werden.

Lurie schreibt in einem fiktiven Brief an sich selbst, der Teil seiner unveröffentlichten Erinnerungen *In Riga* ist, „... das Gemälde, in welchem du skrupellos wechselweise die Geschichte deiner Vergangenheit [die Läuse der Lager, d. Vf.] und die Erfahrungen der amerikanischen Realität Ende der 1950er/Anfang der 60er Jahre [Liberty, d. Vf.] übereinandergelagert hast, bis alle diese ungleichen, im Verlauf überdeckten und ausgelöschten, kleinen Kapitel in einem vereinten Werk [...] gelierten: Das Wort [...] ‚Jeanne' (der Name deiner schönen, jüngeren Schwester, Rumbula) tauchte immer wieder darin auf."[1] Ebenso erscheinen die Daten „8. Dezember" für die zweite tödliche Aktion in Rumbula gegen seine Mutter, Großmutter, Schwester und Geliebte 1941 und „18. April" für den Tag der Befreiung aus dem Außenlager in Magdeburg 1945.

In einer chaotischen Assemblage von Fotografien, z. B. einer des Rigaer Ghettos, Zeitungsausschnitten, fotografischen Wiedergaben seiner Gemälde, darunter eine seiner *Dismembered Women*, einem Passfoto des Künstlers, einem Judenstern auf einem gelborangenen Fleck mit Farbverläufen, wie er ab September

Any view of Boris Lurie's artistic oeuvre is obstructed by several large and intimidating labels, such as "Holocaust art," "anti-art," and "NO!art." Any attempt to approach his artworks with an open mind is almost doomed to failure due to the unique circumstances in which they were produced.

Boris Lurie was born in Leningrad in 1924, the youngest of Shaina and Ilya Lurie's three children. The following year, the family left the Soviet Union and settled in Riga, the capital of the newly independent state of Latvia. When he was 17 years old, Boris Lurie underwent the traumatic experience of having his family brutally torn apart. In December 1941, his mother, grandmother, and the younger of his two sisters, Jeanne, were waiting in Riga's Large Ghetto for what was supposed to be their "evacuation." Instead, on December 8, they and thousands of others were taken to Rumbula forest, eight kilometers outside the city, where they were made to strip naked in the bitter cold before being forced into pits and shot in the back of the head. Boris Lurie's childhood sweetheart Ljuba Treskunova was also among those killed. Following a similar "Aktion" on November 30, 1941, this was the second part of an atrocity that resulted in the deaths of more than 30,000 Jews. It had taken place even before the death camps in Auschwitz, Bełżec, Sobibór, and Treblinka went into operation in spring 1942.

Eckhart Gillen

Boris Lurie: Our only master is truth

Against all the odds, Boris Lurie and his father Ilya managed to survive the next four years in various various Nazi camps. After a period in the Lenta and Salaspils forced labor camps, they were moved to Stutthof concentration camp, and later to a forced labor subcamp of Buchenwald in Magdeburg that was attached to the Polte-Werke munitions factory.

Fourteen years after the war ended, these traumatic experiences were reflected for the first time in Boris Lurie's painting *Liberty or Lice* (1959 – 60, oil and collage on canvas, 166 x 212 cm, now in the collection of the Israel Museum in Jerusalem). The title of this work can be understood as a sarcastic reference to the choice between lice, which posed a potentially deadly threat in the camps, and the promise of liberty in the new but still unfamiliar homeland of America. In a fictitious letter to himself that is included in his unpublished autobiography *In Riga,* Lurie writes that in this painting "you ruthlessly superimposed alternatively your past history [the lice in the camps] and experiences of the American reality of the late 1950s and early 1960s [liberty] until all these disparate little chapters, covered over and extinguished in the process, jelled into a unified work. [...]

1941 als Zwangskennzeichen der Juden vom NS-Regime eingeführt wurde, und der Fotografie seiner Ehefrau Béatrice Lecornu, von der er sich, während dieses Bild entstand, gerade getrennt hatte, werden zwischen Reklamefetzen und vereinzelten hochhackigen Schuhen, die an die Sammlungen von Schuhen und anderen Habseligkeiten der Häftlinge in den Asservatenkammern der KZs erinnern, buchstäblich unverdaute Erinnerungsbilder und Gegenstände hochgewirbelt und dann wieder in weißen, blauen und roten Farbwirbeln ertränkt.

Lurie selbst bestätigt: „Das Gemälde, wage ich zu sagen, eröffnete dir und deiner Kunst das bewusste Verstehen des Selbst und begründete eine neue Kunstform von vollständiger und waghalsiger und bewusster Ehrlichkeit und Offenheit, die jedoch durch ‚unbewusstes' Handeln, Gestikulieren erreicht wurde, von momentanen Projektionen des Geistes, die sofort auf der Leinwand festgehalten wurden, und das war Kunst, kein Dada oder Antikunst."[2]

Tatsächlich überlagern sich in diesem Gemälde Gegenwart und Vergangenheit ausweglos. Lange vor seiner ersten Reise 1975 zum Tatort Riga, die zum Auslöser wird für eine immense und beeindruckende literarische Aufarbeitung der Vergangenheit in Form einer 700 Seiten umfassenden unveröffentlichten Autobiografie *In Riga*, aus der ich zitiert habe, ist das zunächst „unbewusste" Hantieren mit Bildern der erste Schritt zu einem „bewussten" Verstehen des eigenen Selbst in seinem literarischen Schaffen. Dazu gehören auch Gedichte in baltendeutscher und englischer Sprache sowie ein autobiografischer Rollenroman *House of Anita* (New York 2016).

Im Rückblick aus dem Jahr 1975 bekennt sich Lurie zu einer ernsthaften, ehrlichen, auf Wahrheit und Erkenntnis gerichteten Kunst gegen Dada-Ironie und Antikunst im Sinne etwa des italienischen Realismo, die er mit der von ihm initiierten NO!art-Bewegung zwischen 1960 und 1964 strikt abgegrenzt hat von einer eitlen, selbstgenügsamen Kunstmarktkunst. Denn Kunst wurde für ihn buchstäblich zu einer Überlebenskunst. Bevor überhaupt eine bewusste Aufarbeitung des Erlebten möglich erschien, war die Beschäftigung mit Bildern der erste Schritt, das Verborgene, das im Gedächtnis scheinbar schon Ausgelöschte, Verlorene und Vergessene zu retten.

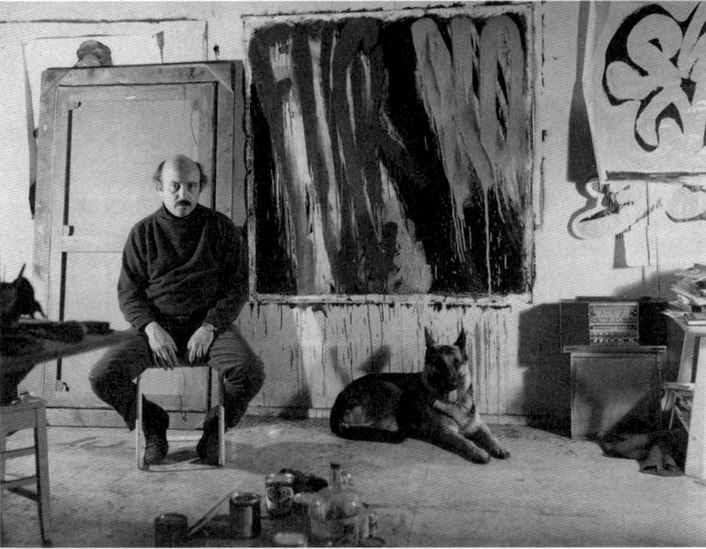

Boris Lurie mit Punch in seinem Atelier / with Punch in his studio

Vor seinen Assemblagen um 1960 hatte Boris Lurie bereits direkt nach seiner Ankunft in New York 1946 begonnen, erste Eindrücke, Figuren, Szenen, Porträts ... mit Bleistift, Kreide, Kohle und Tusche skizzenhaft festzuhalten, die er „War Series" nannte. Ergänzt werden sie durch großformatigere Pastelle, Gouachen und Ölbilder. Darunter befindet sich z. B. ein ergreifendes *Portrait of My Mother Before Shooting* (1947) als Traumerscheinung aus einer fernen, anderen Welt. In der Tradition eines Alfred Kubin, eines James Ensor, Edvard Munch, Ludwig Meidner oder Antonin Artaud gelingen dem Autodidakten, der nur kurze Zeit um 1948 Kurse bei Reginald Marsh an der Arts Students League of New York besucht hatte, eindrucksvolle Szenen aus der Hölle der Lager wie *Entrance* (1946), das Wächter am Eingang einer Lagerbaracke zeigt, die umgestülpte Abfalleimer als Helme und geschulterte Besen als Gewehre tragen. Die Muselmane genannten Häftlinge, welche sich bereits selbst aufgegeben haben, werden in weichen, fließenden Formen in ein magisches Zwielicht getaucht. Alle diese Studien, noch im Stil einer Malerei der Repräsentation mit surrealen

The word [...] 'Jeanne' (your beautiful younger sister's name, Rumbula) kept appearing in it."[1] Two dates can also be found in *Liberty or Lice*: "Dec. 8" – a reference to the second deadly "Aktion" in Rumbula that killed his mother, grandmother, sister, and girlfriend in 1941 – and "April 18", the day in 1945 when the satellite camp in Magdeburg was liberated.

Liberty or Lice presents a chaotic assemblage of photographs (of the Riga ghetto, for example), newspaper clippings, reproductions of paintings (including one of his *Dismembered Women*), a passport photo of the artist himself, a Star of David on a patch of yellow-orange dripping paint (a reference to the identifying badge for Jews that was introduced by the Nazis in September 1941), and a photograph of Lurie's wife Béatrice Lecornu, from whom he had just separated when this picture was taken. Between snippets of advertisements and depictions of single stilettos that recall the collections of inmates' shoes and other confiscated belongings in the concentration camp warehouses, "undigested" memory images and objects surface briefly before being drowned once more in whirls of white, blue, and red. The significance of this work was confirmed by Lurie himself: "That painting, I dare say, opened you and your art up to a conscious understanding of self, while also inaugurating an art form of full and reckless and conscious sincerity and openness, but arrived at via 'unconscious' exercising, gesturing, of instantaneous projections of the mind immediately fixed on canvas; and this was art, not Dada or anti-art."[2]

In this painting, the past and the present are indeed visibly overlapped and shown to be inextricably linked. Boris Lurie's first visit in 1975 to the site of the massacre in Riga triggered an extensive process of examining and coming to terms with his past, culminating in the compilation of an impressive, 700-page autobiography entitled *In Riga* (as yet unpublished), from which the above quotations are taken. Long before this, however, his initially "unconscious" use of images had been the first step towards gaining a "conscious" understanding of his inner self. Lurie's literary output also includes poems in Baltic German and English, as well as the autobiographical novel *House of Anita* (New York: NO!art Publishing, 2016).

In 1975, looking back over his life and his creative practice to date, Lurie reaffirmed his commitment to a serious, honest form of art that was aimed at truth and knowledge, as opposed to Dadaist irony or anti-art in the sense of Italian Neo-Realism, for example. With the NO!art movement he co-founded and led between 1960 and 1964, he drew a clear dividing line between the kind of art he believed in and the vain, self-satisfied art that served the commercial art market. For Lurie himself, art had literally become an art of survival. Before a conscious processing of his traumatic past experiences even seemed possible, he found that working with images was a way of retrieving what was buried deep in his memory – things that appeared to have been forgotten, lost, or erased.

Prior to the assemblages he created from around 1960 onwards, Boris Lurie had made what he called his "War Series" soon after he arrived in New York in 1946. In these sketchily executed works in pencil, chalk, charcoal, and Indian ink, he recorded his first impressions and drew figures, portraits, and small scenes. The drawings were accompanied by a number of large-format pastels, gouaches, and oil paintings. These include the poignant *Portrait of My Mother Before Shooting* (1947), in which Shaina appears like a dreamlike figure from some distant, other world. Following in the painterly tradition of artists such as Alfred Kubin, James

Anklängen, waren für ihn private Bilder, die er zu seinen Lebzeiten nicht ausstellen wollte.

Die Kunst erweist sich hier als ein einzigartiges Medium für die Sichtbarmachung und Verarbeitung von Traumata. Traumatisierte können vergessene Erfahrungen lange vor einer verbalen Formulierung visualisieren, da die Bilder der rechten Gehirnhemisphäre näher stehen, von der angenommen wird, dass sie traumatische Erinnerungen speichern kann, die der linkshemisphärischen, verbalen Repräsentation noch nicht zugänglich sind. Die beste Möglichkeit, die zerbrochene Verbindung mit dem inneren Selbst wiederherstellen zu können, ist der Versuch des Traumatisierten, mit seinem Trauma in einen kreativen Dialog zu kommen. Der Künstler tut dies symbolisch, indem er versucht, sein Trauma im Kunstwerk zu objektivieren. Die künstlerische Arbeit mobilisiert die intellektuellen, imaginativen, integrativen und manuellen Fähigkeiten eines Menschen, wirkt der Neigung zu innerer Desintegration entgegen und hilft so dem Betroffenen, wieder ein Gefühl für seine Identität und seinen Selbstwert zu entwickeln. Der Weg in die Vergangenheit, in das Zentrum des Schmerzes, führt also über die Bilder.

Das Malen als somatische, künstlerische Tätigkeit ist weniger Rekonstruktion von Vergangenheiten als Erfindung, Wiederbelebung, Wiederfinden, Suchbewegung, Überprüfung, Verwerfung, Spurensuche, um zu beobachten, was sich herauskristallisiert, und am Ende eine Konstruktion als spekulative Zusammenfügung mit offenem Ausgang, wie wir am Beispiel seiner Assemblage *Liberty or Lice* gesehen haben.

Boris Lurie arbeitete inmitten der New Yorker Kunstszenen des Abstrakten Expressionismus, des Neodadaismus, der Neuen Figuration, der Pop-Art um 1960, in denen er sich, wie viele Zeugnisse belegen, auf gleicher Augenhöhe mit namhaften Kollegen wie Rothko, Rauschenberg, Warhol bewegte und vielfältige Kontakte pflegte. Obwohl er mit den avanciertesten Kunstformen arbeitete, ging es ihm nie um „aesthetic labels", denn diese sind „neither true nor important", sondern darum, mit seiner Kunst etwas zu bewirken und zu verändern, vor allem aber seine eigene Situation besser begreifen zu können. Als Überlebender des Holocaust lebte er ja unwiderruflich in einer anderen Welt, auf einem anderen Planeten, in einem anderen Wertesystem. Eine Verständigung mit den Zeitgenossen, die das Lagersystem nicht erlebt hatten, scheint fast unmöglich. Allein die Kunst vermochte da vielleicht eine Brücke auf die andere Seite zu schlagen.

Susan Sontag beschrieb 1977 in ihrem Essay *In Platons Höhle* ihre Erfahrung als 12-Jährige mit Aufnahmen aus Bergen-Belsen und Dachau, die sie im Juli 1945 zufällig in einer Buchhandlung in Santa Monica entdeckte: „Nichts, was ich jemals gesehen habe – ob auf Fotos oder in der Realität –, hat mich so jäh, so tief und unmittelbar getroffen. Und seither erschien es mir ganz selbstverständlich, mein Leben in zwei Abschnitte einzuteilen: in die Zeit, bevor ich diese Fotos sah [...] und die Zeit danach – obwohl noch mehrere Jahre verstreichen mußten, bis ich voll und ganz begriff, was diese Bilder darstellten. [...] Als ich diese Fotos betrachtete, zerbrach etwas in mir. Eine Grenze war erreicht, und nicht nur die Grenze des Entsetzens; ich fühlte mich unwiderruflich betroffen, verwundet, aber etwas in mir begann sich zusammenzuballen; etwas starb; etwas weint noch immer."[3]

Vor dem Hintergrund dieser Äußerung kann man ermessen, welche Weichenstellung seines Lebens Boris Lurie 1941 als 17-Jähriger erfahren musste. Schlim-

Ensor, Edvard Munch, Ludwig Meidner, or Antonin Artaud, the self-taught Lurie – he only briefly attended the Art Students League of New York around 1948, where he studied with Reginald Marsh – produced striking images of the hellish reality of life in the camps. *Entrance* (1946), for example, shows two inmates standing guard at the entrance to a camp barracks, wearing upturned buckets as helmets and carrying brooms over their shoulders as "rifles." These *Muselmänner* – the name given to severely emaciated inmates who had resigned themselves to their fate – are depicted with flowing forms and and are steeped in a muted, magical half-light. Lurie regarded all of these studies, which were painted in a representational style with surreal touches, as private images that he never wished to exhibit.

For Boris Lurie, art proved to be a uniquely powerful medium in which to visualize and process trauma. Traumatized individuals are able to visualize forgotten experiences long before they can express them verbally; this is because the images are located closer to the right cerebral hemisphere, where traumatic memories can be stored that are not yet accessible to left-hemispheric, verbal representation. The best way for a traumatized person to repair the broken link to their inner self is to enter into a creative dialogue with their trauma. The artist does this symbolically by attempting to objectify his trauma in an artwork. Artistic practice mobilizes a person's intellectual, imaginative, and integrative capacities as well as their manual skills; it counteracts the tendency towards inner disintegration and in this way helps the affected person to re-establish a sense of their own identity and self-worth. The journey into the past, to the heart of the painful experience, thus leads through images.

Painting as a somatic, creative act has less to do with reconstructing the past than with inventing, reviving, relocating, searching, examining, dismissing, and looking for clues, then seeing what this all crystallizes into. The resulting image of the past is ultimately a construction – a speculative, open-ended combination of multiple elements, as we have seen with Lurie's assemblage *Liberty or Lice*.

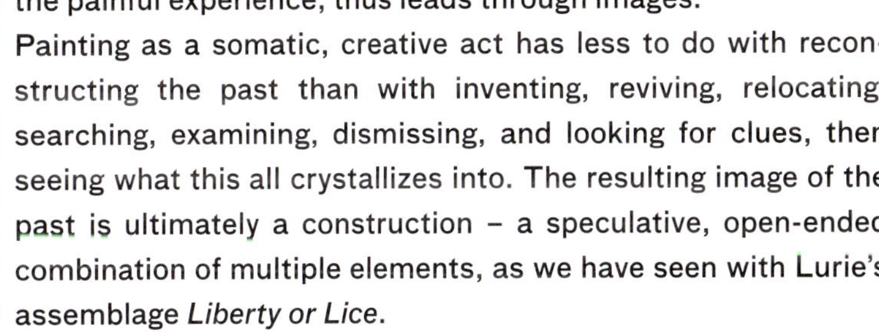

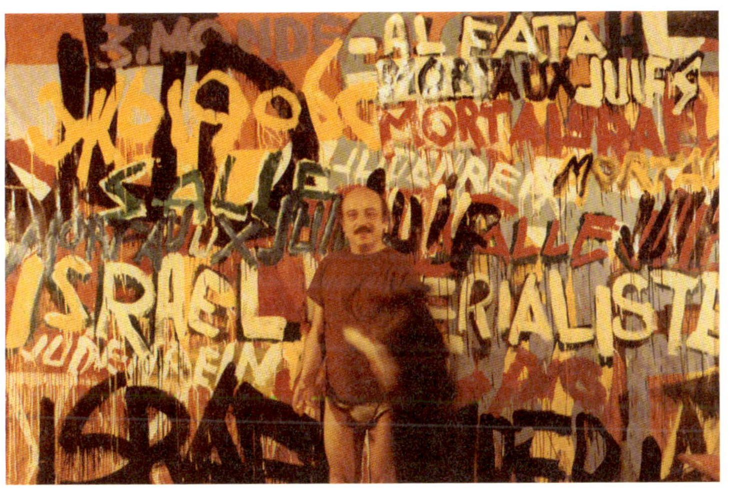

Boris Lurie in seinem Atelier / in his studio, ca. / ca 1970

Working in New York around 1960, Boris Lurie was surrounded by the art scenes of Abstract Expressionism, Neo-Dada, New Figuration, and Pop Art; documentary evidence puts him on an equal footing with well-known colleagues such as Rothko, Rauschenberg, and Warhol, and he had a large network of contacts. Although he experimented with the most progressive forms of art, Lurie was never interested in "aesthetic labels," as he considered these "neither true nor important"; he wanted his art to have an effect and bring about change. Above all, however, he wanted to gain insights into his own situation. As a Holocaust survivor, he was always going to inhabit a different world, a completely different planet, to those around him, and he lived by a different set of values. Understanding and communicating with contemporaries who had not experienced the camp system seemed well-nigh impossible. Art was the only means possible of building a bridge to the other side.

In her essay *In Plato's Cave,* Susan Sontag describes how in July 1945, when she was 12 years old, she came across photographs of Bergen-Belsen and Dachau in a bookstore in Santa Monica: "Nothing I have seen – in photographs or in real life – ever cut me as sharply, deeply, instantaneously. Indeed, it seems plausible to

mer als die erlebten Verbrechen, die erlittene Gewalt der Täter, war es für Boris Lurie und seine Leidensgenossen, die Gleichgültigkeit seiner Zeitgenossen zu ertragen. In den Vereinigten Staaten hatten zwar alle irgendwann einmal nach Kriegsende die schrecklichen Fotos von Lee Miller oder Margaret Bourke-White in der *Life* oder anderen Journalen gesehen, die gewöhnlich inmitten von Werbung der Konsumindustrie platziert waren. Danach wurden sie vergessen bis zum Eichmann-Prozess 1961 in Jerusalem, der die mediale Aufmerksamkeit wieder auf den Genozid an den europäischen Juden richtete.

In diesem Zusammenhang sprach Susan Sontag davon, dass nach den ersten Publikationen der Fotografien von nationalsozialistischen Konzentrationslagern 1945 ein „gewisser Sättigungsgrad" eingetreten sei. Die „anteilnehmende" Fotografie habe „mindestens ebensoviel dazu getan, unser Gewissen abzutöten, wie dazu, es aufzurütteln."[4]

Lurie griff genau dieses Phänomen auf mit seinem *Saturation Painting (Buchenwald)*, 1960 – 63 (Collage, Fotografie und Zeitung auf Leinwand, 91 × 91 cm). Es zeigt im Zentrum einer vom Keilrahmen abgenommenen schmutzigen Leinwand ein Foto von Margaret Bourke-White, das sie nach ihrem Eintreffen mit General George S. Pattons 3. Army im Lager Buchenwald am 13.4.1945 im Auftrag des *Life*-Magazins aufgenommen hatte. Es handelt sich um Gefangene hinter Stacheldraht, die bei ihrer Befreiung völlig apathisch den alliierten Befreiungskräften entgegenstarren. Das ikonisch gewordene Bild erschien erstmals am 26.12.1960 im *Life*-Magazine unter dem Titel *Grim Greeting at Buchenwald*. Lurie hat es aus der Magazinpublikation herausgeschnitten. Es wird von zwölf pornografischen Pin-up-Fotos umrahmt. Als wolle er den Zynismus der amerikanischen „Affluent Society", für die alle Bedürfnisse wie Liebe und menschliche Nähe und alle Bilder, unabhängig von ihrer moralischen Bedeutung, zu Waren geworden sind, auf den Begriff bringen.

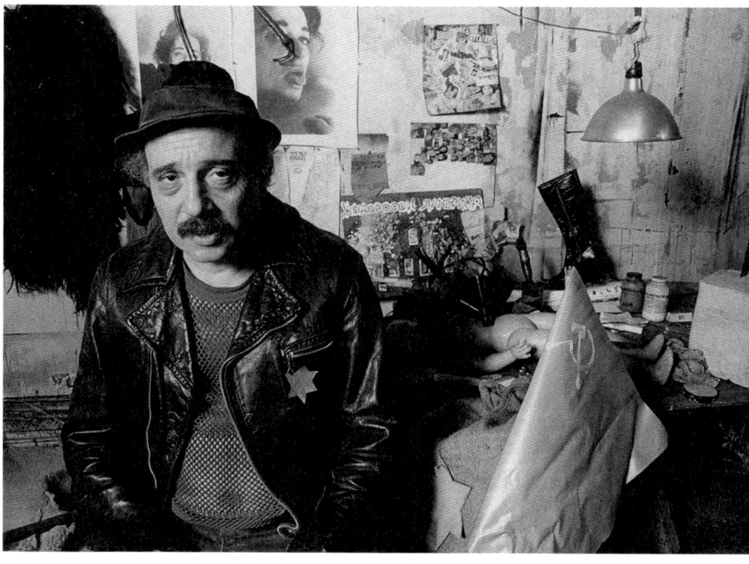
Boris Lurie in seinem Atelier / in his studio, 1977

Das Wort „Saturation" zielt auf eine Bilderflut, die falsche Bedürfnisse und Wünsche in uns stimulieren soll. Lurie will inmitten eines Kunstbetriebs, der für ihn als Überlebenden die notwendigen Inhalte des Kunstschaffens durch seine Merkantilisierung permanent entwertet, den Betrachter mit seiner Assemblage bewusst ästhetisch verstören. Die Vernichtung der Körper im KZ-System setzt sich fort in der Entwertung von Schönheit, Sinnlichkeit und Sexualität der Frauen. Lurie bringt diesen Zusammenhang hier auf den Punkt lange vor Pier Paolo Pasolinis ähnlich lautenden Anklagen in seinen „Freibeuterbriefen" am Ende der 1960er Jahre.

Parallel zu der berühmten Ausstellung *The Art of Assemblage* (MoMA, 4.10. – 12.11.1961), für die Alfred Barr Jr. und sein Kurator William Seitz bereits Werke von Lurie ausgewählt hatten, die dann doch nicht gezeigt wurden, entstand die wohl am meisten verstörende Arbeit von Boris Lurie: *Flatcar, Assemblage, 1945 by Adolf Hitler*, ca. 1962 (Offsetdruck, 41 × 61 cm). Hier verwendete Lurie ein anonymes Foto, das lange Zeit Margaret Bourke-White zugeschrieben wurde, und stellte daraus einen Offsetdruck her mit der Bildlegende, die Adolf Hitler als Autor einer Assemblage ausweist, die aus den kreuz und quer übereinandergeworfenen nackten Leichen auf der offenen Ladefläche eines Anhängers sich zusammensetzt.

me to divide my life into two parts, before I saw those photographs [...] and after, though it was several years before I understood fully what they were about. [...] When I looked at those photographs, something broke. Some limit had been reached, and not only that of horror; I felt irrevocably grieved, wounded, but a part of my feelings started to tighten; something went dead; something is still crying."[3] This statement gives us a sense of the life-changing impact of what Boris Lurie experienced as a 17-year-old in 1941.

For Boris Lurie and his fellow survivors, the indifference of their contemporaries was often harder to bear than the crimes committed against them or the violence they had experienced. In the United States, just about everyone had seen the shocking photographs taken by the likes of Lee Miller or Margaret Bourke-White, which appeared in *Life* magazine and other publications – often sandwiched between adverts for consumer goods – soon after the war ended. After that, however, they were largely forgotten until the Eichmann trial was held in Jerusalem in 1961, focusing media attention once again on the genocide of the European Jews.

In this context, Susan Sontag pointed out that in the decades following the first publication of photographs of the Nazi concentration camps in 1945, a "saturation point" had been reached. "Concerned" photography had "done at least as much to deaden conscience as to arouse it."[4]

Lurie addresses precisely this phenomenon in his *Saturation Painting (Buchenwald)* (1960 – 63, collage, photographs, and newspaper on canvas, 91 x 91 cm). Near the center of a dirty piece of unstretched canvas is a photograph taken by Margaret Bourke-White when she arrived in Buchenwald on April 13, 1945, having been commissioned by *Life* magazine to accompany General George S. Patton's Third Army. It features a group of survivors standing behind a barbed-wire fence during the liberation of the camp, staring out impassively at the Allied rescuers. This iconic image was first published in a special issue of *Life* magazine on December 26, 1960, where it was captioned *Grim Greeting at Buchenwald*. Lurie cut it out of the magazine and framed it with 12 pornographic pin-up photos. He appears to be portraying the cynicism of affluent American society, in which all human needs – such as the need for love and closeness – and all images, irrespective of their moral significance, have become commodities. The term "saturation" points to the flood of images that are intended to create false needs and desires within us. Faced with an art industry where the tenets of artistic practice that were so crucially important to him as a Holocaust survivor were constantly being devalued by commercialization, Lurie created this assemblage with the specific intention of offending viewers' aesthetic sensibilities. The destruction of the body within the concentration camp system was, he believed, being continued in the devaluation of women's beauty, sensuality, and sexuality. This connection was established by Lurie long before Pier Paolo Pasolini made similar accusations in his *Scritti corsari* (1975).

Parallel to the groundbreaking exhibition *The Art of Assemblage* (Museum of Modern Art, New York City, October 4 – November 12, 1961), for which MoMA director Alfred H. Barr, Jr. and curator William C. Seitz selected works by Lurie that ended up not being exhibited, he created what is perhaps his most disturbing piece: *Flatcar, Assemblage, 1945 by Adolf Hitler* (ca 1962, offset print, 41 x 61 cm). His printed work is based on a picture by an unknown photographer that for a long time was falsely attributed to Margaret Bourke-White; Lurie's title

Um 1960, in einem Moment, in dem die autonome Kunst sich zunehmend in der Aktionskunst aufzulösen droht, die in den 1960er Jahren auf eine Aufhebung der Differenz von Kunst und Leben zielt, erklärt Boris Lurie Adolf Hitler zum größten Aktionskünstler. Denn, wenn Kunst in das Leben überführt werden soll, dann ist Hitler der größte, mächtigste und wirksamste Künstler gewesen, der Künstler mit den am weitesten reichenden Folgen.

„Wer ist der größte Künstler dieses Jahrhunderts? Ist es Duchamp (!!), ist es Picasso (!!!), Boris Lurie (!!!) oder ist es doch Adolf Hitler? Letzterer scheint mir der wahrscheinlichste Kandidat für diesen erlauchten Titel zu sein: Der größte Künstler der Zerstörung, der lebende (ja, lebende) Spuren seiner Meisterwerke hinterlassen hat. [...] Geschaffene Kunstwerke werden vergehen, aber bei einem zerstörerischen Künstler, der das Leben selbst umformte [...] wird die Wirkung seines Werkes Generationen überdauern. [...] Zwar erklärte Duchamp, dass sein ganzes Leben Kunst sei, Hitler jedoch nahm das wirkliche Leben und formte es nach seinen Vorstellungen."[5]

Lurie demonstriert mit seinem Exempel einer extremen Konzeptkunst die fatale Konsequenz einer politischen Avantgarde der 1960er Jahre, die statt Analyse Aktion forderte. Er nimmt experimentell eine Position vorweg, die z. B. von Dieter Kunzelmann, Mitglied der Künstlergruppe SPUR in München, die er 1962 verlässt, um durch permanente Aktionen aus der defensiven Rolle des sich verfolgt fühlenden Künstlers ausbrechen zu können. Mit seiner *Subversiven Aktion* und gezielten Regelverletzungen, einer Mischung aus dadaistischer Provokation und politischer Manifestation, sollte der Unterschied zwischen Leben und Kunst aufgehoben werden.

Fast dreißig Jahre später greift der Künstler Matti Braun diese Idee 1998 mit dem Künstlerbuch *Adolf Hitler, Installationen und Happenings* wieder auf, das Hitlers Massenhappenings „würdigt", die Frontlinien seiner Schlachten als „Abstraktionen" rubriziert und Leichenfelder als „Amorphe Installation" bezeichnet.

Boris Lurie dagegen geht genau den umgekehrten Weg. Er will aus dem Rohmaterial des Lebens, aus dem Schmerz, den das Leben ihm zugefügt hat, Kunst machen. Durch seinen Willen, seinen Intellekt und seine künstlerischen Fähigkeiten wollte er sein vergangenes Leben, das so unwahrscheinlich und absurd war, mit und dank seiner Kunst verstehen, verarbeiten, transformieren und lernen, es zu ertragen. Einzig im Moment des Erinnerns, im Eingedenken vermag Kunst den Toten gerecht zu werden. Lurie ging es immer und ausschließlich um die Aufdeckung der Wahrheit über das Leben, über die Fortdauer der Gewaltverhältnisse und die Gleichgültigkeit des Publikums angesichts dieser Tatsachen. Aus dieser Grundhaltung heraus sind alle Provokationen und Aktionen der NO!art-Bewegung zu verstehen, die andernorts gut dokumentiert sind.

Im Sinne von Adorno, mit dem Lurie die Frage teilte, „ob nach Auschwitz noch sich leben lasse, ob vollends es dürfe, wer zufällig entrann und rechtens hätte umgebracht werden müssen", hat in den nach Auschwitz produzierten Kunstwerken das „perennierende Leiden [...] soviel Recht auf Ausdruck wie der Gemarterte zu brüllen".[6]

Boris Lurie lebte in Manhattan in seinem „New Yorker Ersatz-Ghetto von Riga", an den Wänden hingen ein Stadtplan von Riga und die Fotografie von seiner Jugendliebe Ljuba Treskunova. Parallel zum Prozess gegen Eichmann in Jerusalem schreibt Lurie im „Involvement Show Statement" zur Eröffnung der

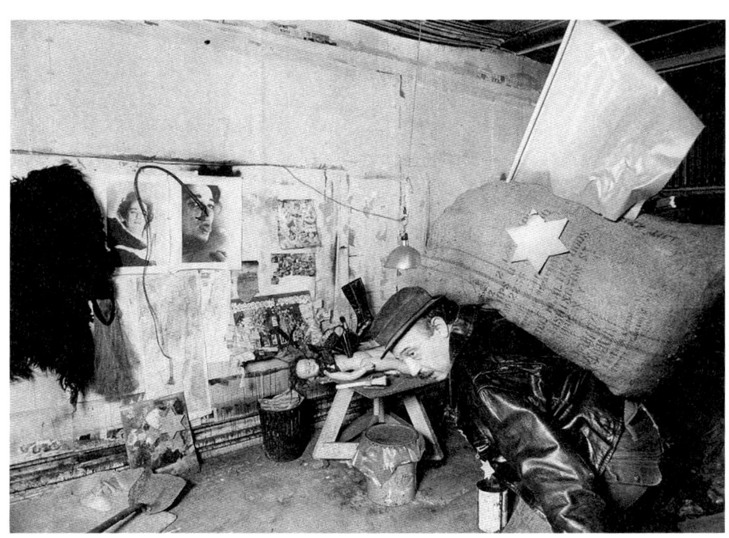

Boris Lurie in seinem Atelier 2 / in his studio 2, 1977

credits Adolf Hitler as the author of an "assemblage" consisting of naked corpses stacked on an open flatcar.

In the early 1960s, at a time when autonomous art was in danger of being subsumed into action art (a mode of practice aimed at lifting the barrier between art and life) Boris Lurie declared Adolf Hitler to be the greatest action artist. If art was to be incorporated into life, he reasoned, then Hitler had been the best, most powerful, and most effective artist – the one whose practice had the farthest-reaching consequences: "Who is the great artist of this century? Is it Duchamp (!!), is it Picasso (!!!), Boris Lurie (!!!!), or is it Adolf Hitler? The last one seems to me the most likely candidate to this august title: The Great Artist of Destruction who left living (yes, living) traces of his masterpieces. (...) Constructed works will crumble, but the destructive artist, molding life itself ... the effect of his work will stand for generations (...). So then Duchamp said all life was art, but Hitler took real life and molded it to his liking."[5]

With this example of a highly extreme form of conceptual art, Lurie demonstrated the fatal consequences of an avant-garde political stance in the 1960s that called for action rather than analysis. His experimental approach to this issue anticipated a position taken up by the likes of Reiner Kunzelmann, a member of the artists' group SPUR in Munich. Kunzelmann left the group in 1962, intending to use targeted actions to break out of the defensive role of an artist who feels persecuted. The distinction between art and life was to be eliminated by means of "Subversive Aktion" and deliberate violations of accepted rules – a mixture of Dadaist provocations and political manifestations.

Almost 30 years later, the German-Finnish artist Matti Braun revived this idea with his artist's book *Adolf Hitler, Installationen and Happenings* (1998), which not only acknowledged Hitler's mass "Happenings", but also categorized the front lines of his battlegrounds as "abstractions," and described fields of corpses as an "amorphous installation."

Boris Lurie took the exact opposite approach. His aim was to create art from the raw material of life, from the pain that life had inflicted upon him. He wanted to use his individual will, his intellect, and his artistic abilities to understand, process, and transform his previous life experiences, which were so improbable and absurd; with and through his art, he hoped to learn how to cope with his past. Only through the act of remembering, through commemoration, could art do justice to the dead. Lurie's abiding and exclusive concern was to reveal the truth about life and the continuation of violence in the present day, while showing the general apathy of the audience towards this reality. It is a fundamental position that underlies all of the NO!art movement's provocations and actions, the details of which have been well documented elsewhere.

In the sense intended by Theodor W. Adorno – who, like Lurie, questioned "whether it is even permissible for someone who accidentally escaped and by all rights ought to have been murdered, to go on living after Auschwitz" – in the artworks produced after Auschwitz, "[p]erennial suffering has as much right to express itself as the martyr has to scream."[6]

Boris Lurie lived in Manhattan, in a studio he called his "New York surrogate Riga Ghetto"; on the walls hung, among other things, a map of Riga and a photo-

gleichnamigen Ausstellung in der March Gallery 1961: „Wir wollen Kunst schaffen, nicht zerstören, aber deutlich sagen, was wir meinen – und dies auf Kosten guter Manieren. Ihr werdet hier keine Geheimsprachen finden, keine raffinierten Ausflüchte, keine stillen Verschwiegenheiten, keine Botschaften, die an ausgewählte Hörer gerichtet sind. Kunst ist ein Werkzeug für Einflussnahme und Mahnung. Wir wollen sprechen, schreien, damit jeder es verstehen kann. Die Wahrheit ist unser Lehrmeister."[7]

1 Boris Lurie: *In Riga,* S. 296. Diese bisher nicht veröffentlichten autobiografischen Aufzeichnungen, die Boris Lurie von 1975 bis in die 1990er Jahre verfasste, sind im Besitz der Boris Lurie Art Foundation.
2 Ebd.
3 Susan Sontag: *Über Fotografie,* Frankfurt am Main 2003, S. 25 f.
4 Ebd., S. 26.
5 Boris Lurie: *In Riga* [Deutsche Übersetzung, nach: *KZ – Kampf – Kunst. Boris Lurie: NO!art,* Ausstellungskatalog, NS-Dokumentationszentrum der Stadt Köln, 27. 8. – 2. 11. 2014, hrsg. von der Boris Lurie Art Foundation, New York 2014, S. 29, Vorwort von Dr. Werner Jung].
6 Theodor W. Adorno: *Negative Dialektik,* Frankfurt am Main 1973, S. 355.
7 Boris Lurie: „Involvement Show Statement", 1961, zit. nach: Boris Lurie und Seymour Krim: *NO!art. Pin-ups, Excrement, Protest, Jew-Art,* Köln/Berlin 1988, S. 39 [Übersetzung der Redaktion].

graph of his childhood sweetheart, Ljuba Treskunova. In 1961, parallel to the Eichmann trial in Jerusalem, he wrote in a statement for the opening of the *Involvement Show* at the March Gallery: "We want to build art and not destroy it, but we say exactly what we mean – at the expense of good manners. You will find no secret languages here, no fancy escapes, no hushed, muted silences, no messages beamed at exclusive audiences. Art is a tool of influence and urging. We want to talk, to shout, so that everybody can understand. Our only master is truth."[7]

1 Boris Lurie, *In Riga*, p. 296. These unpublished autobiographical notes, written between 1975 and the 1990s, are held by the Boris Lurie Art Foundation.
2 Ibid.
3 Susan Sontag, 'In Plato's Cave,' in idem, *On Photography* (New York: Picador, 2001), pp. 3 – 24, here p. 20.
4 Ibid., p. 21.
5 Boris Lurie, *In Riga*.
6 Theodor W. Adorno, *Negative Dialectics* [1966], trans. Dennis Redmond (2001), paragraphs 354 – 8, available online at <<http://members.efn.org/~dredmond/ndtrans.html>>; accessed April 18, 2017. See also the published translation by E. B. Ashton: Adorno, *Negative Dialectics*, trans. E. B. Ashton (New York: Continuum, 1973), pp. 362f.
7 Boris Lurie, 'Involvement Show Statement' (1961), in Boris Lurie and Seymour Krim (eds.), *NO!art. Pin-ups, Excrement, Protest, Jew-Art* (Berlin/Cologne: Edition Hundertmark, 1988), p. 39.

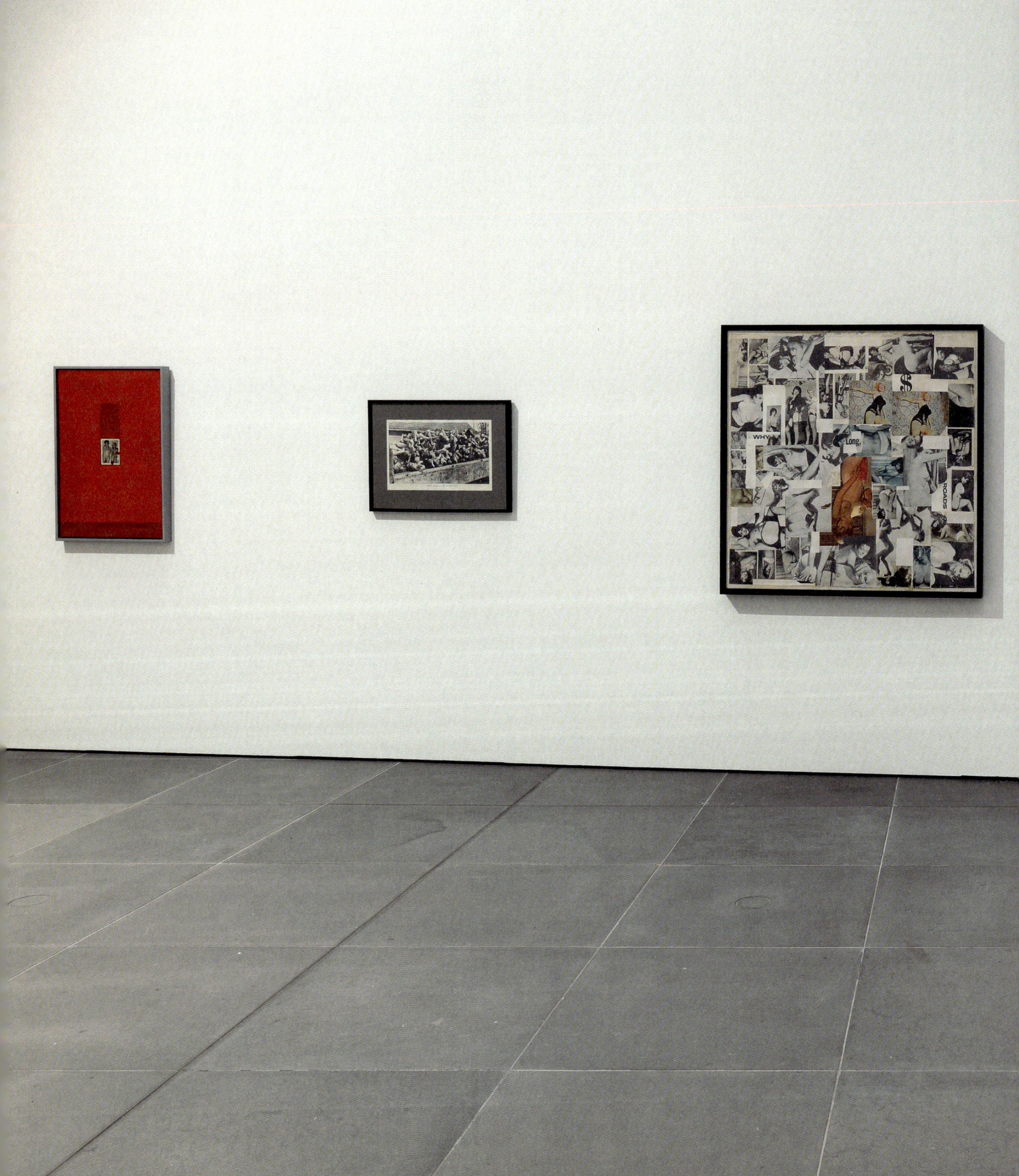
WHY
Long.
ROADS

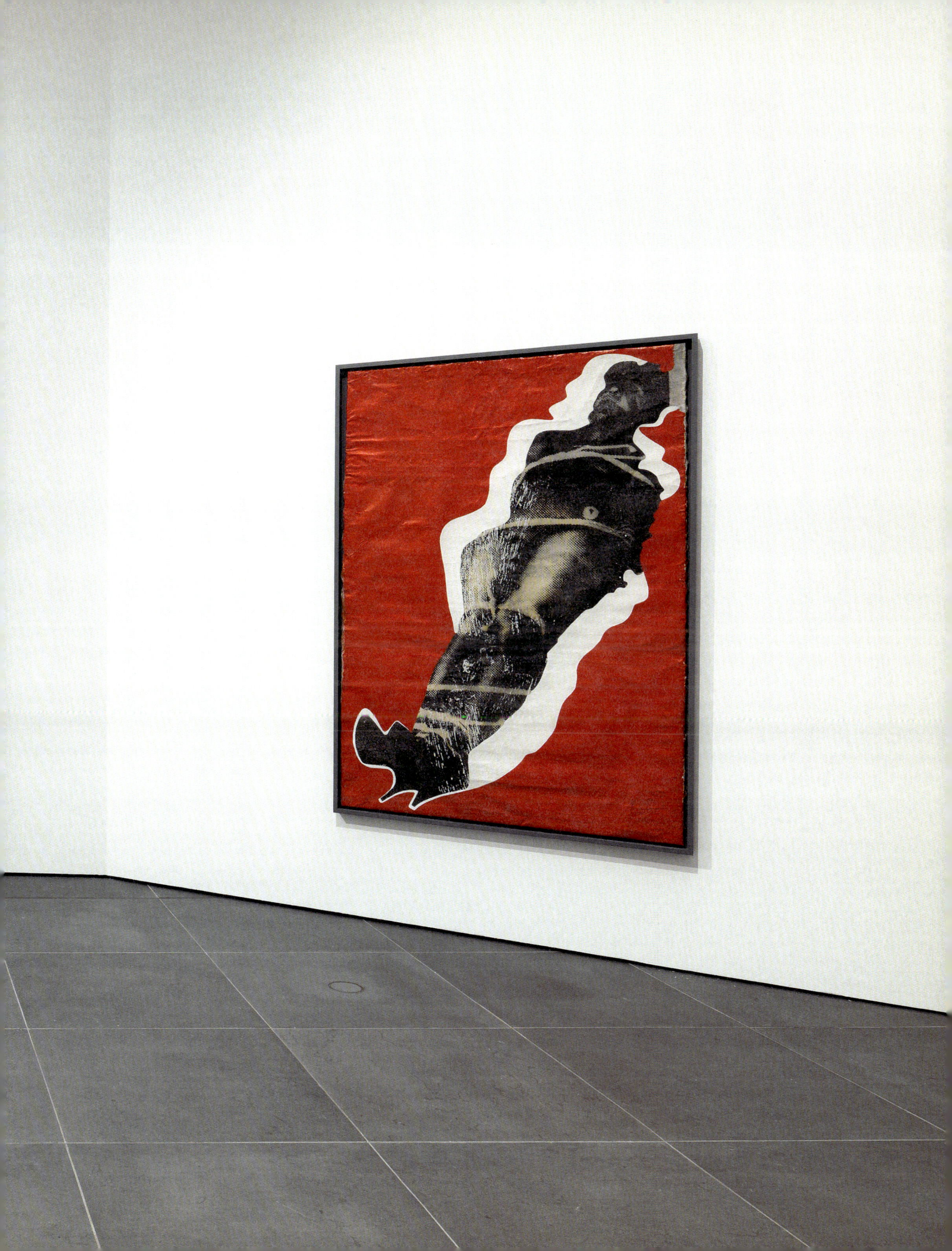

Dismembered Women

Die Serie *Dismembered Women* entstand kurz nach Boris Luries Ankunft in New York, in der Zeit zwischen 1947 und 1956. Zwei unterschiedliche Stilrichtungen kennzeichnen diese malerische Folge: Teilweise stark figurativ angelegte Arbeiten mischen sich mit abstrakteren Gemälden. Die Serie zeigt ausschließlich weibliche Figuren, die einerseits Luries ambivalentes Frauenbild, andererseits seine Erfahrungen im Zweiten Weltkrieg zum Ausdruck bringen: „Es war meine Reaktion auf New York und auf Amerika. Fette und zerstückelte Weiber. Fett und doch zerstückelt. All das nach dem Hunger und Krieg in Europa. Ganz sicher sind in diesen Bildern auch Spuren der Rigaer Rumbula-Massengräber zu finden, wo Zehntausende erschossen wurden. Ich malte zerstückelte Weiber. Ganz einfach und skulpturell modelliert."[1]

Während sich die realistisch gezeichneten Frauenfiguren noch mit der Tradition des Abstrakten Expressionismus in Verbindung bringen lassen und entfernt an Frauenbildnisse Willem de Koonings erinnern, sprechen die abstrakter gehaltenen Arbeiten eine andere Bildsprache. Bei *Combat* (1951) lassen die Farbgebung und die schwarz umrandeten Formen der kompakten Körper eine Nähe zu Arbeiten Fernand Légers erkennen. Die zumeist gesichtslosen, deformierten und zerstückelten Frauenkörper sind zu Objekten geworden. Sie sprechen von Enteignung, Macht und Gewalt. So ist bei *Dismembered Stripper* (1956) noch ein weiblicher Körper zu erkennen, wogegen bei *Combat* (1951) eine menschliche Figur nur noch erahnt werden kann. Formal ähnelt die plakative Farbigkeit dieses Gemäldes der Arbeit *Love Series: Bound on Red* (ca. 1963) und kann auch im Zusammenhang politischer Plakat- und Propagandakunst gesehen werden. Die Dialektik zwischen Angezogen- und Abgestoßensein, zwischen Attraktivität und Abscheu sowie die Gegenüberstellung von gemeinhin Unvereinbarem wird in diesen Bildern wie auch in später folgenden Serien thematisiert und in Szene gesetzt – der von Lurie als sexueller Fetisch häufig verwendete, hochhackige Stöckelschuh wird hier beispielsweise mit ungelenken, fettleibigen Frauenkörpern kombiniert. Diese eher figurativ angelegten Gemälde aus der Serie *Dismembered Women* rufen gleichsam Assoziationen an Körperdarstellungen Francis Bacons hervor, in dessen Arbeiten Fleisch als zentrales Motiv für den geschundenen und verstümmelten Körper steht und die Gefährdungen der menschlichen Existenz vermittelt. CM

1 Boris Lurie in: „NO!art. Dietmar Kirves im Gespräch mit Boris Lurie, dem Mitbegründer der NO!art", in: *neue bildende kunst. Zeitschrift für Kunst und Kritik*, Nr. 1/95, Berlin 1995, S. 48f.

Dismembered Women

The *Dismembered Women* paintings were made shortly after Lurie's arrival in New York, between 1947 and 1956. The series is characterized by two stylistic tendencies, as strongly figurative works mix with more abstract pictures. They all feature female figures, expressing both Lurie's ambivalent view of women and his experiences in World War II:

"It was my reaction to New York and to America. Fat, dismembered women. Fat but dismembered nonetheless. All of that after the hunger and war in Europe. These pictures certainly contain traces of the Rumbula mass graves in Riga, where tens of thousands were shot. I painted dismembered women. Quite simple and sculpturally modelled."[1]

While the realistically rendered women can be linked to the tradition of Abstract Expressionism, distantly recalling pictures of women by Willem de Kooning, the more abstract works speak a different visual language. In *Combat* (1951) the colors and black outlines reveal an affinity with the work of Fernand Léger. The mostly faceless, deformed, and carved up female bodies have become objects. They speak of dispossession, power, and violence. In *Dismembered Stripper* (1956), a female body is still identifiable, whereas the human figure in *Combat* (1951) can only be guessed at. The bold color scheme of this painting relates in formal terms to *Love Series: Bound on Red* (ca 1963) and can also be viewed in connection with political poster and propaganda art.

As in later series, these pictures address and stage the dialectic of attraction and revulsion, while juxtaposing elements usually considered incompatible. High-heeled stiletto shoes, a sexual fetish often seen in Lurie's work, is combined here with ungainly, obese female bodies. These more figurative paintings in the *Dismembered Women* series recall the work of Francis Bacon, where flesh is a central motif, standing for the abused and mutilated body, speaking of the vulnerability of human existence.

CM

1 Boris Lurie in "NO!art. Dietmar Kirves im Gespräch mit Boris Lurie, dem Mitbegründer der NO!art" in *neue bildende kunst. Zeitschrift für Kunst und Kritik*, 1/95, Berlin 1995, p. 48f.

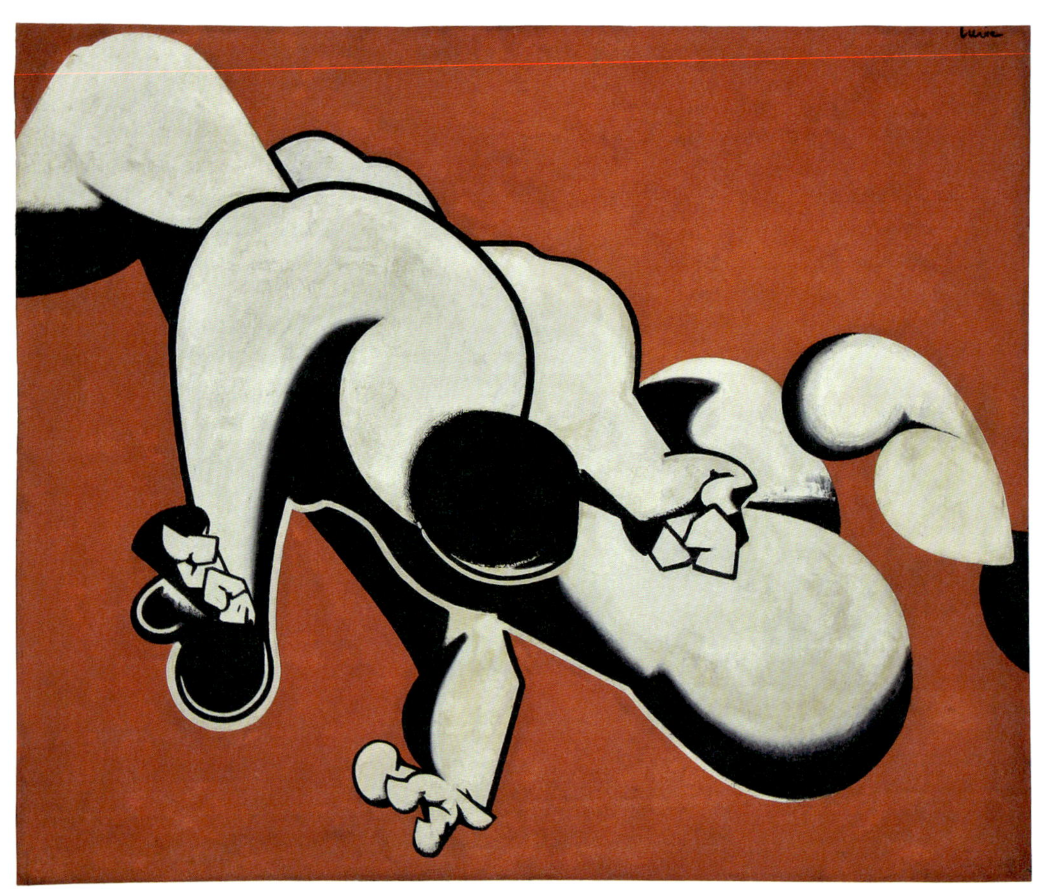

 Combat, 1951

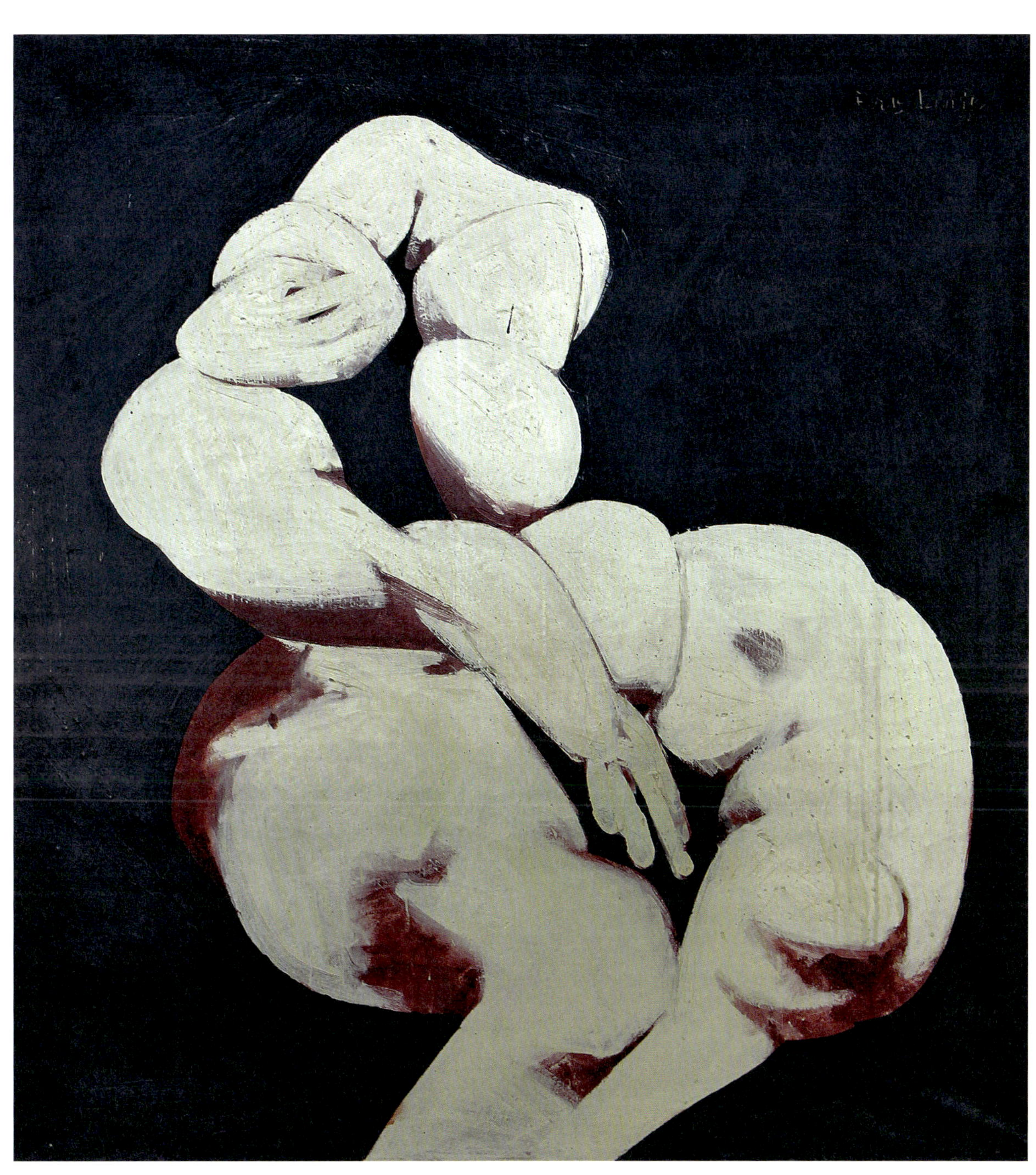

Dismembered Stripper, 1956

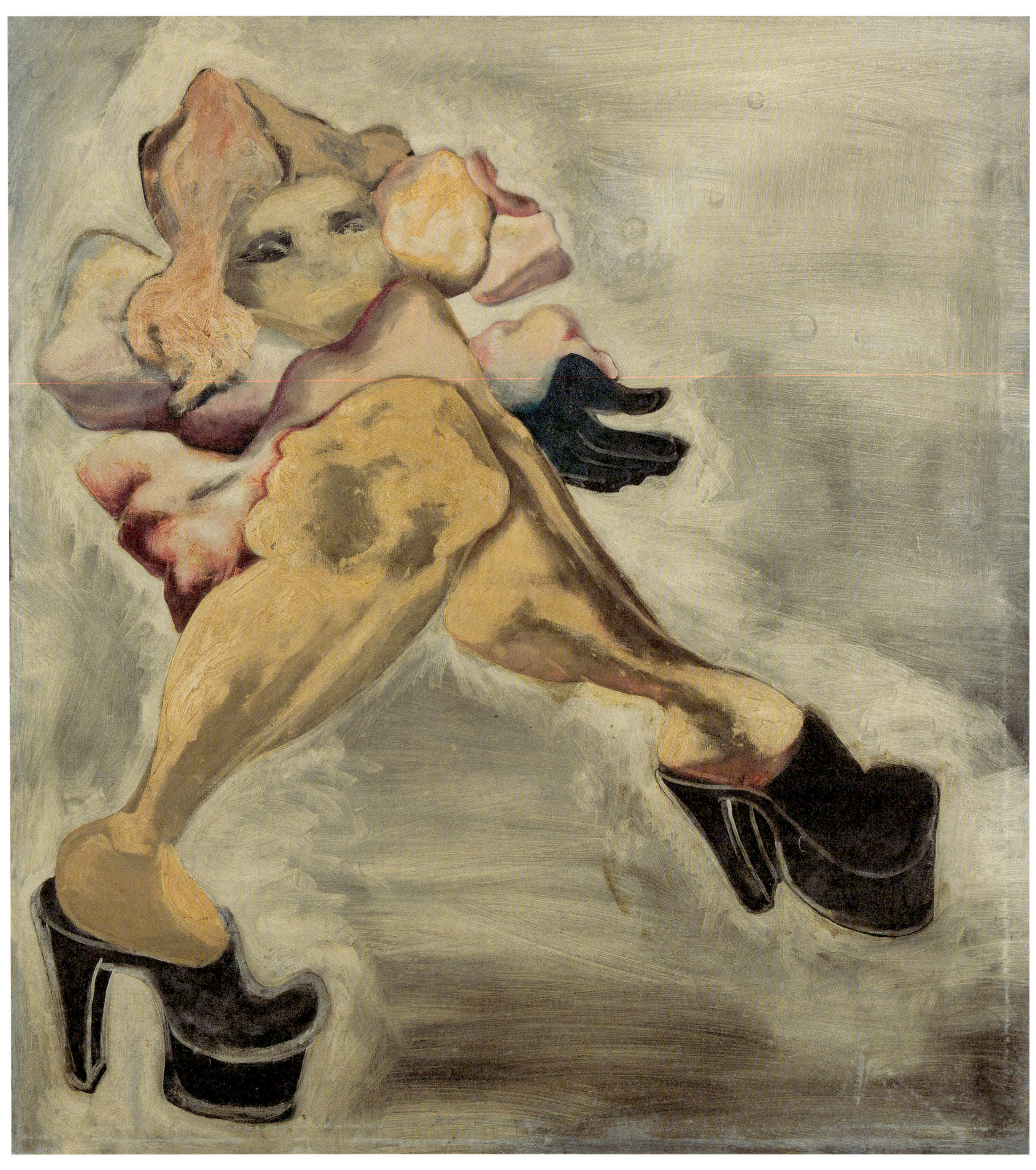

 Dismembered Woman, ca. / ca 1955

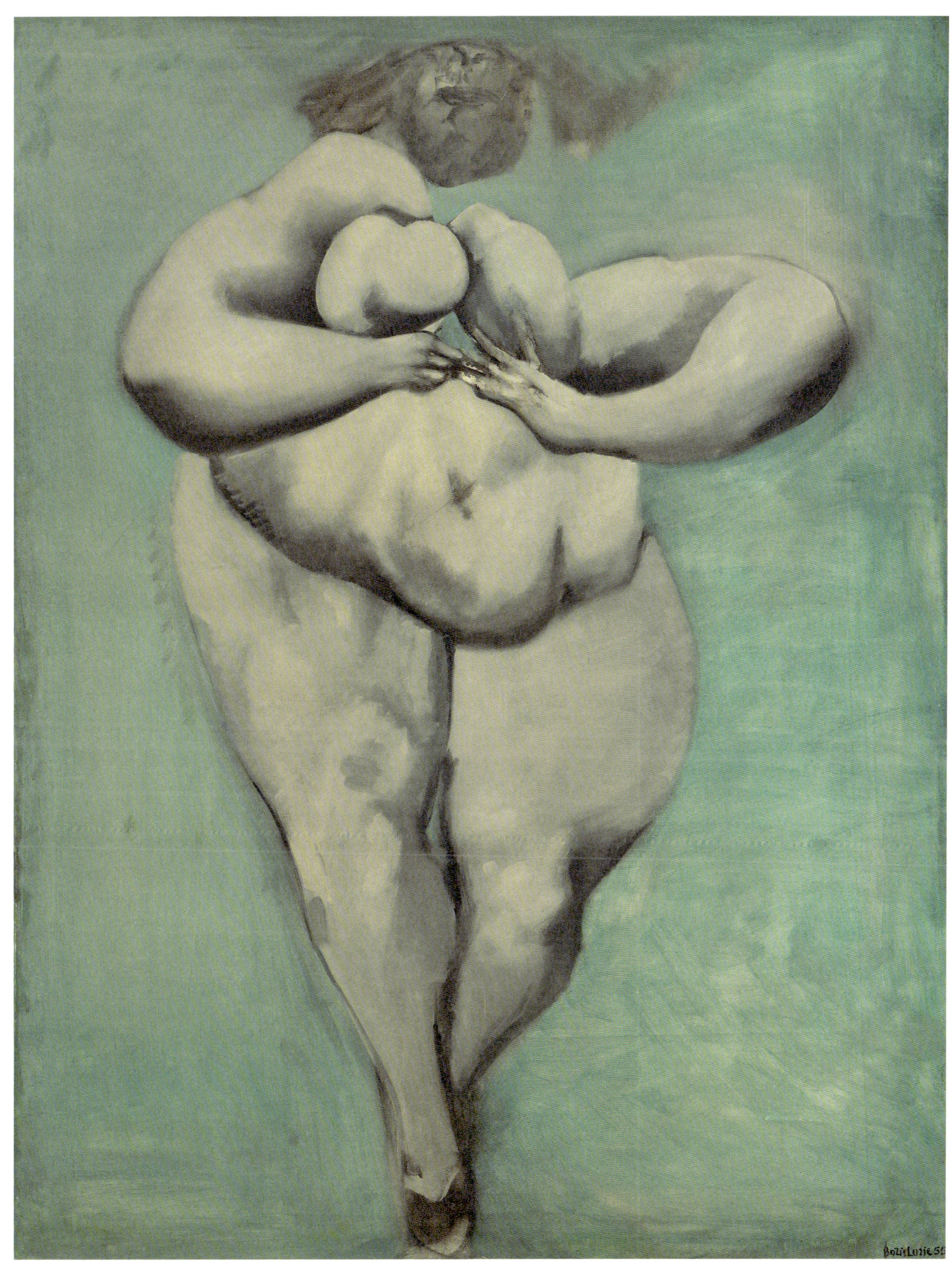

Dismembered Woman: Nude, Stepping, 1955

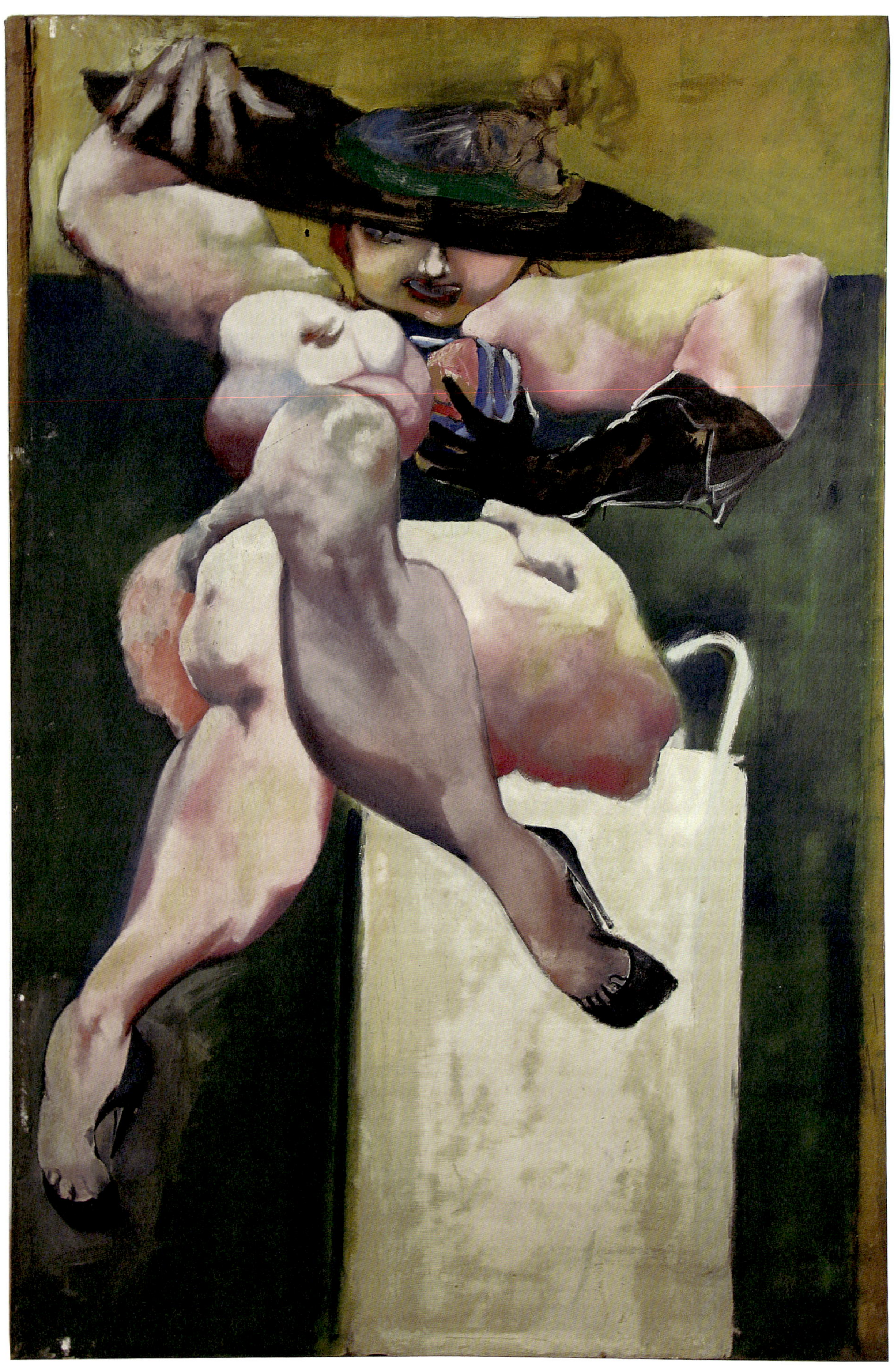

 Dismembered Woman: The Stripper, 1955

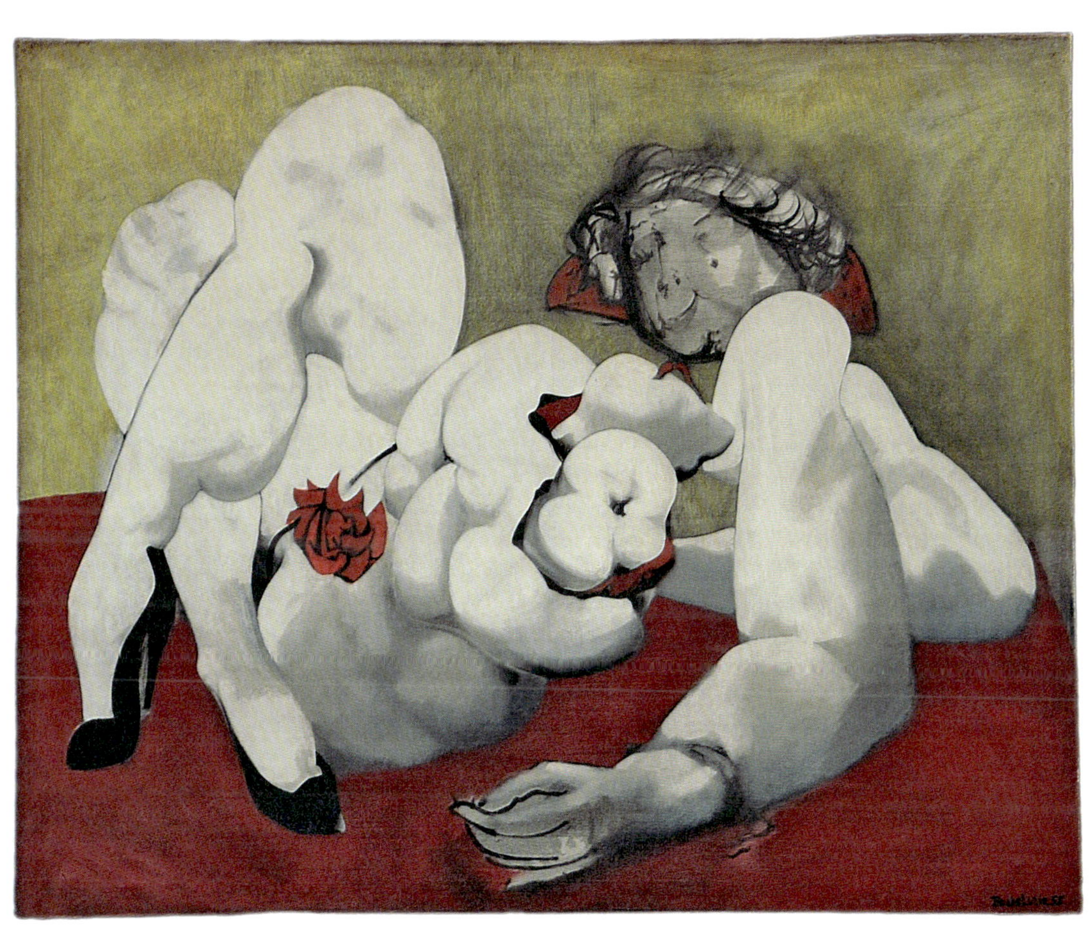

Dismembered Woman, 1955

Trauma

Seit Ende der 1950er Jahre entstehen Collagen – die sogenannten *Saturation Paintings*[1], die in mehrfacher Hinsicht eine „Sättigung“, vielleicht auch eine „Übersättigung“ mit Bildern des Holocausts andeuten. Boris Lurie verwendet hier erstmals historische Fotografien aus den Vernichtungslagern und kombiniert diese mit Pin-ups. Es sind Fotografien, die bereits 1945 in amerikanischen und britischen Zeitschriften und Magazinen in unmittelbarer Nachbarschaft zu Abbildungen von Stars, Mode, Kosmetik usw. abgedruckt wurden.

Indem Lurie Fotografien geschundener und gequälter Menschen oder toter Körper aus den Konzentrationslagern mit Bildern sexueller Provokation wie beispielsweise in *Railroad to America (Railroad Collage)* (1963) in Beziehung setzt, schafft er eine schockierende Bildrealität. Für den Offsetdruck *Flatcar, Assemblage, 1945 by Adolf Hitler* (ca. 1962) verwendet der Künstler zum wiederholten Mal die Fotografie aufeinandergestapelter Leichen in einem offenen Transportwagen aus dem befreiten Konzentrationslager Buchenwald. Erst durch die Bildunterschrift des Künstlers wird sie zu einem Kunstwerk, das als Readymade bezeichnet werden könnte. Durch die Betitelung stellt Boris Lurie einen geradezu ungeheuerlichen Zusammenhang zwischen Kunst und Vernichtung her. Dafür nimmt er die avantgardistische Gleichung von „Kunst = Leben“ wortwörtlich. So gesehen, verstand er das Vernichtungswerk Adolf Hitlers als „große Kunst“, wenn er bemerkt: „Zwar erklärte Duchamp, dass sein ganzes Leben Kunst sei, Hitler jedoch nahm das wirkliche Leben und formte es nach seinen Vorstellungen.“[2] Neben diesem puren Zynismus persifliert Lurie mit derartigen Aussagen auf schonungslose Art und Weise auch andere Künstler und Kunstrichtungen. Diese konzeptionell angelegte Arbeit gehört zu den erschütterndsten Werken des Künstlers.

Boris Lurie verweist mit diesen Arbeiten sehr deutlich auf Diskrepanzen zwischen seinen Lebenserfahrungen, Erinnerungen und aktuellen Lebensumständen: auf die Kluft zwischen der Erfahrung von Verfolgung, Internierung und menschenverachtender Demütigung und deren medialer Darstellung, auf das „Nebeneinander“ unterschiedlicher Lebensrealitäten und nicht zuletzt auf eine immer wieder von ihm konstatierte, oberflächliche und voyeuristisch verzerrte Rezeption des Holocausts. In diesem Sinne geht es auch immer um die Inszenierung des Blicks – des Künstlers, des Betrachters, des Fotografen – und nicht zuletzt um den der medialen Verwendung. Boris Lurie stellt damit die unerbittliche Frage, wie die NS-Verbrechen in den Medien verbreitet wurden und offenbart mit der ihm eigenen ästhetischen Radikalität die Beziehung zwischen den Greueltaten im Zweiten Weltkrieg und kapitalistischen, konsumorientierten und patriarchalen Systemen.

CM

1 Saturation wird in deutscher Sprache im Sinne von „Farbsättigung“ verwendet.

2 Boris Lurie in: Wolfgang Leidhold, „Die Moderne Kunst und der politische Diskurs. Eine Begegnung mit Boris Lurie“, in: *KZ – Kampf – Kunst. Boris Lurie: NO!art*, Ausstellungskatalog, NS-Dokumentationszentrum der Stadt Köln, hrsg. von der Boris Lurie Art Foundation, New York 2014, S. 29f.

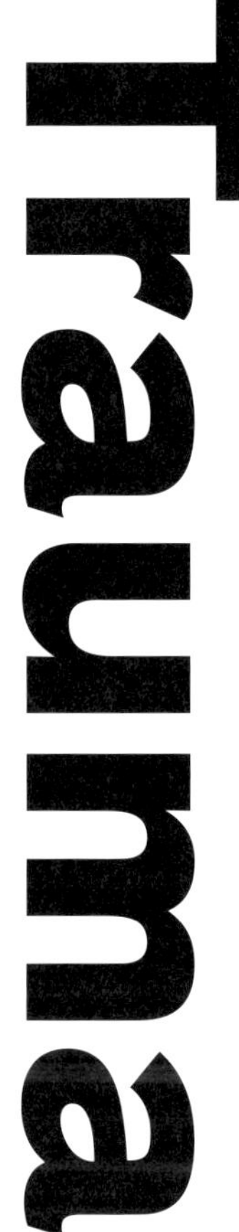

From the late 1950s onwards, Lurie made the *Saturation Paintings*, collages that speak of saturation in both senses,[2] perhaps even an over-saturation of images of the Holocaust. This was the first time Lurie had used historical pictures from the death camps, combining them with pin-ups. The photographs in question had already been printed in American and British magazines in 1945, alongside pictures of stars, fashions, cosmetics, etc.

By relating pictures of abused and tortured people or dead bodies from the death camps with images of sexual provocation, as in *Railroad to America (Railroad Collage)* (1963), Lurie created a shocking visual reality. For the offset print *Flatcar Assemblage, 1945 by Adolf Hitler* (ca 1962), Lurie used a picture of corpses piled up on an open railroad car after the liberation of Buchenwald concentration camp, a photograph he also used in several other works. With the artist's caption, it becomes an artwork that could be described as a readymade. With his choice of title, Lurie makes a positively monstrous link between art and annihilation, taking literally the avant-garde equation of "art = life." In this light, he understands Adolf Hitler's work of destruction as "great art" when he notes: "So then Duchamp said all life was art, but Hitler took real life and molded it to his liking."[3] Beside its pure cynicism and radically negative view of art, Lurie's statement is also a merciless parody of other artists and art movements. These conceptual pieces are among Lurie's most harrowing works.

With these works, Lurie points very clearly to discrepancies between his life experiences, memories, and current life conditions: to the gap between the experience of persecution, internment, inhuman humiliation, and their representation in the media; to the "co-existence" of different life realities; and, not least, to the superficial and voyeuristically distorted reception of the Holocaust – a recurring theme in his work. Among others, then, Lurie's work is thus always about staging the gaze – the gaze of the artist, of the viewer, of the photographer, and, not least, the gaze of media exploitation. In this way, Lurie raises the grim question of how the crimes of the Nazis were spread via the media, using a radical aesthetic to expose the links between the atrocities of World War II and capitalist, consumerist, and patriarchal systems. CM

1 As in saturated colors, but also in the sense of being completely permeated.

2 Boris Lurie, in Wolfgang Leidhold, "Die Moderne Kunst und der politische Diskurs. Eine Begegnung mit Boris Lurie" in *KZ – Kampf – Kunst. Boris Lurie: NO!art*, exhibition catalogue, NS-Documentation Center of the City of Cologne, ed. Boris Lurie Art Foundation (New York 2014), p. 29f.

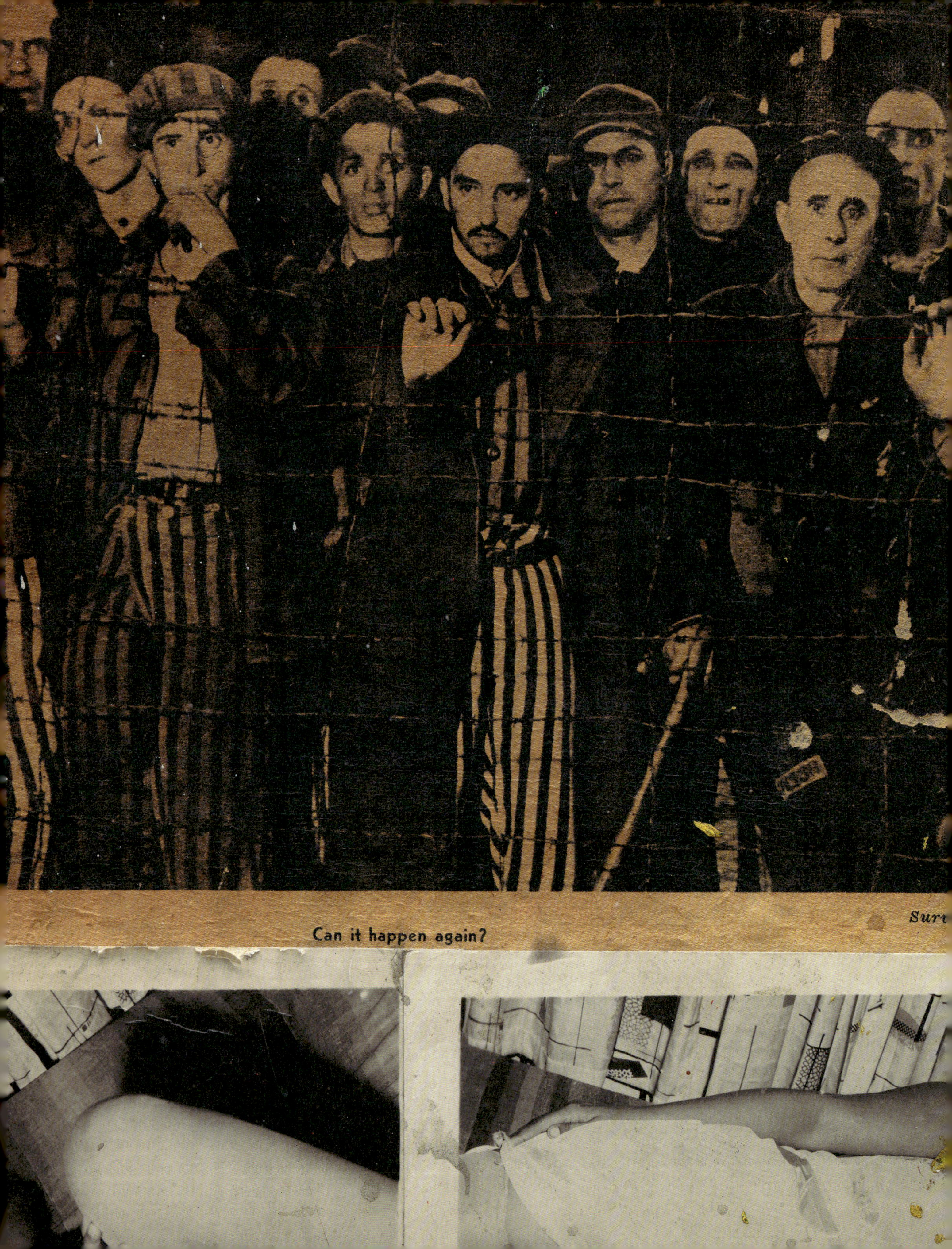

Can it happen again?

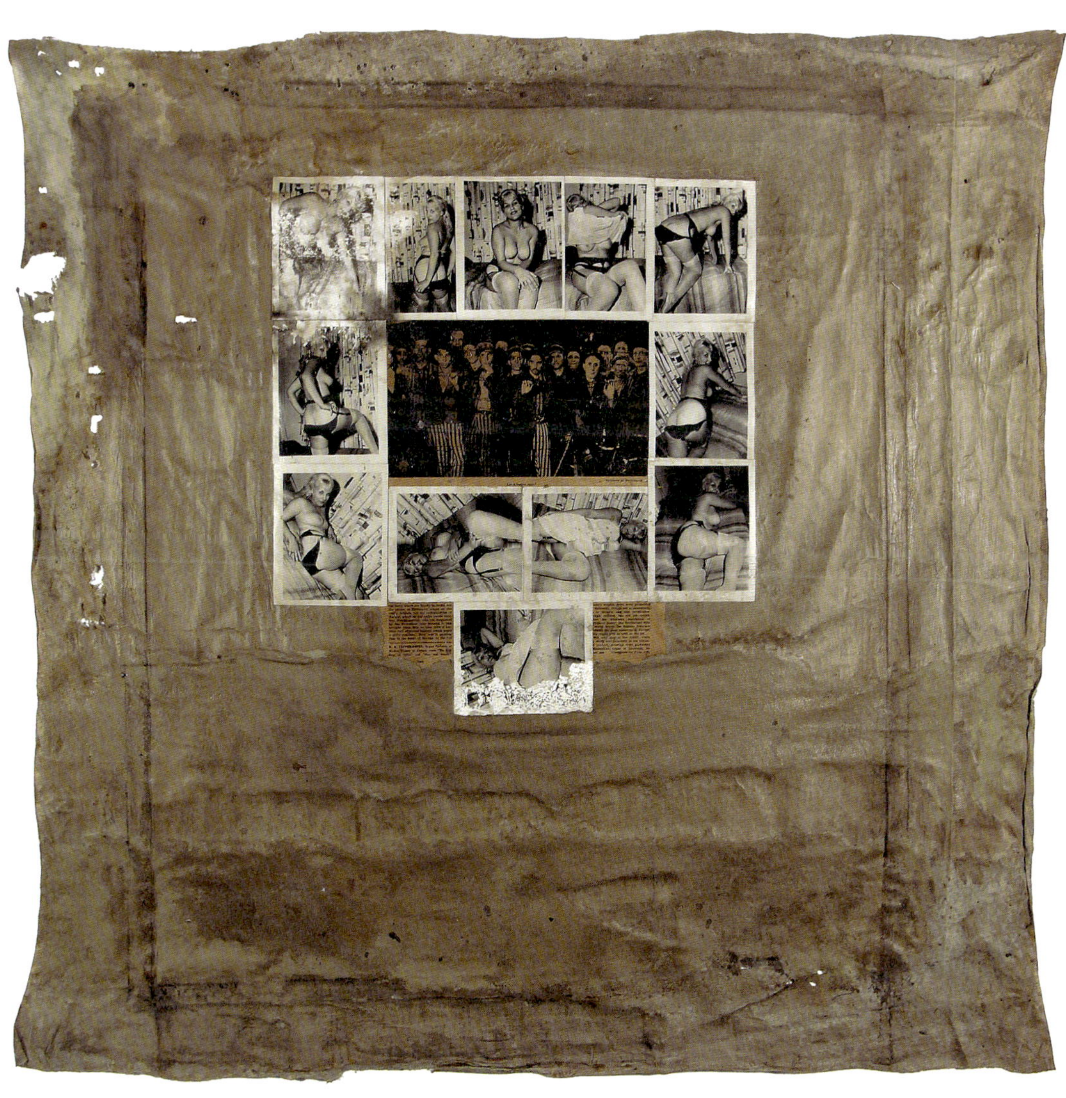

Saturation Painting (Buchenwald), 1960 – 63

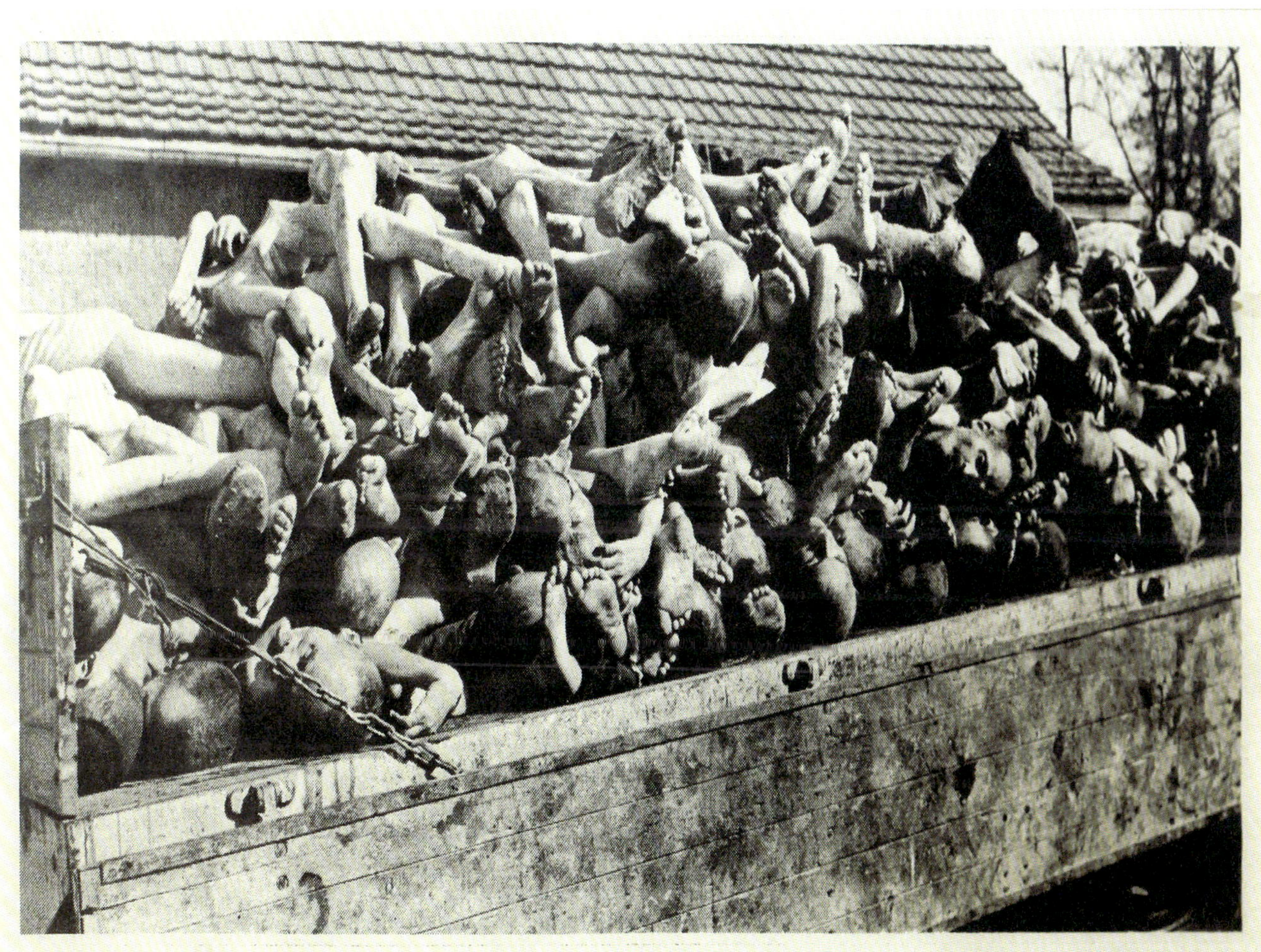

Flatcar, Assemblage, 1945 by Adolf Hitler, ca. / ca 1962

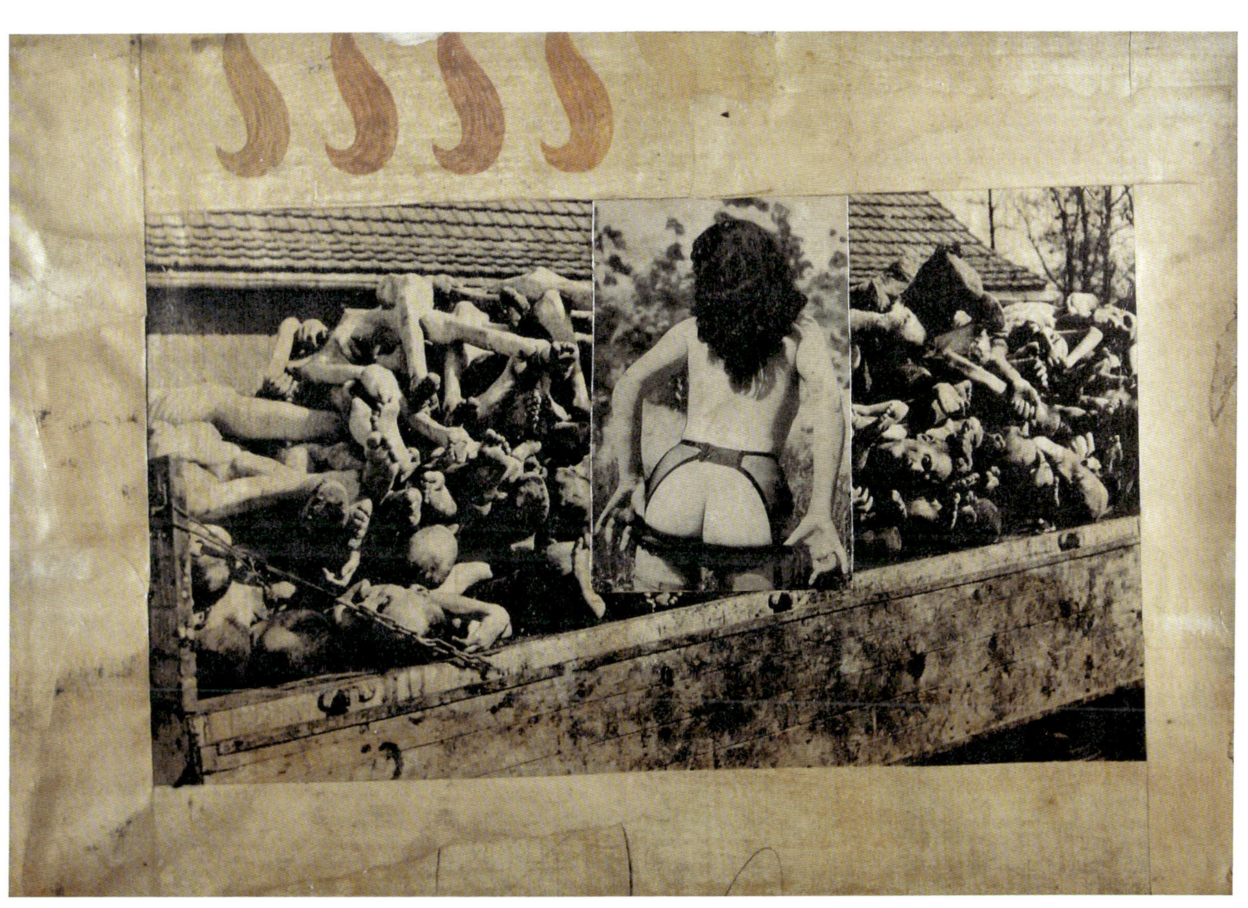

Railroad to America (Railroad Collage), 1963

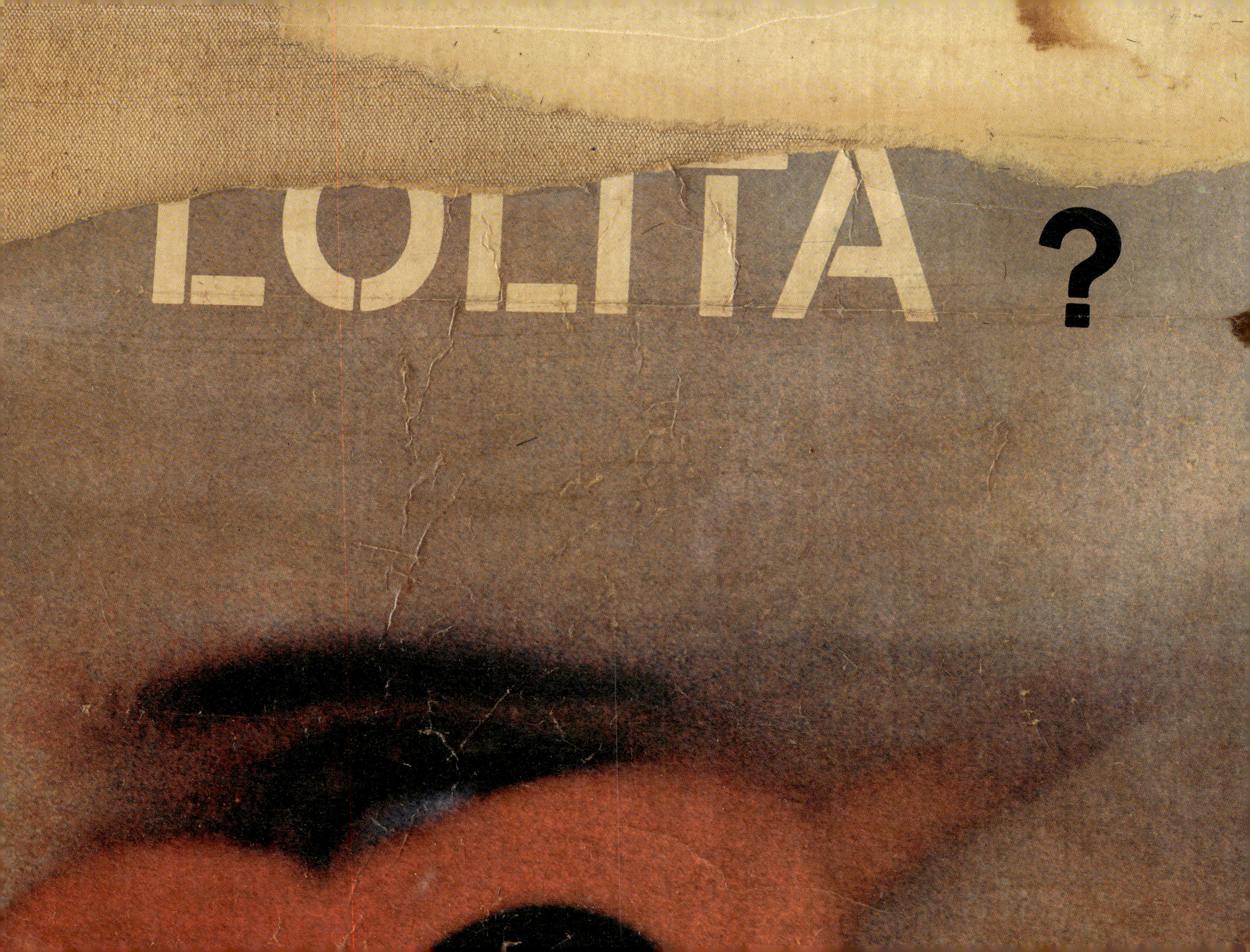
LOLITA ?

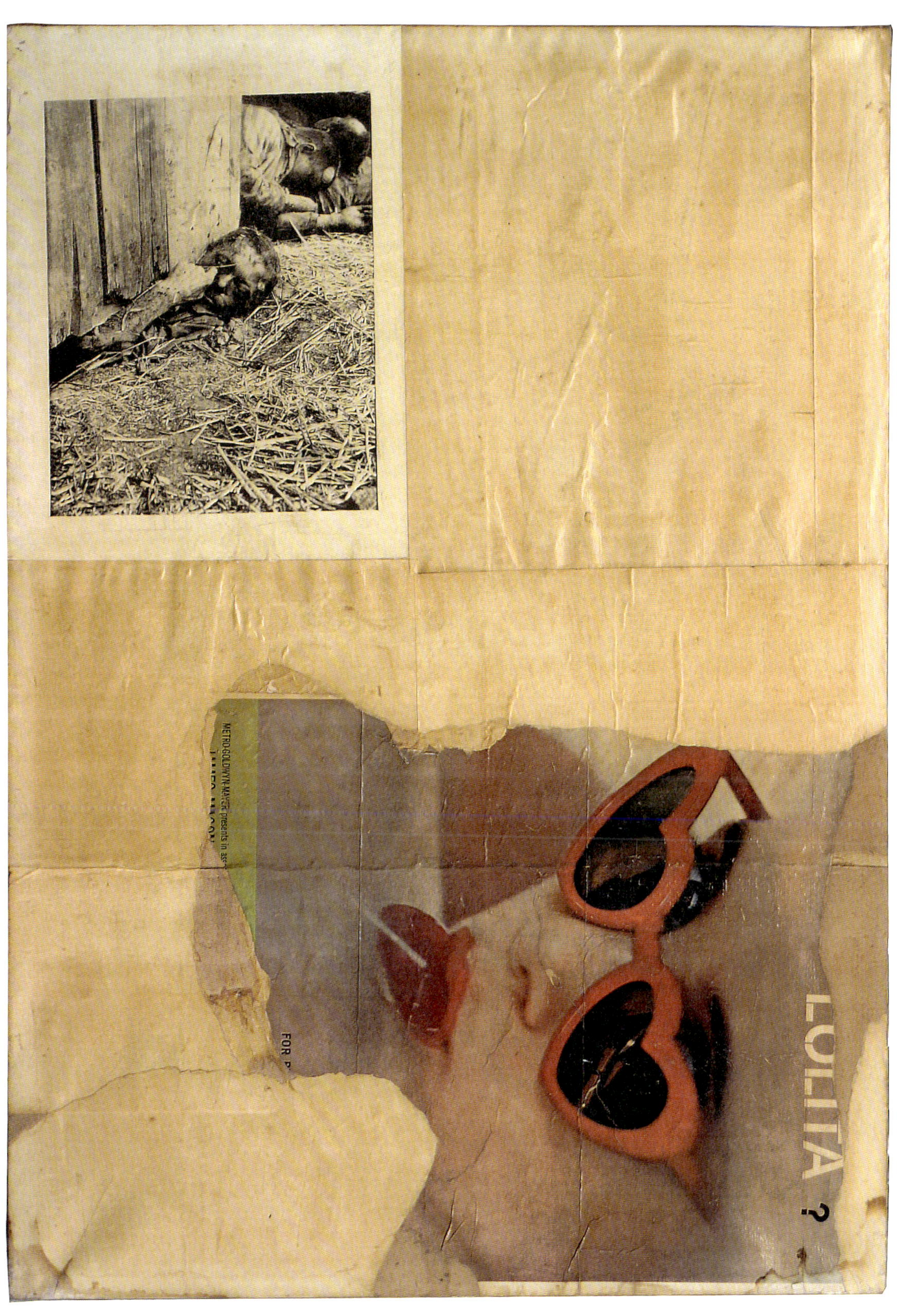

Lolita, 1962–63

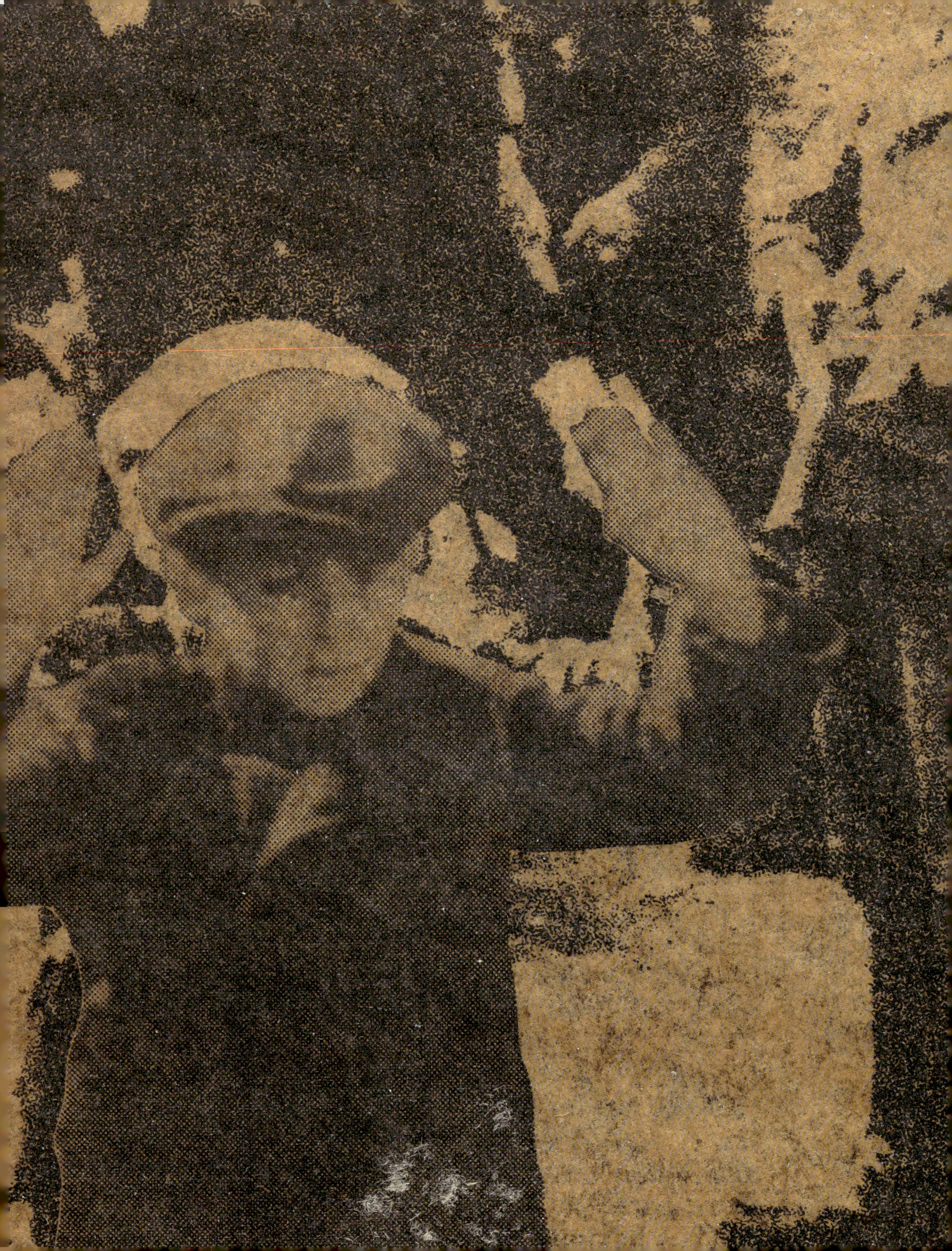

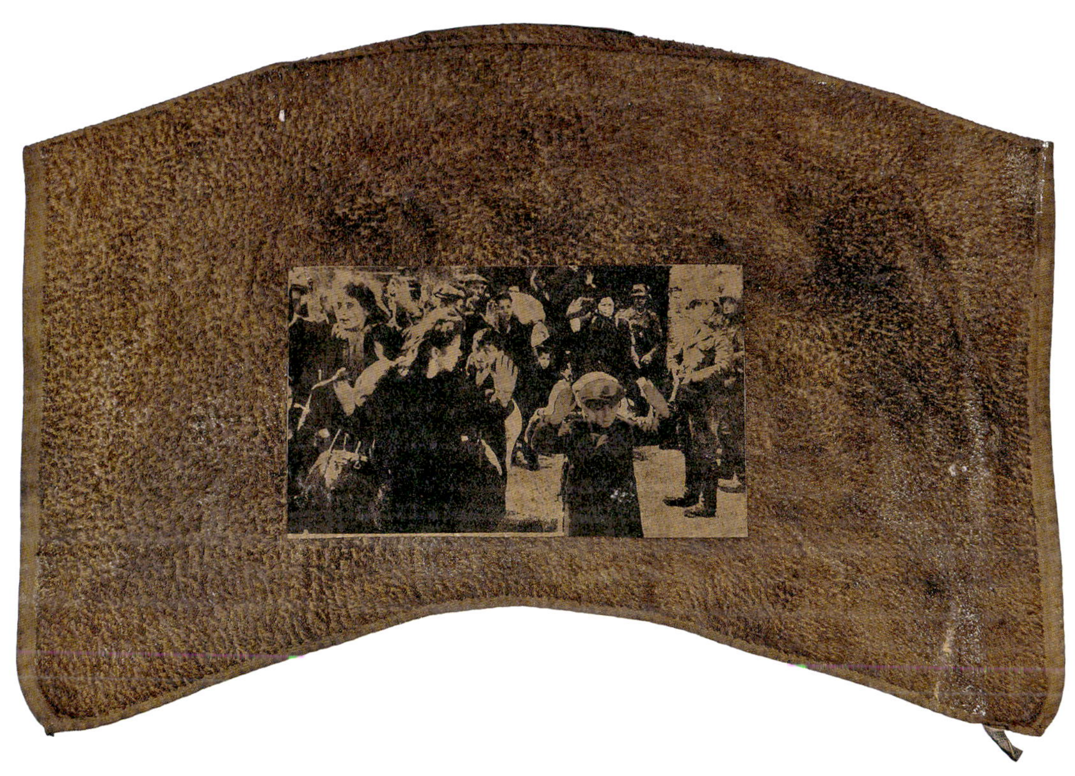

Untitled (Saturation Painting), ca. / ca 1963

Familie

Boris Luries Lebenserfahrung mit dem Holocaust spiegelt sich in zahlreichen seiner Arbeiten wider – ein Trauma, das letztlich sein gesamtes Werk und seine Sicht auf die Rezeption des Holocausts prägt. In seinen Zeichnungen, Collagen und Gemälden mischen sich Erinnerungsbilder grauenvoller Erlebnisse mit Bildern des „Danach". Die traumatische Familiengeschichte des Künstlers bildet dabei die Folie sowohl für die um 1946 entstandenen Zeichnungen als auch für das Porträt seiner Mutter – *Portrait of My Mother Before Shooting* (1947): Im Dezember 1941 wurden die Mutter von Boris Lurie, seine Großmutter, seine jüngere Schwester und seine Jugendliebe bei einem Massaker im Wald von Rumbula, in der Nähe von Riga (Lettland), ermordet. Dabei handelte es sich um eine der größten Erschießungsaktionen des Holocausts. Boris Lurie und sein Vater Ilja überlebten die Internierung im Rigaer Ghetto, die Arbeitslager Lenta und Salaspils sowie das Konzentrationslager Stutthof und ein Außenlager von Buchenwald. Während der insgesamt vierjährigen Lagerhaft gelang es Lurie, eine Mappe mit Familienfotos aus der elterlichen Wohnung zu retten. Darunter befand sich unter anderem auch eine Fotografie, die Lurie als 12-Jähriger von seinem Vater aufgenommen hatte. Diese Fotografie hing später – zwischen zahlreichen Zeitungsausschnitten, Pin-ups, eigenen Kunstwerken und allen möglichen anderen Papieren – neben dem *Portrait of My Mother Before Shooting* an der Wand seines Ateliers. Das Gemälde entstand aus der Erinnerung an seine Mutter, kurz nachdem Lurie mit seinem Vater Ilja 1946 in New York angekommen war.

Das Gesicht eines Menschen ist untrennbar mit seiner Identität verbunden. Boris Lurie ehrt und bewahrt mit diesem Porträt das auf schamlose und abscheuliche Weise ausgelöschte Gesicht seiner Mutter.

Zur gleichen Zeit begann der damals 22-jährige Boris Lurie mit einer Reihe von tagebuchartigen Zeichnungen, Tusche- und Aquarellarbeiten, die seine Erinnerungen und furchtbaren Erfahrungen im Ghetto und in den Konzentrationslagern sowie seine frühe New Yorker Zeit festhielten. Diese von ihm selbst als „private Zeichnungen" benannten Arbeiten verstand er nie als Teil seines künstlerischen Werks. Demzufolge wurden sie auch zu Lebzeiten des Künstlers nicht ausgestellt. Erst fünf Jahre nach Luries Tod wurden sie erstmals in einer Ausstellung in New York der Öffentlichkeit gezeigt.

CM

Family

Many of Boris Lurie's works reflect his life experience with the Holocaust – a trauma that ultimately shaped his entire oeuvre and his view of how the Holocaust has been perceived. In his drawings, collages, and paintings, memories of horrific events mix with pictures of what came afterwards. The artist's traumatic family history forms the backdrop for the drawings made around 1946 and for his *Portrait of My Mother Before Shooting* (1947): In December 1941, Lurie's mother, his grandmother, his younger sister, and his teenage girlfriend were murdered in a massacre at Rumbula forest, near Riga (Latvia), one of the largest single shootings of the Holocaust. Lurie and his father Ilja survived internment in the Riga Ghetto, the labor camps at Lenta and Salaspils, and the concentration camps at Stutthof and Buchenwald. Through his four years of incarceration, Lurie managed to hide and keep a folder of family photographs from his parents' apartment. They include a photograph of Lurie aged 12 taken by his father. Later, this photograph hung – among numerous newspaper clippings, pin-ups, artworks and all manner of other papers – on the wall of his studio beside his *Portrait of My Mother Before Shooting*. This painting based on memories of his mother was made shortly after Lurie arrived in New York with his father in 1946.

A person's face is inseparably connected to their identity. With this portrait, Boris Lurie honors and preserves the shamelessly and horrifically erased face of his mother.

At the same time, aged 22, Lurie began a series of journal-like drawings, works in ink and watercolor that record his memories and terrible experiences in the ghetto and in the concentration camps, as well as his early New York period. These "private drawings", as he called them, were works that he never saw as part of his oeuvre. Consequently, they were never exhibited during his lifetime. They were not shown in public until five years after his death in an exhibition in New York.

CM

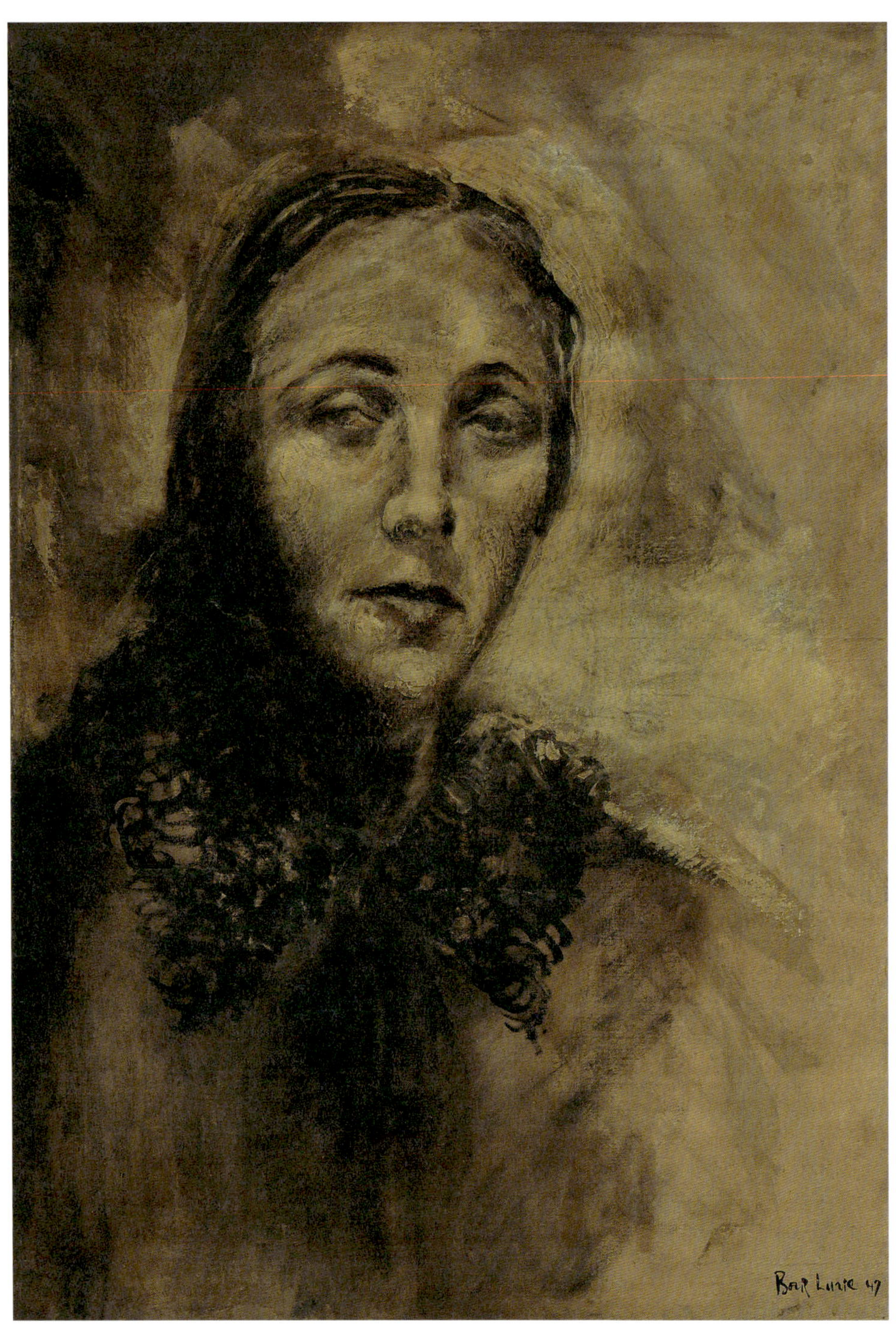

Portrait of My Mother Before Shooting, 1947

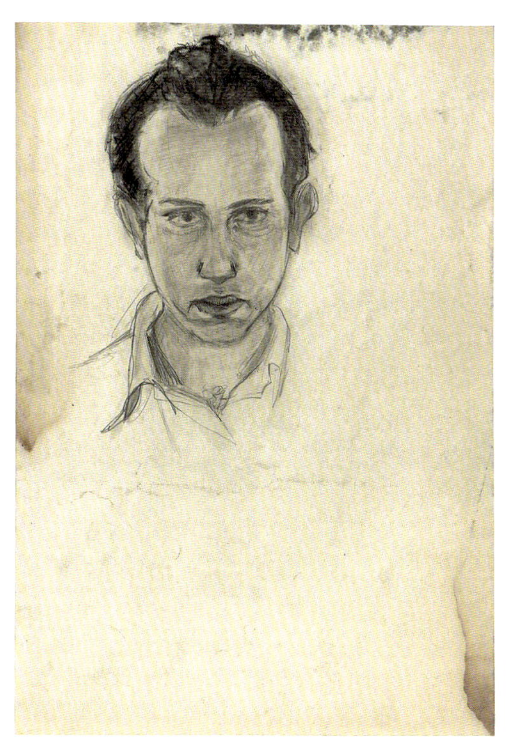

Untitled, ca. / ca 1946

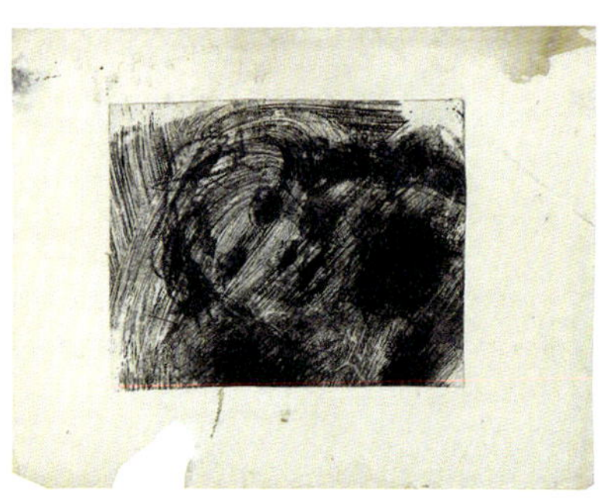

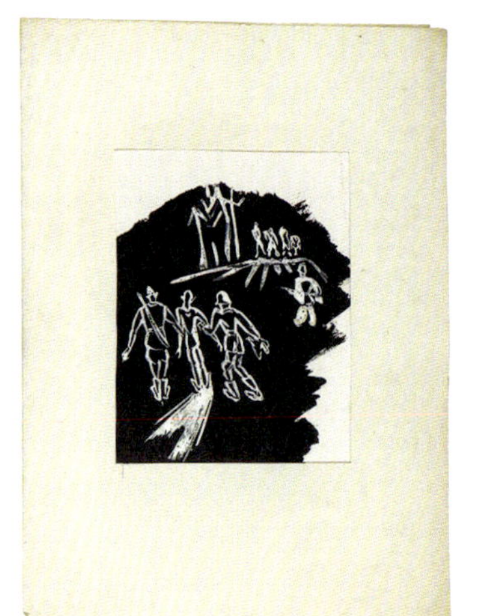

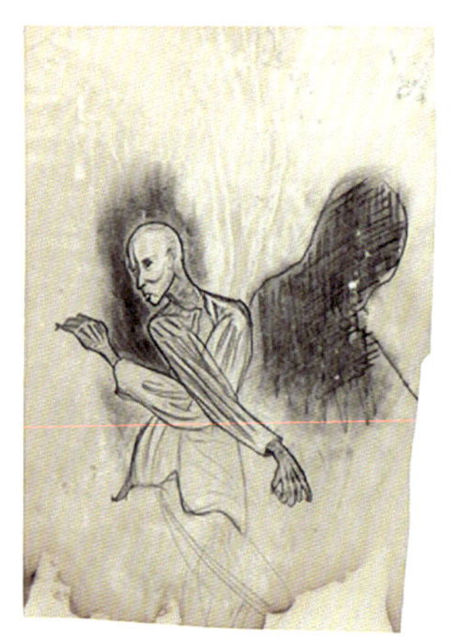

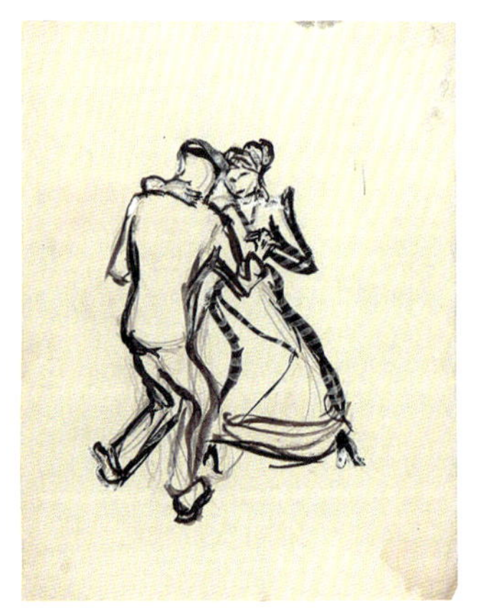

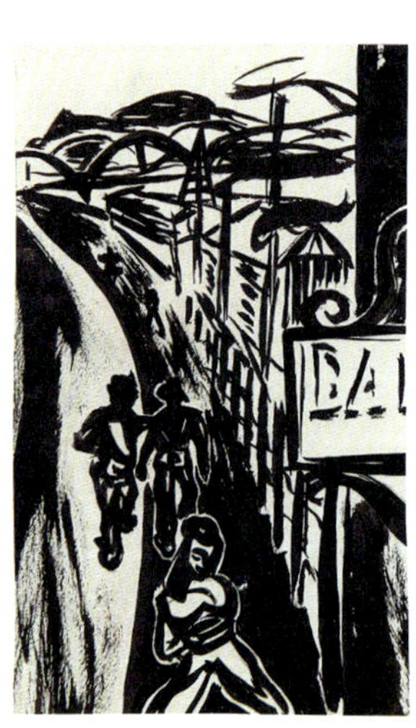

Untitled, ca. / ca 1946

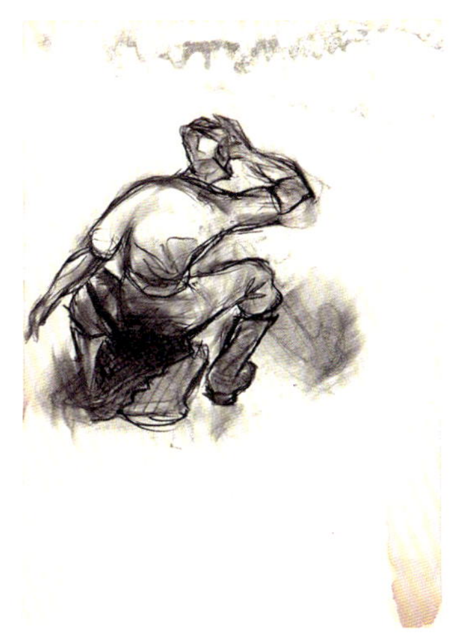
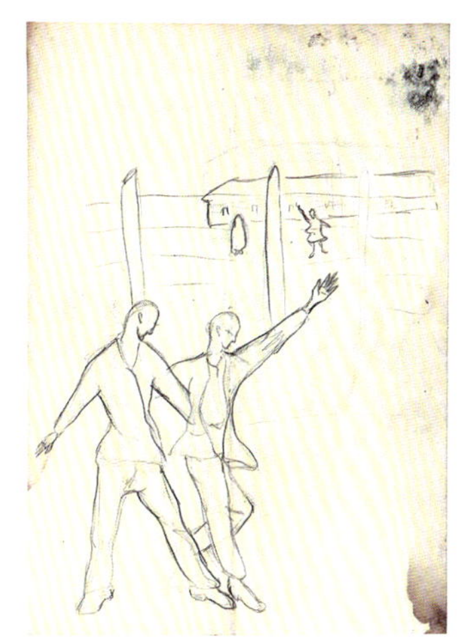
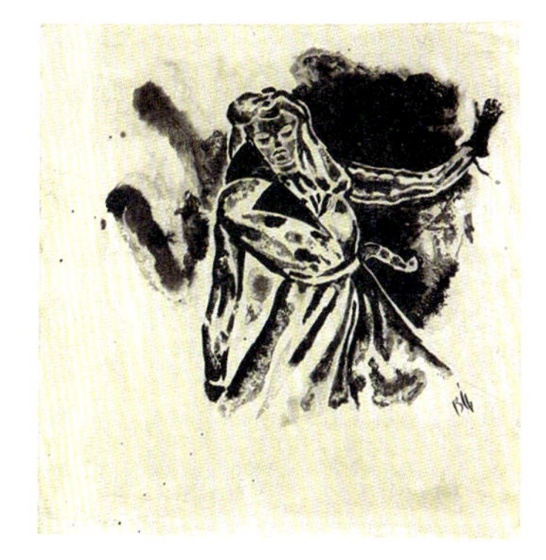
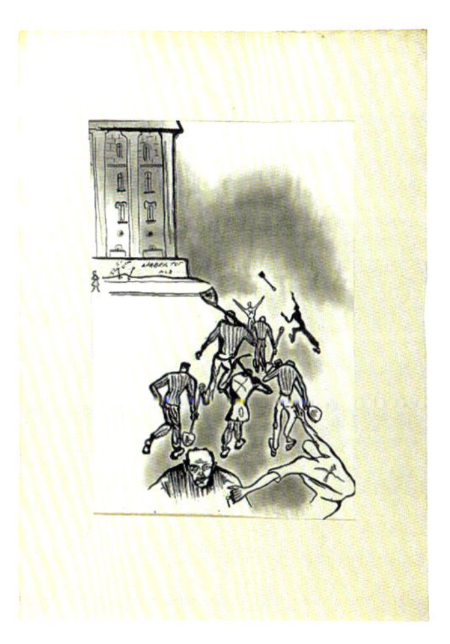
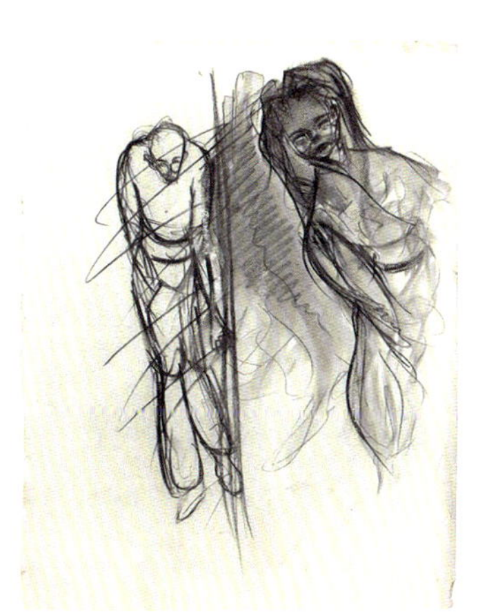
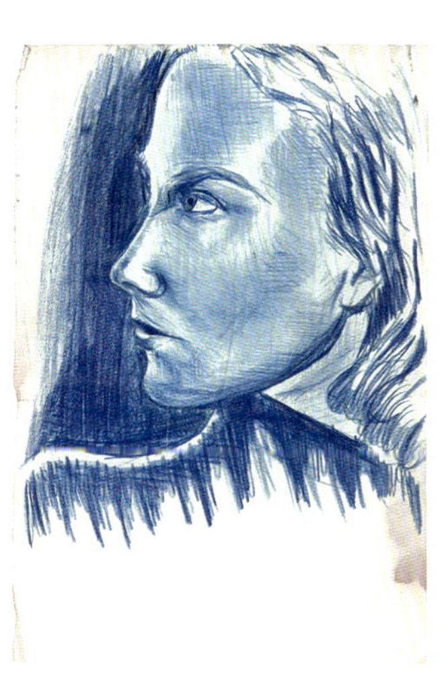

Untitled, ca. / ca 1946

Adieu Amérique

In einer Reihe von Werken Boris Luries taucht der Schriftzug „Adieu Amérique" auf. Auch eine Einzelausstellung des Künstlers in einer New Yorker Galerie im Herbst 1960 trug diesen Titel. Er steht für den nicht realisierten Wunsch des Künstlers, die Vereinigten Staaten in Richtung Frankreich oder Italien zu verlassen. Nicht zuletzt die imperialistische Politik seiner neuen Heimat hatte ihn zutiefst enttäuscht.

Als eine der politisch offenkundigsten Arbeiten kann die Collage *Lumumba is Dead (Adieu Amérique)* (1959 – 61) gelten. Malerei tritt hier zugunsten des „Bildermachens" vollkommen zurück. Zahlreiche, sehr unterschiedliche Bildmaterialien sind zueinander in Beziehung gesetzt und durchdringen sich gegenseitig: Bestellbögen für Pin-ups, Anzeigen für Damenunterwäsche, Tierbilder, erotische Spielkarten, Comics, Heiligenfiguren, Abbildungen sadomasochistischer Szenen, Hakenkreuze in verschiedenen Größen, diverse Zeitungsausschnitte und die Einladung zu einer Gedenkveranstaltung für die in Lettland ermordeten Juden. In unmittelbarer Nähe dazu ist in Großbuchstaben „December" zu lesen, der Monat, in dem Luries Mutter 1941 ermordet wurde. Das zentral gesetzte, gegenläufige Hakenkreuz überschreibt ein gezeichnetes Porträt von Adolf Eichmann sowie einen Zeitungsartikel mit dem Titel „Adieu Amérique". Die titelgebenden Worte „Lumumba is Dead" sind auf die linke und rechte Bildhälfte aufgeteilt.

Der 1960 von den USA unterstützte Putsch gegen den ersten demokratisch gewählten Premierminister des unabhängigen Kongo, Patrice Lumumba, und dessen durch die USA forcierte Ermordung 1961 gehören zu den strittigsten Ereignissen des Kalten Krieges. Den wirtschaftlichen Interessen der ehemaligen Kolonialmacht Belgien und denen der USA stand Lumumbas entschiedener Kampf entgegen, seinem Land politische und wirtschaftliche Unabhängigkeit zu verschaffen.

Boris Lurie projiziert in *Lumumba is Dead (Adieu Amérique)* die nationalsozialistische Machtherrschaft auf die gegenwärtige Politik der USA und will verdeutlichen, dass totalitäre Strukturen auch in demokratischen Gesellschaften weiterhin Bestand haben. Die Gegenüberstellung von Sexualität und staatlich organisierter Gewalt ist dabei einerseits Ausdruck seines bedingungslosen politischen Protests, und andererseits veranschaulicht sie in aller Radikalität seine Illusionslosigkeit.

Wie stark sich Boris Lurie mit seinem künstlerischen Schaffen der jeweiligen Zeitgeschichte annähert, wird auch anhand der Collagen *NO with Mrs. Kennedy* (1963) und *Oswald* (1963) deutlich. Letztgenannte entsteht unmittelbar nach der Ermordung John F. Kennedys und zeigt den Mörder des Präsidenten, Lee Harvey Oswald. Beide Collagen stehen für Luries kritisches Verhältnis gegenüber dem US-amerikanischen Politikgeschehen insbesondere während des Kalten Krieges und der Kuba-Krise zu Beginn der 1960er Jahre.

Seine radikale Kritik an einer Gesellschaft, die zu dieser Zeit gekennzeichnet war durch Puritanismus, Repression, Sexismus und historische Ignoranz, war dabei immer begleitet von seiner Suche nach einem „wahrhaftigen" Leben ohne Selbsttäuschung und Tröstungsversuche als Überlebender des Massenmords an den europäischen Juden in Europa. CM

Adieu Amérique

A number of Lurie's works include the words "Adieu Amérique" that were also used as the title for his solo show at a New York gallery in the fall of 1960. They stand for Lurie's unrealized wish to leave the United States for France or Italy, due not least to his deep disappointment over the imperialist politics of his new home country.

One of Lurie's most obviously political works is the collage *Lumumba is Dead (Adieu Amérique)* (1959 – 61). Here, painting takes a back seat to "picture making," interrelating and intermingling very different image materials: order forms for pin-ups, ads for women's underwear, animal pictures, erotic playing cards, comics, figures of saints, sadomasochist scenes, swastikas in various sizes, newspaper clippings, and the announcement of an event commemorating the Jews murdered in Latvia. Right next to this, in capital letters, stands "DECEMBER," the month in which Lurie's mother was murdered in 1941. The centrally placed reversed swastika overwrites a portrait of Adolf Eichmann, and a newspaper article with the headline "Adieu Amérique." The words in the title "Lumumba is Dead" are divided between the left and right halves of the picture.

The US-supported putsch in 1960 against the first democratically elected prime minister of Congo, Patrice Lumumba, and his murder in 1961, also with US involvement, were some of the most controversial events in the Cold War. The economic interests of the former colonial power Belgium and the United States were at odds with Lumumba's determined struggle to establish political and economic independence for his country.

In *Lumumba is Dead (Adieu Amérique)*, Lurie projects the Nazi regime onto the contemporary politics of the United States, aiming to highlight the way totalitarian structures continue to exist even in democratic societies. The juxtaposition of sexuality and state-organized violence is an expression of his unconditional political protest, but it also radically illustrates his lack of illusions.

How closely Lurie followed current events in his art is made clear by the collages *No with Mrs. Kennedy* (1963) and *Oswald* (1963). The latter was made immediately after the assassination of John F. Kennedy and shows the president's killer, Lee Harvey Oswald. Both of these collages stand for Lurie's critical stance towards political events in the United States, especially during the Cold War and the Cuban Missile Crisis of the early 1960s. His radical critique of a society marked at the time by puritanism, repression, sexism, and ignorance of history was always accompanied by his search for a "true" life without self-deception or attempts at consolation as a survivor of the mass murder of the European Jews. CM

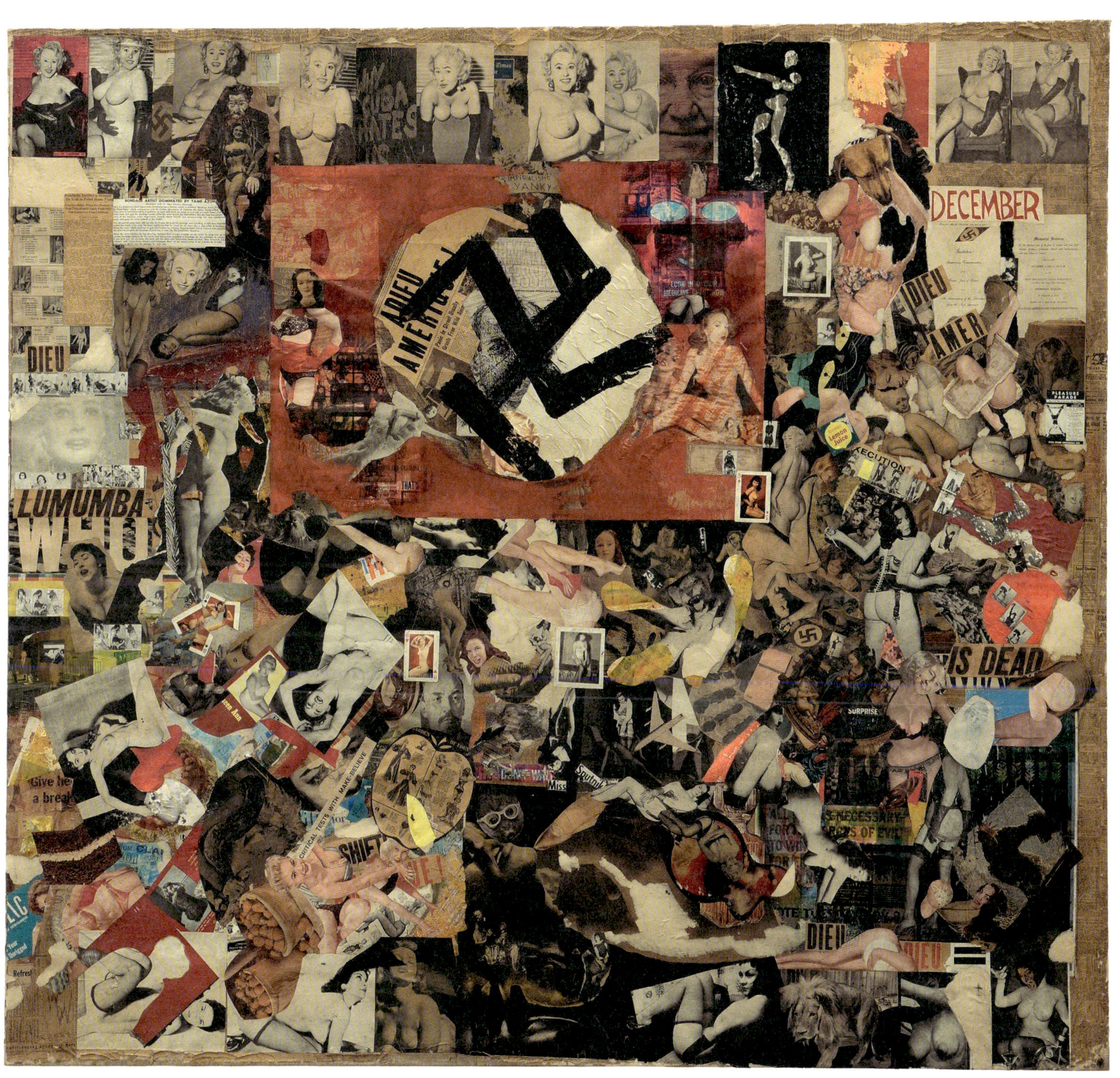

Lumumba is Dead (Adieu Amérique), 1959 – 61

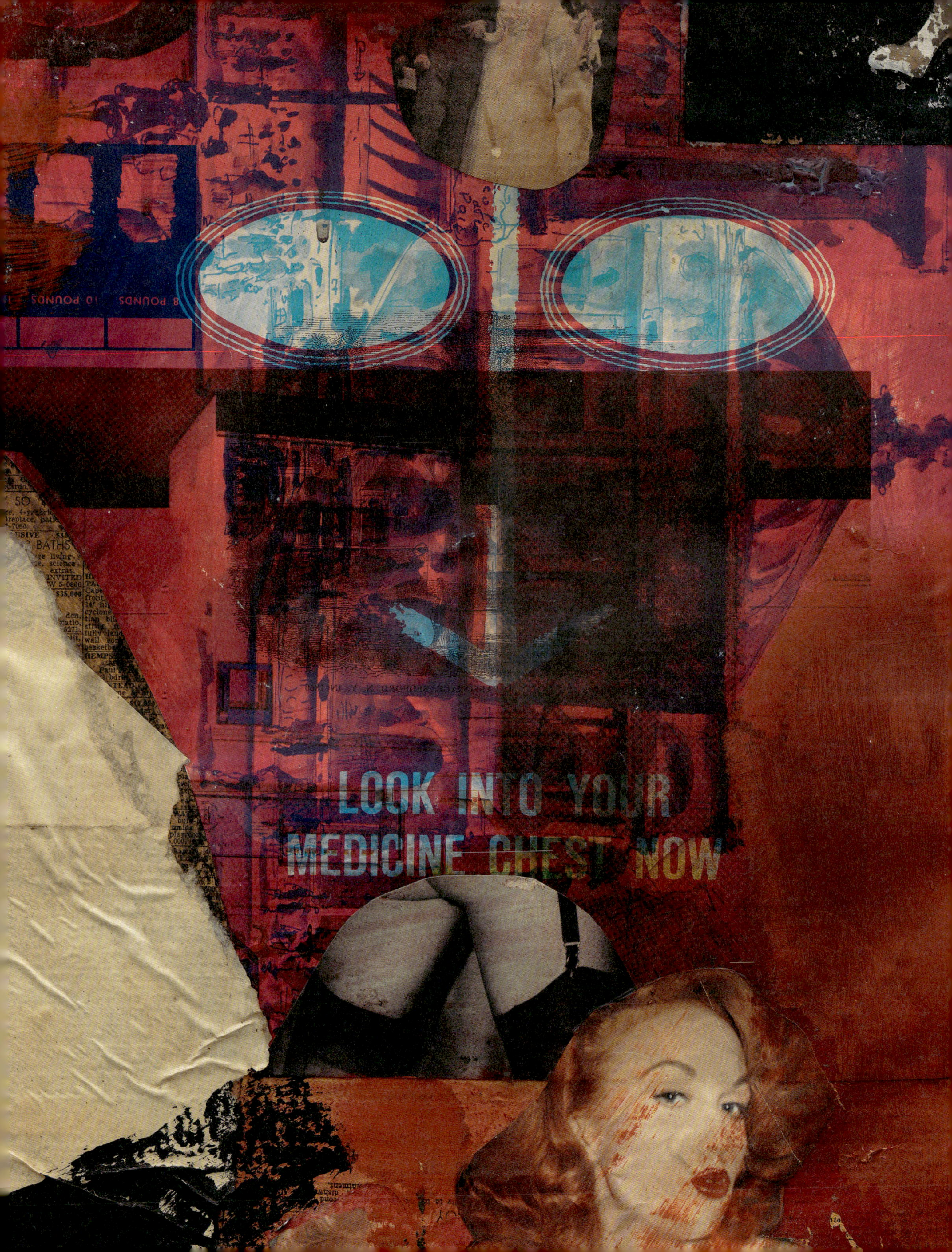
LOOK INTO YOUR
MEDICINE CHEST NOW

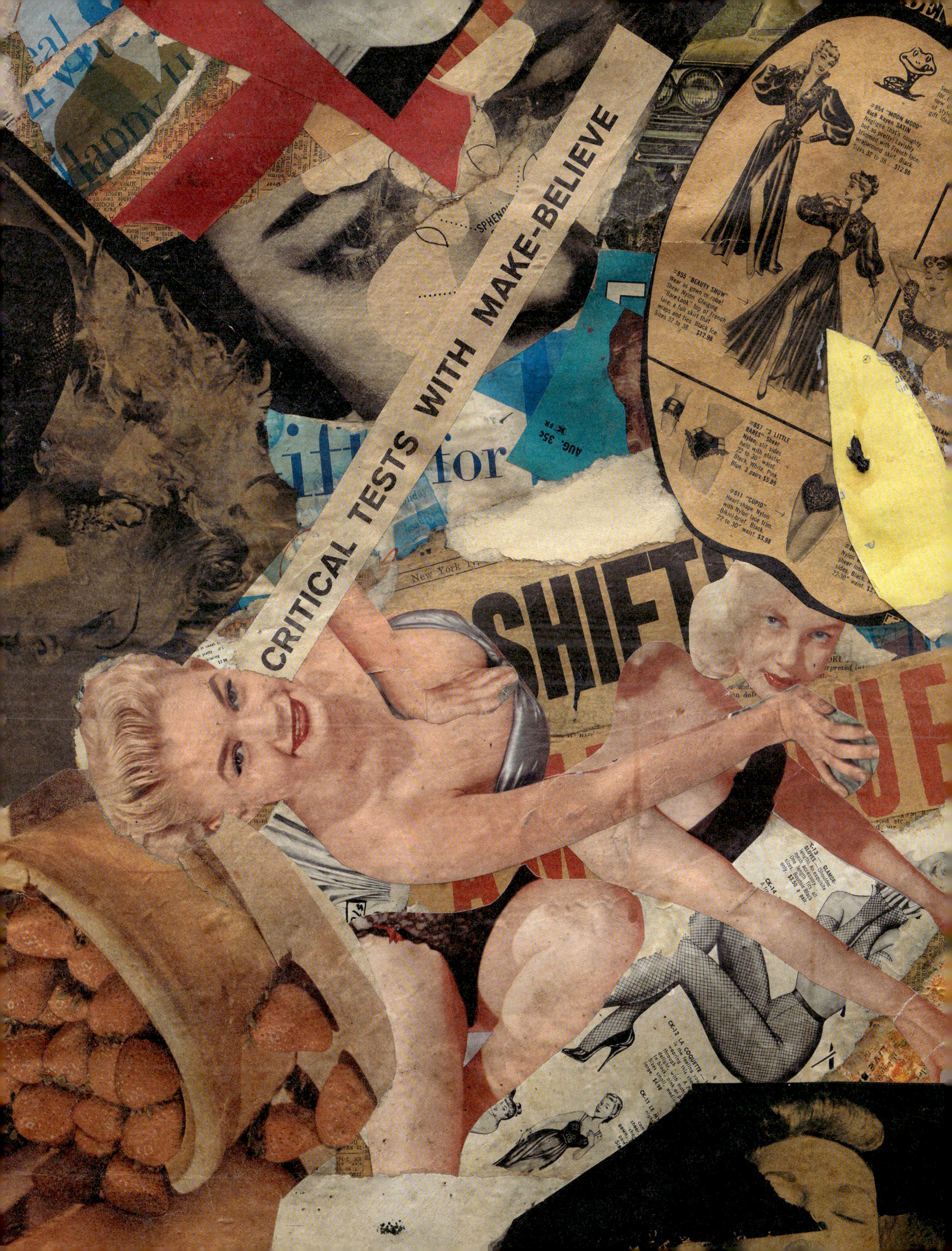
CRITICAL TESTS WITH MAKE-BELIEVE
SHIFT

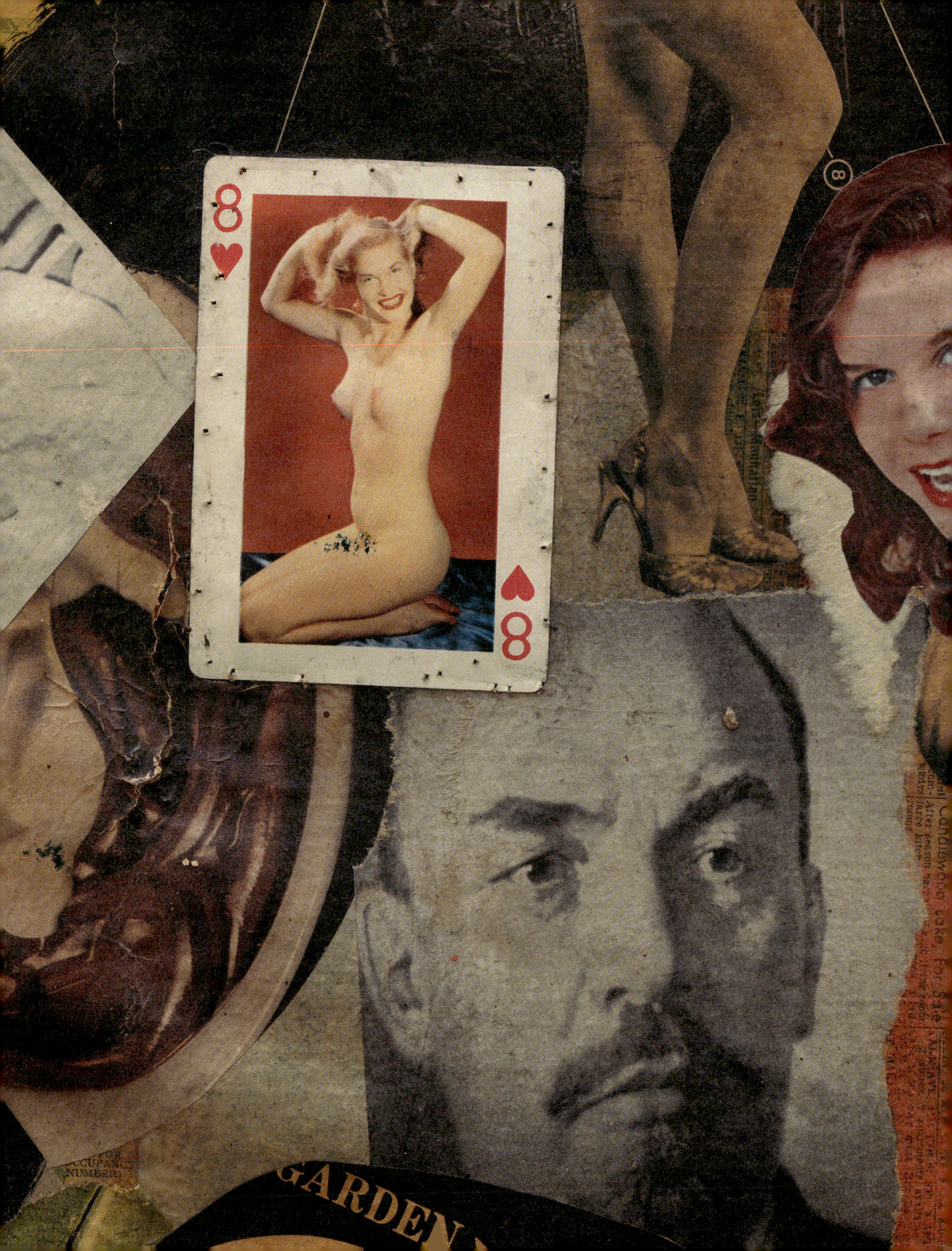

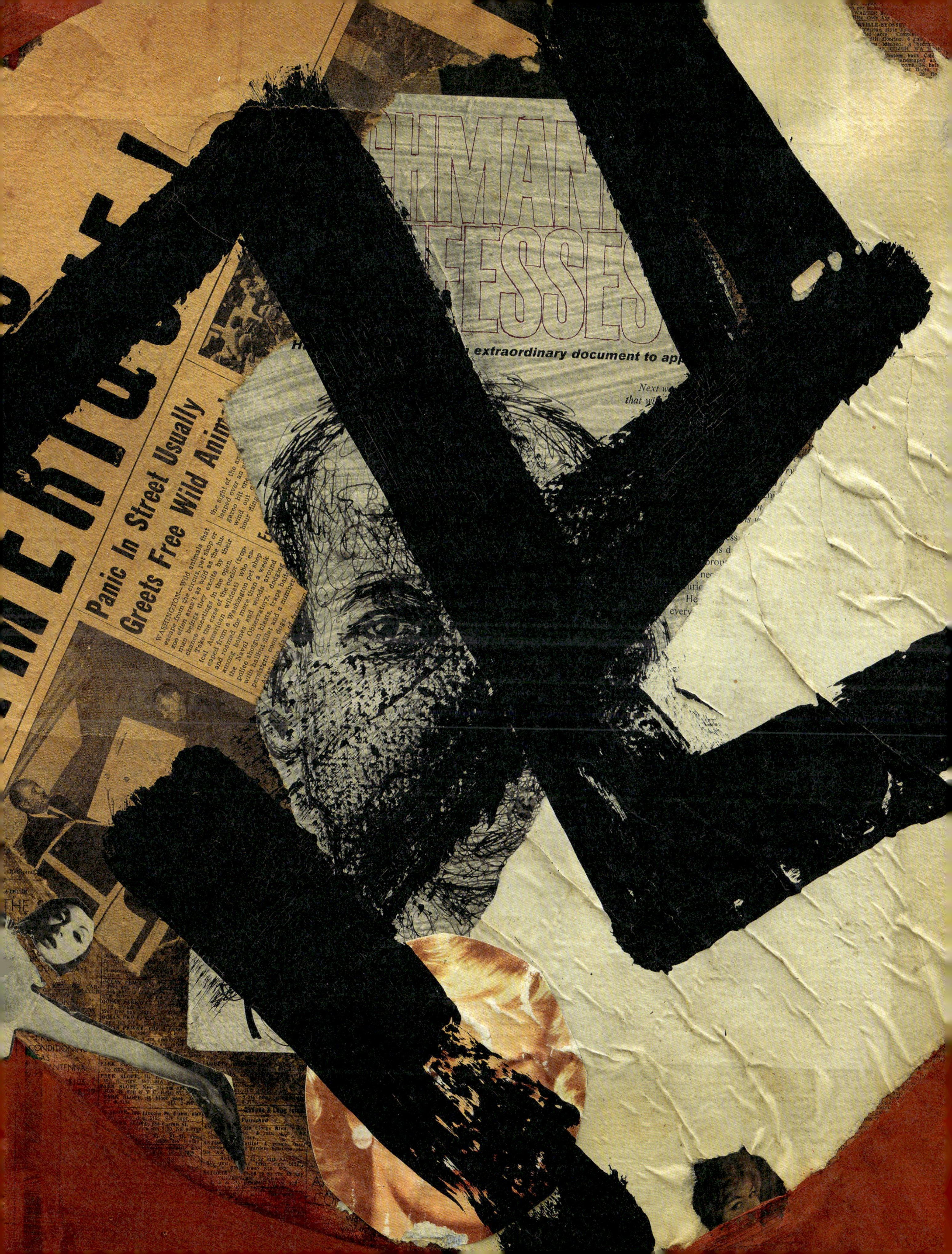

Panic In Street Usually
Greets Free Wild
extraordinary document to

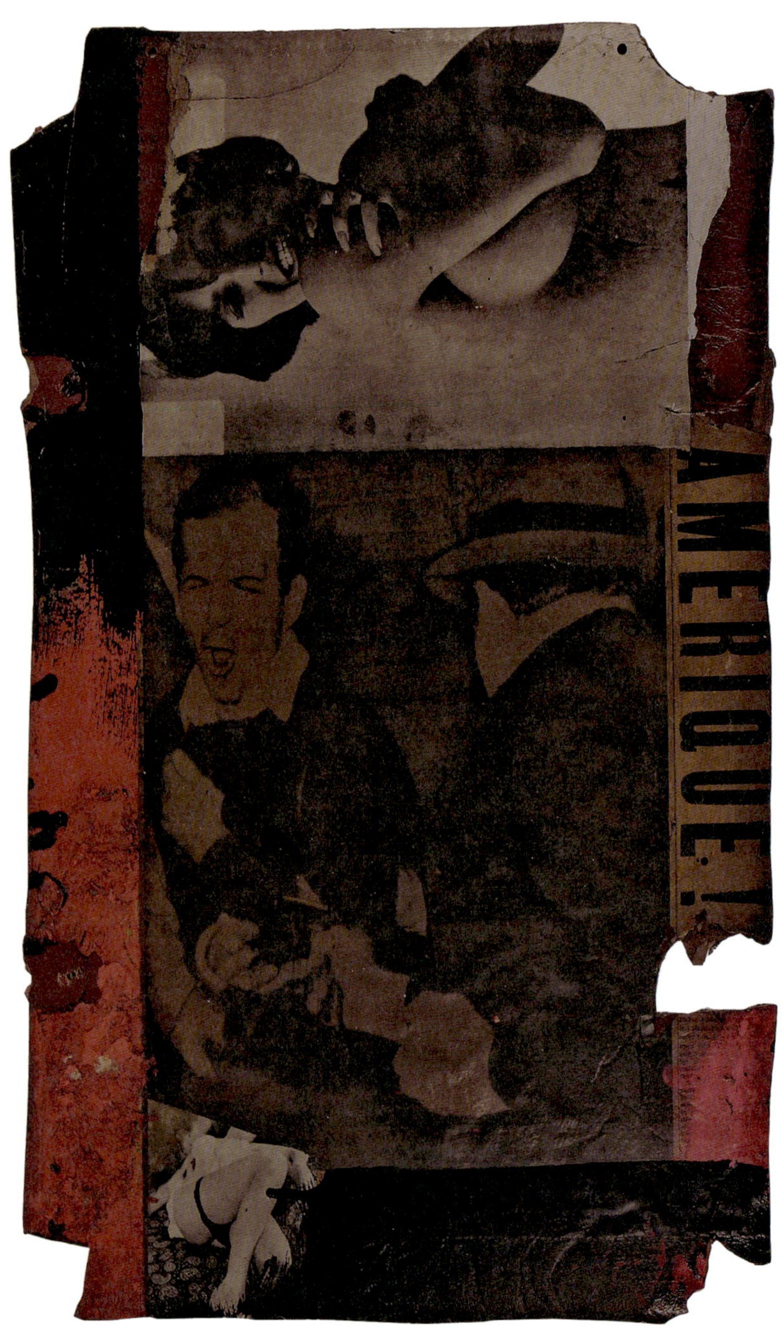

 Oswald, 1963

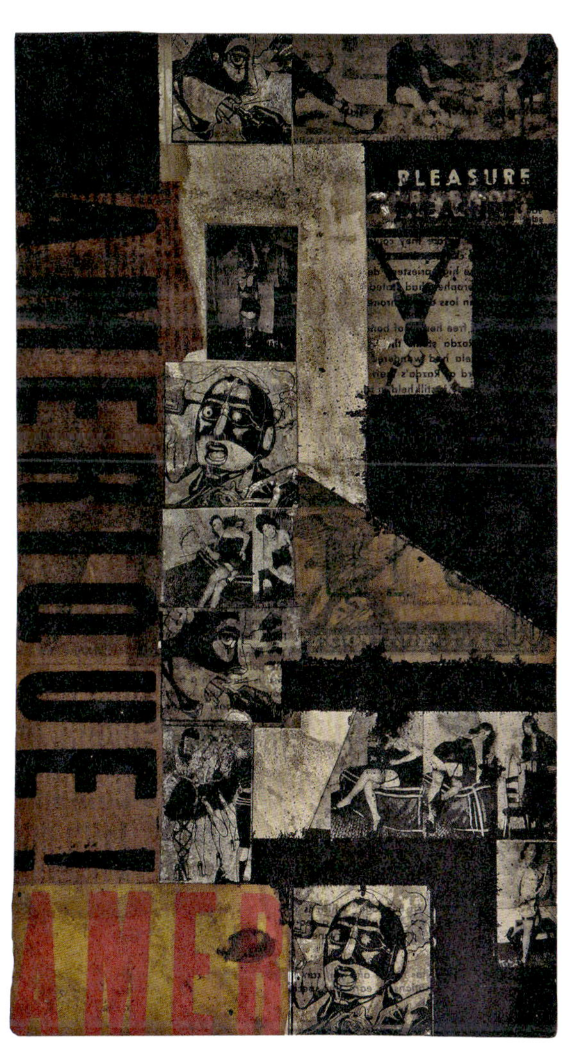

Amérique Amer (Pleasure), ca. / ca 1963

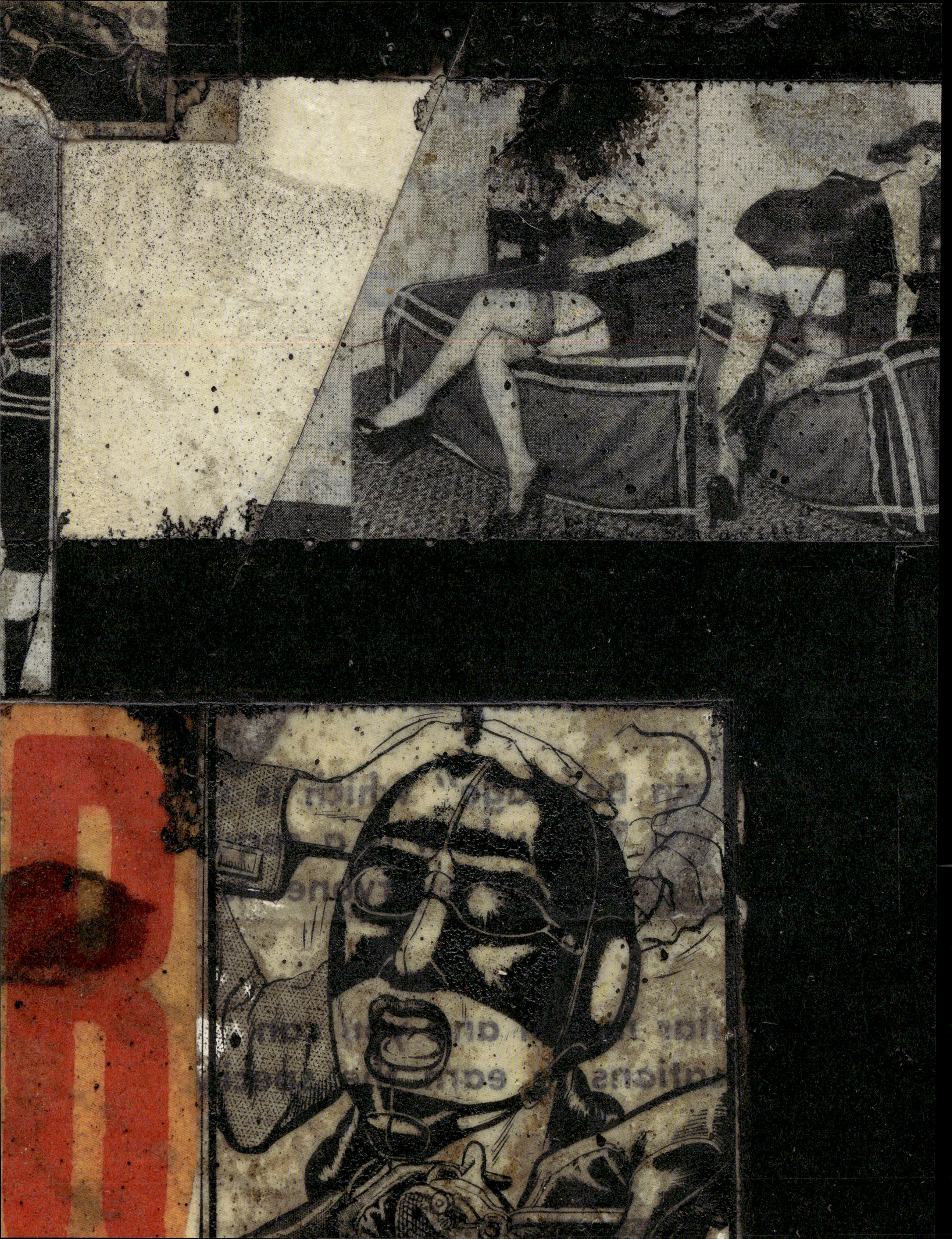

PLEASURE

PLEASURE

Passage, Übergang, Transfer – Begriffe, die sich in vielerlei Hinsicht im Werk von Boris Lurie wiederfinden. Sie beziehen sich sowohl auf künstlerische Transfertechniken als auch auf „Zustände eines Dazwischen" – auf den Übergang von einer traumatisierenden Vergangenheit in eine für Lurie zum großen Teil befremdende Gegenwart, auf fließende Übergänge von gesellschaftlichen Machtstrukturen sowie auf die Übertragung, Erlebtes in Kunst zum Ausdruck zu bringen. In *Suzy Sweet* (1963) attackiert Lurie mit der Familie und dem Glauben zwei Eckpfeiler der amerikanischen Gesellschaft. Die Darstellung von Vater und Tochter beim Tischgebet hinter einem mächtigen Thanksgiving-Truthahn ist von Pin-ups umrahmt. Sie überführen das Familienidyll jener Verlogenheit, die in der zentralen Lolita-Figur von „Suzy Sweet" personifiziert scheint.

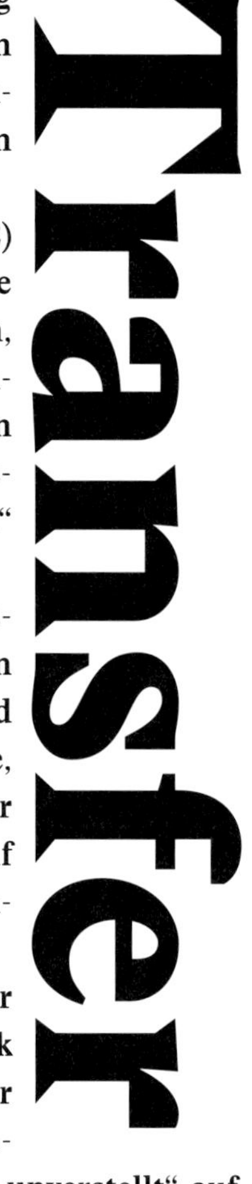

Ein vordergründig „leiserer" Ton ist in der Arbeit *Salad* (1962) angeschlagen. Unter Mehrfachverwendung bestimmter Motive gestaltet Lurie das Bild einer in zarter Farbigkeit gehaltenen, scheinbar harmlosen, bürgerlichen Welt. Umringt von Konsumgütern, lachenden Gesichtern mit hochtoupierten Haarfrisuren und gestellten Posen, lustigen Festen mit reich garniertem Gemüsekuchen, wird das medial vermittelte Bild einer „heilen" Welt widergespiegelt.

Die in Transfertechnik hergestellten Arbeiten sind in enger Auseinandersetzung Luries mit Arbeiten seines Künstlerkollegen Robert Rauschenberg entstanden. Bei der Transfertechnik wird die Druckfarbe eines gedruckten Motivs (z. B. einer Fotokopie, eines Ausdrucks oder einer Zeitschriftenseite) auf einen zuvor mit Lösungsmitteln behandelten Untergrund übertragen. Auf diese Weise können unterschiedlichste Bild- und Schriftelemente in die Gestaltung einfließen.

Rauschenberg brachte vermutlich als einer der ersten Künstler über die Transfer-Zeichnung Realitätsfragmente in sein Werk ein – eine Möglichkeit, die Lurie schätzte und für sich nutzbar machte. Letztlich konnte diese Technik jedoch seinem Anspruch, Ausschnitte der Wirklichkeit ästhetisch weitgehend „unverstellt" auf die Leinwand zu bringen, auf Dauer nicht genügen. In diesem Sinne zeigt die Collage *Torn Pinups* (ca. 1962 – 63) auch weniger eine strenge Komposition als eine vielmehr dem Zufall überlassene Anordnung der einzelnen Bildelemente. Die wahrscheinlich aus einem Heft mit Abbildungen von Pin-ups herausgerissenen erotischen Darstellungen scheinen wie zufällig auf den ungespannten, mit Farbe bearbeiteten Stoff herabgefallen zu sein. CM

Passage, transition, transfer – concepts with many links to Boris Lurie's oeuvre. They refer both to specific transfer techniques used by artists and to "intermediary states" – the transition from a traumatic past into a present Lurie mostly found disconcerting; the fluid transitions within social power structures; and the transfer involved in expressing experience in art. In *Suzy Sweet* (1963), Lurie attacks the family and religious belief, two pillars of American society. The portrayal of father and daughter saying grace behind a giant Thanksgiving turkey is framed by pin-ups, convicting the family idyll of the kind of hypocrisy personified by the central Lolita figure of "Suzy Sweet."

On the surface, *Salad* (1962) strikes a "quieter" note. Using specific motifs multiple times, Lurie creates the picture of a seemingly harmless bourgeois world in gentle colors: consumer goods, laughing faces with big hair and fake poses, funny parties with richly garnished tarts – reflecting the media image of a world where all is well.

The works made using transfer techniques are a result of Lurie's close engagement with the work of his fellow artist Robert Rauschenberg. With this technique, the ink from a printed motif (e. g. a photocopy, printout, or newspaper page) is transferred to a surface treated with solvents. In this way, a wide range of image and text elements can find their way into the design.

Rauschenberg was one of the first artists to introduce fragments of reality into his work via the solvent transfer process – a possibility that Lurie appreciated and put to his own uses. Ultimately, however, this technique was unable to uphold its claim to bring excerpts from reality onto the canvas in aesthetically "undisguised" form. In this sense, the collage *Torn Pin-ups* (ca 1962 – 63) shows less a rigorous composition than an arbitrary arrangement of individual elements. The erotic images, probably torn from a book of pin-ups, seem to have fallen at random onto the unstretched, painted fabric. CM

Transfer

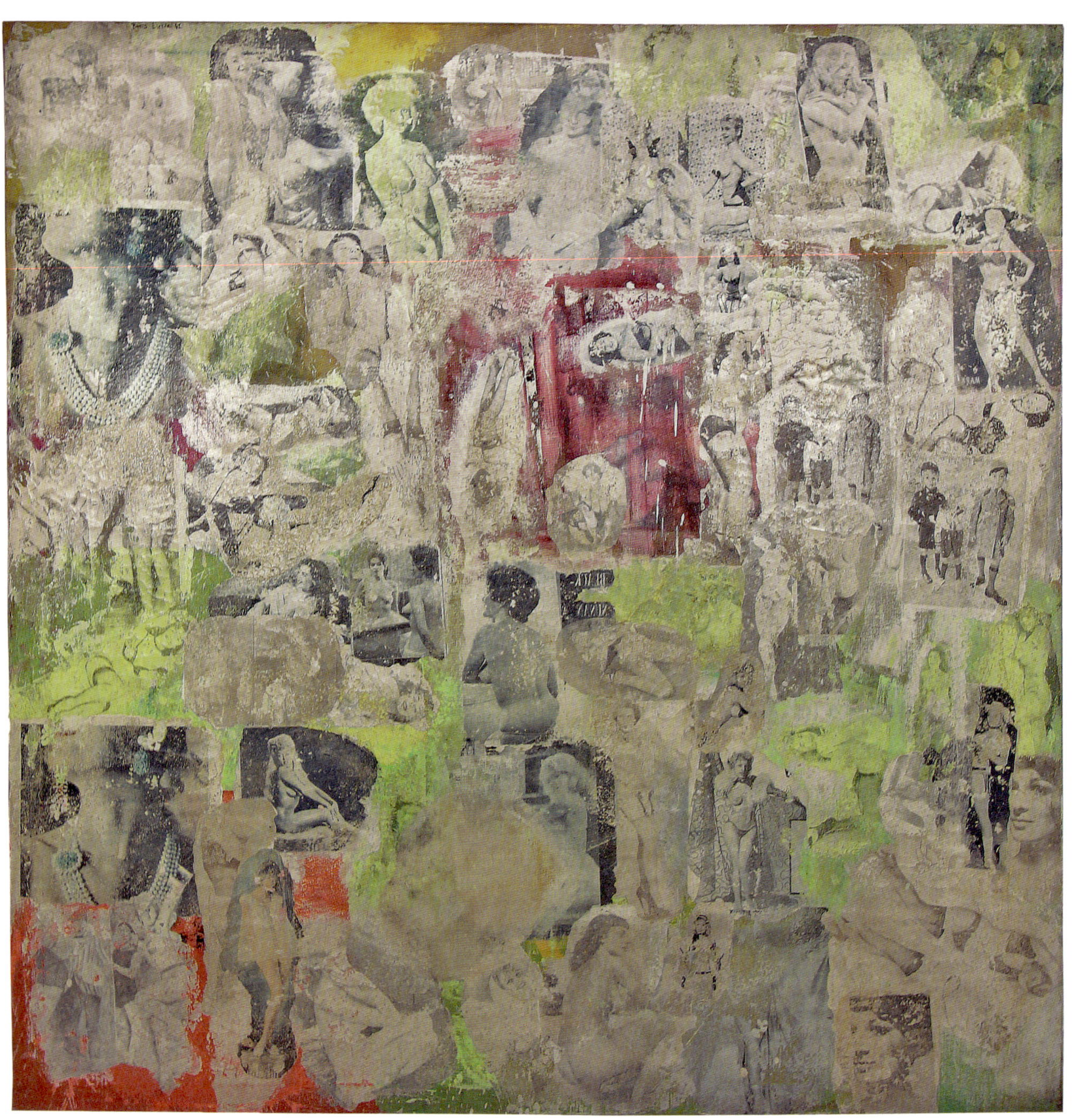

 Black Susan, 1962

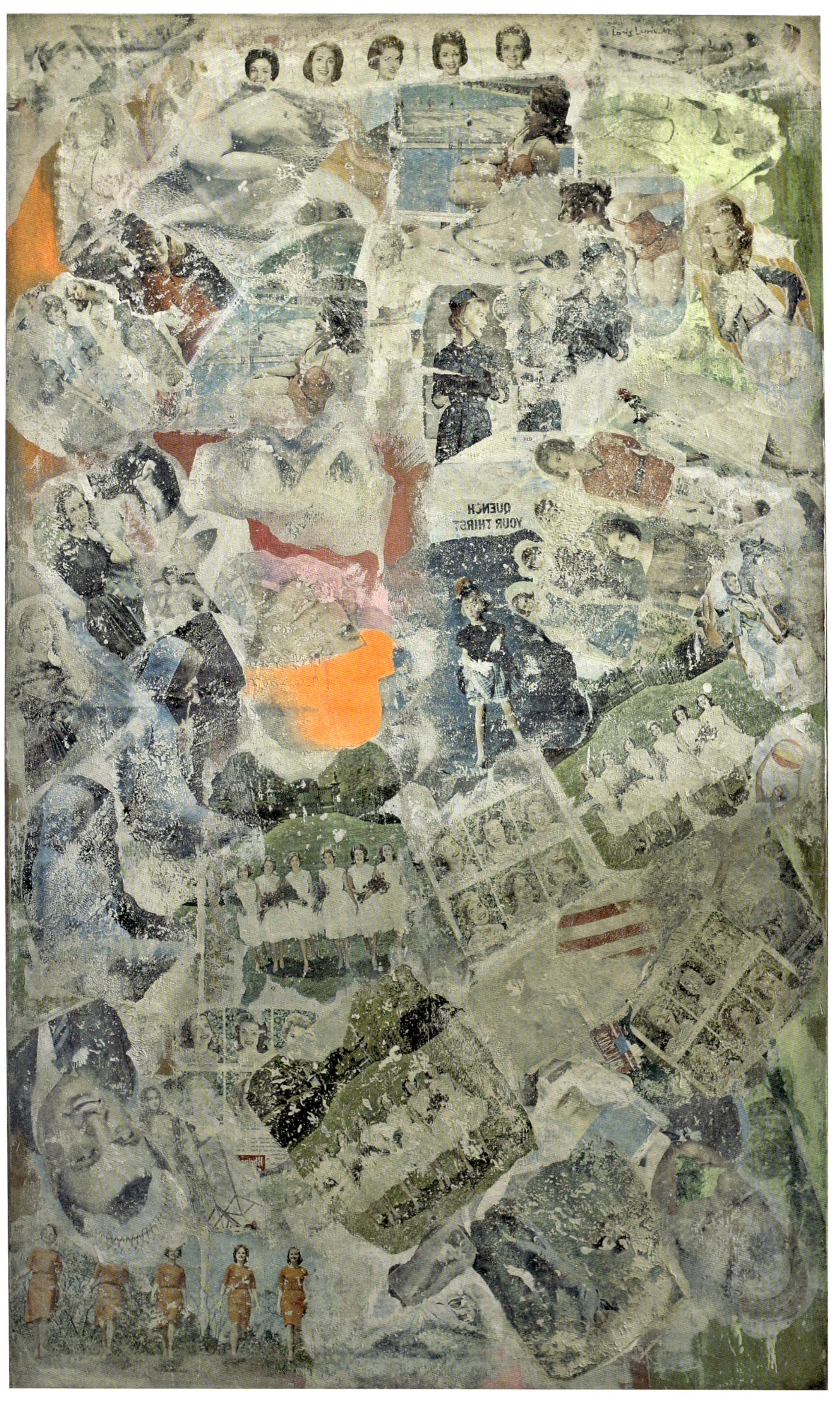

Quench Your Thirst, 1962

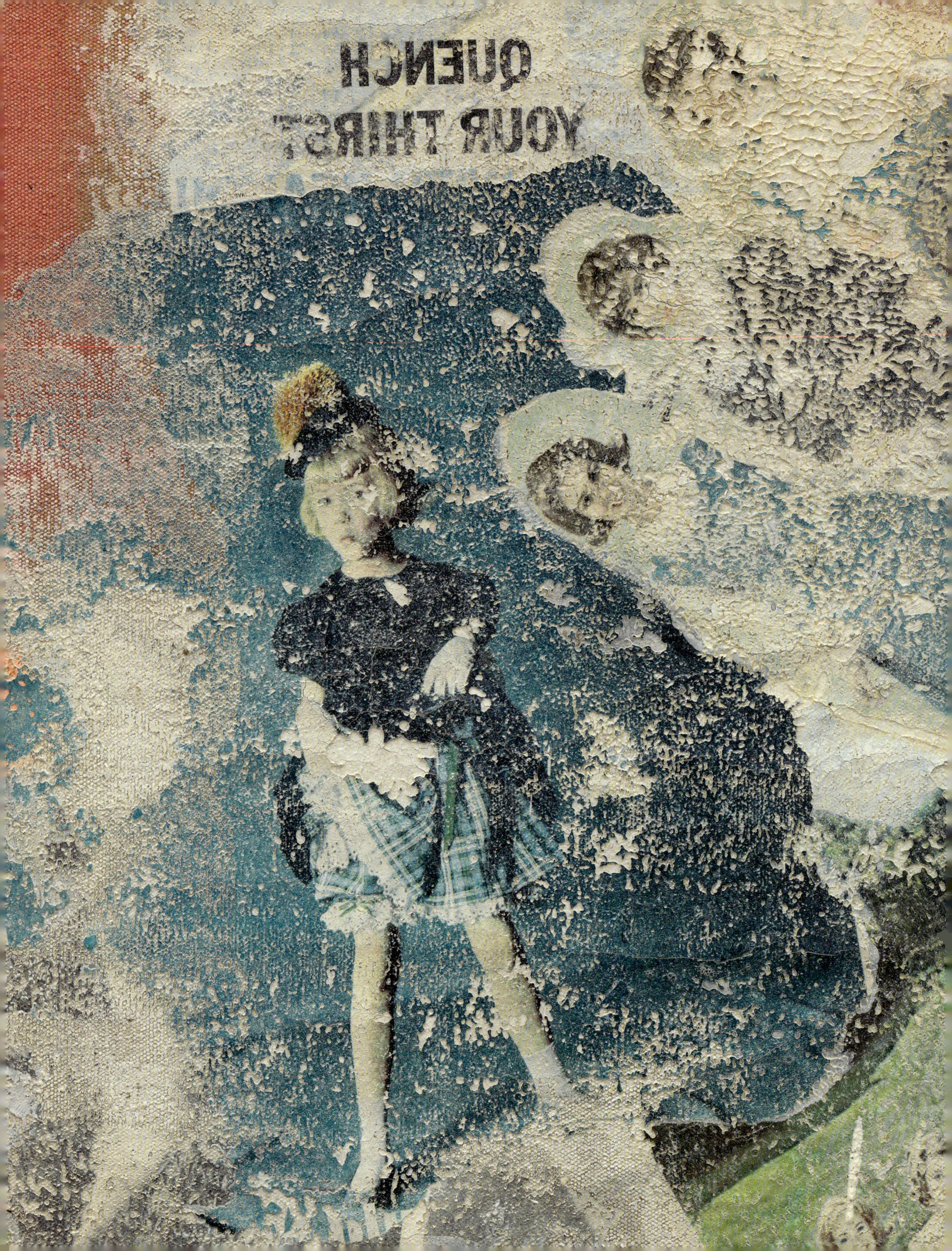
QUENCH
YOUR THIRST

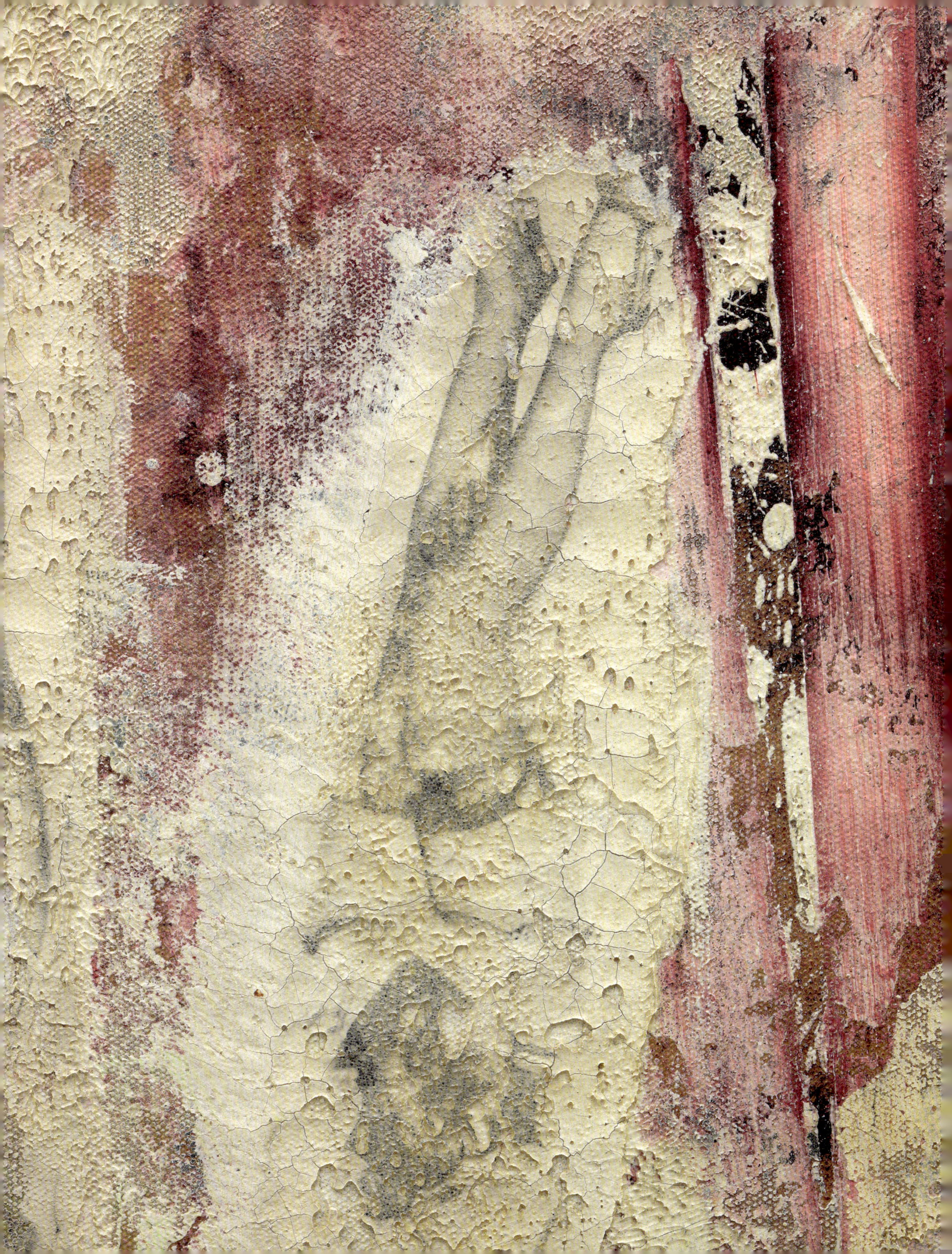

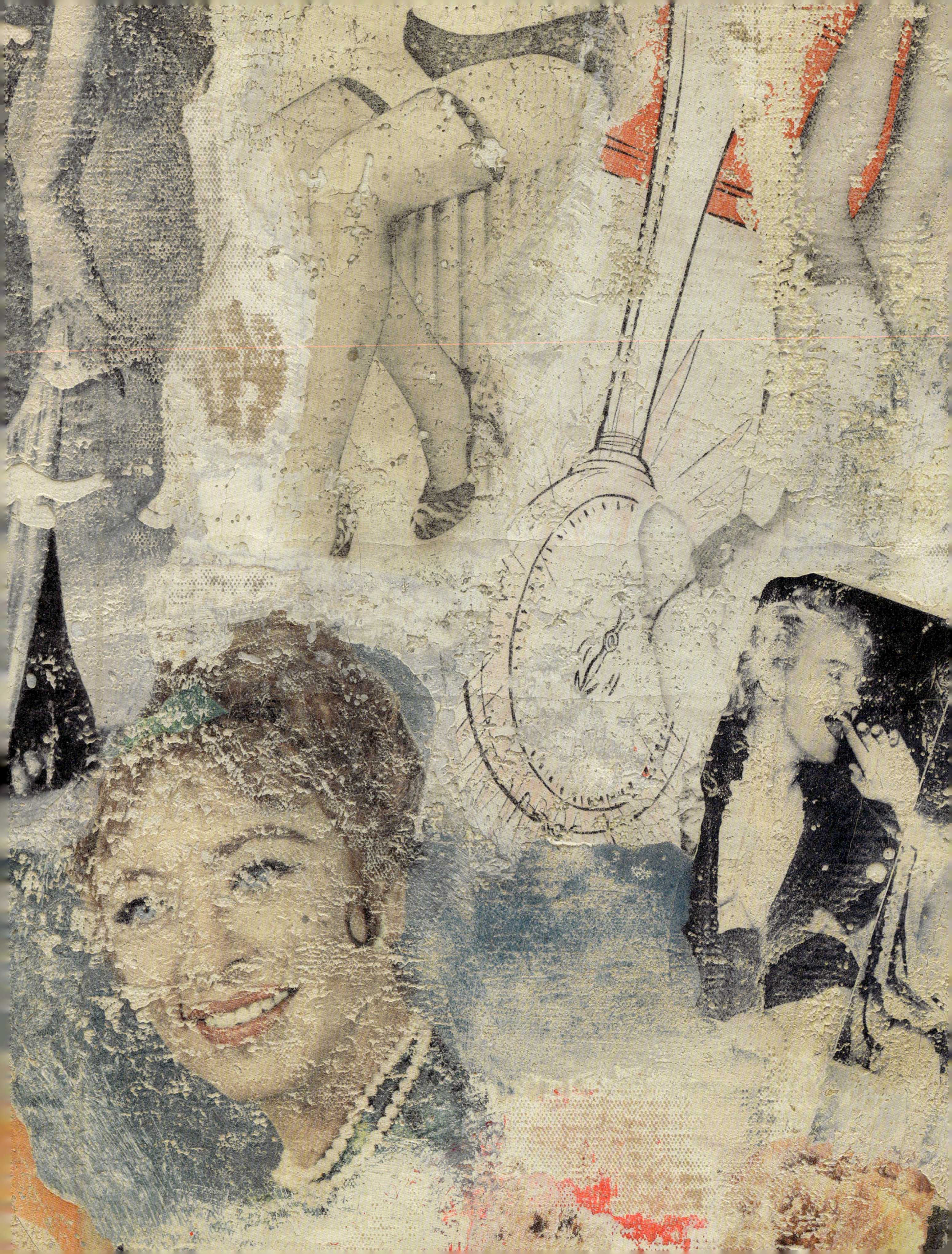

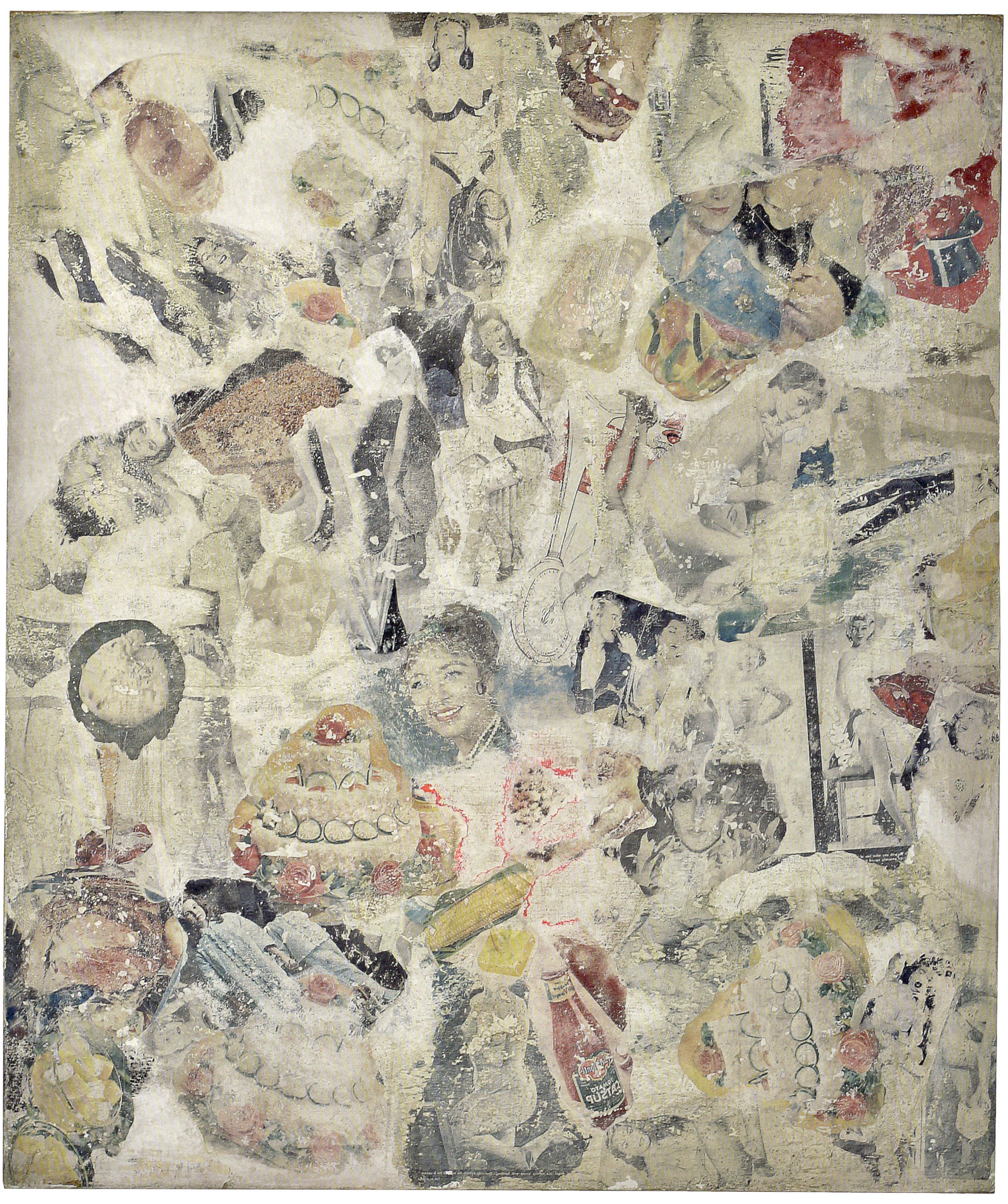

Salad, 1962

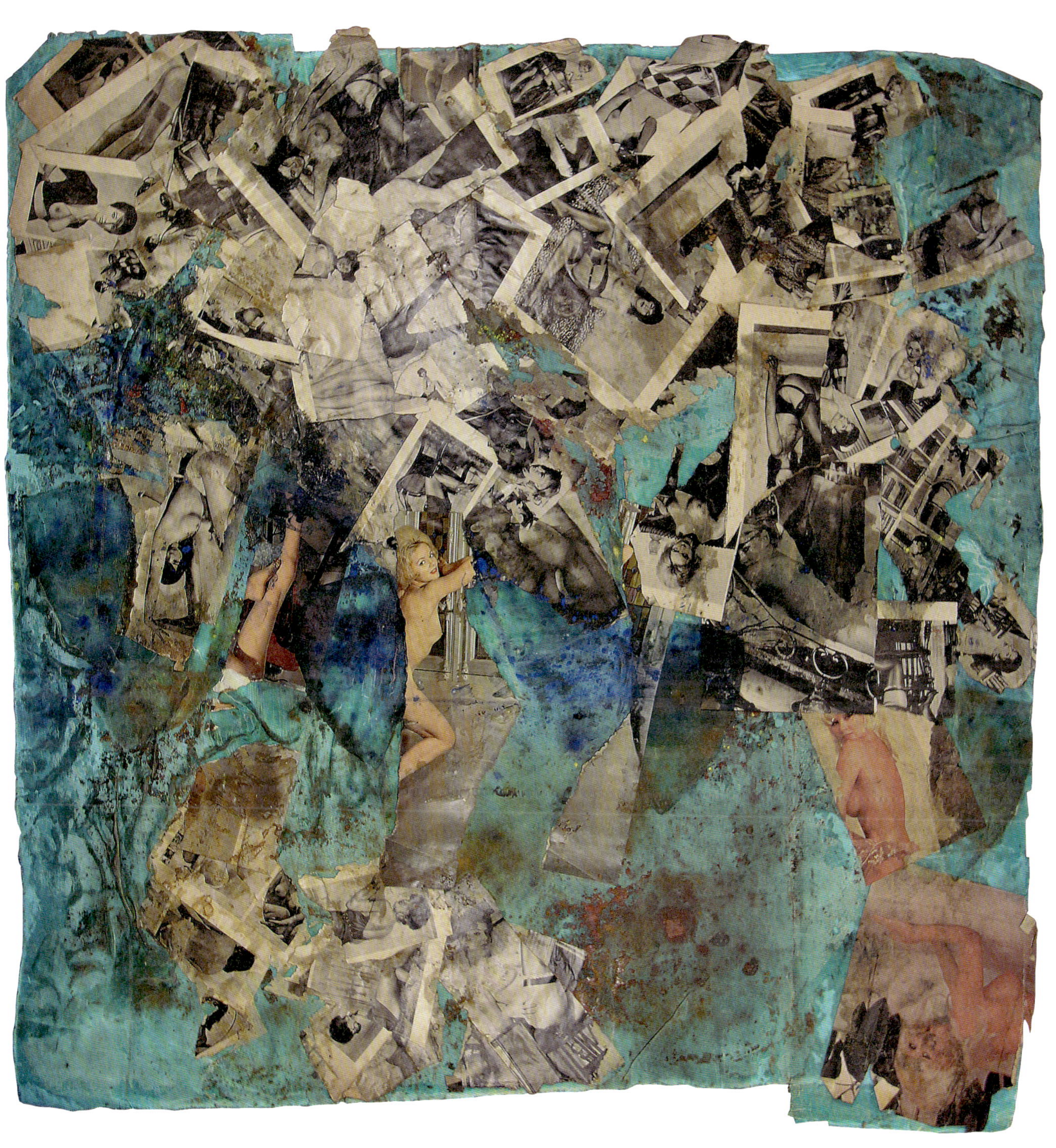

Torn Pinups, ca. / ca 1962 – 63

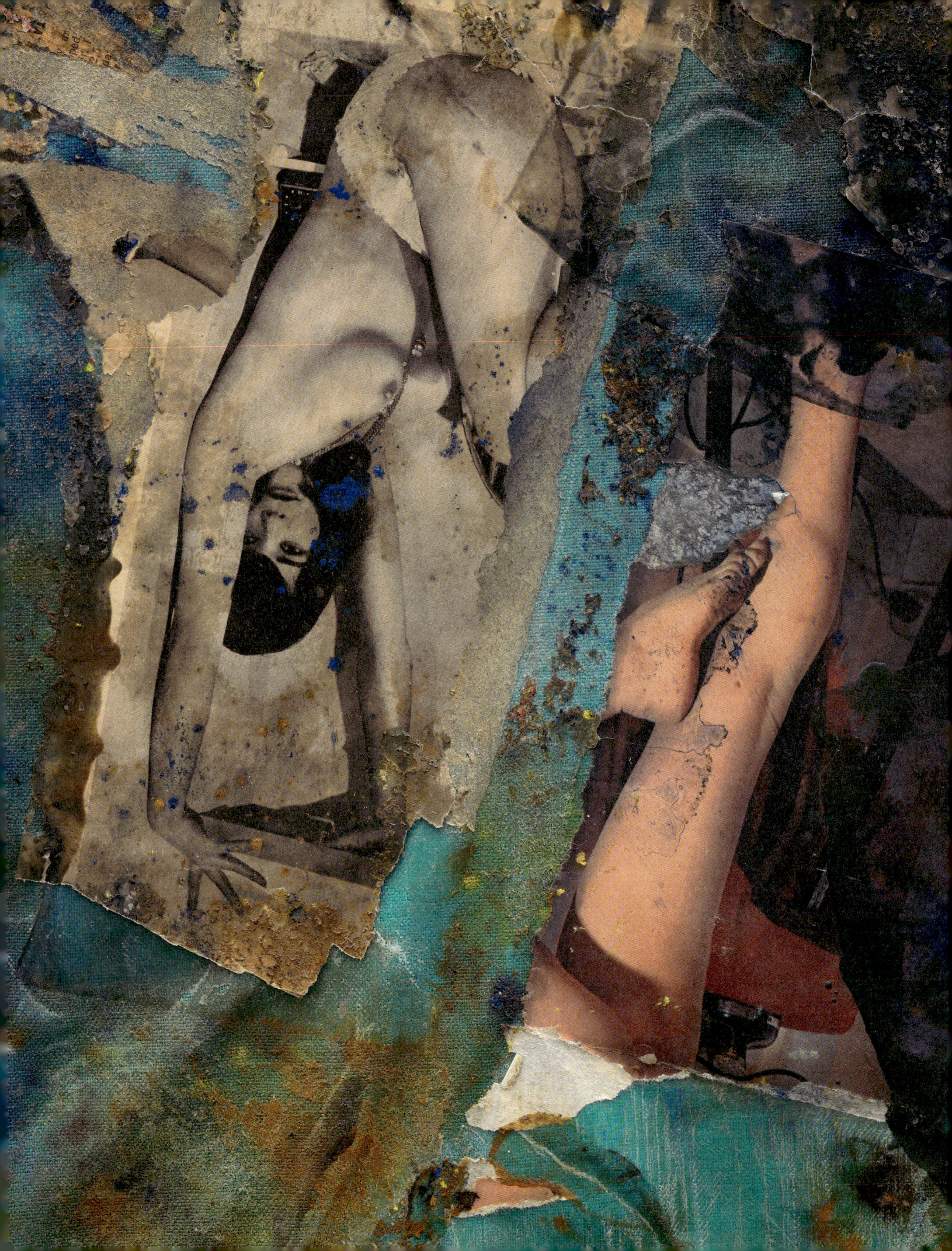

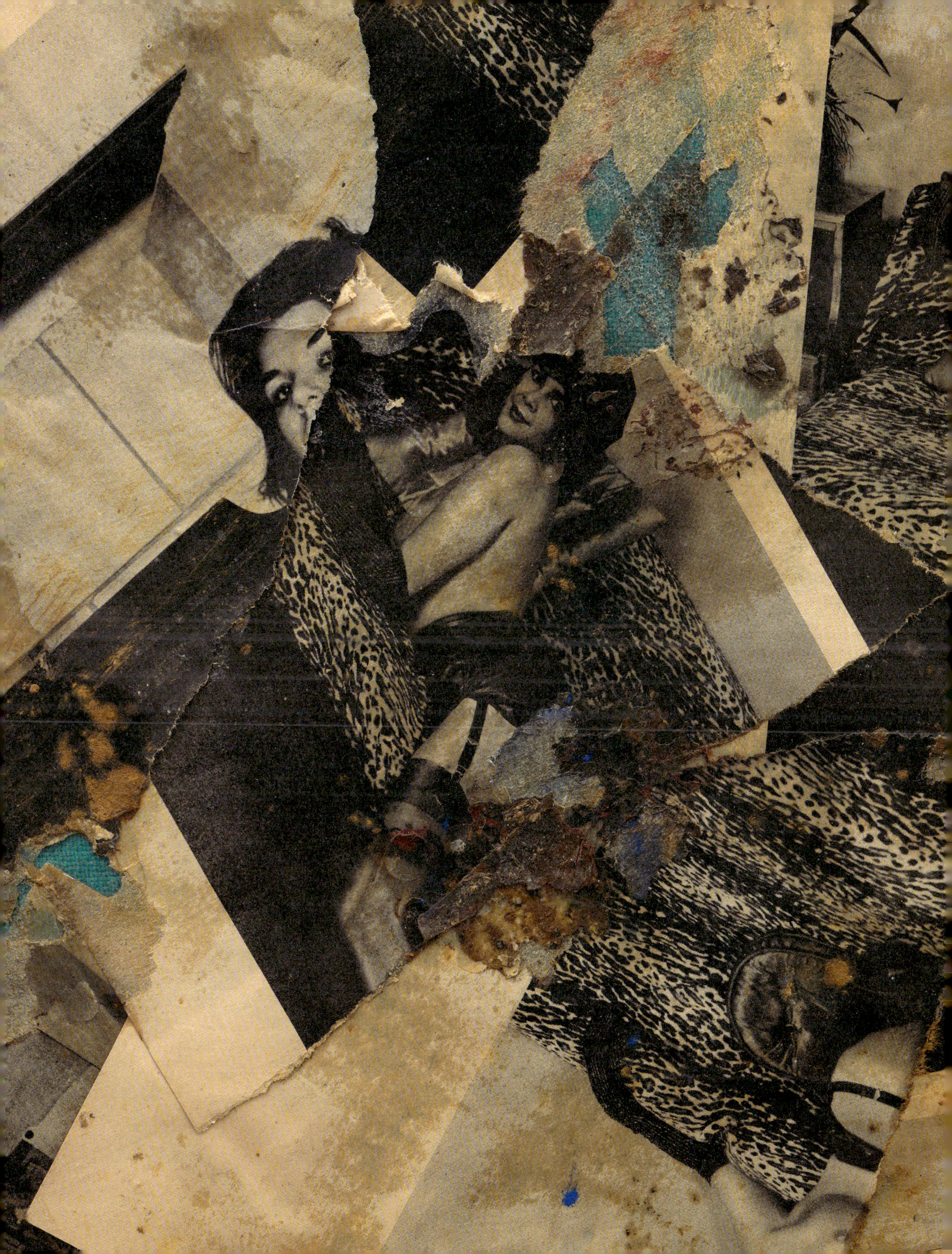

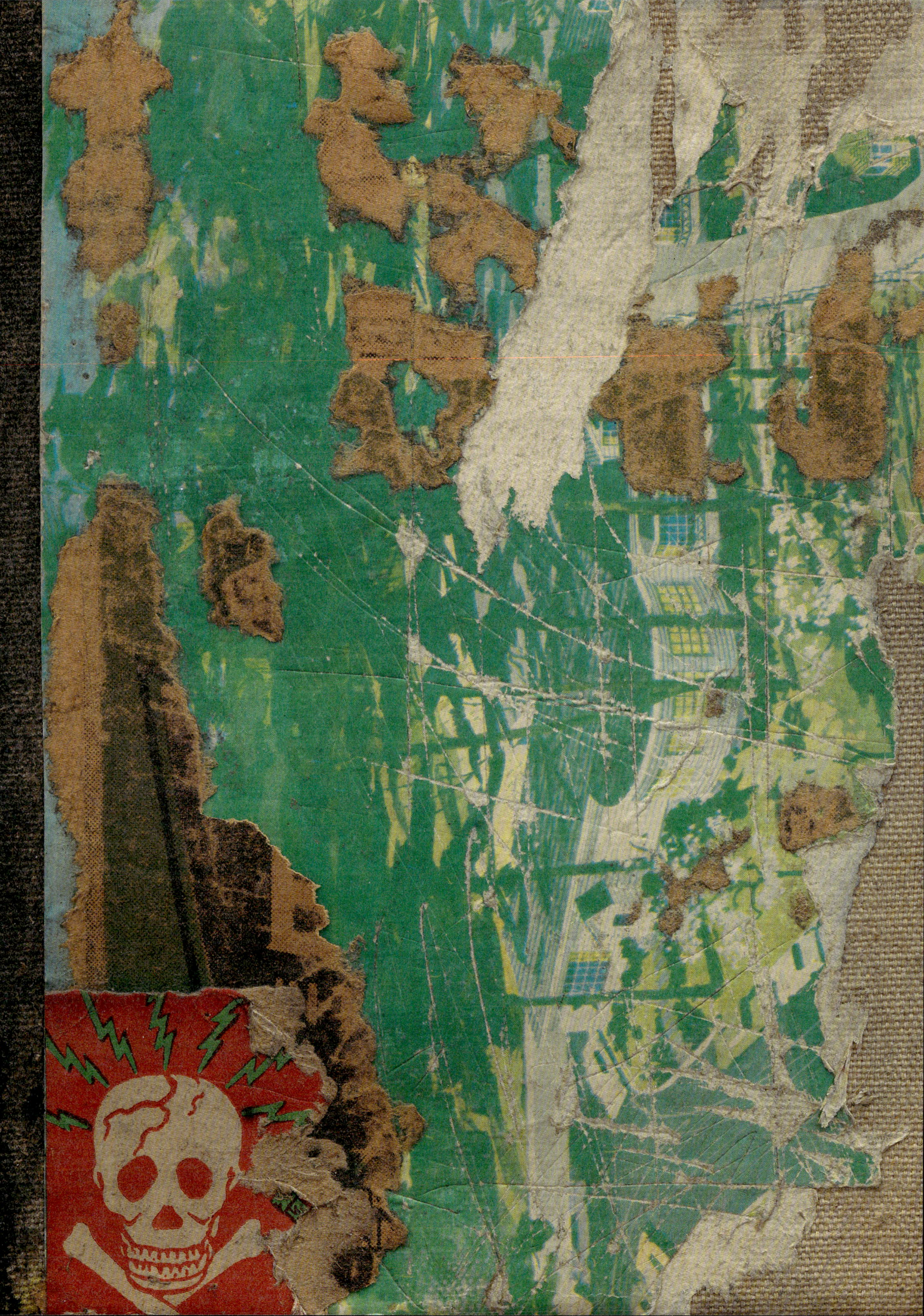

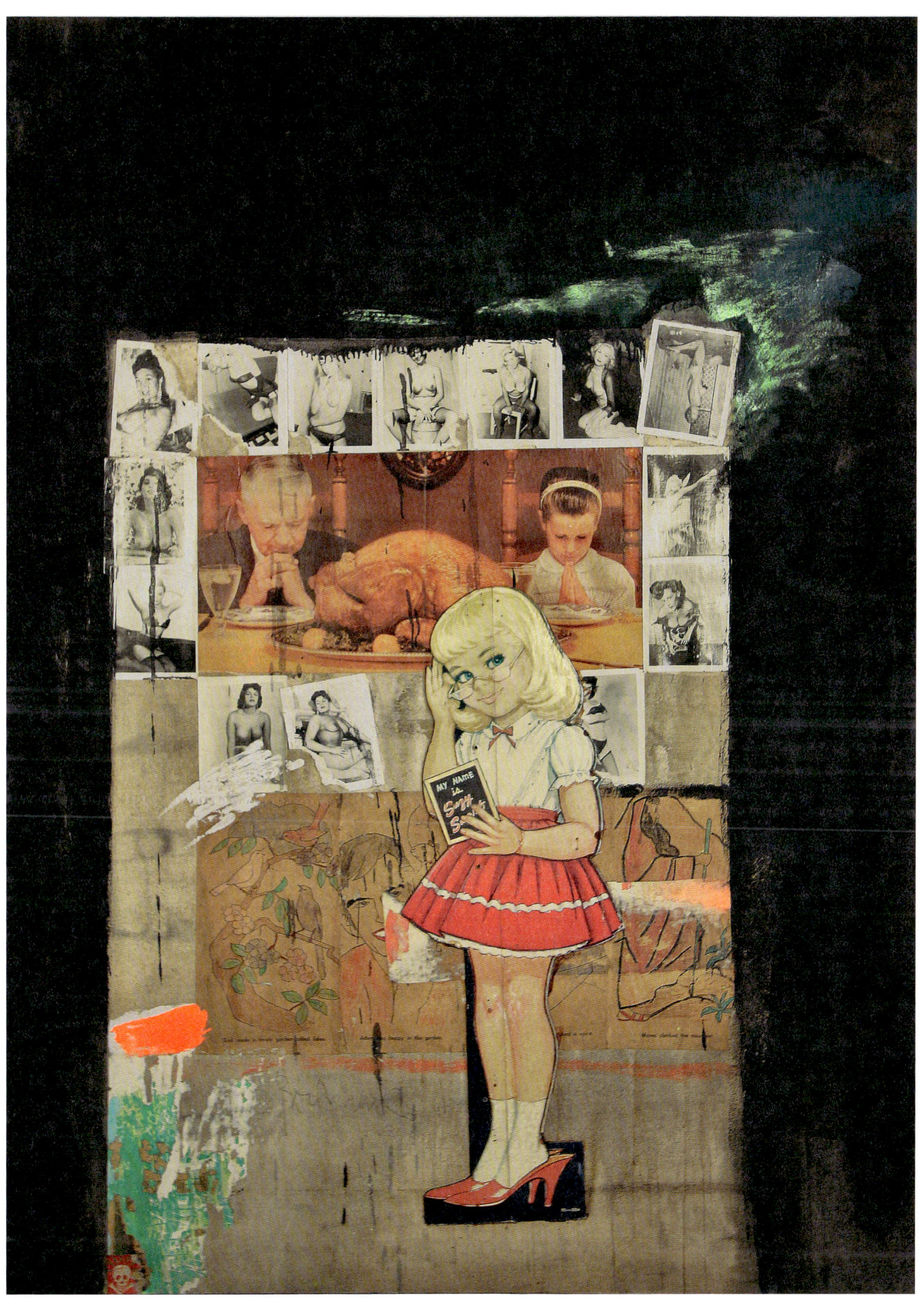

Suzy Sweet, 1963

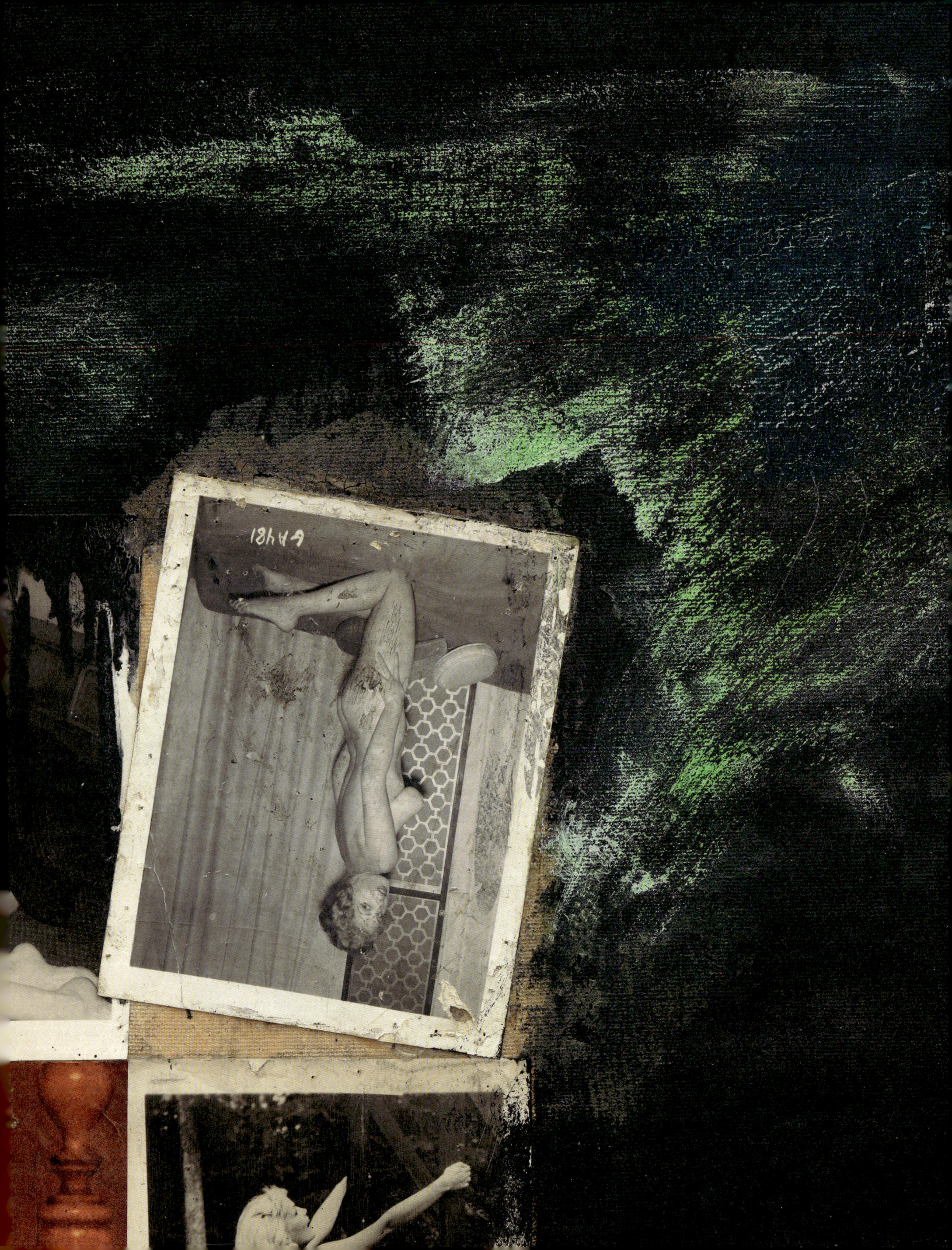

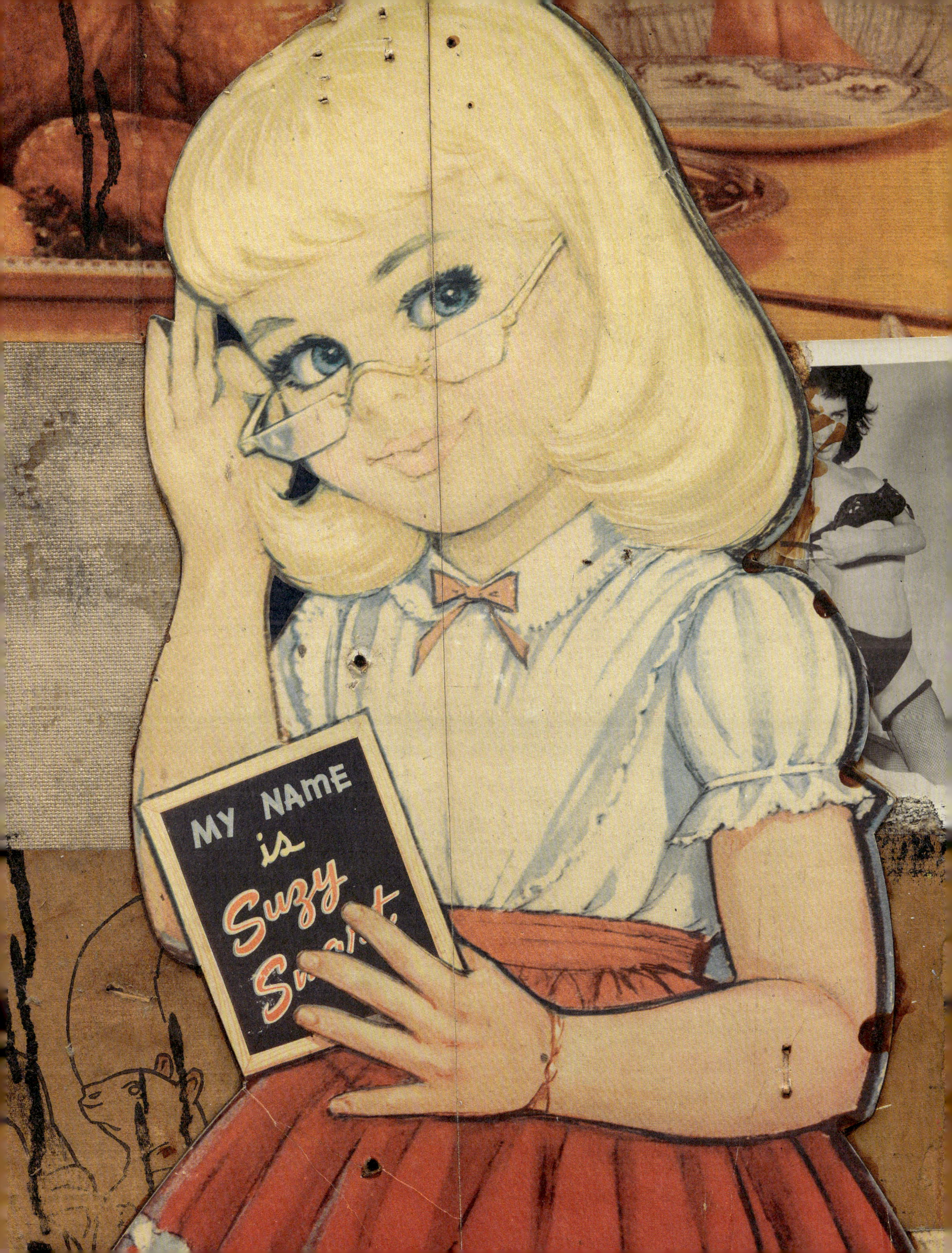
MY NAME
is
Suzy

Männermagazine und Pornohefte dienten Boris Lurie als Vorlagen für seine Pin-up-Collagen. Er sammelte sie in obsessiver Weise, pflasterte seine Atelierwände mit den „Girlies“ und trug sie teilweise in mehreren Schichten auf Leinwände auf. Bei der „Verarbeitung“ der Pin-ups verwendete er verschiedenste künstlerische Techniken: Übermalung, Verwischung, Kopier-, Reiß- und Transfertechniken.

Lurie bringt in diesen Arbeiten sein ambivalentes Verhältnis zum anderen Geschlecht zum Ausdruck, kommentiert aber gleichzeitig das in den USA medial vermittelte Frauenbild der 1960er Jahre, das von (sexueller) Gleichberechtigung noch sehr weit entfernt war. „Das Pin-up – ein Begriff, der im Zweiten Weltkrieg geprägt wurde, als amerikanische Soldaten Bilder von Betty Grable und Rita Hayworth an die Wände ihrer Quartiere hängten – war in der Nachkriegszeit ein sichtbares Symbol für den ‚male backlash‘ (männlicher Gegenschlag), die Aufrechterhaltung des männlichen Herrschaftsanspruchs. Pin-ups zeigten das Ideal passiver weiblicher Sexualität. Sie wurden zu einem allgegenwärtigen Bild der visuellen Kultur, so dass es beinahe unumgänglich war, dass sie auch die zeitgenössischen Künstler beeinflussten.“[1]

Pinups

Indem Lurie beispielsweise durch die Übermalung fotografischer Vorlagen besonders die Brüste und Hände der abgebildeten Frauen hervorhebt, deren Gesichter aber vollkommen unkenntlich macht, verdinglicht und anonymisiert er sie. Einerseits bieten sie die Projektionsfläche männlichen Begehrens, andererseits wird ihre Benutzbarkeit als „Ware“, auf die Macht und Kontrolle ausgeübt werden kann, deutlich. Obwohl sich der Künstler immer wieder gegen patriarchalische Vorstellungen und Herrschaftsverhältnisse ausspricht, schwingen entgegengesetzte Töne mit: „Wir waren gegen die unterdrückte Sexaggressivität der Männer. Die damalige nichtbürgerliche Kunstszene war nämlich vollkommen von Sexwut erfüllt, die man mit Alkohol auslöschte. Das heißt, in meinen Pin-ups gab es auch Wut gegen die Frauen. Bei mir persönlich standen die Pin-up-Konglomerationen auch für die Massengräber wie z. B. in Riga, wo meistens Frauen erschossen wurden.“[2]

Mit *Altered Photos: Shame!* (1963) richtet Lurie den Fokus auf einen etwas anderen Zusammenhang: Im Vergleich mit einem Großteil seiner Arbeiten kann diese als besonders malerisch bezeichnet werden. Sie erinnert beispielsweise an die Farbfeldmalerei der US-amerikanischen Künstler Ad Reinhardt und Mark Rothko. Luries Malerei will jedoch anderes: Sie wendet sich gegen ein Kunstsystem, welches soziale, gesellschaftliche und politische Themen ausklammert und sich stattdessen selbst feiert. So platziert er inmitten des Gemäldes eine Fotografie, die zwei unbekleidete Frauen zeigt. Vor der Kamera posierend, bedecken sie nur scheinbar überrascht, eher belustigt ihre Scham. Mit der Betitelung *Altered Photos: Shame!* stellt Boris Lurie jedoch generell die Frage nach Scham und Schuld – wie sich die Gesellschaft und der Einzelne darauf beziehen, wie Scham und Schuld bewertet werden.

CM

1 Simon Tayler in: „Die NO!art-Bewegung in New York, 1960 bis 1964“, in: *NO!art*, Ausstellungskatalog, Neue Gesellschaft für Bildende Kunst, Berlin 1995, S. 32.

2 Boris Lurie in: „NO!art. Dietmar Kirves im Gespräch mit Boris Lurie, dem Mitbegründer der NO!art“, in: *neue bildende kunst. Zeitschrift für Kunst und Kritik*, Nr. 1/95, Berlin 1995, S. 49.

Pinups

Men's magazines and pornography served Lurie as sources for his "pin-up collages." He collected them obsessively, plastered his studio walls with them and applied them to canvases, sometimes in several layers. When "processing" the pin-ups, he used a wide range of artistic techniques: overpainting, blurring, copying, tearing, and solvent transfer. In these works, Lurie expresses his ambivalent relationship to the opposite sex while also commenting on the media image of women in 1960s America – an image still far removed from (sexual) equality. "The 'pin-up' – an expression coined during World War II, when American servicemen displayed pictures of Betty Grable and Rita Hayworth on their barracks' walls – was a conspicuous symbol of the post-war male backlash. Promoting an ideal of passive female sexuality, pin-ups were such a ubiquitous form of visual culture, it was almost inevitable that they would influence contemporary artists."[1]

By overpainting photographic source images in such a way that the breasts and hands are emphasized while the faces are rendered completely unrecognizable, for example, he objectified and anonymized the women. On the one hand, they offer surfaces for the projection of male desire, while also stressing their exploitability as "commodities" over which power and control are exerted. Although Lurie repeatedly spoke out against patriarchal ideas and power relations, there are also resonances that are at odds with this:

"We were against the repressed sexual aggression of the men. At the time, the non-bourgeois art scene was totally filled with a sexual rage that people would drown in alcohol. Which is to say that in my pin-ups there was also anger against women. For me personally, the pin-up conglomerations also stood for mass graves, as in Riga, where mostly women were shot."[2]

With *Altered Photos: Shame!* (1963), Lurie adopts a slightly different focus compared to most of his work, it can be described as particularly painterly. Although it recalls the color field painting of American artists like Ad Reinhardt and Mark Rothko, Lurie's work has a different aim: it opposes an art system that ignores social, societal and political themes and celebrates itself instead. In the middle of the painting, he places a photograph showing two unclad women. Posing for the camera, they cover their modesty, only seemingly surprised, more amused. The title *Altered Photos: Shame!* raises the question of shame and guilt in general – how shame and guilt are judged, and how society and the individual relate to them. CM

1 Simon Taylor, "THE NO!art MOVEMENT IN NEW YORK, 1960 – 1964", published in German in NO!art, exhibition catalogue, Neue Gesellschaft für Bildende Kunst, Berlin 1995. Final draft in English: http://text.no-art.info/en/taylor_%20no-art-movement.pdf

2 Boris Lurie in „NO!art. Dietmar Kirves im Gespräch mit Boris Lurie, dem Mitbegründer der NO!art", in *neue bildende kunst. Zeitschrift für Kunst und Kritik*, 1/95, Berlin 1995, p. 49.

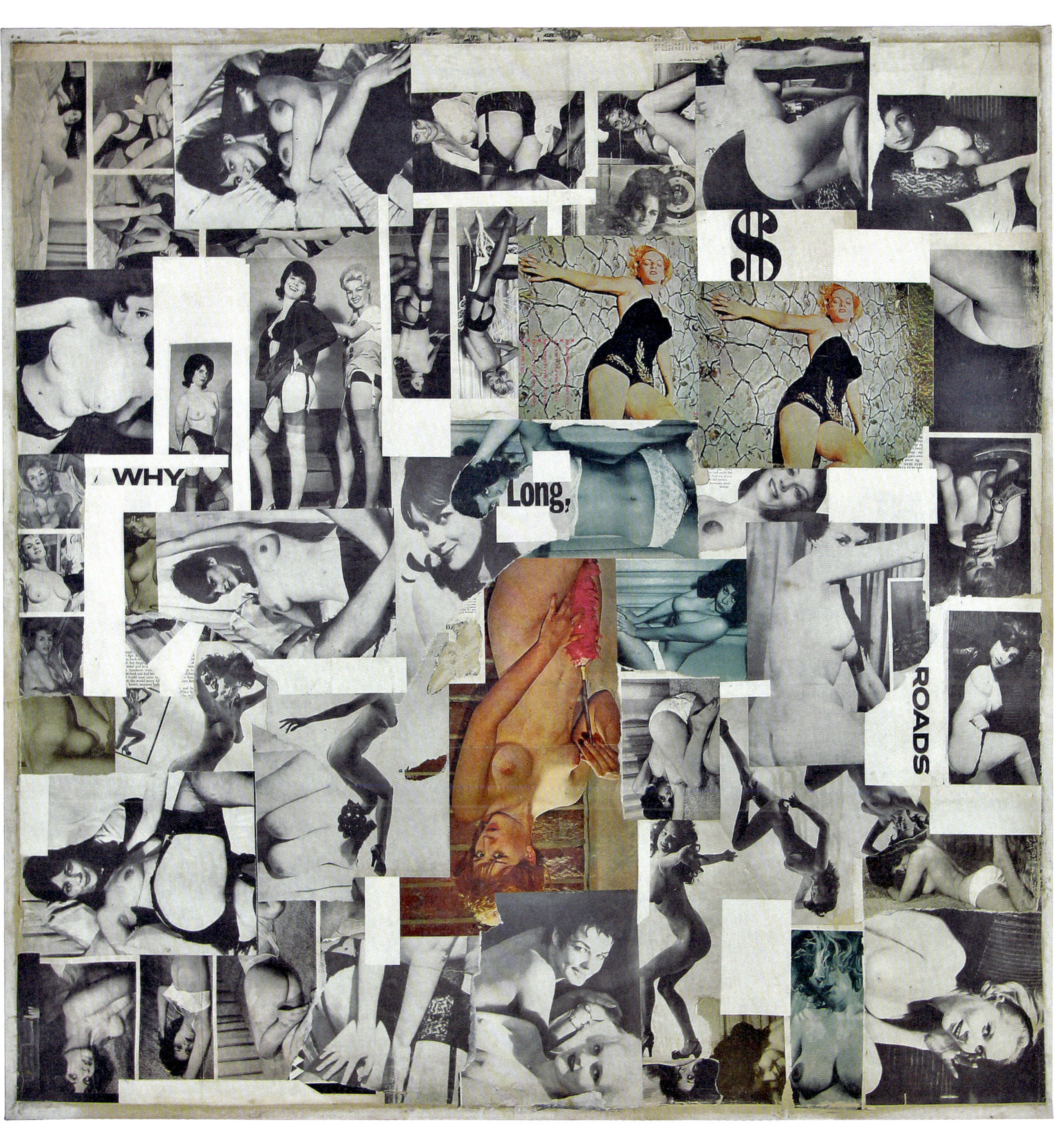

Large Pinup: Why Long Roads?, ca. / ca 1964

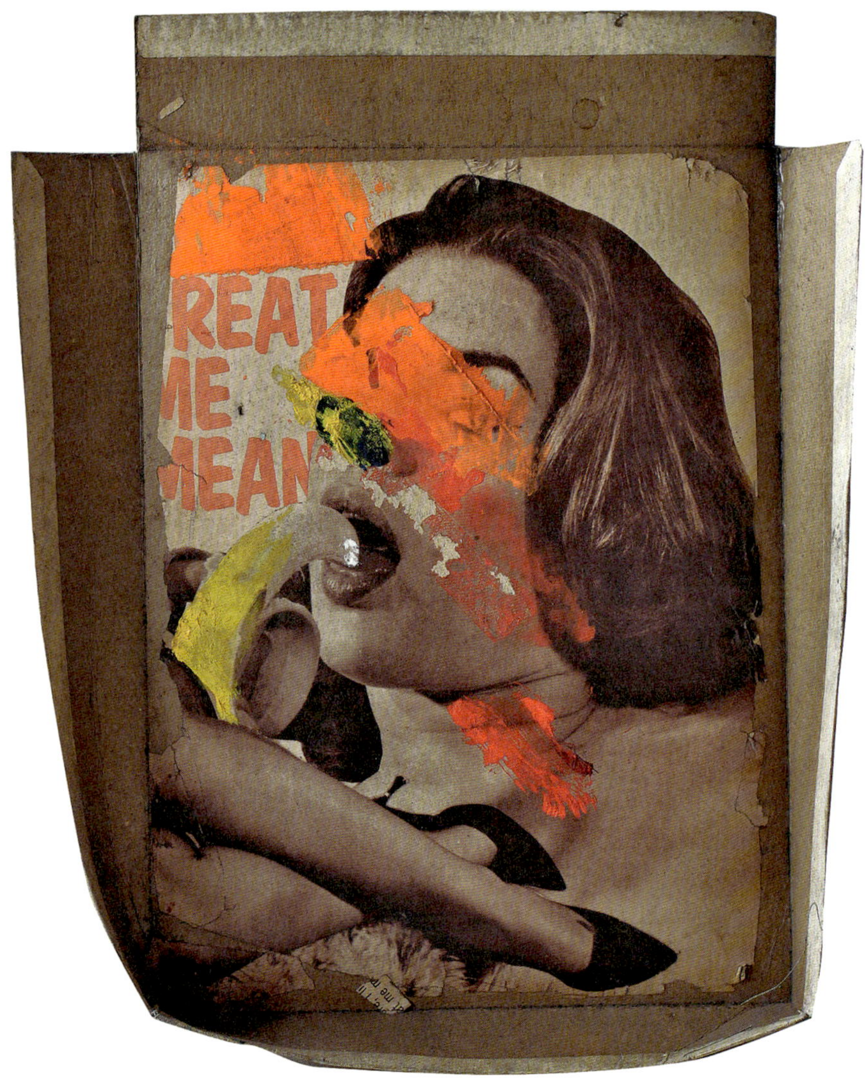

 Untitled, ca. / ca 1963

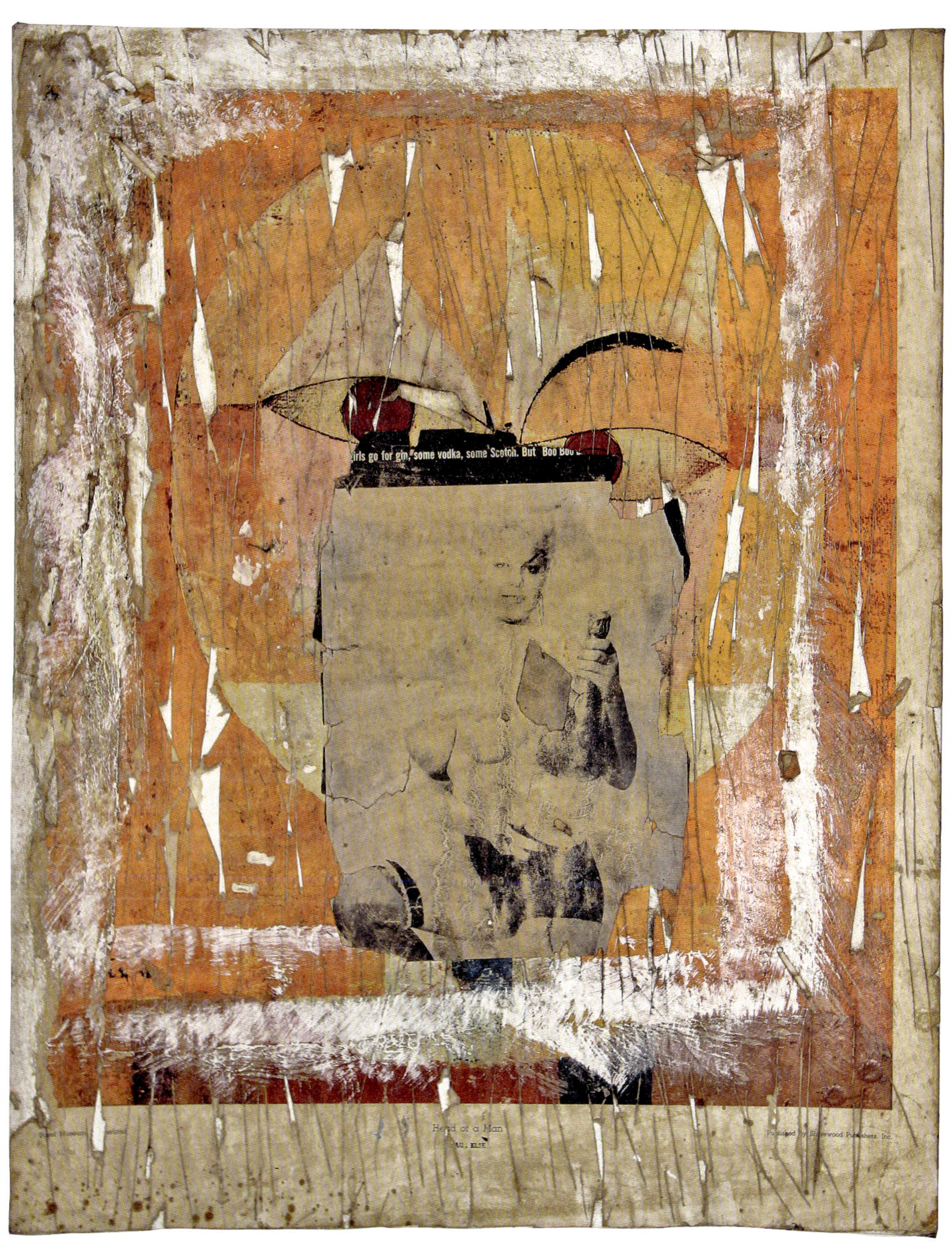

Untitled (Deliberate Pinup), ca. / ca 1975

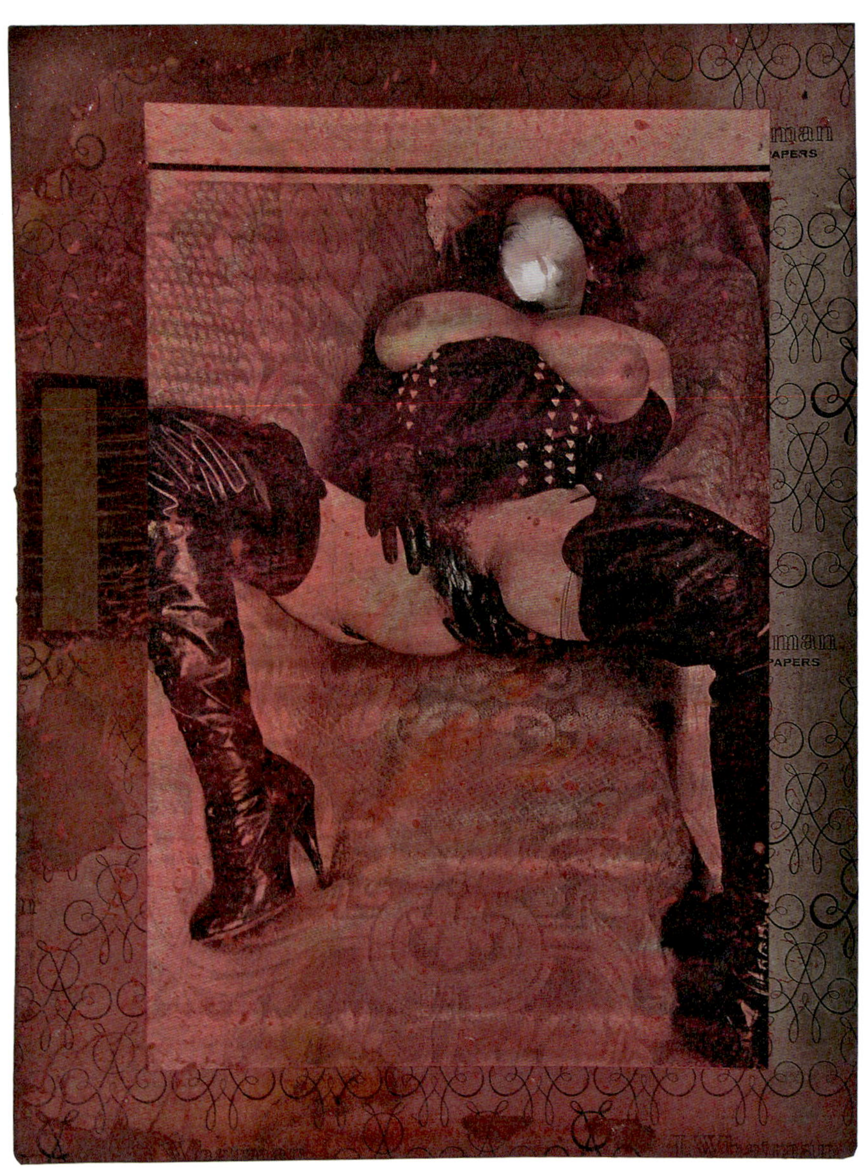

 Untitled (Deliberate Pinup), ca. / ca 1975

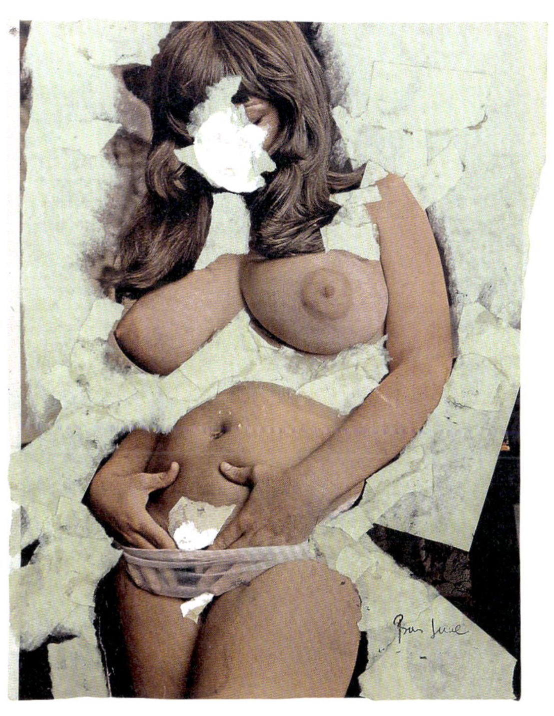

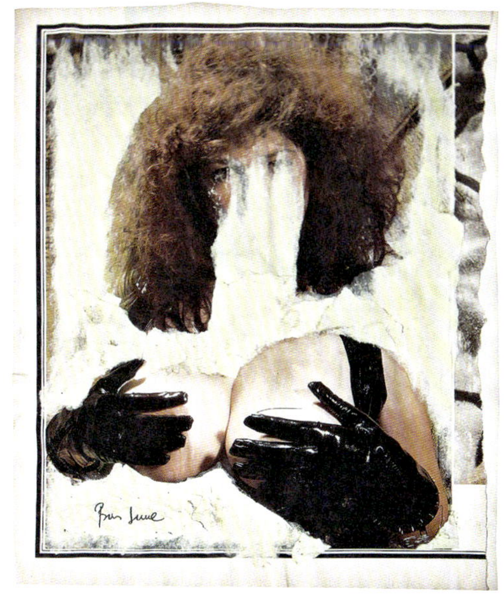

Untitled, Mitte der 1970er Jahre / mid-1970s

Untitled, Mitte der 1970er Jahre / mid-1970s

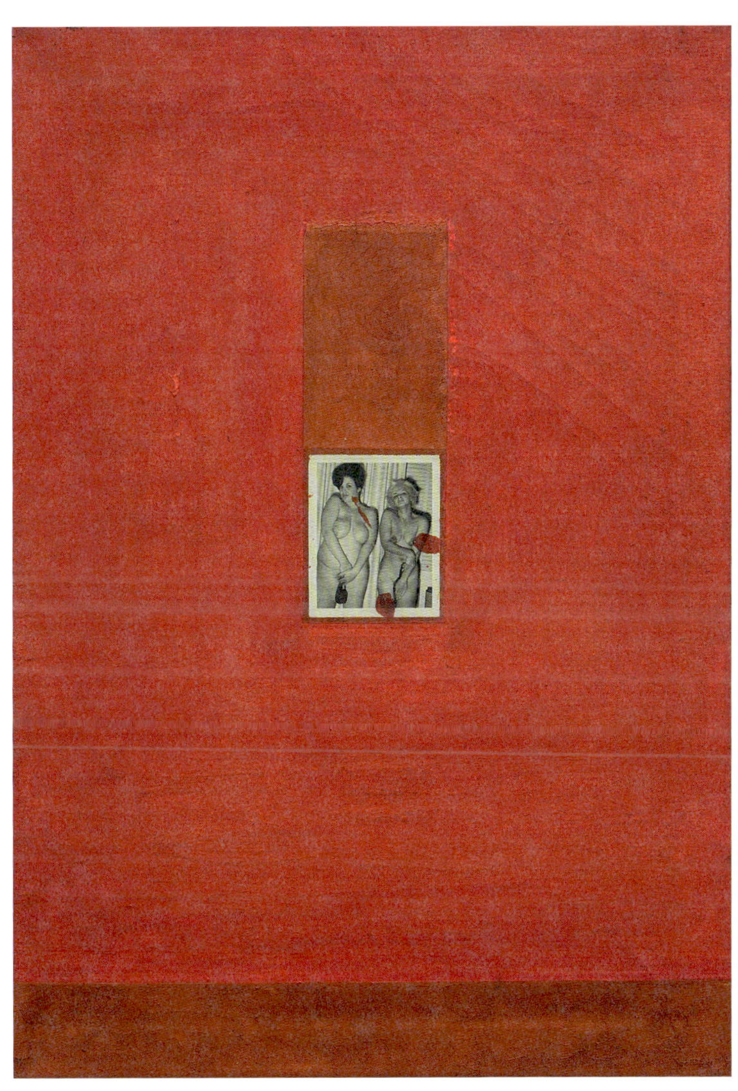

Altered Photos: Shame!, 1963

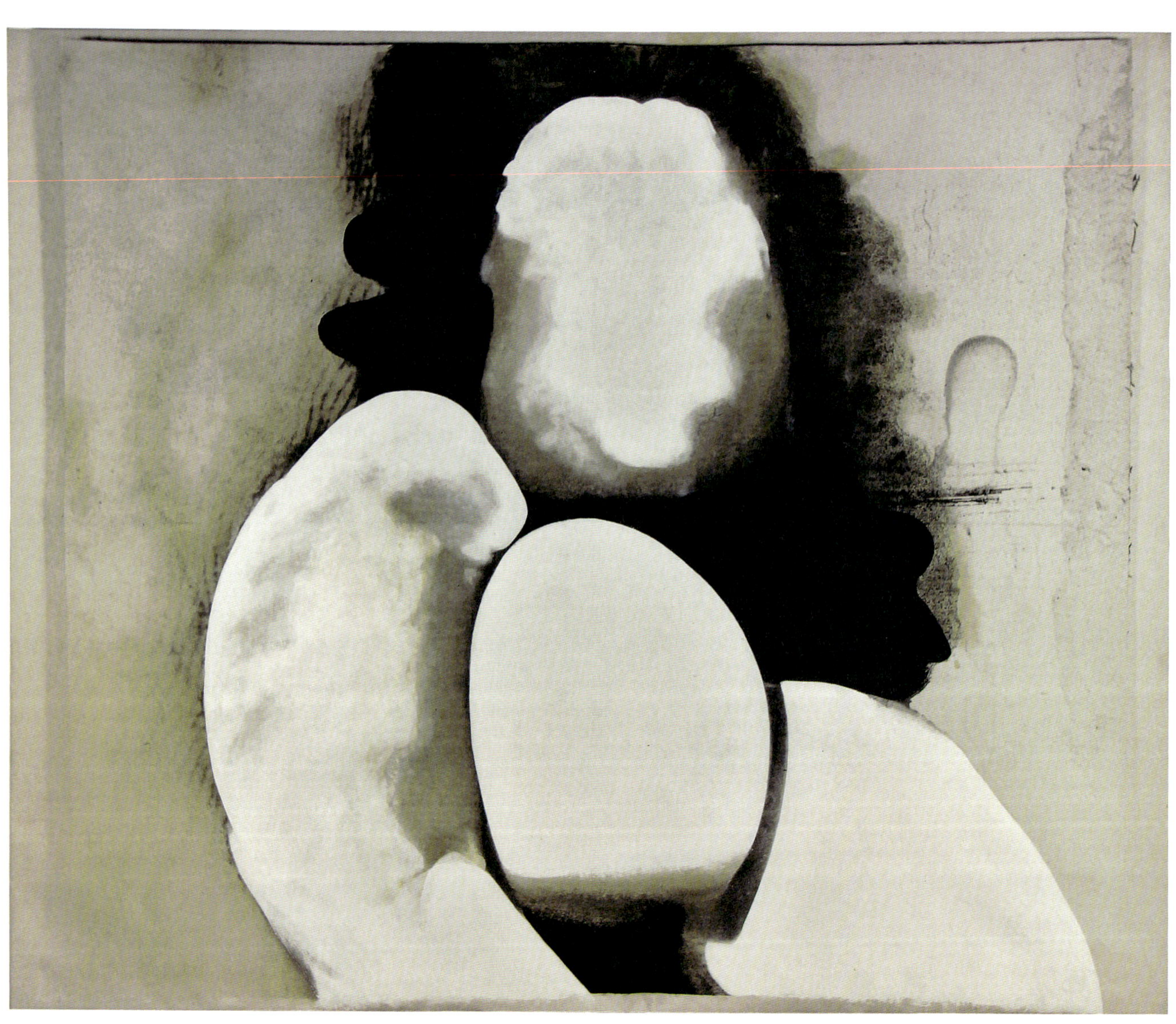

 Altered Photos: Pinup (Dismembered Figure), ca. / ca 1963

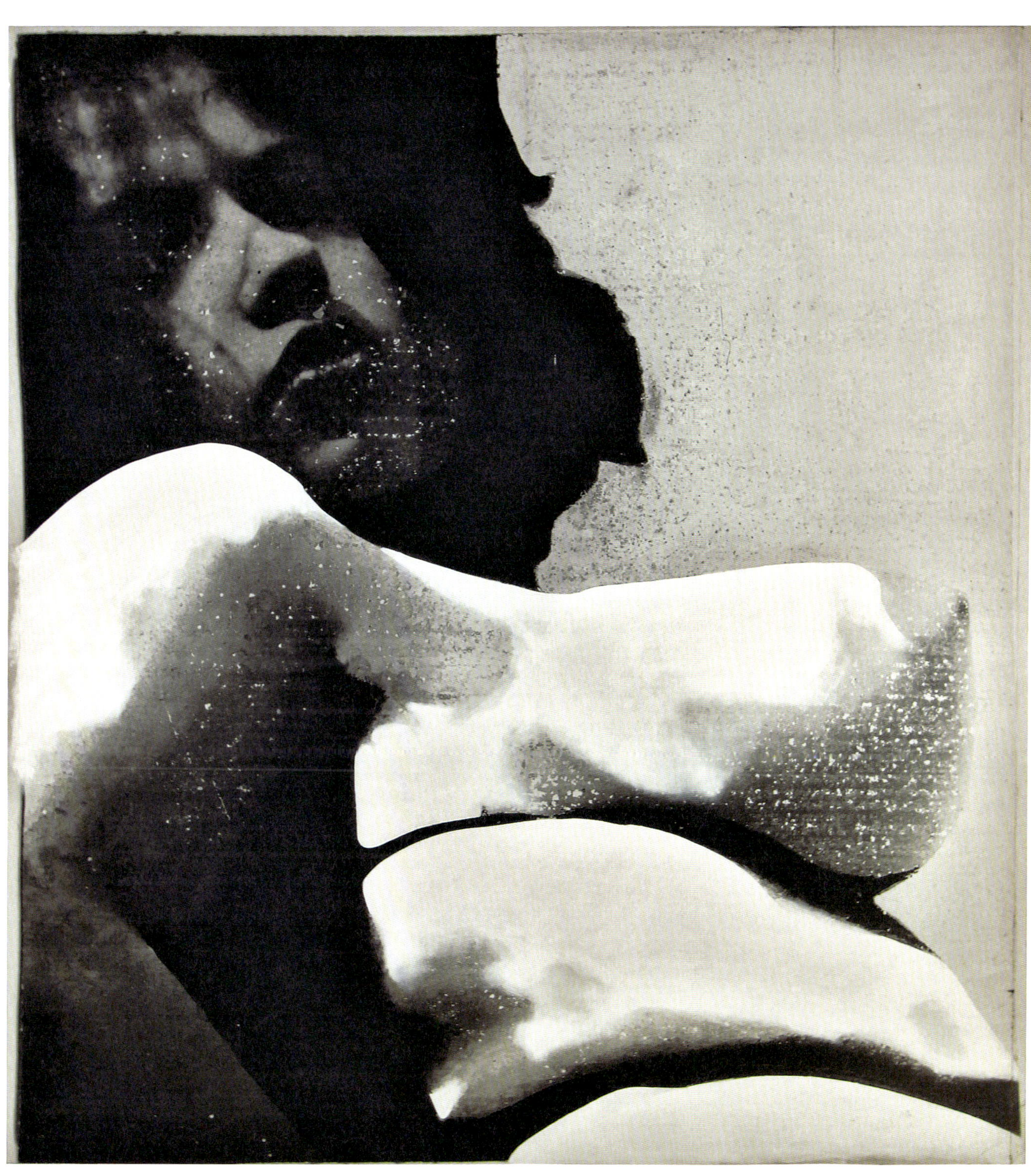

Altered Photos: Pinup (Body), ca. / ca 1963

Love Series

Von Liebe zu sprechen, ist angesichts der Darstellungen sado-masochistischer Praktiken eine Provokation. Die *Love Series* enttäuscht alle romantischen Erwartungen an das Verhältnis von Mann und Frau radikal. Gefesselte und geknebelte Frauen, aber auch Männer, die vor dominanten Frauen knien oder ihre Lackstiefel lecken, waren wie ein Schlag ins Gesicht der prüden USA. Aus der losen Reihe überwiegend kleiner Bilder ragt das große *Bound on Red* (ca. 1963) heraus. Eine gefesselte Gestalt liegt diagonal im Bildfeld. Durch das Blow-up werden die Rasterpunkte des ursprünglichen Druckverfahrens überdeutlich. Wie schon in der Serie der *Dismembered Women* stechen die Stöckelschuhe im Vordergrund hervor. Die Bondage-Szene, deren Figur merkwürdig zwischen Frau und Mann changiert, ist stark grafisch gehalten. Mit ihrer schwarz-weiß-roten Farbigkeit wirkt die Darstellung wie ein Plakat, das die Szene aus den engen Zirkeln Gleichgesinnter in die Öffentlichkeit trägt.

Die Bilder von Unterwerfung, Demütigung und Schmerz, die Boris Lurie in BDSM-Magazinen fand, wurden im Kontext seiner Bildwelt zum Ausdruck realer gesellschaftlicher und politischer Verhältnisse. Es gehörte zu den Grundüberzeugungen der kritischen Generation der 1960er Jahre, dass nur der sexuell befreite Mensch die politische Freiheit gewinnen könne. Der autoritäre Charakter dagegen zeichnete sich in dieser Sicht durch Triebunterdrückung und eine von Ängsten besetzte Sexualität aus. Dadurch war er zur Unterwürfigkeit gegenüber Autoritäten und zum Hass auf alles Schwache disponiert. Sado-Masochismus wurde in dieser Wahrnehmung zum Ausweis autoritärer Strukturen. In der populären wie der Hochkultur, etwa in Pier Paolo Pasolinis Film *Salò oder die 120 Tage von Sodom* (1975), wurde der Zusammenhang zwischen Faschismus und Sado-Masochismus dargestellt.

Damit empfahl sich der Sado-Masochismus auch für Boris Lurie als metaphorisches System, um über seine Holocaust-Traumatisierung sprechen zu können. Ab den 1970er Jahren arbeitete er an seinem Roman *House of Anita*, der in der Tarnung einer verstörenden SM-Fantasie seine Erfahrungen in den Konzentrationslagern ebenso thematisiert wie die New Yorker Kunstszene, die Lurie in ihren Strukturen als faschistisch erlebte. Bis zu seinem Tod beschäftigten den Künstler regelrecht obsessiv die Zusammenhänge zwischen Sexualität, Gewalt und Demütigung. In einem Interview von 2004 machte er auf ein Foto in seinem Atelier aufmerksam, das nackte jüdische Frauen kurz vor ihrer Erschießung im Jahre 1941 zeigte. „Heute kann man sowas zum Beispiel auf den Fotos aus dem Abu-Ghraib-Gefängnis in Irak sehen. Das sagt viel über die Gesellschaft aus. Die Starken unterdrücken die Schwachen und die Folterer ziehen ein gewisses Vergnügen aus ihren Taten, ein sexuelles Vergnügen."[1] Die Vorstellung, dass sich auch seine Mutter, seine Großmutter, seine Schwester und seine Geliebte im Wald von Rumbula nackt ausziehen mussten, bevor sie getötet wurden, war für den Künstler besonders quälend. TH

1 Boris Lurie zit. nach: Tal Sterngast: „Schocktherapie. Frauen als Figur in Boris Luries Werk", in: *Keine Kompromisse! Die Kunst des Boris Lurie*, Ausstellungskatalog, Jüdisches Museum Berlin, 26.2.–31.7.2016, S.127.

Love Series

Talking about love in connection with depictions of sadomasochistic practices is in itself a provocation. The radical portrayals in Boris Lurie's *Love Series* thwart any romantic expectations viewers may have of male-female relationships. Images of women who are bound and gagged, but also of men kneeling before dominant female figures or licking their patent leather boots, were like a slap in the face of the prudish United States in the 1960s. In this loose series of mainly small-sized pictures, one large-format work stands out: *Bound on Red* (ca 1963), in which a reclining, bound figure lies diagonally across the picture plane. In the blown-up image, the halftone dots of the original printed reproduction are clearly visible. Here, as in Lurie's *Dismembered Women* series, the stiletto-heeled shoes are prominent in the foreground. This bondage scene, involving a figure that oscillates between male and female, has a strongly graphic quality. With its black, white, and red coloring it resembles a poster, which transports the scene out of the close circles of like-minded individuals and into the public realm.

In Boris Lurie's artworks, the images of subjection, humiliation, and pain taken from BDSM magazines were used to reflect contemporary social and political conditions. One of the core beliefs of the critical 1960s generation was the notion that only a sexually liberated person could attain political freedom. An authoritarian character, on the other hand, was characterized by suppressed desires and fears regarding sexuality; this made him or her prone to be subservient to authority and to hate anything regarded as weak. Sadomasochism was thus perceived to be an identifying feature of authoritarian structures. Representations of the connection between fascism and sadomasochism were found in both popular and high culture, for example in Pier Paolo Pasolini's film *Salò, or the 120 Days of Sodom* (1975).

For Boris Lurie, therefore, sadomasochism also suggested itself as a metaphorical system he could use to talk about his Holocaust trauma. From the 1970s onwards he worked on the novel *House of Anita;* in the guise of a disturbing S&M fantasy, it enabled him to address his experiences not only in the concentration camps but also in the New York art scene, which Lurie regarded as fascist in terms of its structures. For the rest of his life he obsessively explored the relationship between sexuality, violence, and humiliation. In an interview from 2004, he drew attention to a photograph in his studio that showed naked Jewish women shortly before they were shot and killed in 1941, saying: "Today one can see it in the photos from Abu Ghraib in Iraq, for example. It's an expression of society. The way the strong ones suppress the weak and the torturer gets a certain pleasure from it, a sexual pleasure."[1] For Boris Lurie, it was particularly agonizing to know that his mother, grandmother, sister, and girlfriend had also been forced to strip naked in the forest of Rumbula before they were murdered.
TH

1 Boris Lurie, quoted in Tal Sterngast, "Shock Treatment: Figures of Women in Boris Lurie's Work," in *No Compromises! The Art of Boris Lurie*, exh. cat. Jewish Museum Berlin, February 26–July 31, 2016 (Bielefeld/Berlin: Kerber Verlag, 2016), pp. 126–34, here p. 127.

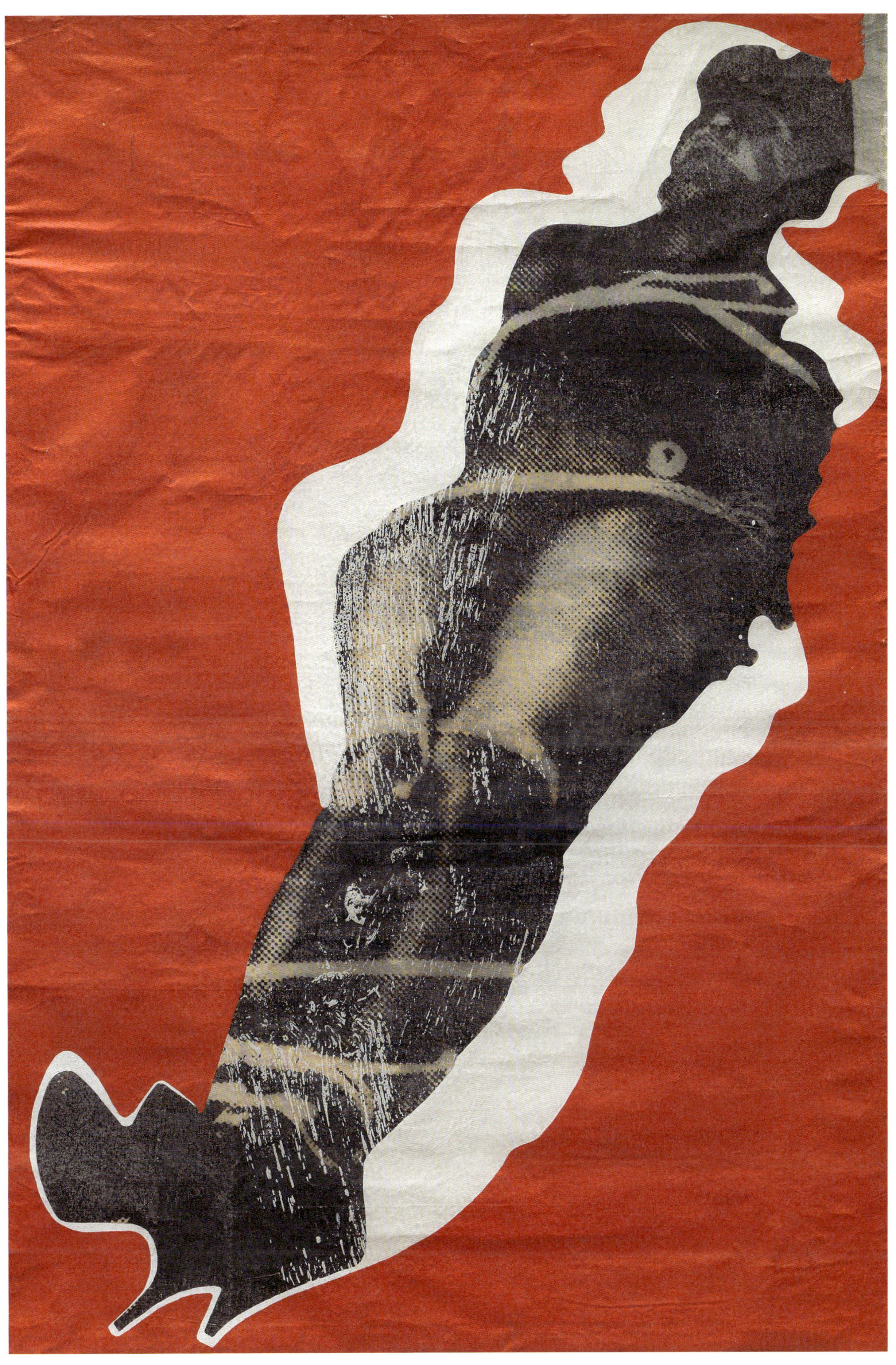

Love Series: Bound on Red, ca. / ca 1963

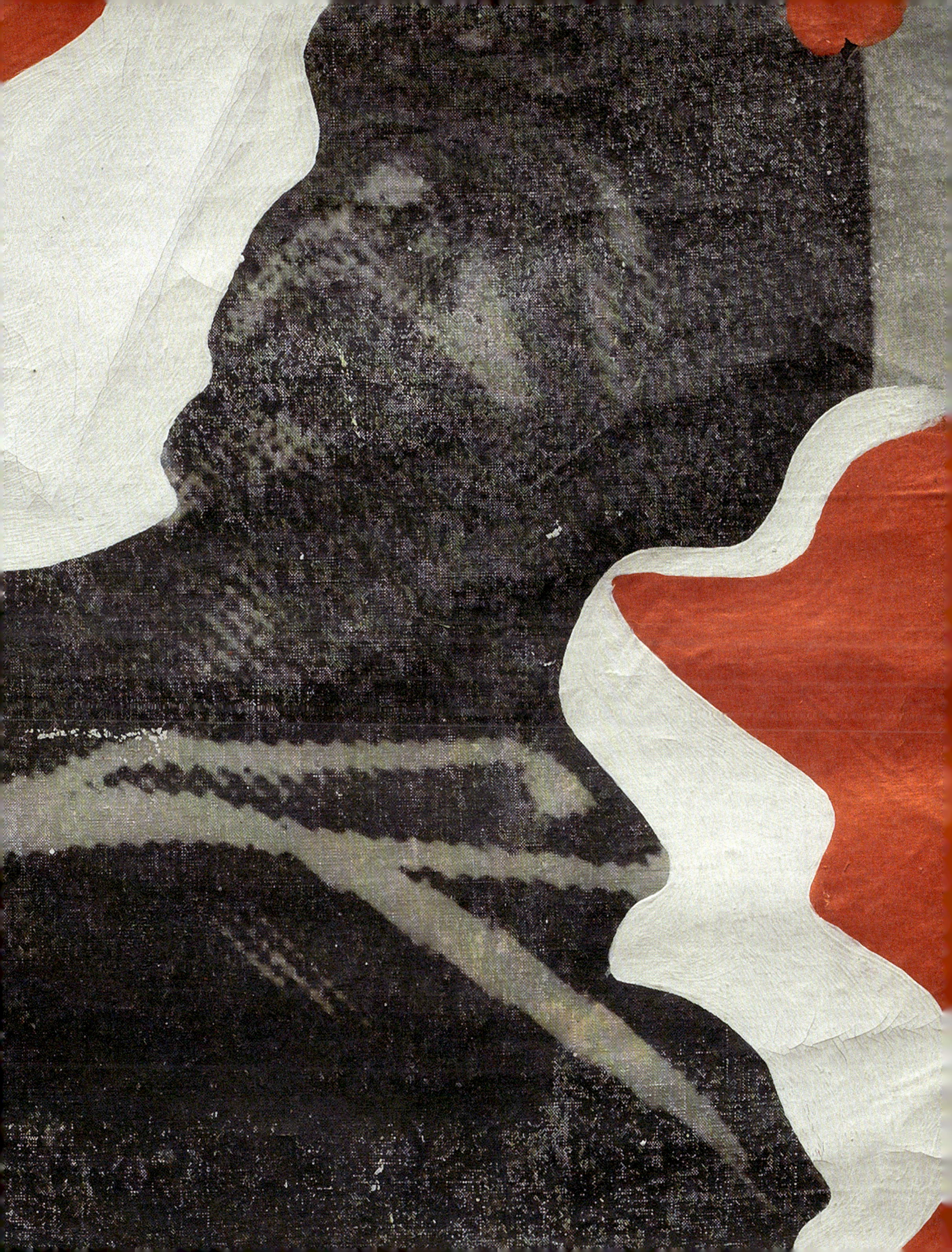

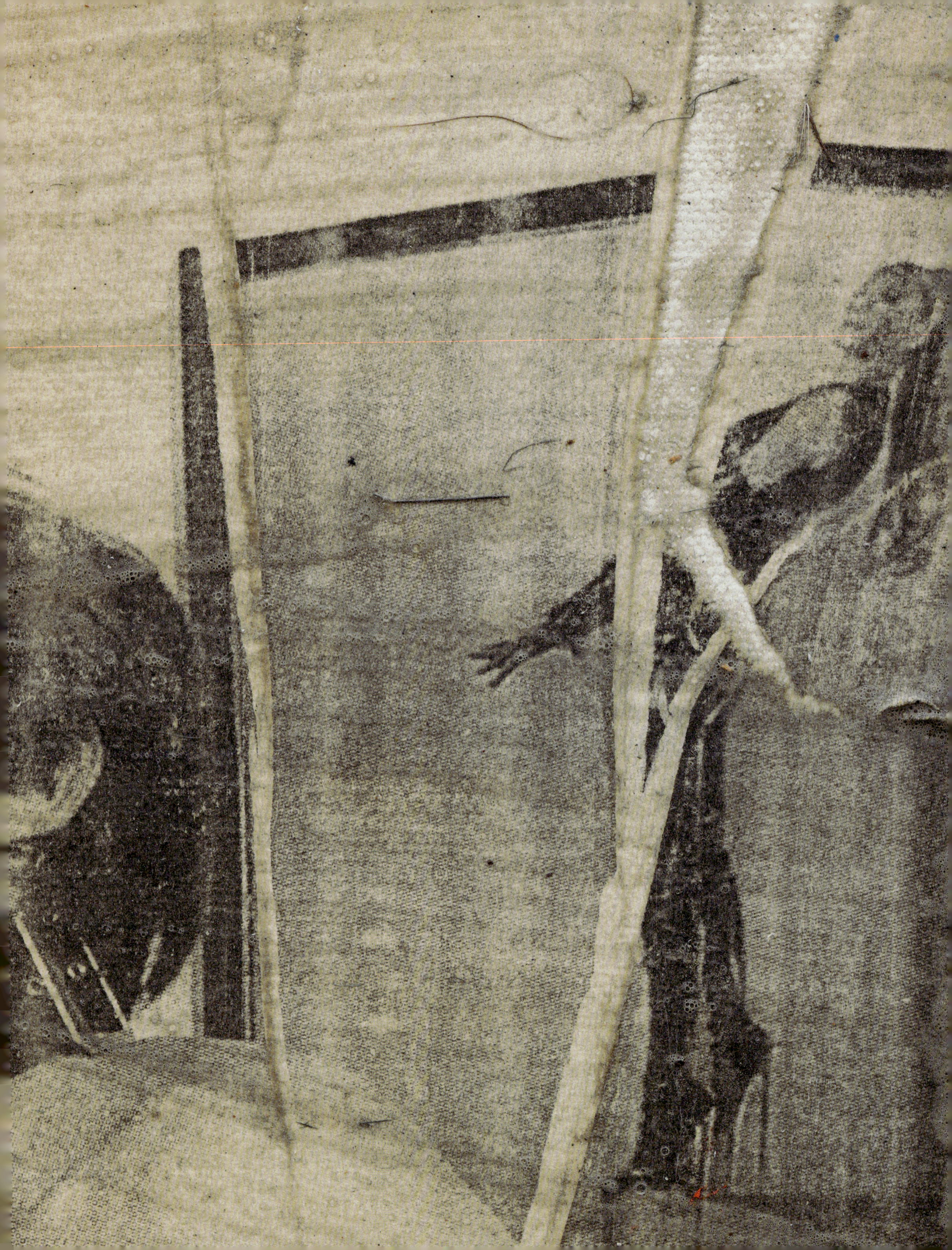

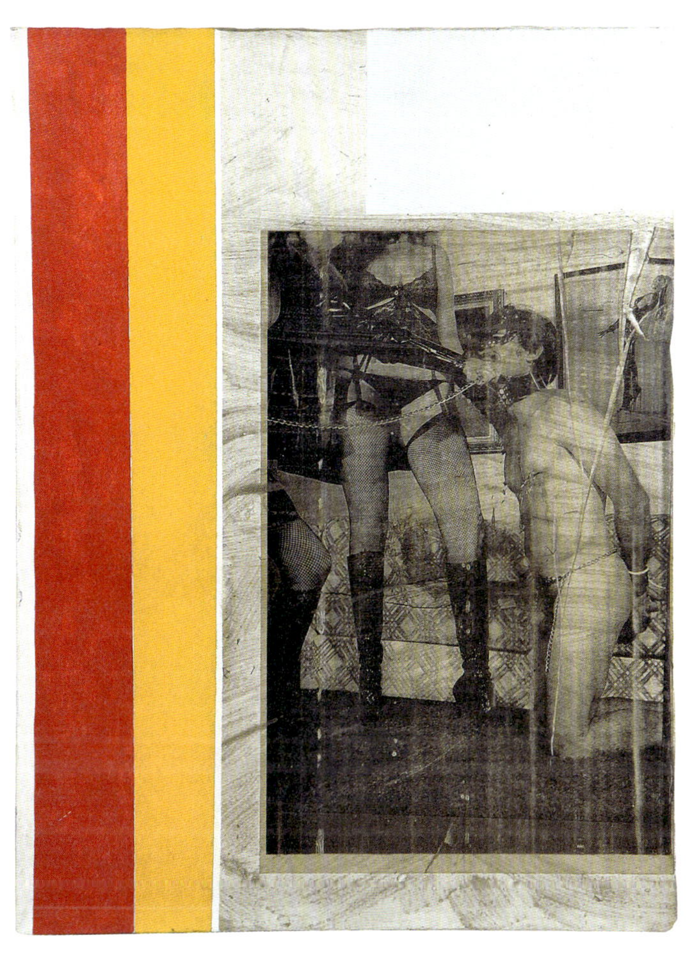

Untitled (Deliberate Pinup), ca. / ca 1971–73

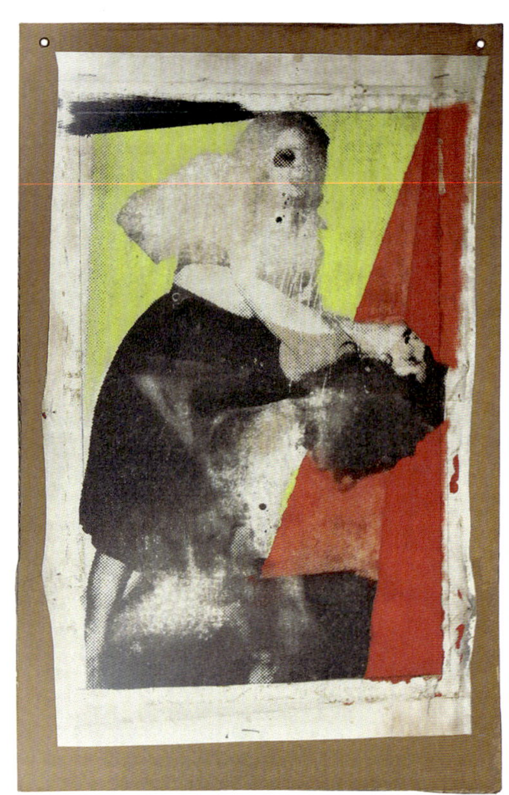

 Love Series: Figthing Females, ca. / ca 1963

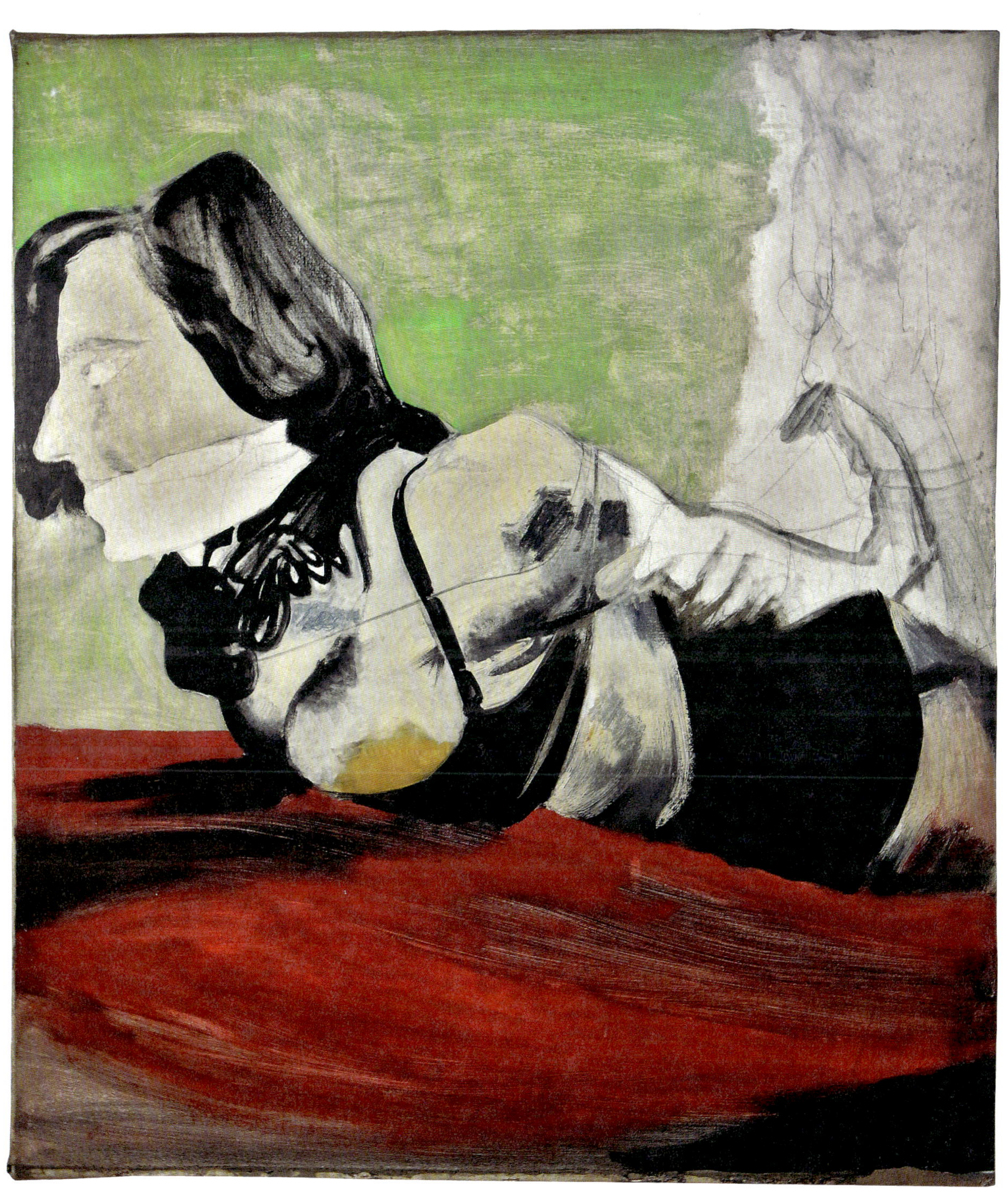

Untitled (On Stomach), ca. / ca 1963

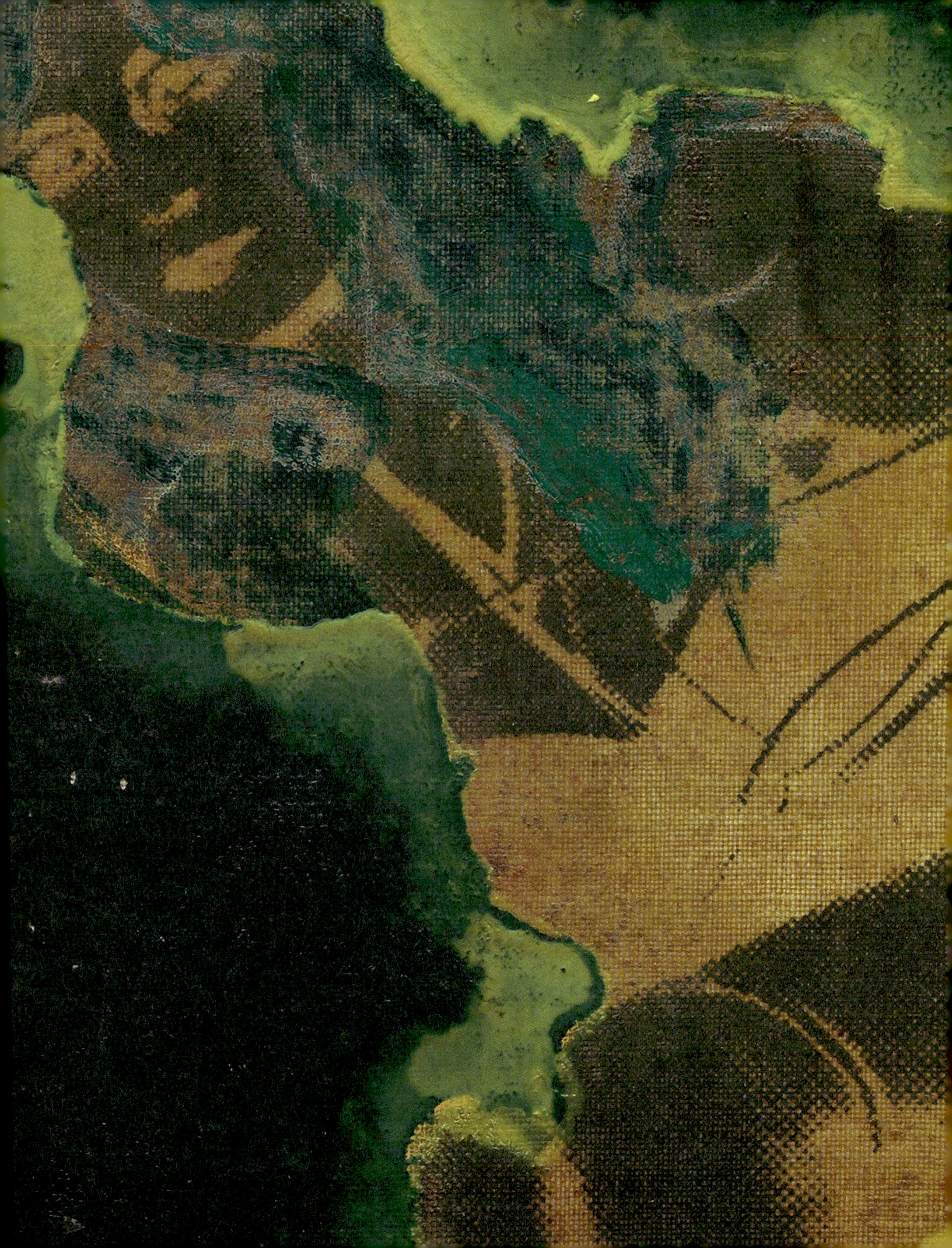

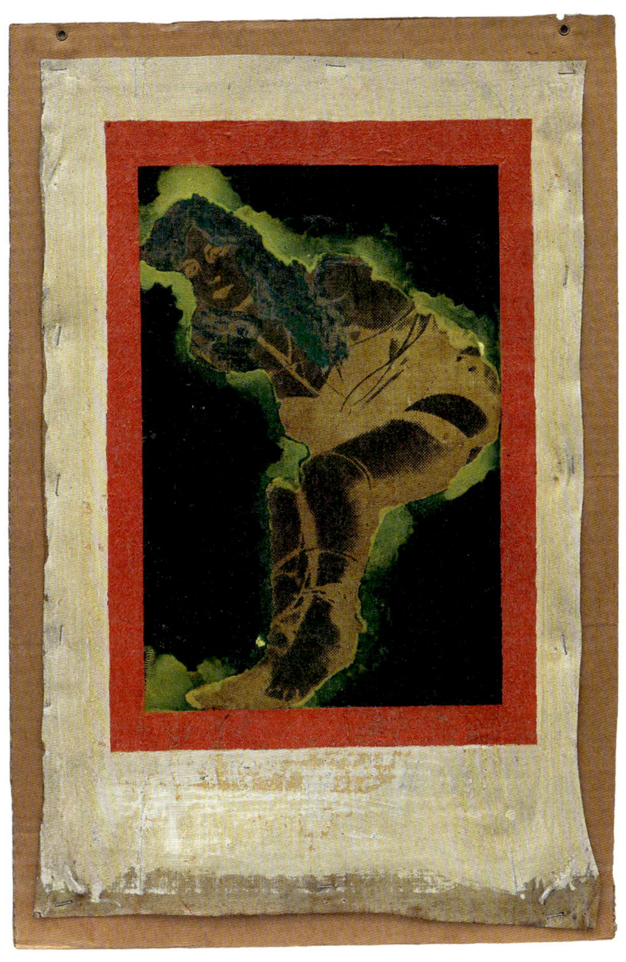

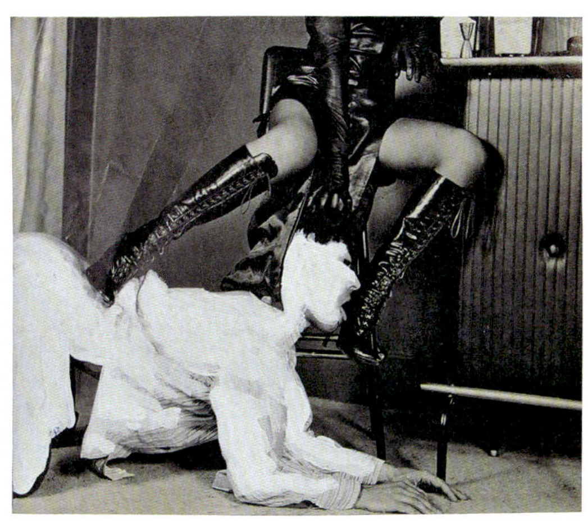

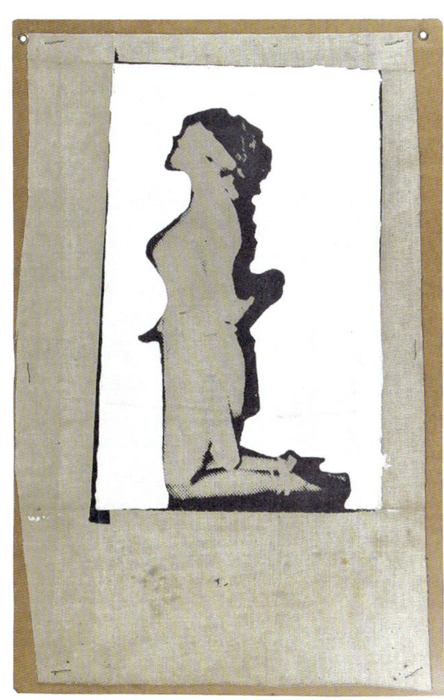

Love Series, ca. / ca 1963   *Love Series: Bound and Gagged*, ca. / ca 1963   *Love Series: Posed*, ca. / ca 1963

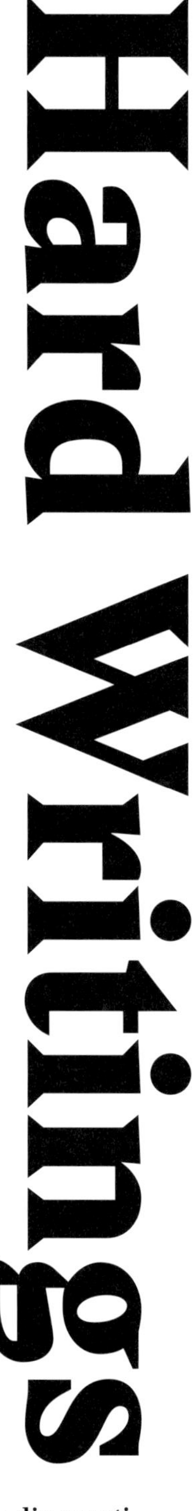

In seinen *Hard Writings* kombinierte Boris Lurie Schrift und Bild. Die Collagetechnik hatte von Anfang an auch fragmentierte Texte und vereinzelte Wörter in Luries Kunst eingebracht. Die Isolierung von Wort und Bild in den *Hard Writings* untersucht quasi experimentell das Spannungsverhältnis zwischen den beiden Zeichensystemen. Wie in einem humanistischen Emblem konstituieren Wort und Bild ein Rätsel, das sich allerdings bei Lurie nicht immer auflösen lässt. Zwischen Wörtern wie „SLAVE", „LICK" oder „PISS" und collagierten Pin-ups lässt sich der Zusammenhang zwar leicht herstellen, doch bleibt etwa bei den beiden Verben unklar, ob es sich vielleicht um Imperative handelt, mit denen die Betrachter zu sexuellen Handlungen aufgefordert werden. In *Hard Writings: PLEASE* und *Hard Writings: SLAVE* greift Lurie in die Typografie ein und provoziert dadurch semantische Doppeldeutigkeiten: Da der Damenkopf mit hochtoupierter Frisur sich zwischen die ersten vier und die letzten beiden Buchstaben des Wortes „PLEASE" schiebt, entsteht ein neues Wort: „PLEA", das mit „Vorwand" oder „Ausrede" übersetzt werden kann. In *Hard Writings: SLAVE* scheint das „L" heruntergerutscht und teilweise hinter das Bild mit dem Pin-up geraten zu sein. Die restlichen Buchstaben ergeben nun das neue Wort „SAVE". Auch ohne solche Interventionen des Künstlers kommt es zu Mehrdeutigkeiten. In *Hard Writings: LOAD* greift Boris Lurie jenes Foto aus Buchenwald auf, das bereits für *Flatcar* und für *Railroad to America* Verwendung gefunden hatte. Die aufgestapelten Leichen lassen sich auch im figurativen Sinn als Last, Belastung oder Bürde verstehen. Gleichzeitig meint das Verb „to load" auch das Laden eines Gewehrs oder einer Fotokamera, ähnlich wie mit beiden Instrumenten im Deutschen wie im Englischen „geschossen" werden kann.

Die Werkgruppe der *Hard Writings*, die vor allem in den Jahren 1972 bis 1974 entstand, ist durch eine sehr strenge formale Gestaltung ausgezeichnet, die aus der Typografie zu erwachsen scheint. Der Einfluss der in den USA omnipräsenten Werbeästhetik ist unverkennbar. Billboards, Plakate und Verpackungen konkurrierten um die Aufmerksamkeit der Konsumenten. Diesem Wettbewerb stellte sich die Kunst von Boris Lurie. Seine *Hard Writings* sparen deshalb auch nicht mit visuellen Reizen: Sex sells. Auch andere amerikanische Künstler arbeiteten mit den aus der Konsumwelt geborgten Reizen: Ed Ruscha zum Beispiel, der schon Anfang der 1960er Jahre die auratische Kraft isolierter Wörter und Trademarks für seine Kunst entdeckt hatte.

Die Bezeichnung „Hard Writing" spielt offensichtlich auf „Hard Edge" (Harte Kante) an. So bezeichnete die US-amerikanische Kunstkritik seit 1958 eine Stilrichtung, die sich im Unterschied zum Abstrakten Expressionismus durch scharfkantig voneinander getrennte Farbflächen auszeichnet. Barnett Newman, Ad Reinhardt, Kenneth Noland oder Ellsworth Kelly sind Künstler, deren Werk mit „Hard Edge" in Verbindung gebracht wurde. Boris Luries *Hard Writings* zeigen lediglich in der klaren Flächen- und Farbkomposition Ähnlichkeiten. Die Einbeziehung von Text und Pin-ups sprengt jedoch die idealistische Hermetik der „Hard Edge"-Malerei. TH

Hard Writings

In Boris Lurie's *Hard Writings* series, words are juxtaposed with images. While fragmented texts and isolated words were incorporated into his art from the very beginning through the use of collage, the isolation of words and images in the *Hard Writings* is a quasi-experimental investigation into the tension between these two representational systems. As in a humanistic emblem, the word and image constitute a puzzle, although in Lurie's art the puzzle cannot always be solved. While it is easy to make a connection between collaged pin-ups and words such as "SLAVE," "LICK," or "PISS," it is not clear, for example, whether these terms are nouns or verbs in the imperative mood, calling upon the viewer/reader to perform sexual acts. In *Hard Writings: PLEASE* (ca 1963–72) and *Hard Writings: SLAVE* (ca 1972), Lurie intervenes in the typography to produce semantic ambiguity: in *Hard Writings: PLEASE*, the head of a woman with a beehive hairdo is interposed between the first four and the last two letters of this word, creating the new word "PLEA"; in *Hard Writings: SLAVE*, the letter L appears to have dropped down and is partly hidden behind the pin-up image, so that the remaining letters produce the word "SAVE." Ambiguity is also generated without any such interventions by the artist. In *Hard Writings: LOAD* (1972), for example, which incorporates the same photograph of Buchenwald that was used in *Flatcar* (ca 1962) and *Railroad to America* (1963), the piled corpses can be understood literally as a "load" in the sense of a cargo, but also figuratively as a burden or weight. At the same time, the verb "to load" refers to putting ammunition into a gun or film into a camera, just as both instruments can be used to "shoot."

The works in the *Hard Writings* series, most of which were created between 1972 and 1974, have an austere formal quality that appears to derive from the typographic design. The influence of the advertising aesthetic that was by then omnipresent in the United States is clearly evident here. Billboards, posters, and packaging designs were all vying for consumers' attention, and Boris Lurie's art faced up to this competition. His *Hard Writings* are therefore not short on visual stimuli: sex sells, after all. Other American artists were also borrowing motifs from consumer culture: in the early 1960s, for example, Ed Ruscha discovered the auratic force of isolated words and trademarks, and put these to effective use in his own art.

The term "Hard Writing" clearly plays on "hard edge," the name given by American art critics from around 1958 to an abstract painting style which, in contrast to Abstract Expressionism, was characterized by sharply defined areas of bold, flat color. Barnett Newman, Ad Reinhardt, Kenneth Noland, and Ellsworth Kelly are among the artists associated with this new style of painting. Boris Lurie's *Hard Writings* show similarities to this movement only in terms of their distinctly planar arrangement and their color composition. The incorporation of text and pin-up images, however, removes them from the idealistic hermeticism of hard-edge painting.

TH

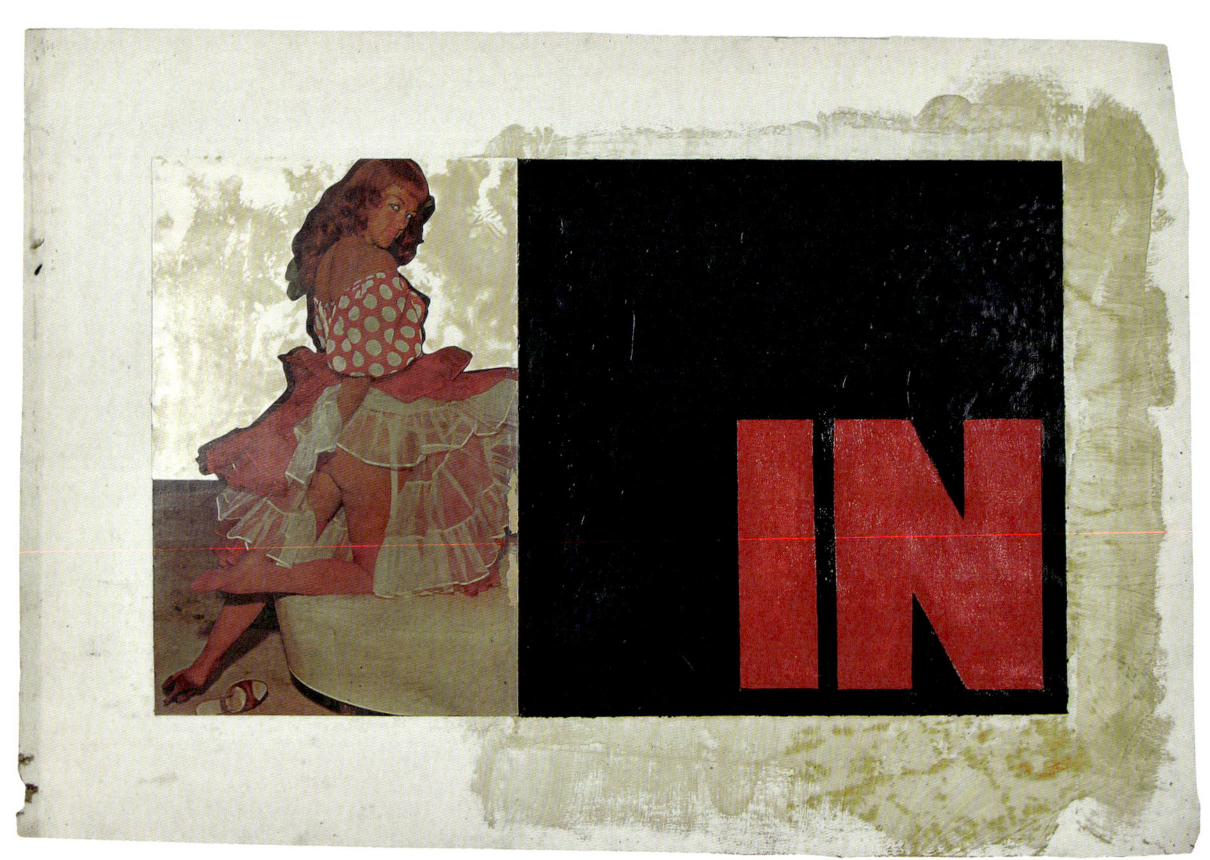

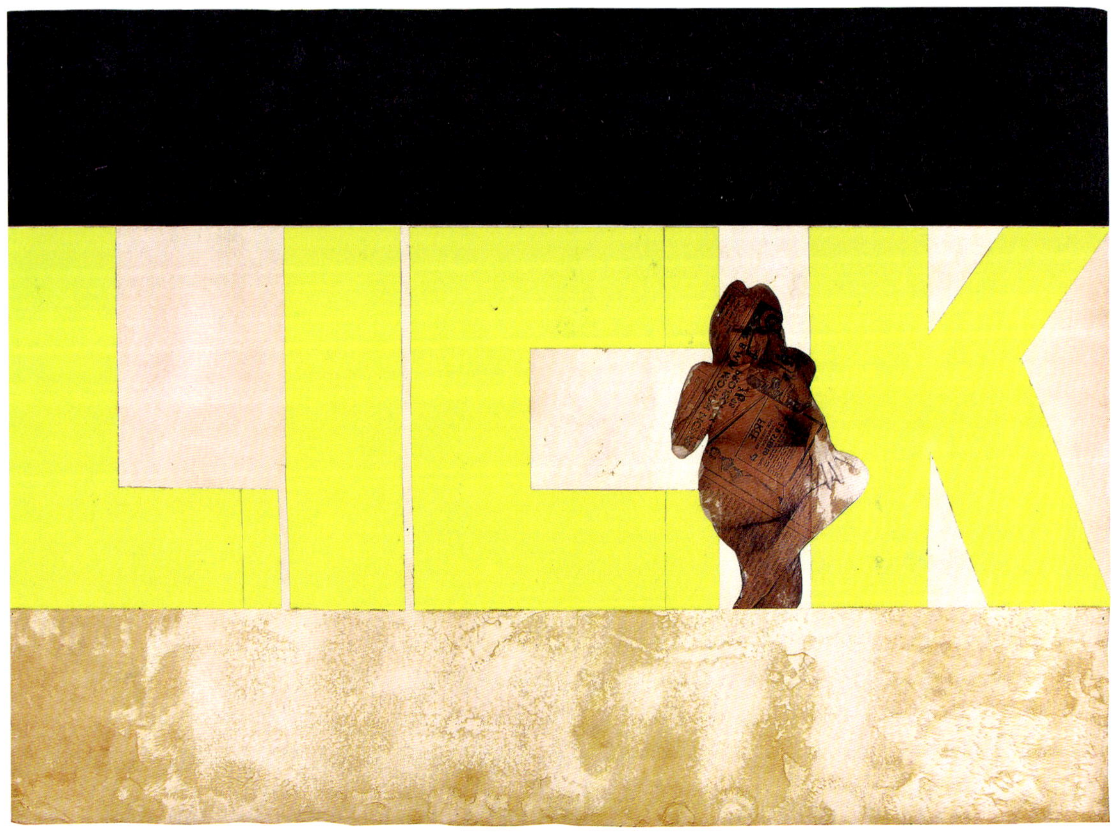

 Hard Writings: IN, ca. / ca 1972 – 73 *Hard Writings: LICK*, ca. / ca 1972

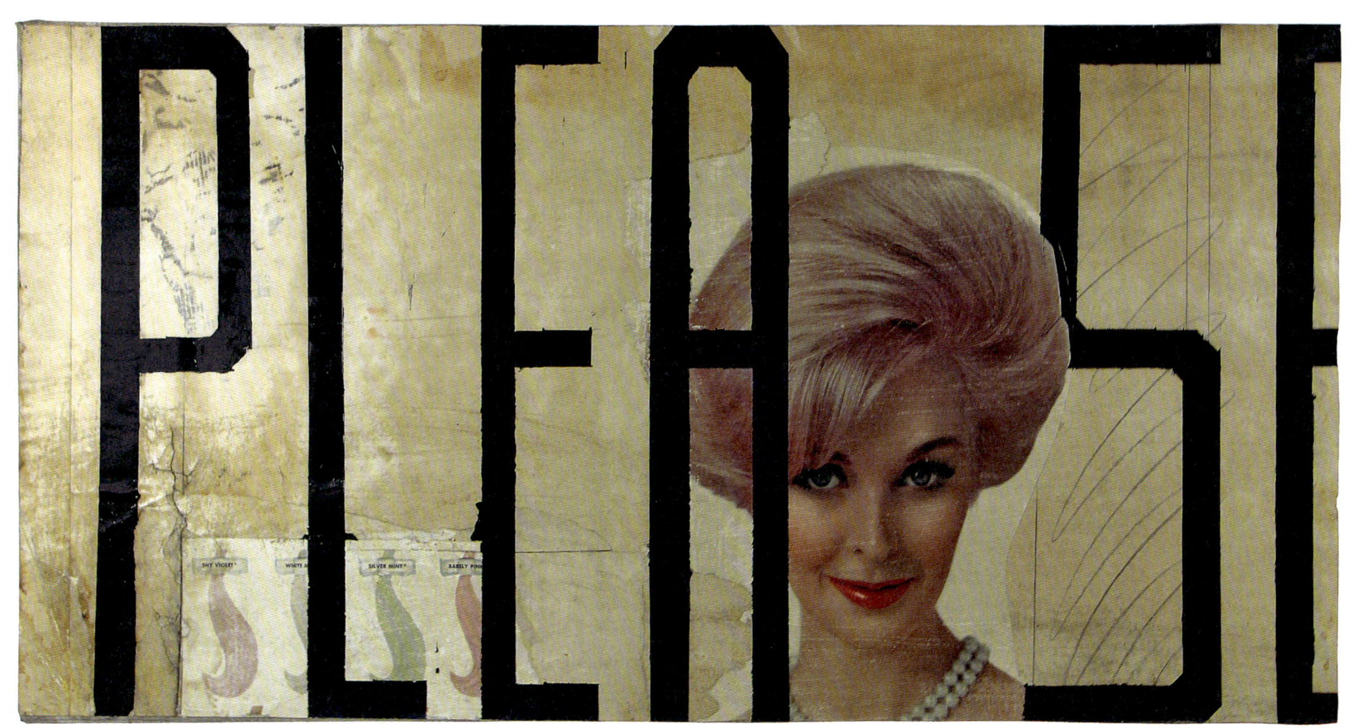

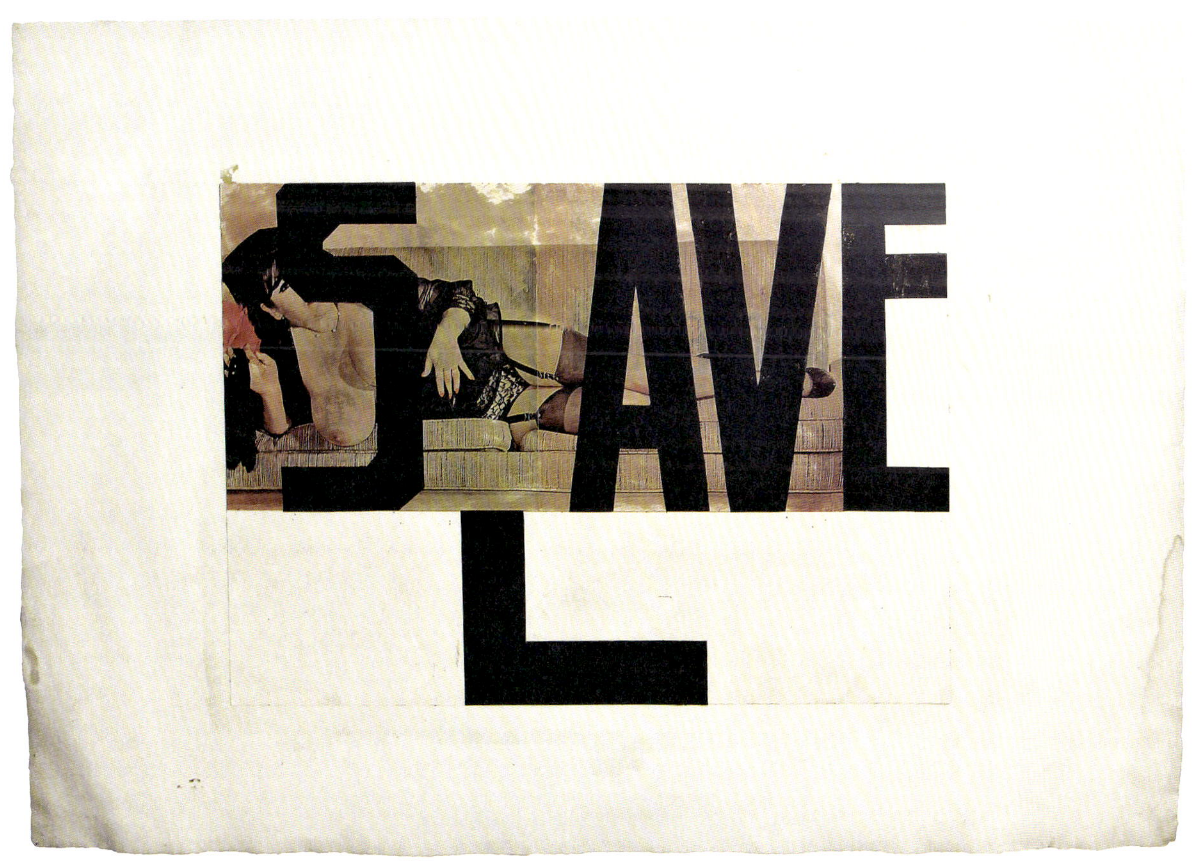

Hard Writings: PLEASE, ca. / ca 1963 – 72 *Hard Writings: SLAVE*, ca. / ca 1972

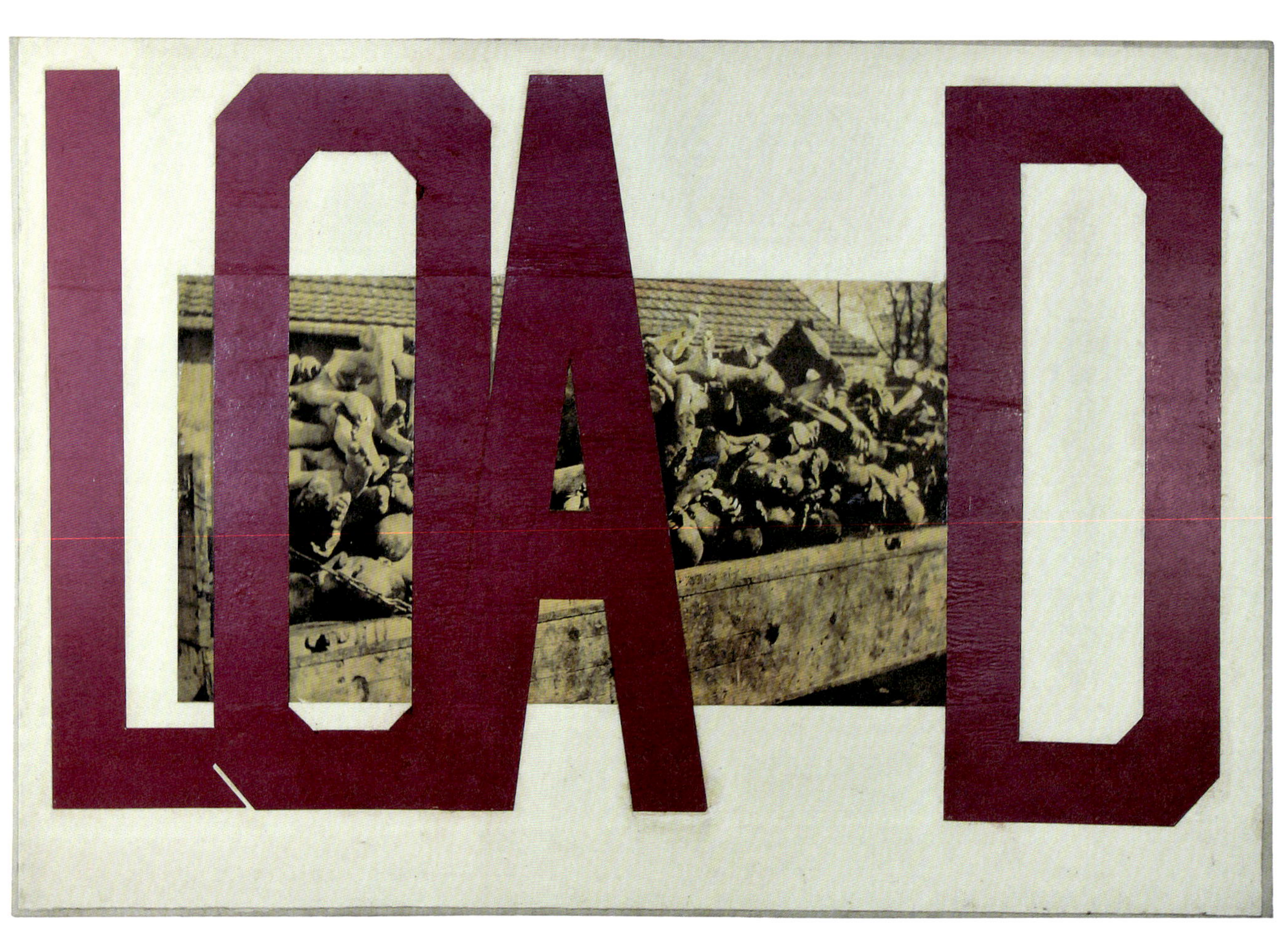

 Hard Writings: LOAD, 1972

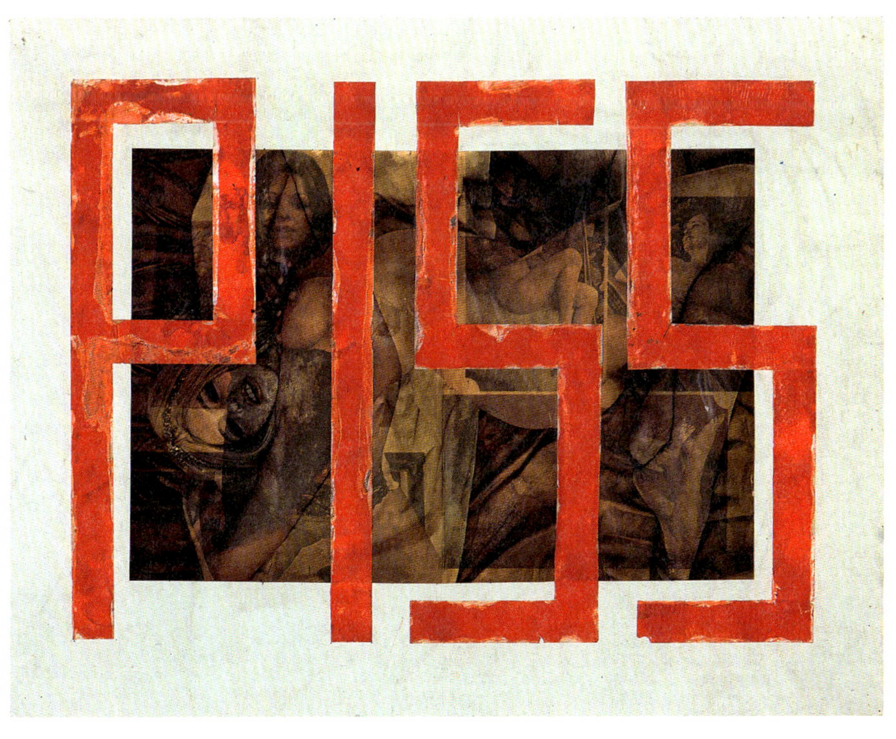

Hard Writings: PISS, ca. / ca 1972–73

Bilder, die Nein sagen und nichts als Nein sagen. In diesen Arbeiten von Boris Lurie kam die NO!art auf den Punkt. Wem das Nein gilt, bleibt zunächst offen. Es ist nicht ausdrücklicher Gegenstand des Bildes. Erst im Zusammenhang von Ausstellungen und begleitenden Statements füllte sich die Leerstelle mit Inhalt. Der Protest richtete sich gegen Imperialismus und Militarismus, gegen Ausbeutung und Kapitalismus, gegen jede Form von Unterdrückung und Ungerechtigkeit. Ganz allgemein galt das „NO" der US-amerikanischen Gesellschaft mit ihrem Konsumismus und Konformismus, ihrer Prüderie und Bigotterie. Vor dem Hintergrund von Boris Luries Biografie bedeutete das Nein auch einen konkreten Appell, den Holocaust nicht zu vergessen.

Das Nein galt nicht der Kunst selbst. Es begründete keine Anti-Kunst, verpflichtete jedoch Kunst zur gesellschaftlichen und politischen Stellungnahme. Formalistischen Experimenten erteilte das „NO" dagegen eine klare Absage. Wenn Boris Lurie dennoch das „NO" stilistisch durchdeklinierte, so bewies er damit eigentlich nur, wie egal ihm alle Formfragen waren, die sich zu einem Ismus verabsolutierten. Das Spektrum der Lösungen ist entsprechend breit und reicht von einer bemalten Schallplatte über Malerei auf Linoleum bis hin zu einem gelben Karton, aus dem das Wörtchen dreimal ausgeschnitten ist. Die Leichtigkeit, mit der Lurie immer neue Varianten ersann, immunisiert die Serie der „NO"-Bilder gegen Pathos und Verkrampfung. Mithilfe von Schablonen und Stempeln ließ sich das „NO" multiplizieren. Was zur Litanei hätte erstarren können, wird ein lebendiges Muster und semantisches Vexierbild, da es auch die Umkehrung „ON" zu lesen gibt. Eine gesprühte Variante von 1963 ist besonders interessant, da Lurie hier eine Technik wählte, die geeignet war, Kunst auf die Straße zu tragen. „NO!art" wurde so zur potenziellen Street Art.

Einige Arbeiten ähneln durch die Kombination von strenger Typografie mit erotischem und pornografischem Bildmaterial der Werkgruppe der *Hard Writings.* Das Foto einer von zwei Händen weit geöffneten Vagina erscheint unter einem harten, schwarzen „NO" in Versalien. Offen bleibt, wie sich das Nein auf die schamverletzende Darstellung bezieht. Protestiert der Künstler damit gegen die Erniedrigung der Frau? Oder erfüllt das Motiv der gespreizten Vulva eine apotropäische Funktion, wie sie aus verschiedenen Kulturen überliefert ist? Soll das abschreckende Foto etwa visuell bannen, wogegen sich das „NO" verbal verwahrt?

Boris Luries „NO"-Bilder sagen vor allem auch Nein zur Kunst als Ware. Ein Vorwurf, den die NO!art vor allem an die Pop-Künstler richtete, die damals den Markt eroberten. „NO" und „Anti-Pop" waren eins. Auch die in Gips nachgebildeten Scheißehaufen von Sam Goodman und Boris Lurie, die sie 1964 in der Galerie von Gertrude Stein präsentierten, meinten im doppelten Sinne des Wortes das „große Geschäft" der Pop-Künstler und ihrer Galeristen. Wie ein Menetekel erscheint auf einer weißen Leinwand von Boris Lurie das Wort „sold" (verkauft). In der Realisierung des Tauschwerts hat sich der Zweck des Kunstwerks erfüllt. In diesem ironischen Kunstwerk ist die Kritik Luries an seinen geschäftstüchtigen Kollegen Bild geworden. TH

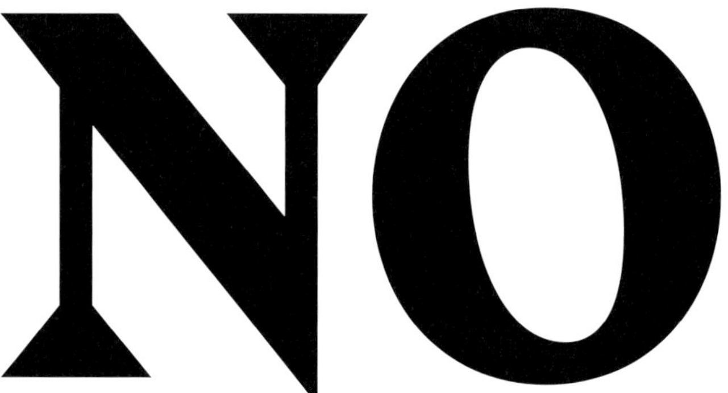

Pictures that say NO, and nothing but NO. In this series of works by Boris Lurie, NO!art gets straight to the point. The question of who or what the NO applies to is left open. It does not appear in the picture as an explicit theme. Only in connection with exhibitions and accompanying statements does the blank space begin to fill with content. Boris Lurie's protests were aimed at imperialism and militarism, exploitation and capitalism, and all forms of repression and injustice. In a more general sense, the NO applied to American society with its consumerism, conformity, prudery, and bigotry. Viewed against the background of his own biography, it was also a direct appeal not to forget the Holocaust.

The NO did not apply to art itself. But while it did not constitute an anti-art position, it did obligate art to take a social and political stance. Formalist experiments, on the other hand, were firmly rejected by the NO. The fact that Boris Lurie produced many stylistic variations on the NO theme only proved how little he cared about questions of form that were often absolutized into isms. The solutions he came up with covered a correspondingly broad spectrum, ranging from a painted LP to painting on linoleum, to a piece of yellow cardboard out of which the little word NO has been cut three times. The NO could also be multiplied with the aid of stencils and rubber stamps. The ease with which Lurie devised new variations immunized his NO pictures against pathos and forcedness. What could easily have degenerated into a tedious litany evolved into a lively pattern, and also became a semantic puzzle with the inclusion of the reverse form "ON". A sprayed version from 1963 is particularly interesting, as Lurie here chose a technique that could be used to transport art into the streets. In this way, NO!art could potentially become Street Art.

N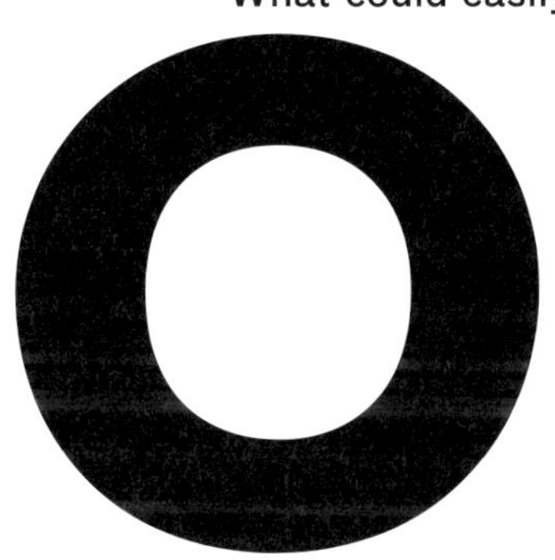

Some of Lurie's NO works recall his series of *Hard Writings* due to the combination of bold typography and erotic or pornographic images. In one such work, a photograph of two hands exposing a vagina appears beneath the word "NO" in bold black capital letters. It is not immediately obvious how this "NO" relates to the obscene image. Is the artist protesting against the humiliation of the woman? Or does the motif of the splayed vagina have an apotropaic function, as it does in various cultural traditions? Is the shocking photograph perhaps intended to visually ward off what the "NO" verbally averts?

Boris Lurie's NO pictures firmly rejected the idea of art as a commodity. This was a criticism levelled by the NO!art movement above all at the Pop artists who were dominating the market at that time. NO and anti-Pop were two sides of the same coin. The painted plaster *Shit Sculptures* presented by Sam Goodman and Boris Lurie at Gallery Gertrude Stein in 1964 also alluded to the "dirty business" the Pop artists and their gallerists were involved in. On a white canvas by Boris Lurie, the word "sold" appears like a warning; the purpose of the artwork is fulfilled in the realization of its exchange value. With this ironic piece, Lurie clearly expresses his disapproval of his market-oriented colleagues. TH

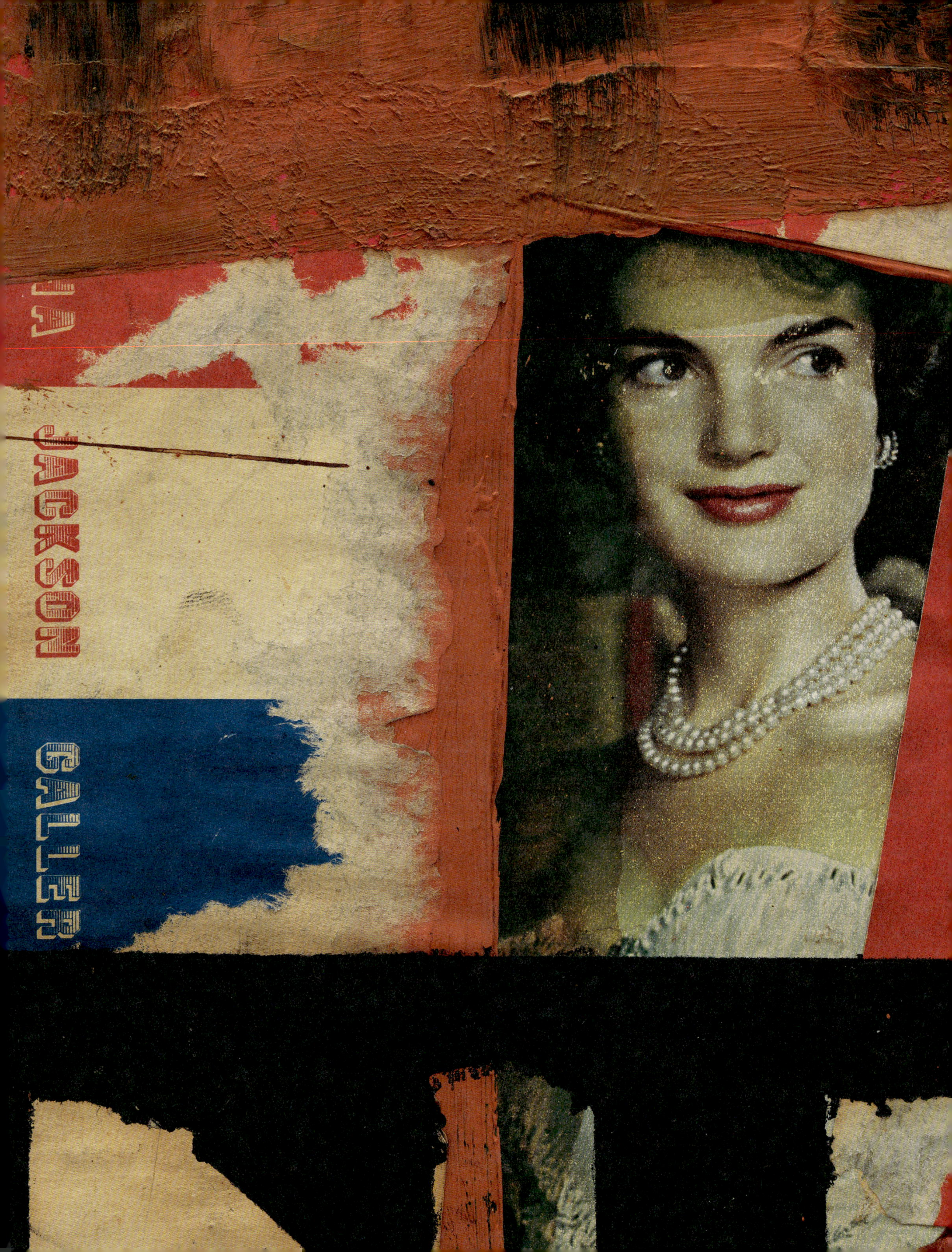
JACKSON
GALLER

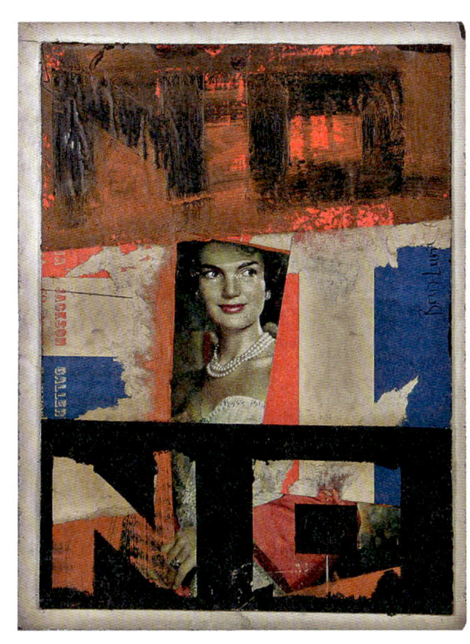

NO with Mrs. Kennedy, 1963

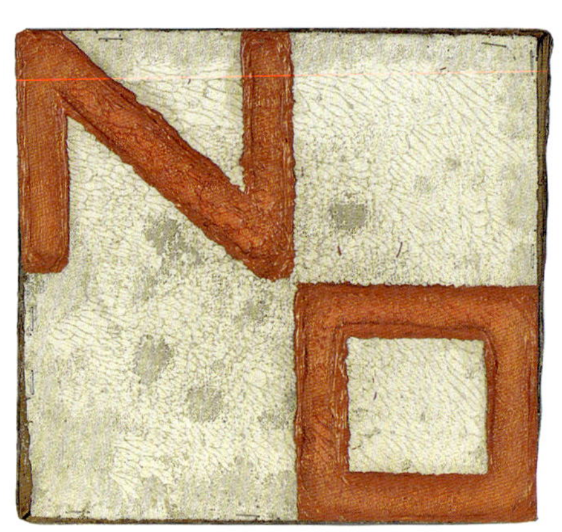

NO in Orange, ca. / ca 1962

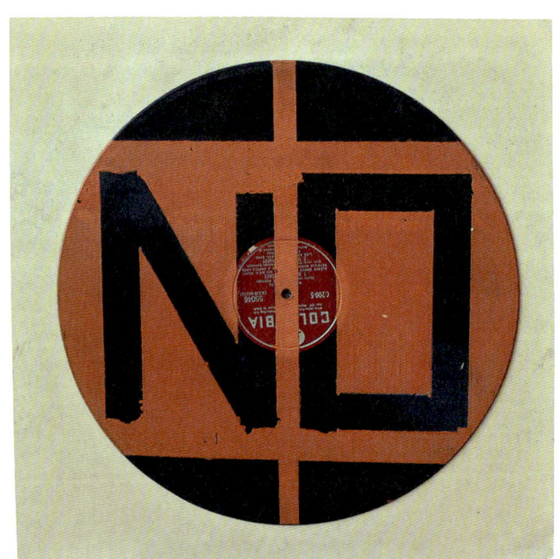

NO Record, 1962

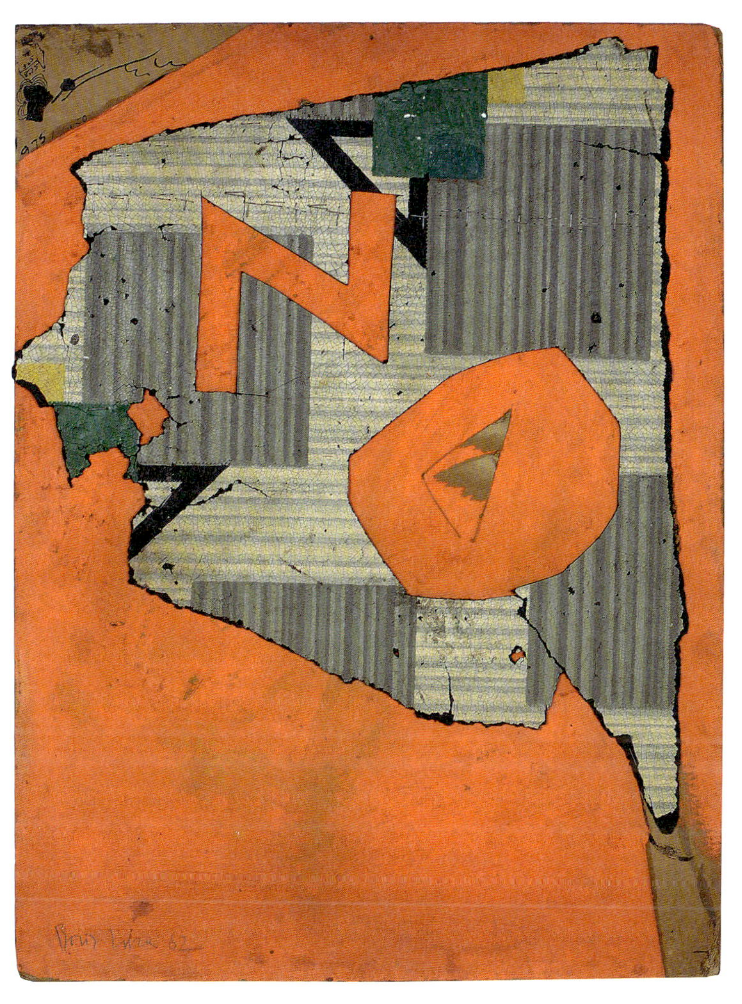

NO with Linoleum, 1962

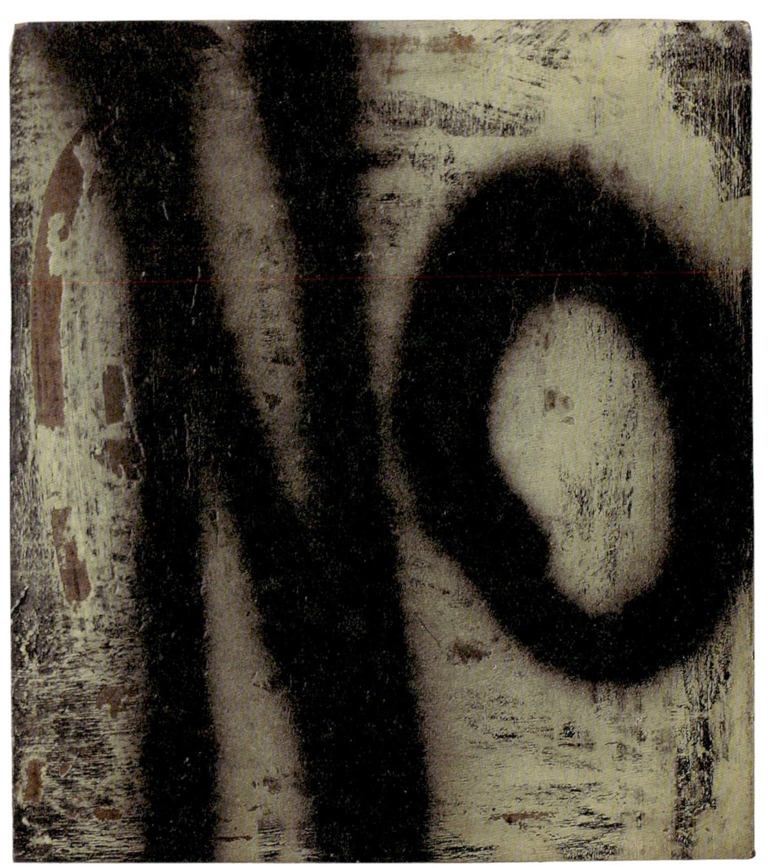

 NO Sprayed, 1963

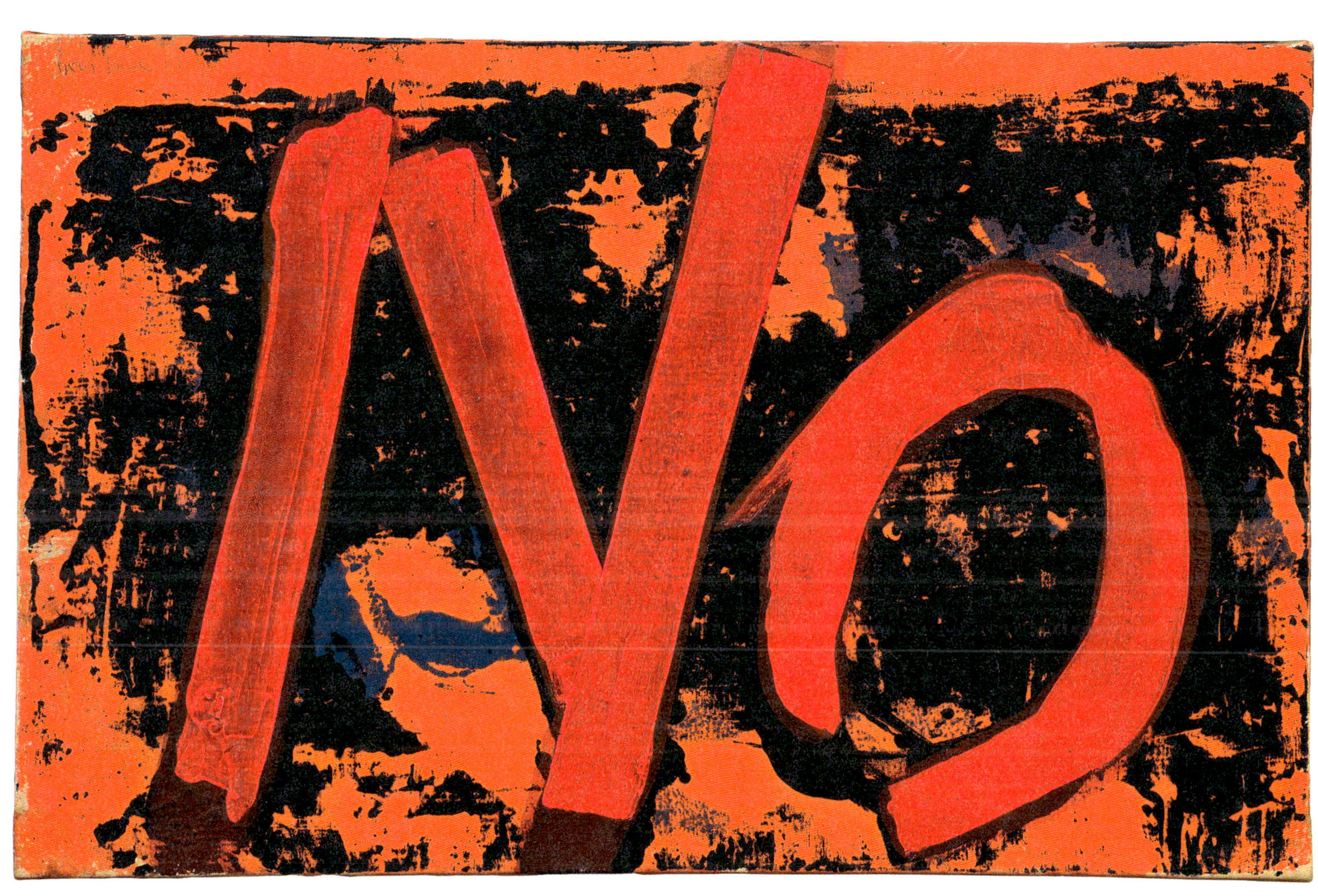

Feel Painting NO with Red and Black, 1963

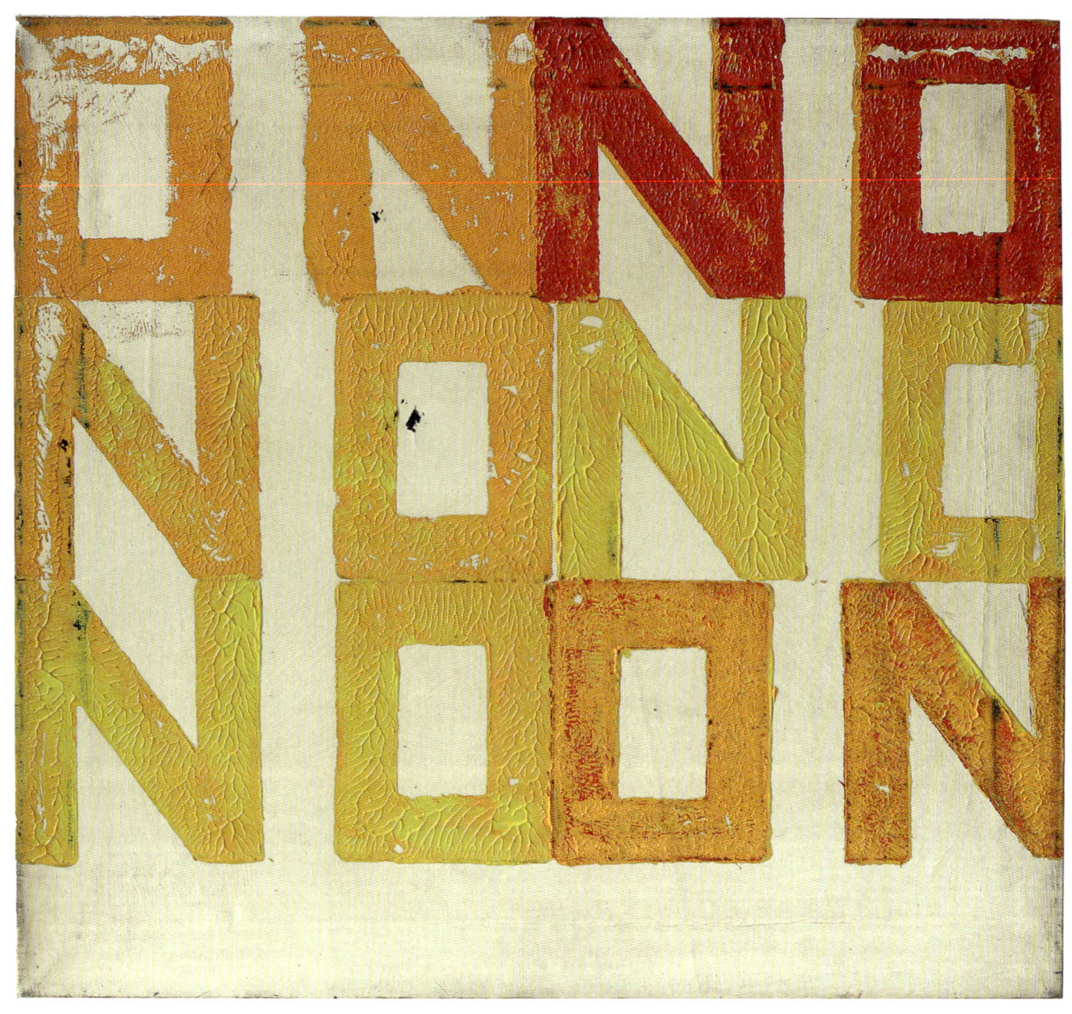

 NO-ON, 1962

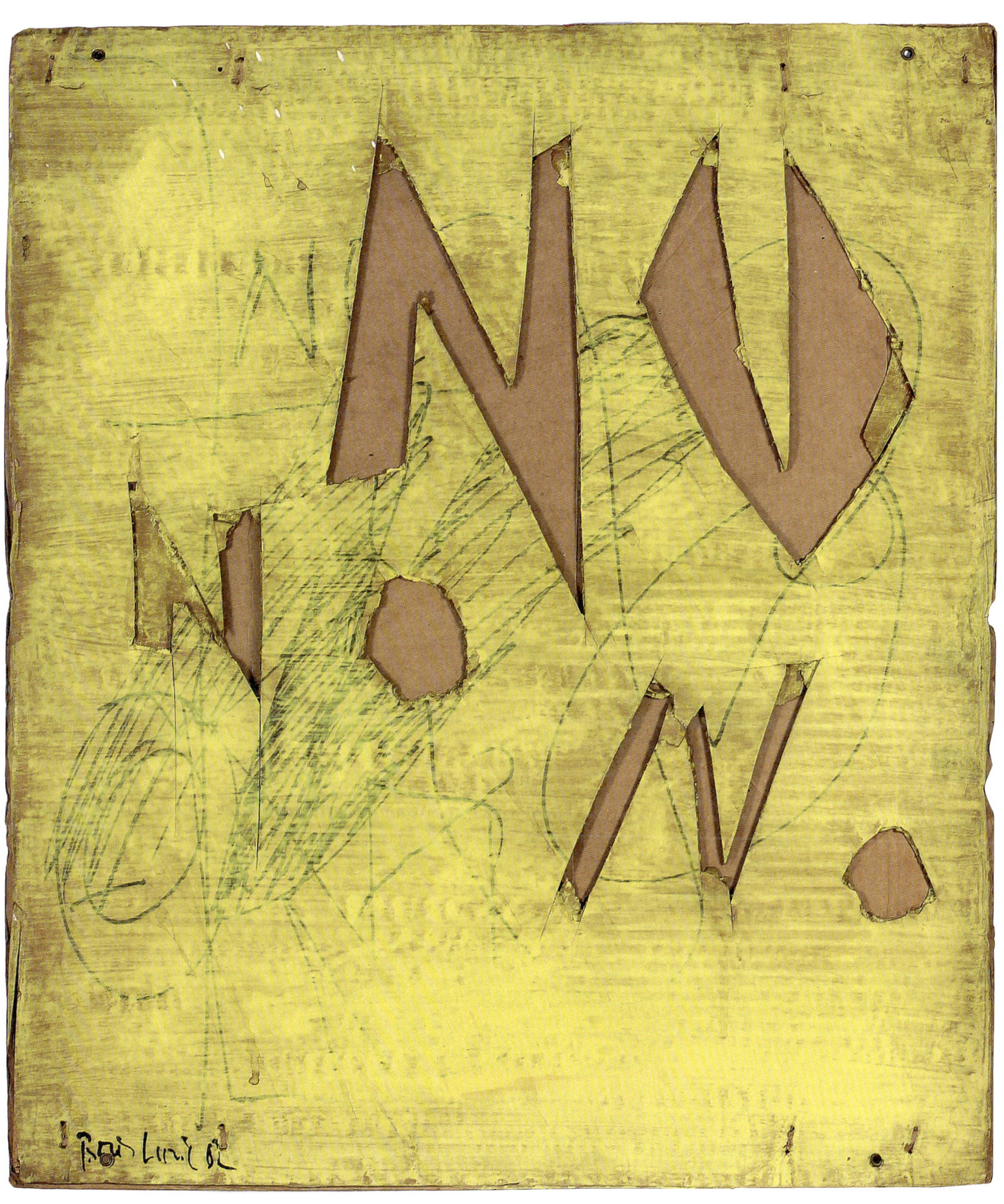

Yellow NO Cutouts, 1962

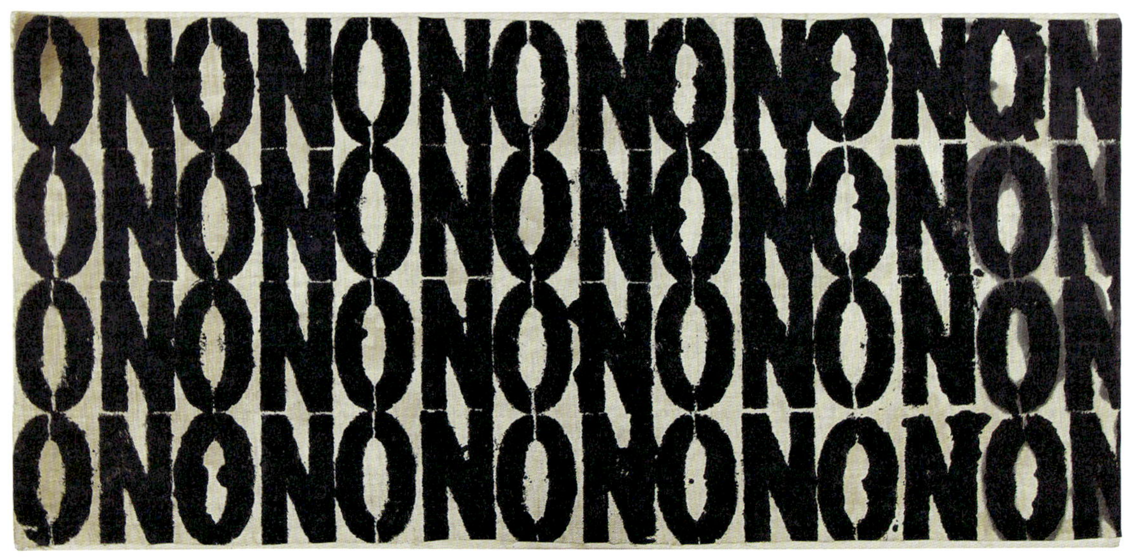

Stenciled NOs, 1969

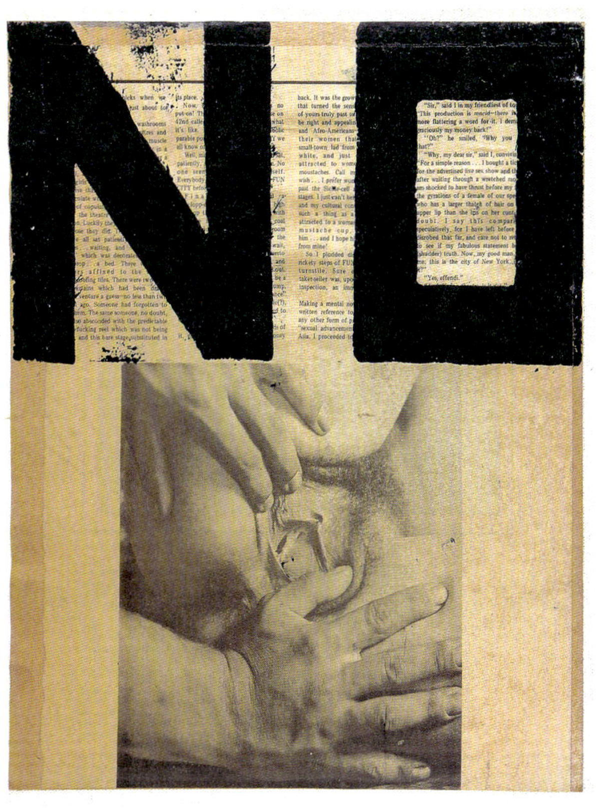

Hard Writings: NO on Pinup, ca. / ca 1972

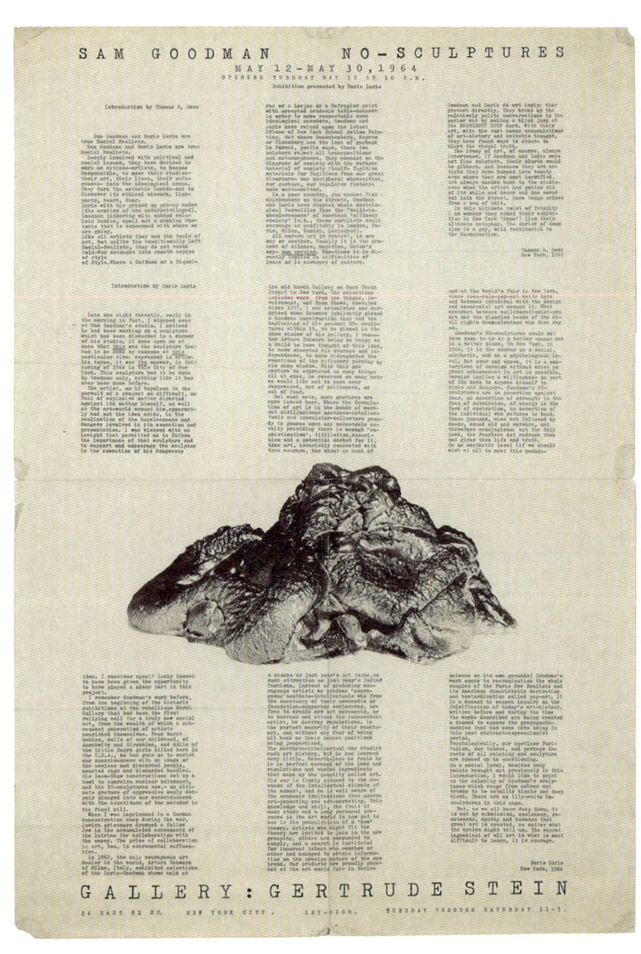

SAM GOODMAN NO-SCULPTURES

MAY 12 - MAY 30, 1964

OPENING TUESDAY MAY 12 AT 10 P.M.

Exhibition presented by Boris Lurie

Introduction by Thomas B. Hess

Introduction by Boris Lurie

Boris Lurie
New York, 1964

GALLERY: GERTRUDE STEIN

24 EAST 81 ST. NEW YORK CITY. LE5-0600. TUESDAY THROUGH SATURDAY 11-5.

Gallery Gertrude Stein: NO Sculptures (Shit) Show Poster, 1964

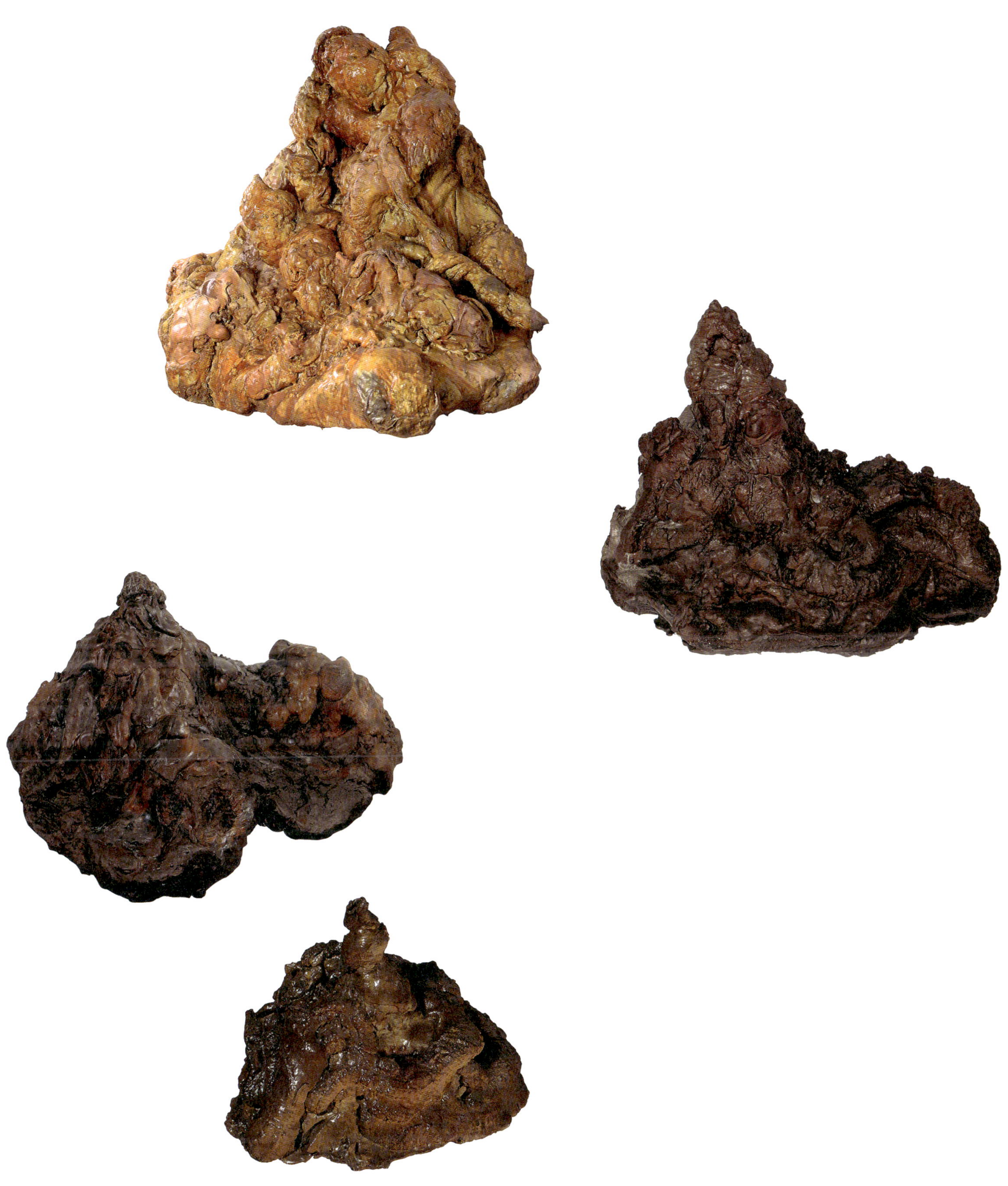

Sam Goodman und / and Boris Lurie, *NO Sculpture (Shit Sculpture)*, 1964

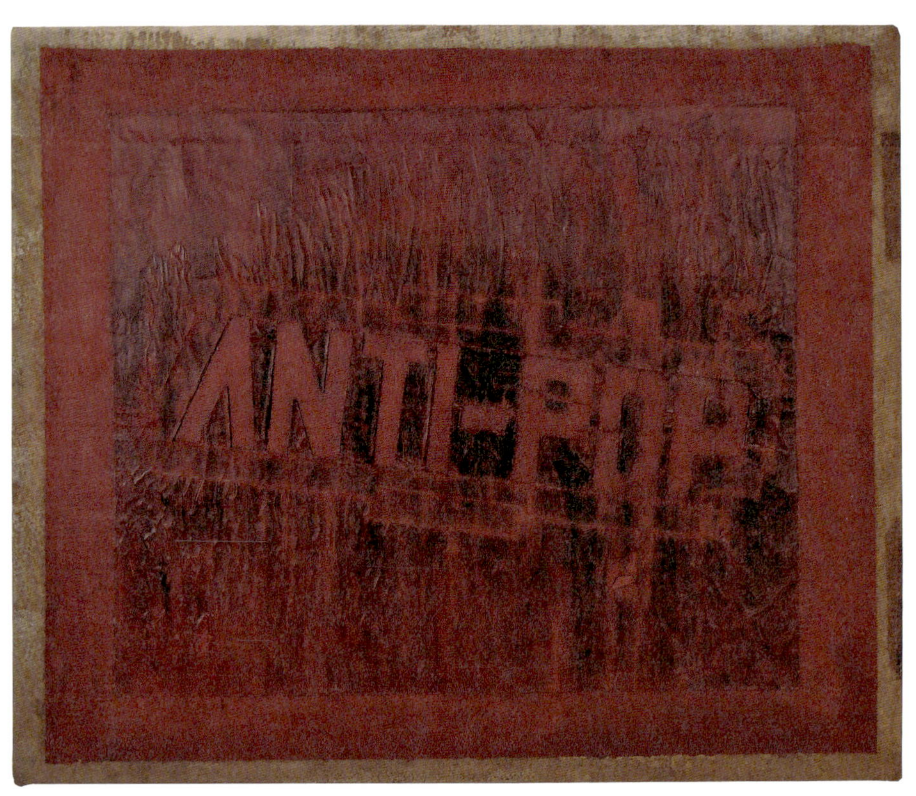

 Anti-Pop Stencil, 1964

Sold, 1972

Boris Lurie: Um im Angesicht des Negativen zu verweilen

Der Holocaust und das Problem der visuellen Repräsentation

Peter Weibel

Eine Annäherung an das Werk von Boris Lurie werde ich im Folgenden über die Geschichte der modernen Kunst als Krise der visuellen Repräsentation versuchen. In der modernen Kunst wurden mehrere Antworten auf die Frage gegeben, wie traumatische Ereignisse und Erfahrungen, die zu grausam sind, um gesellschaftlich akzeptiert zu werden, künstlerisch dargestellt werden können. Der Untertitel meines Essays benennt einen Sonderfall dieses Problems, nämlich: Wie kann man mit Mitteln der Kunst auf den Holocaust reagieren? Antworten boten die Abstraktion, die Zerstörung der Darstellungsmittel und am Ende eine neue Passion für das Reale. Dieses Reale allerdings ist für die klassischen Formen der Repräsentation und Symbolisierung der Realität nicht zugänglich.

Repräsentationsprobleme der klassischen Kunst

Die Geschichte der Kunst ist jahrhundertelang als System der visuellen Repräsentation erzählt worden. Man muss also zuerst einmal zu definieren versuchen, was Repräsentation eigentlich heißt. Um 1500 hat Leonardo da Vinci in seinem *Traktat über die Malerei* das Programm der Repräsentation sehr genau formuliert: Der Maler verfügt über Punkt, Linie, Fläche und die Simulation des Volumens auf der Fläche. Das sind die Darstellungsmittel, mit denen er die sichtbare Form der Dinge, d. h. der Gegenstandswelt, repräsentieren kann. Das ist das klassische Programm der visuellen Kunst. Genauso beschrieb Leonardo da Vinci dies:

„Vom ersten Anfang der Wissenschaft der Malerei: Der Anfang der [Wissenschaft der] Malerei ist der Punkt, dann folgt die Linie, das Dritte ist die Fläche, das Vierte der Körper, der sich in diese Oberfläche kleidet, und zwar gilt dies von demjenigen, welches vorgestellt wird, das heißt vom nachgeahmten Körper selbst; denn die Malerei geht in Wahrheit nicht weiter, als bis zur Fläche [oder Oberfläche], bei und vermöge deren der Körper dargestellt wird, als Figur jeglicher sichtbaren Sache.“[1]

Nach einiger Zeit begannen Probleme mit diesem Kunstkonzept sichtbar zu werden. 300 Jahre nach Leonardo definierte Immanuel Kant in seinem Werk

Peter Weibel

Boris Lurie: Tarrying with the Negative

The Holocaust and the Problem of Visual Representation

This essay approaches Boris Lurie's oeuvre via the history of modern art as a crisis of visual representation. Modern art offers several answers to the question of how traumatic events and experiences that are too horrific to be socially acceptable can be portrayed. The subtitle names a special case of this problem – artistic responses to the Holocaust. These have included abstraction, the destruction of the means of representation, and finally a new passion for the real. For classical forms of representing and symbolizing reality, however, this real is not accessible.

Problems of Representation in Classical Art

For centuries, the history of art has been told as a system of visual representation. To begin with, then, we must try to define what representation actually means. Around 1500, in his *Treatise on Painting*, Leonardo da Vinci formulated the program of representation in very precise terms: the painter has at his disposal point, line, plane, and the simulation of volume on the plane. These are the means of portrayal with which he can represent the visible form of things, the world of objects. Such is the classic program of visual art. Da Vinci put it like this:
"The science of painting begins with the point, then comes the line, the plane comes third, and the fourth the body in its vesture of planes. This is as far as the representation of objects goes. For painting does not, as a matter of fact, extend beyond the surface; and it is by its surface that the body of any visible thing is represented."[1]
Some time later, problems with this concept of art began to emerge. Three hundred years after Leonardo, in his *Critique of the Power of Judgement,*[2] Immanuel Kant defined the concept of beauty, distinguishing between art and nature:[3] "A natural beauty is a *beautiful thing*; artistic beauty is a *beautiful presentation* of a thing."[4] Presentation here means representation. And representation means we are able to portray our idea of the world, of what the world is like, and that we can produce this portrayal using painterly means. Consequently, representation means that the painter uses painterly means to produce a portrayal which he considers to be real. In Kant's definition, a peculiar shift becomes apparent which, although very important, has largely escaped art history to date: paradoxically, in his definition of art, he no longer speaks of beautiful things. The adjective "beautiful" has shifted from things to the representation of these things. The beauty of art is now only a beautiful representation, not a fact of beautiful things that exist. Kant himself identified the contradiction in his aesthetic system: "Fine art shows its superiority precisely in this, that it describes things beautifully that in nature we would dislike or find ugly."[5] This is antinomy. Art makes what is ugly beautiful. "The Furies, diseases, devastations of war, and so

Kritik der Urteilskraft[2] den Begriff der Schönheit und unterschied dabei zwischen Kunst- und Naturschönheit[3]: „Eine Naturschönheit ist ein schönes Ding; die Kunstschönheit ist eine schöne Vorstellung von einem Dinge".[4] „Vorstellung" heißt Repräsentation. Vorstellung, Darstellung oder Herstellung – alle Begriffe haben mit Repräsentation zu tun. Repräsentation bedeutet, dass wir unsere Vorstellung von der Welt, wie sie sei, darstellen und diese Darstellung mit malerischen Mitteln herstellen können. Repräsentation heißt folglich, der Maler stellt mit malerischen Mitteln eine Vorstellung dessen her, von dem er glaubt, dass es die Wirklichkeit sei. In Kants Definition wird eine merkwürdige Verschiebung ersichtlich, die, obwohl sie sehr wichtig ist, leider der Kunstgeschichte bisher entgangen ist. Mit Immanuel Kant ist auf ein sehr schönes logisches Paradoxon hinzuweisen. Er spricht in seiner Kunstdefinition nicht mehr von schönen Dingen. Das Adjektiv „schön" hat sich von den Dingen auf die Vorstellung über diese Dinge verschoben. Kunstschönheit ist nur mehr eine schöne Vorstellung, nicht ein Faktum von schönen Dingen, die sind. Kant selbst hat den Widerspruch in seinem ästhetischen System entdeckt: „Die schöne Kunst zeigt darin eben ihre Vorzüglichkeit, daß sie Dinge, die in der Natur häßlich oder mißfällig sein würden, schön beschreibt".[5] Das ist die Antinomie. Die Kunst macht das Hässliche schön. „Die Furien, Krankheiten, Verwüstung des Krieges u. dgl. können, als Schädlichkeiten, sehr schön beschrieben, ja sogar im Gemälde vorgestellt werden […]."[6] Daher kommt es zu einer Einschränkung der Darstellung und Vorstellung, zu einem ersten Repräsentationsverbot. Nur eine Art Hässlichkeit kann nicht der Natur gemäß vorgestellt werden, „nämlich diejenige, welche Ekel erweckt".[7]

Das Problem ist somit formuliert: Wenn ein Ding hässlich oder ein Lebewesen krank ist, dann macht die Kunstschönheit eine schöne Vorstellung daraus. Das darf nicht sein, dass die hässliche Realität, die Ekel erregt, in der Kunst als schön repräsentiert wird. Damit hat Kant zum ersten Mal ein ästhetisches Verbot eingeführt, das wichtige Verbot, dass der Ekel nicht dargestellt werden kann. Für viele Menschen gilt dieses Verbot bis heute: Ekel erregende Barbarei kann nicht repräsentiert werden. Und Kant wird noch deutlicher:

„Auch hat die Bildhauerkunst, weil an ihren Produkten die Kunst mit der Natur beinahe verwechselt wird, die unmittelbare Vorstellung häßlicher Gegenstände von ihren Bildungen ausgeschlossen, und dafür z. B. den Tod […] durch eine Allegorie oder Attribute, die sich gefällig ausnehmen, mithin nur indirekt vermittelst einer Auslegung der Vernunft, und nicht für bloß ästhetische Urteilskraft vorzustellen erlaubt."[8]

Mit anderen Worten: Im Programm der klassischen Repräsentation darf und kann der Holocaust gar nicht dargestellt werden. Das Hässliche, Eklige und Grausame können höchstens allegorisch dargestellt werden. Angesichts des Holocaust ist das Kant'sche Problem noch dringlicher denn je. Boris Lurie stellt sich diesem Problem der Repräsentationskunst als einer der ersten Künstler. Die schönen Künste sind dazu verdammt, nur schöne Dinge zu zeigen oder zumindest eine schöne Illusion der Dinge zu vermitteln. Aber wenn die Kunst das Hässliche und Eklige ästhetisch vorstellt, dann wird das Kunstschöne zum Naturschönen, das ja schöne Dinge zeigt. Um Kunst zu bleiben, muss sich Kunst verweigern, zumindest in einigen Zonen der Repräsentation. Kant und seine Nachfolger sind also Gefangene eines Paradoxes, das nur durch Verbote und Ausnahmen beseitigt bzw. aufgelöst werden kann. Die Definition des Kunst-

on are all harmful; and yet they can be described, or even presented in painting, very beautifully."[6] This led to a first restriction on depiction and representation: there is only one kind of ugliness that cannot be represented in accordance with nature, "that ugliness which arouses *disgust*."[7]

Such is the problem: if an object is ugly or if a living thing is diseased, then art makes a beautiful representation out of it. It is not acceptable for ugly reality that arouses disgust to be represented in art as beautiful. In this way, Kant introduced an aesthetic prohibition forbidding the representing of disgust. For many people, this ban still applies today: loathsome barbarism cannot be represented. And Kant put it more clearly still:

"The art of sculpture, too, has excluded from its creations any direct presentation of ugly objects, since in its products art is almost confused with nature. Instead it has permitted [ugly objects] to be presented by an allegory – e.g., death [...] – or by attributes that come across as likable, and hence has permitted them only to be presented indirectly and by means of an interpretation of reason rather than presented for a merely aesthetic power of judgment."[8]

In other words: in the program of classical representation, the Holocaust can not and may not be portrayed. The ugly, the loathsome, and the atrocious can at best be represented allegorically. In the case of the Holocaust, this Kantian problem is more urgent than ever. Boris Lurie was one of the first artists to confront this problem of representative art. The fine arts are doomed to show beautiful things or at least to convey a beautiful illusion of things. But when art represents what is ugly and disgusting in aesthetic form, then artistic beauty becomes natural beauty that shows beautiful things. To remain art, art must refrain, at least from certain areas of representation. Kant and his followers are thus prisoners of a paradox that can only be removed or resolved by means of prohibitions and exceptions. The definition of artistic beauty as a beautiful presentation of things runs the risk of also portraying ugly things as beautiful, and thus of making beautiful paintings of the Holocaust. The anti-art movement has one of its roots in German Idealism: as a reaction to Kantian antinomy, an aesthetics of beauty that excludes the portrayal of the ugly, an aesthetics of ugliness emerged.

Ugliness and Evil as Pillars of Modernism

In the mid-nineteenth century, fifty years after Kant, Karl Rosenkranz, a student of Hegel, formulated his *Aesthetics of Ugliness* (1853). Whereas for Kant, artistic beauty may not portray what is ugly, Rosenkranz called for ugliness to be captured by the term "negative beauty:"

"The concept of ugliness, of negative beauty, thus is a part of aesthetics. There is no other science to which it could be assigned, and so it is right to speak of the aesthetics of ugliness. No one is amazed if biology also concerns itself with the concept of illness, ethics with that of evil."[9]

For Rosenkranz, evil and illness are equivalents of ugliness in art. "The beautiful is the positive condition of its existence, and the comical is the form through which it delivers itself from its purely negative character relative to the beautiful."[10] Rosenkranz speaks here for the first time of a "negative character," a kind of negative representation. Hegel's notion of tarrying with the negative can still be discerned here.[11] This negativity, the legacy of Hegel, becomes, for Boris Lurie, the foundation of his NO!art movement, of his negative art, his anti-art,

schönen als schöne Vorstellung der Dinge läuft Gefahr, auch hässliche Dinge als schön darzustellen, gewissermaßen schöne Gemälde vom Holocaust zu fertigen. Die Anti-Kunst-Bewegung hat eine ihrer Wurzeln im deutschen Idealismus. Als Reaktion auf die Kant'sche Antinomie, eine Ästhetik des Schönen, welche die Darstellung des Hässlichen ausschließt, entsteht eine Ästhetik des Hässlichen.

Das Hässliche und das Böse als Säulen der Moderne

Bereits Mitte des 19. Jahrhunderts, 50 Jahre nach Kant, hat Karl Rosenkranz, ein Hegel-Schüler, seine *Ästhetik des Häßlichen,* 1853, formuliert. Während Kant zufolge das Kunstschöne den Ekel nicht darstellen dürfe, forderte Rosenkranz, das Hässliche im Begriff des „Negativschönen" zu erfassen:
„Der Begriff des Häßlichen als des Negativschönen macht also einen Teil der Ästhetik aus. Es gibt keine andere Wissenschaft, welcher derselbe überwiesen werden könnte, und es ist also richtig, von der Ästhetik des Häßlichen zu sprechen. Niemand wundert sich, wenn in der Biologie auch vom Begriff der Krankheit oder wenn in der Ethik vom Begriff des Bösen [...] gehandelt wird."[9]
Für Rosenkranz sind das Böse und das Kranke gewissermaßen das Pendant zum Hässlichen in der Kunst. „Das Schöne ist die positive Bedingung seiner Existenz, und das Komische ist die Form, durch welche es sich dem Schönen gegenüber von seinem nur negativen Charakter wieder erlöst."[10] Rosenkranz spricht hier zum ersten Mal von einem „negativen Charakter", von einer Art negativen Repräsentation. Hegels Diktum vom Verweilen im Negativen[11] schimmert hier noch durch. Diese Negativität, das Erbe Hegels, wird von Boris Lurie zur Grundlage seiner NO!art-Bewegung, seiner negativen Kunst, seiner Anti-Art, seiner Kunst der negativen Präsentation, und für Theodor W. Adorno zur Grundlage der *Negativen Dialektik,* 1966.
In der Mitte des 19. Jahrhunderts erschienen zwei Werke, deren Veröffentlichung nur wenige Jahre auseinander liegt, die aber dennoch selten gemeinsam zitiert werden – womit die Bedeutung dieser Koinzidenz verloren geht. Es handelt sich um die bereits erwähnte *Ästhetik des Häßlichen*, 1853, von Karl Rosenkranz sowie die im Jahre 1857 erstmals erschienene Gedichtsammlung von Charles Baudelaire mit dem Titel *Die Blumen des Bösen* (*Les Fleurs du mal*)[12]. Das Hässliche und das Böse betraten also gemeinsam die Bühne der Moderne. War bisher Schönheit als das sinnliche Erscheinen einer Idee Gegenstand der Ästhetik, so wurden nun plötzlich das Hässliche und das Böse deren Bestandteile.
Beide Autoren, Rosenkranz und Baudelaire, hießen das Hässliche und das Böse willkommen. Schaut man seine Gedichte näher an, dann erkennt man eindeutig, dass Baudelaire das Böse und alles, was damit in Zusammenhang stand (z. B. das Gemeine, das Vulgäre, das Schreckliche, das Komische), nicht abgelehnt hat. Das Einzige, was in den Gedichten nicht erlaubt ist, das ist Langeweile. Es bleibt also festzuhalten: Nicht nur betreten das Böse und das Hässliche zu Mitte des 19. Jahrhunderts die Bühne der Moderne, diese beiden Erscheinungen werden sogar zu Eckpfeilern der Moderne.[13] Diese Entwicklung zeichnet sich in der bildenden Kunst selbst ab: Ein hässlicher Gegenstand, ein Urinal (Marcel Duchamp, *Fontaine*), wurde 1917 unter dem Titel *Ready-made* als Kunst vorgestellt. Duchamps *Fontaine* markiert den Beginn der Anti-Kunst, eine wichtige Quelle von Boris Lurie.

his art of negative presentation, and, for Theodor W. Adorno, the foundation of *Negative Dialectics* (German original 1966; first English edition 1973).

In the mid-nineteenth century, two works were published just a few years apart, but because they are rarely quoted in the same context the significance of this coincidence is lost. On the one hand, Rosenkranz's *Aesthetics of Ugliness* (1853) and on the other Charles Baudelaire's volume of poems *Les Fleurs du mal* (The Flowers of Evil), first published in 1857.[12] Here, then, ugliness and evil enter the stage of modernity at the same time. Whereas in the past, beauty as the sensory appearance of an idea had been the subject of aesthetics, now ugliness and evil, too, were part of it.

Both authors, Rosenkranz and Baudelaire, embraced the ugly and the evil. A close look at his poems clearly shows that Baudelaire did not reject evil and everything associated with it (e.g., baseness, vulgarity, horror, the comic). The only thing that is not allowed in his poems is tediousness. Evil and ugliness thus not only entered the stage of modern art in the mid-nineteenth century, these two phenomena both become pillars of modernism.[13] This development is reflected in fine art itself: in 1917, an ugly object, a urinal (Marcel Duchamp, *Fountain*), was exhibited as art with the designation "readymade." Duchamp's *Fountain* marks the beginning of anti-art, an important source of inspiration for Boris Lurie.

The everyday, the banal, the base, the disgusting, the grotesque, the obscene, the evil, the ugly, the diabolical – since the mid-nineteenth century, all of these aesthetic categories have been part of art's expanded canon. Around 1900, a further expansion took place when the modern aesthetics of ugliness was extended to include the aesthetics of the primitive. From Ernst Ludwig Kirchner to Pablo Picasso, the primitive is also a foundation of modernism. What is still modern about modernism when the primitive itself is modern is a question that needs to be discussed elsewhere. A famous exhibition in the temple of modernism itself, the Museum of Modern Art in New York, bore the title *Primitivism and Modern Art* (1984). If primitive art influenced modern art, as this exhibition proved, then why is primitivism not considered modern and progressive and why is modern art not considered retrograde?

In the study of the foundations of modernism it has been overlooked that Wassily Kandinsky's book *Concerning the Spiritual in Art And Painting in Particular* (1911) was written under the influence of the Russian philosopher Vladimir Solovyov (as its title already suggests). Solovyov was a Christian mystic, a Platonist whose published works include *The Crisis of Western Philosophy: Against the Positivists* (1874), in which he denounced the West's rationalism, materialism, positivism, and faith in facts, called for a spiritual Renaissance in Russia, and advocated the importance of the intuitive and the spiritual in art. With Solovyov, a pre-modern Russia exerted its influence on Kandinsky, one of the fathers of modernism. Is this not paradoxical? Kandinsky took on Solovyov's critique of the West. Art history twists the facts and turns Kandinsky, a student of this traditionalist discontent with the West, into a founder of modernism in the West. These are strange matters.

Modernism – a Product of the Collapse of Representation?

Kandinsky's second book, published in 1926, sheds even more light on the development of modern art. Under the title *Point and Line to Plane. Contribution to the*

Das Alltägliche, das Banale, das Gemeine, das Eklige, das Groteske, das Obszöne, das Böse, das Hässliche, das Diabolische – all diese ästhetischen Kategorien sind seit Mitte des 19. Jahrhunderts Teil der Kunst. Der Kanon der Kunst hat sich seit 1850 erweitert. Um die Jahrhundertwende erfolgte eine abermalige Erweiterung, als das Primitive Teil der Moderne wurde. Die Ästhetik des Hässlichen wurde erweitert um die Ästhetik des Primitiven. Von Ernst Ludwig Kirchner über Pablo Picasso gehört das Primitive ebenfalls zu einem Fundament der Moderne. Was allerdings an der Moderne noch modern sei, wenn das Primitive selbst modern ist, das ist eine Frage, die an anderer Stelle zu diskutieren wäre. Eine berühmte Ausstellung im Tempel der Moderne selbst, dem Museum of Modern Art in New York, trug den Titel *Primitivism and Modern Art*, 1984. Wenn die primitive Kunst die moderne Kunst beeinflusst hat, wie die Ausstellung beweist, warum gilt dann der Primitivismus nicht als modern und fortschrittlich und die moderne Kunst nicht als rückschrittlich?
Nachdem die Grundlagen der Moderne nie ernsthaft erforscht worden waren, hat man übersehen, dass Wassily Kandinskys Buch *Über das Geistige in der Kunst. Insbesondere in der Malerei,* 1911, unter dem Einfluss des russischen Philosophen Wladimir Solowjow entstand, wie schon der Buchtitel verrät. Solowjow war ein christlicher Mystiker, ein Platonist und veröffentlichte u. a. das Buch *Die Krise der westlichen Philosophie. Gegen die Positivisten*, 1874, in dem er Rationalität, Materialismus, Positivismus und Faktengläubigkeit des Westens anprangerte, eine spirituelle Renaissance in Russland orderte und für die Bedeutung des Intuitiven, des Geistigen in der Kunst plädierte. Mit Solowjow nahm ein vormodernes Russland Einfluss auf Kandinsky, einen der Väter der Moderne. Ist das nicht paradox? Solojows Kritik am Westen übernahm Kandinsky. Die Kunstgeschichte, offensichtlich nicht die Kunstwissenschaft, verdreht die Fakten und macht Kandinsky, einen Schüler des traditionalistischen Unbehagens am Westen, zu einem Begründer der Moderne im Westen. Das sind merkwürdige Dinge.

Die Moderne – ein Produkt des Kollapses der Repräsentation?

Das zweite Buch Kandinskys von 1926 ist für die Entwicklung der modernen Kunst noch erhellender. In diesem Buch mit dem Titel *Punkt und Linie zu Fläche. Beitrag zur Analyse der malerischen Elemente* führt er das Programm von Leonardo da Vinci zwar an, bringt es jedoch nicht zu Ende. Das Repräsentationsprogramm heißt Punkt, Linie und Fläche als Darstellungsmittel der Gegenstandswelt. Aber Kandinsky hört bei der Hälfte des Satzes von Leonardo auf. Er reduziert das Programm. Er verwendet Punkt, Linie, Fläche nicht zur Darstellung der sichtbaren Formen der Dinge. Die moderne Kunst begnügt sich mit der Selbstdarstellung der Darstellungsmittel Punkt, Linie, Fläche. „Abstraktion“ ist ein euphemistisches Wort. Im Gegensatz zu früher konzentriert sich die moderne Kunst nun nicht mehr auf die Nutzung der malerischen Elemente zur Repräsentation, sondern auf die malerischen Elemente der Repräsentation selbst. Die moderne Kunst begnügt sich mit der Selbstdarstellung der Darstellungsmittel und verbannt deswegen den Gegenstand aus dem Bild. Es war nicht mehr erlaubt, die Darstellungsmittel anzuwenden, um im Gemälde den Gegenstand darzustellen – ein zweites Verbot nach Kant also. Die Gegenstandswelt wurde zurückgewiesen. Aber gleichzeitig kam 1913 mit Duchamp der reale Gegenstand in die Kunst herein, zusammen mit dem Bösen und Hässlichen. Wenn sich in der Kunst die

Analysis of the Pictorial Elements (first English edition 1947), he mentions Da Vinci's program, but he doesn't quote it in full. The program of representation is point, line, and plane as means of portraying the world of objects. But Kandinsky stops after half of Leonardo's phrase. He reduces the program. He does not use point, line, plane to represent the visible form of things. Modern art contents itself with the self-portrayal of point, line, and plane as means of representation. "Abstraction" is a euphemistic term. Whereas in earlier times, art concentrated on the use of painterly means of representation, modern art focuses on these painterly means themselves, contenting itself with the self-representation of the means of representation and banishing the object from the picture – a second ban after Kant. The world of objects was rejected. At the same time, however, the real object entered art with Duchamp in 1913 (*Roue de bicyclette*), together with the evil and the ugly. In art, when the painterly means of representation represent themselves, objects do the same, as Duchamp shows.

From 1913, then, one saw a total collapse of art's system of representation. On the one hand, there was the ban on representation in art, i. e., the banishment of the object from painting, and on the other hand, real objects entered art. The painters themselves declared representation to be at an end, as made clear by Alexander Rodchenko's first monochrome paintings (*Pure Red Color, Pure Yellow Color, Pure Blue Color*, 1921). Now, rather than serving to represent flowers, color is presented as color. Color is no longer a means of representation, but only a concrete material. Rodchenko called this the "end of depiction" – the end of representation. Between 1913 and 1920, the painters themselves terminated the program of representation, replacing it with reality. After World War I, art-as-representation was dead,[14] but of course art per se was not dead; what had died was representational art.

With Duchamp's urinal, ugliness explicitly entered the stage of aesthetics, disguised as a provocation of the jury, submitted under a pseudonym, intended as anti-art. Before Rodchenko, Duchamp had already declared the end of representation, the end of art. In a speech act, he declared everyday items, found objects, to be artworks, as readymades, industrially mass produced rather than handcrafted, an echo of the industrial revolution. This was the birth of anti-art. The contrary positions and opposing tendencies of object art and abstraction are reflected in the new ethic and aesthetic: it is no longer the sublime that is valid and desirable (as it was for Kant or the Romantics); instead, there is an idealization of the ordinary, the trivial, the banal, and the ugly (e.g., in Pop Art). The banal, lowly, trivial object is elevated to the status of art,[15] while at the opposite pole there was an evocation of the spiritual, the intellectual, the abstract, the supernatural, and the metaphysical. These are the twin paradoxes within which art has moved since the abolition of representation.

The first half of the twentieth century can be said to have been marked by a paradoxical program, a contradiction: on the one hand abstraction, a withdrawal from the world of objects, and on the other, the entry of reality into art in direct form. After 1945, everything that had previously been representation became reality: instead of painted objects there were real objects; instead of painted portraits there was Body Art and performance; instead of painted animals there were real hares and horses; instead of painted landscapes there was Land Art; instead of painted machines there were actual machines; instead of painted interiors there were installations; and so forth.

malerischen Darstellungsmittel selbst darstellen, kommt es auch zur Selbstdarstellung der Dinge in der Kunst, was an Duchamp sichtbar wird.

Ab 1913 war also der totale Zusammenbruch des Repräsentationssystems der Kunst zu beobachten. Einerseits herrschte das Verbot der Repräsentation in der Kunst, d. h. die Verbannung des Gegenstands aus der Malerei, andererseits ist der reale Gegenstand in die Kunst eingezogen. Die Maler selbst erklärten die Repräsentation für beendet, wie die ersten monochromen Bilder von Alexander Rodtschenko (*Reine Farbe Rot, Reine Farbe Gelb, Reine Farbe Blau*, 1921) deutlich werden lassen. Farbe dient nicht mehr zur Darstellung von Blumen, sondern Farbe wird als Farbe präsentiert. Die Farbe ist kein Darstellungsmittel mehr, sondern nur konkretes Material. Rodtschenko hat dies „Ende der Darstellung" genannt – Ende der Repräsentation. Zwischen 1913 und 1920 haben die Maler selbst das Repräsentationsprogramm beendet und an dessen Stelle die Realität gesetzt. Kunst als Repräsentation war bereits nach dem Ersten Weltkrieg tot,[14] aber selbstverständlich war nicht die Kunst an sich tot, gemeint war damit nur die Repräsentationskunst.

Mit Duchamps Urinal, einem Pissbecken, betrat explizit das Hässliche die Bühne der Ästhetik, gedeckt als Provokation einer Jury, eingereicht unter Pseudonym, gedacht als Anti-Kunst. Vor Rodtschenko hatte Duchamp bereits das Ende der Repräsentation verkündet, das Ende der Kunst. Er hat Alltagsgegenstände, Massenware der Industrie, Ready-mades, gefertigte, gefundene und fertige Objekte, Found objects, industrielle, nicht handwerkliche Fertifikate – ein Echo der industriellen Revolution – in einem Sprechakt zu Kunstwerken erklärt. Hier läutet die Geburtsstunde der Anti-Art. Duchamp wollte allerdings nicht, dass, wie der Lauf der Zeit zeigt, aus der Anti-Kunst Kunst würde. Die konträren Positionen und gegensinnigen Tendenzen von Objektkunst und Abstraktion wiederholen sich auch im Ethischen und Ästhetischen. Gültig und erstrebenswert ist nicht mehr das Sublime wie bei Kant oder der Romantik, verklärt werden das Gewöhnliche, Triviale, das Banale und Hässliche, z. B. in der Pop-Art. Die banale, konkrete, niedrige, triviale Gegenstandswelt wird in den Rang der Kunst erhoben.[15] Auf der anderen Seite geschah die Anrufung des Spirituellen, Geistigen, Abstrakten, Übersinnlichen und Metaphysischen. Das sind die beiden Paradoxe, in denen sich die Kunst seit der Abschaffung der Repräsentation bewegt.

Man kann sagen, die erste Hälfte des 20. Jahrhunderts war von einem paradoxen Programm, einem Widerspruch gekennzeichnet: einerseits Abstraktion, Austritt aus der Gegenstandswelt, andererseits Eintritt der Realität in die Kunst direkt und pur. Nach 1945 wird alles, was bisher Repräsentation war, Realität: Statt gemalten Gegenständen gibt es reale Objekte, statt gemalten Porträts gibt es Body Art und Performance, statt gemalter Tiere gibt es reale Hasen oder Pferde, statt gemalter Landschaften gibt es Land Art, statt gemalter Maschinen gibt es reale Maschinen, statt gemalter Interieurs gibt es Installationen usw.

Die Geschichte der Kunst als System visueller Repräsentation ist im 20. Jahrhundert an ihr Ende gelangt, was fälschlicherweise als Ende der Kunst deklariert wird. Die Menschheit hat Ereignisse, Seinsweisen und Kunstwerke produziert, die mit den klassischen Vorstellungen des Humanismus und der Ästhetik inkompatibel und inkommensurabel sind. In der Welt haben sich das radikal Böse und der radikale Ekel[16] eingenistet. Die Reaktionen darauf sind grosso modo: 1. Abbildung des Horrors als figurative Malerei, 2. Abbild- und Repräsentationsverbot: Selbstdarstellung der Darstellungsmittel (Abstraktion), 3. Selbst-

In the twentieth century, the history of art as a system of visual representation came to an end, and this was falsely declared as the end of art. People produced events, ways of being, and works of art that were incompatible and incommensurable with classical notions of humanism and aesthetics. Radical evil and radical nausea established themselves in the world.[16] Roughly speaking, the reactions to this were as follows: firstly, representation of horror in figurative painting; secondly, a ban on depiction and representation, self-representation of the means of representation (abstraction); thirdly, self-destruction of the means of representation; fourthly, replacement of representation by reality (*Nouveau réalisme*, object art, assemblages, environments, installations); fifthly, new forms of action; and sixthly, a passion for the real (real bodies, real audience).

At the Zero Point of Meaning and Existence

In 1945, after World War II ended, not only the cities were in ruins – but after 60 million dead, the Holocaust, the Gulag, and nuclear annihilation, any belief in traditional humanism also lay in ruins. Europe was at ground zero of meaning and existence. As a result, books, films, and art movements were given names like *Being and Nothingness* (Jean-Paul Sartre, 1943), *The Chips Are Down* (Sartre, 1947), *Endgame* (Samuel Beckett, 1956), *The Plague* (Albert Camus, 1947), *Kaputt* (Curzio Malaparte, 1944), *Writing Degree Zero* (Roland Barthes, 1953), *Germany, Year Zero* (Roberto Rossellini, 1948), *Movimento Nucleare* (1951), ZERO (1958) or *Nul* (1961). After the cataclysms and catastrophes, from Auschwitz to Hiroshima, after all of the loss and upheaval, persecution and displacement, mutilation and extermination, the notion of a tabula rasa became the artistic point of departure for the neo-avant-gardes: absurd theatre, neo-dada, nonsense, nihilism.

Were we to be given the choice of asking the question "How do we react to the Holocaust?", an answer could be derived from the historical sources of the avant-gardes. We can react with abstraction, i.e., by banishing reality, or we can react with super-realism, showing things as they are. These are the two paths laid out by modern art following the collapse of representation.

Trauma and Reaction Formation

The traumas of World War II are a precondition for and wellspring of the European neo-avant-gardes, whose art can be interpreted as a response to these traumas. Traumatic experiences, all forms of destruction and annihilation (shooting, dispossession, deportation, rape, torture, internment, mass murder), profoundly disturbed the way the victims perceived themselves and the world. The wounds of physical and psychological violence, horror and helplessness, generated post-traumatic symptoms. Talking about personal traumatic experiences proved equally difficult for both the speaker and the listener. This was the situation art found itself in with regard to the Holocaust. The trauma of World War II marked not only the war generation, but also the following generation. How do people react to and work through trauma?

In her 1936 book *Das Ich und die Abwehrmechanismen* (first published in English under the title *The Ego and the Mechanisms of Defense* in 1937), Anna Freud describes ten types of defense: repression, regression, isolation, undoing,

zerstörung der Darstellungsmittel, 4. Ersetzen der Repräsentation durch Realität (Nouveau Réalisme, Objektkunst, Assemblagen, Environments, Installationen), 5. Neue Handlungsformen der Kunst, 6. Passion für das Reale: reale Körper, reales Publikum.

Am Nullpunkt des Sinns und des Seins

1945, nach dem Ende des Zweiten Weltkrieges, waren nicht nur die Städte zerstört, sondern mit 60 Millionen Toten nach sieben Jahren Krieg, nach dem Holocaust, dem Gulag und der atomaren Vernichtung war auch der Glaube an Menschlichkeit, Humanismus und Kultur zerstört. Europa befand sich am Nullpunkt des Sinns und des Seins. Bücher, Filme und Kunstbewegungen hatten daher Titel wie: *Das Sein und das Nichts* (Jean-Paul Sartre, 1943), *Das Spiel ist aus* (Jean-Paul Sartre, 1947), *Endspiel* (Samuel Beckett, 1956), *Die Pest* (Albert Camus, 1947), *Kaputt* (Curzio Malaparte, 1944), *Am Nullpunkt der Literatur* (Roland Barthes, 1954) oder *Deutschland im Jahre Null* (Roberto Rossellini, 1948), *Movimento Nucleare* (1951), ZERO (1958) oder *Nul* (1961). Nach den Kataklysmen und Katastrophen von Auschwitz bis Hiroshima, nach den Verlusten und Verwerfungen, Verfolgungen und Vertreibungen, Verstümmelungen und Vernichtungen wurde die Idee der Tabula rasa zum künstlerischen Ausgangspunkt der Neo-Avantgarden: Absurdes Theater, Neo-Dada, Nonsens, Nihilismus.
Wenn wir die Wahl haben, zu fragen, wie reagieren wir auf den Holocaust? – so können wir aus den historischen Quellen der Avantgarden eine Antwort ableiten. Wir können mit Abstraktion darauf reagieren, d.h. mit Verbannung der Wirklichkeit, oder wir können darauf mit einem Superrealismus antworten, indem wir die Dinge zeigen, wie die Dinge sind. Diese beiden Schienen hat die moderne Kunst vorgelegt, nachdem die Repräsentation zusammengebrochen war.

Trauma und Reaktionsbildung

Die Traumata des Zweiten Weltkrieges sind Voraussetzung und Quellgrund der europäischen Neo-Avantgarden. Die neo-avantgardistische Kunst kann als Reaktionsbildung auf Traumata interpretiert werden. Traumatisierende Erlebnisse, alle Formen der Zerstörung und Vernichtung wie Erschießung, Enteignung, Deportation, Vergewaltigung, Folter, Lagerhaft und Massenmord haben in vielfacher Weise Selbst- und Weltbilder erschüttert. Verletzungen und Verwundungen durch körperliche und psychische Gewalt riefen Entsetzen und Hilflosigkeit hervor, die posttraumatische Symptome erzeugten. Traumatisierende Erfahrungen zu thematisieren, stellt sich für den Sprechenden gleichermaßen wie für den Zuhörenden als schwer heraus. In dieser Situation befand sich die Kunst angesichts des Holocaust. Das Trauma des Zweiten Weltkriegs hat nicht nur die Kriegs-, sondern auch die nachfolgende Generation geprägt. Die meisten Menschen reagierten mit Abwehrmechanismen – so auch die Kunst. Das Ich entfaltet mehrere Strategien von Abwehrmechanismen gegen traumatisierende Erfahrungen. In ihrem Buch *Das Ich und die Abwehrmechanismen*, 1936, nennt Anna Freud 10 Typen der Abwehr: Verdrängung, Regression, Isolierung, Ungeschehenmachen, Projektion, Introjektion, Wendung gegen die eigene Person, Verkehrung in das Gegenteil, Sublimierung oder die Verschiebung des Trieb-

projection, introjection, turning against the self, reversal into the opposite, sublimation or displacement of instinctual aims, and reaction formation. *Reaction formation* is the term used by Freud to denote a certain kind of defense mechanism against unacceptable drives or events. The ego safeguards itself against the return of the repressed with behavior that is at odds with what it actually desires. What is to be repressed, the awful experience, is turned into its opposite by reaction formation: an attempt is made to neutralize the negative event in a kind of positive transferal. Most people reacted with defense mechanisms – and art did the same. The ego develops several strategies of defense against traumatic experiences.
Take, for example, the name of the film *Hiroshima, mon amour* (dir.: Alain Resnais, script: Marguerite Duras, 1959): although it may refer to the parallel plot, it is striking that *Hiroshima, mon horreur* or *Hiroshima, mon terreur* would have been a more obvious title. This is an example of inversion. By the process of reaction formation, repressed experiences are turned into their opposite and thus dealt with. The ego flees and avoids the unbearable situation that arouses unpleasure by reaction formation that transforms unpleasure into pleasure.[17] Reaction formation is a regressive and reactive ego alteration that seeks to undo an event or turn an occurrence or mental impulse into its opposite. In its efforts to fend off unwanted memories and experiences, the ego makes use of the mechanisms of inversion. After 1945, artists deployed defense mechanisms to process traumas. They transformed an aggressive turn of events against themselves into a turn against art. This explains the way artists responded to the destruction of culture by the Nazis by destroying canvases, pianos, and so forth – developments in European neo-avant-gardes that show it to be literally art after war, art about traumatic experiences, about grief and pain, about displacement and forgetting, about memory and repression. Boris Lurie shared these traumatic experiences with the European avant-garde and was thus closer to them than to the affirmative American art scene. The neo-avant-garde was thus not just a formal repetition of the historical interwar avant-gardes, but rather a "reaction formation" in response to the breakdown of civilization during World War II. Several distinct phases of reaction formation in postwar art can be identified.

Phase 1: Semi-Realistic Representation

After the war, there was nothing but destroyed landscapes and cities, destroyed houses and people. In an initial reaction, painting and sculpture were marked by attempts to portray the traumas of destruction figuratively. In a kind of pre-modern painting and sculpture, artists turned to subject-centered expressive art in order to represent devastation and turmoil, pain and grief.

Phase 2: Abstraction

The crisis of representation and the uncertainty about whether it was possible to depict such barbaric horrors in figurative ways led to abstractions in painting and sculpture. Informel and Tachism are evidence of representation being reduced to the means of representation, which were then deformed and distorted. The crimes against humanity that had been experienced seemed indescribable and unrepresentable. This led to a crisis, to rejection and prohibition of repre-

ziels und Reaktionsbildung. Als *Reaktionsbildung* bezeichnet Anna Freud eine bestimmte Art von Abwehrreaktion gegen inakzeptable Triebe oder Ereignisse. Das Ich sichert sich gegen eine Rückkehr des Verdrängten durch ein Verhalten ab, das dem eigentlichen Verlangen entgegensteht. Was verdrängt werden soll, die horrible Erfahrung, wird durch die Reaktionsbildung ins Gegenteil verkehrt: Das negative Ereignis wird in einer Art positiver Übertragung zu neutralisieren versucht. Nehmen wir als Beispiel den Titel des Films *Hiroshima, mon amour* (Regie: Alain Resnais, Drehbuch: Marguerite Duras, 1959). Obgleich der Titel des Films durch die Parallelhandlung motiviert sein kann, ist es doch auffallend, dass als Titel *Hiroshima, mon horreur* oder *Hiroshima, mon terreur* naheliegender wären. Hier haben wir ein Beispiel von Inversion. Die unterdrückten Erfahrungen werden durch Reaktionsbildung in ihr Gegenteil verkehrt und dadurch bewältigt. Das Ich flüchtet und vermeidet die unerträgliche Situation, die Unlust erregt, durch Reaktionsbildung, die Unlust in Lust verwandelt.[17] Die Reaktionsbildung ist eine regressive und reaktive Ich-Veränderung, die ein Ereignis ungeschehen machen soll bzw. einen Vorfall oder eine psychische Regung in ihr Gegenteil verkehrt. Das Ich bedient sich bei der Abwehr unerwünschter Erinnerungen und Erfahrungen der Inversion. Die Künstler übten sich nach 1945 in Abwehrmechanismen, um Traumata zu verarbeiten. Sie transformierten die aggressive Wendung gegen die eigene Person zur Wendung gegen die Kunst. Dadurch erklärt sich, dass Künstler auf die Zerstörung der Kultur durch die Nazis mit der Zerstörung von Leinwänden, Klavieren etc. antworteten. Diese Phasen der Entwicklung der europäischen Nachkriegskunst zeigen, dass es sich bei den Neo-Avantgarden tatsächlich und buchstäblich um eine Kunst nach dem Krieg handelt, eine Kunst über traumatisierende Erfahrungen, über Trauer und Schmerz, über Vergessen und Verdrängung, über Erinnerung und Repression. Boris Lurie teilt die traumatisierenden Erfahrungen mit den europäischen Neo-Avantgarden und steht ihnen daher näher als dem affirmativen amerikanischen Kunstbetrieb. Die Neo-Avantgarde ist also nicht eine rein formale Wiederholung der historischen Avantgarden vor dem Zweiten Weltkrieg. Die Neo-Avantgarde ist eine „Reaktionsbildung" auf die Zivilisationsbrüche während des Zweiten Weltkrieges. Wir können mehrere Phasen dieser Reaktionsbildungen in der Nachkriegskunst feststellen.

Phase 1: Semi-realistische Repräsentation

Nach dem Krieg gab es nichts als zerstörte Landschaften und Städte, zerstörte Häuser und Menschen. Malerei und Skulptur waren in einer ersten Reaktion von dem Versuch geprägt, die Traumata der Destruktion figurativ darzustellen. In einer Art vormoderner Malerei und Bildhauerei wandten sich Künstlerinnen und Künstler einer subjektzentrierten Ausdruckskunst zu, um Verwüstungen und Verwerfungen, Schmerz und Trauer zu repräsentieren.

Phase 2: Abstraktion

Die Krise der Repräsentation und die Verunsicherung darüber, ob das Grauen der Barbarei überhaupt figurativ darstellbar sei, führten zu Abstraktionen in Malerei und Skulptur. Informel und Tachismus sind Belege für die Reduktion auf die Darstellung der Darstellungsmittel, die nun selbst verformt und verzerrt

sentation. But abstract painting and sculpture were still an art of subjective expression in the spectrum of pain and trauma, of despair and hope.

Franceso Lo Savio, *Metallo Nero Opaco*, 1960

Phase 3: Material Pictures or the Crisis of the Easel Painting

It was not until the 1950s and the Italian material pictures that the process began in which artistic means of representation were questioned, replaced, and ultimately destroyed; materials like cement, wood, PVC, and sackcloth were used instead of oil paint and canvas, showing the easel painting at its zero point. This radical probing of the means of representation themselves paved the way for the turn from subject-centered to object-centered representation. The crisis of representation became a "crisis of the easel painting."[18] Representation was vehemently rejected, and with it the idea of the image itself. All that remained of the easel painting was the panel. This is exemplified by the work of Francesco Lo Savio and Armando. In 1956 Armando painted a charred human head titled *Tête noire II*, a figurative depiction of the annihilation of people in wartime.

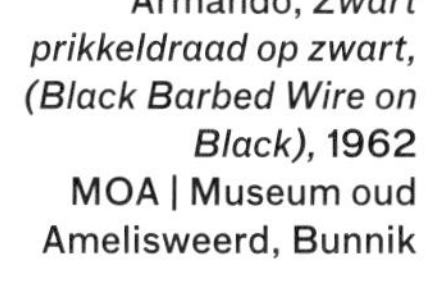

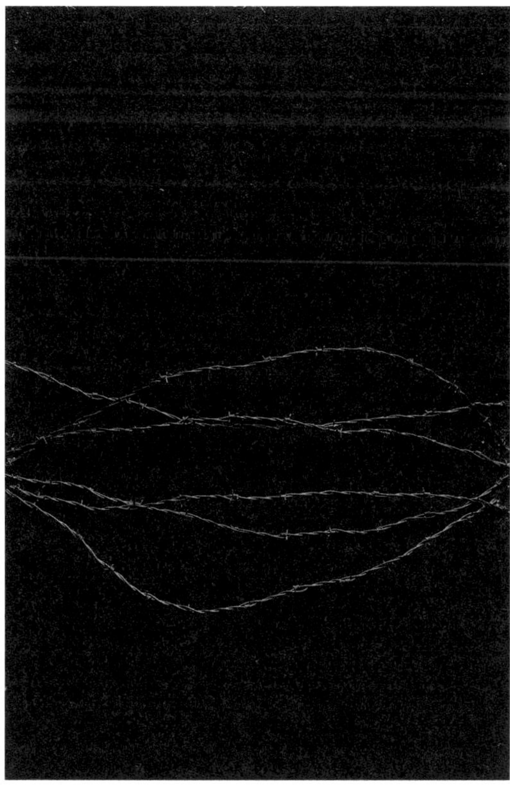

Armando, *Zwart prikkeldraad op zwart, (Black Barbed Wire on Black)*, 1962 MOA | Museum oud Amelisweerd, Bunnik

His work titled *Zwart prikkeldraad op zwart* (Black Razor Wire on Black, 1962) consists of a black board with razor wire attached to its lower third. Rather than painting figurative pictures of destruction, Armando now presented a picture object, performing the turn from representation to reality. The black board embodies the tabula rasa after 1945, a dominant experience that also served other artists as a point of departure, e.g., *Tabula rasa* by Mangelos (1951–56), which is also a black panel, or more precisely a black canvas, on which "Tabula rasa" is written.[19] This work defines itself in the context of the above-mentioned zero point of meaning and existence. At the same time, it evokes a school blackboard with writing on it. This helps to explain Joseph Beuys's obsessive use of blackboards densely covered with writing and drawings. These works are clearly also based on the experience of the tabula rasa, which Beuys sought to process or work through not in paintings or pictures, but with writing and conceptualization. Razor wire also plays a key part in works by other artists marked by war, including Wolf Vostell and Bazon Brock. In one of the very first happenings, *Die Linie von Hamburg* (The Line of Hamburg) – a blend of performance painting and action art staged in Hamburg in 1959 in collaboration with Friedensreich Hundertwasser – we see Bazon Brock opening a book entitled *We Have Not Forgotten* in such a way that a picture of razor wire in the book overlaps with painted lines in the room.

Phase 4: Self-Destruction of the Means of Representation

The crisis of representation was formulated by Theodor W. Adorno in two now famous passages: firstly, the verdict that "to write poetry after Auschwitz is bar-

werden. Die erlebten Verbrechen gegen die Menschheit schienen unbeschreibbar und unrepräsentierbar. Es kam zur Krise, zur Verweigerung und zum Verbot der Repräsentation. Abstrakte Malerei und Skulptur waren noch immer subjektive Ausdruckskunst des Spektrums von Schmerz und Trauma, von Verzweiflung und Hoffnung.

Phase 3: Materialmalerei oder die Krise des Tafelbildes

Erst in den 1950er Jahren begann mit der italienischen Materialmalerei der Prozess, die künstlerischen Darstellungsmittel zu hinterfragen, zu ersetzen und schließlich zu zerstören. In der italienischen Materialmalerei der 1950er Jahre wurden als Trägermedien anstelle von Leinwand und Ölfarben Materialien wie Zement, Holz, PVC, Sackleinen verwendet, wodurch das Tafelbild an seinem Nullpunkt gezeigt wird. Diese radikale Auseinandersetzung mit den Darstellungsmitteln bot die Voraussetzung für die Wende von der subjektzentrierten zur objektzentrierten Repräsentation. Die Krise der Repräsentation wurde zu einer „Krise des Tafelbildes".[18] Die Repräsentation wurde vehement zurückgewiesen und damit die Idee des Bildes selbst. Vom Tafelbild blieb nur die Tafel, das Bild verschwand. Beispielhaft hierfür sind die Werke von Francesco Lo Savio oder Armando. Unter dem Titel *Tête noire II* hat Armando 1956 einen verbrannten schwarzen Kopf gemalt und somit die Vernichtung der Menschen durch den Krieg noch figurativ dargestellt.

Mangelos, *Tabula rasa,* 1951–56
Courtesy Ilija & Mangelos Foundation und / and Galerie Frank Elbaz

Die Arbeit mit dem Titel *Zwart prikkeldraad op zwart* (Black Razor Wire on Black) von 1962 besteht aus einer schwarzen Tafel, in deren unterem Drittel realer Stacheldraht angebracht ist. Armando malt also nicht mehr figurativ Bilder der Vernichtung, sondern präsentiert ein Bildobjekt mit realem Stacheldraht. Armando hat also die Wende zum Materialbild und von der Repräsentation zur Realität vollzogen. Die schwarze Tafel verkörpert die Tabula rasa nach 1945. Eine dominierende Erfahrung, die auch anderen Künstlern als Ausgangspunkt diente, z. B. die Arbeit *Tabula rasa* von Mangelos[19], 1951–56, die ebenfalls eine schwarze Tafel, genauer eine schwarze Leinwand ist, auf der „Tabula rasa" geschrieben steht. Diese Arbeit definiert sich im Kontext des zitierten Nullpunkts des Sinns und des Seins. Sie gemahnt zugleich an eine Schultafel und an die Schrift auf einer Tafel. Wir verstehen nun die obsessive Verwendung von dicht beschriebenen und vollgezeichneten Schultafeln von Joseph Beuys. Diese haben offensichtlich ebenfalls die Erfahrung der Tabula rasa als Quelle, die Beuys nicht durch Gemälde oder Bilder, sondern durch Schrift und Konzeptualisierung verarbeiten bzw. durcharbeiten wollte. Der Stacheldraht spielt auch eine zentrale Rolle in Arbeiten von ebenfalls kriegsgeprägten Künstlern wie Wolf Vostell und Bazon Brock. Schon bei einem der ersten Happenings der Welt *Die Linie von Hamburg*, eine Mischung aus Schaumalerei und Aktionskunst, 1959 gemeinsam mit Friedensreich Hundertwasser in Hamburg veranstaltet, sehen wir Bazon Brock, wie er das Buch mit dem

Bazon Brock, Friedensreich Hundertwasser, *Die Linie von Hamburg,* 18.–20. Dezember 1959, Hochschule für Bildende Künste Hamburg

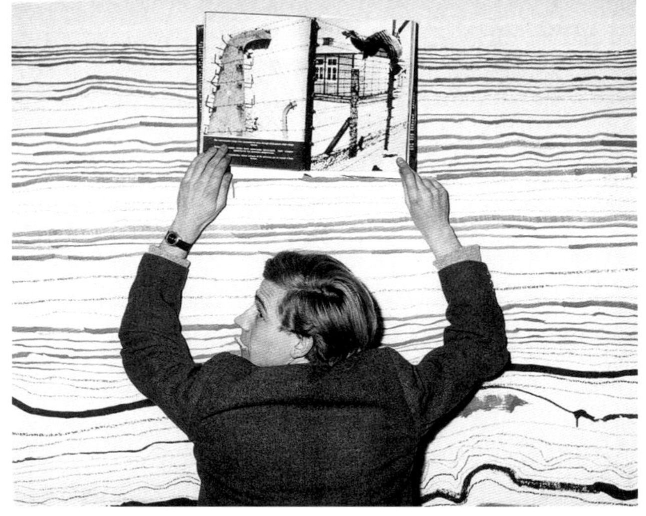

baric" and, secondly, declaring "all post-Auschwitz culture is garbage" in his book *Negative Dialectics* (German original 1966, first English edition 1973). In the face of barbaric destruction, he argues, culture had failed. The classic means of representation, the entire program of cultural representation, did not prevent barbarism. In a kind of reaction formation, as prisoners of trauma, artists thus transferred the real destruction they had experienced and observed to the means of representation themselves that had been capable neither of preventing barbarism nor of portraying it as such. In accordance with the logic of the paradigm shift from representation to reality, the portrayal of destruction became real destruction – the destruction of the means of representation themselves. Lurie's NO!art is closely related to this tradition.

This phase constitutes the actual crisis of representation: the destruction of the means of representation themselves. From then on, art no longer depicted destroyed cities and people, but the destroyed means of representation as well. The breakdown of civilization was reflected in a break with the classic means of representation: canvases, films, and books were slashed, burned, and destroyed, pianos were smashed. From the auto-destruction of a sculpture at the MoMA by Jean Tinguely in 1960 (*Homage to New York*) to the Destruction in Art Symposium (DIAS) in London in 1966, or Gustav Metzger's *South Bank Demonstration* of 1961, his first performance of auto-destructive art, art was marked by self-amputation, auto-aggression, and auto-destruction. The real destruction of Europe, by internal and external forces, was mirrored and repeated in the self-destruction of art. As reaction formations in the wake of trauma, the artistic practices of destruction and self-destruction repeated the preceding destruction of buildings, values, and people. One need only recall Niki de Saint-Phalle's shooting pictures (*Tirs*) in the 1961 exhibition *Feu à volonté.* The experience of people being shot at was no longer represented figuratively, as in Andrzej Wróblowski's painting *Execution IV* (1948), but was transferred directly to the medium of representation – by shooting at the canvas. The destruction wrought by barbarism was repeated in the auto-destruction of the means of representation. The reaction formation of inversion took place, repeating what had damaged the ego.

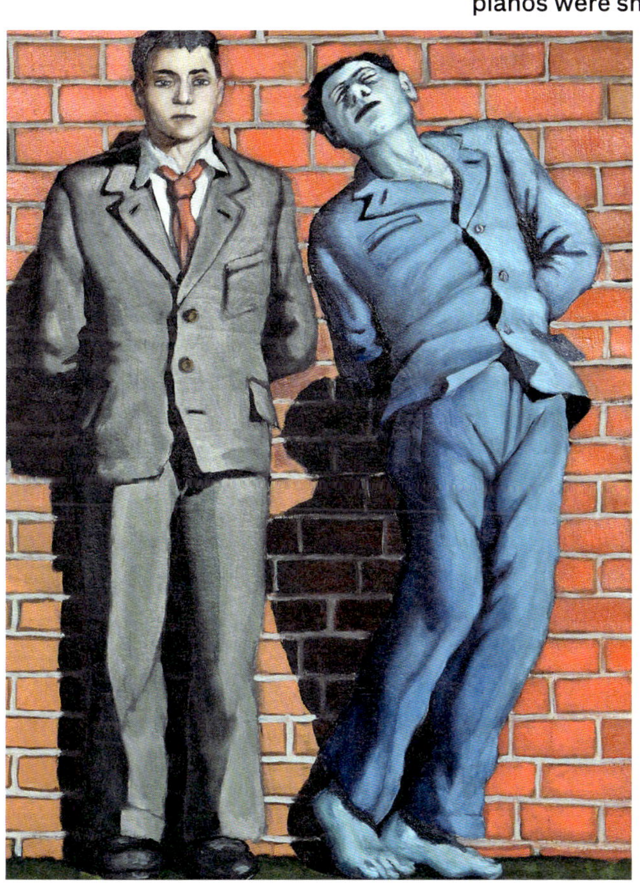

Andrzej Wróblewski, *Rozstrzelanie IV –Execution IV,* 1949
Polish Army Museum, Warsaw

To a large extent, post-war art reveals itself as a therapeutic reaction formation (see Beuys's installation *Zeige deine Wunde,* Show Your Wound, 1974/75) and thus as a prisoner of trauma. Just as, in the era of civilization's breakdown, art was burned, consumed by destructive rage, the postwar artists perpetuated this work of destruction as an inverse reaction formation. The example of Arman makes this clear: his "accumulations" of real objects refer to the photographic documents of piles of eyeglasses, shoes, and clothes in the death camps. His object *Papierkorb* (Recycle Bin, 1964) illustrates Adorno's contention that all culture is garbage. Artists including Alberto Burri and Joseph Beuys used materials associated with the war, like felt, tarpaulins, and combustible fuels. The language of art bore the traces of the upheavals and devastations that had been experienced. This self-destruction of the means of representation showed art to be a prisoner of trauma.

Titel *We have not forgotten* so aufschlägt, dass sich die Abbildung von Stacheldraht aus dem Buch mit den gemalten Linien im Raum überlagert.

Phase 4: Selbstzerstörung der Darstellungsmittel

Die Krise der Repräsentation hat Theodor W. Adorno in zwei berühmt gewordenen Passagen definiert, nämlich 1. dem Verdikt, dass man nach Auschwitz keine Gedichte schreiben könne, und 2. der Erklärung der Kultur zu Müll in seinem Buch *Negative Dialektik*, 1966. Die Kultur habe angesichts der barbarischen Zerstörung versagt. Die klassischen Mittel der Repräsentation, das ganze kulturelle Repräsentationsprogramm hat die Barbarei nicht verhindert. In einer Art von Reaktionsbildung, als Gefangene des Traumas, übertragen daher die Künstlerinnen und Künstler die erfahrene und beobachtete reale Zerstörung auf die Darstellungsmittel selbst, welche die Barbarei weder verhinderten noch als solche repräsentieren könnten. Daher wird die Abbildung der Destruktion – gemäß der Logik des paradigmatischen Wechsels von der Repräsentation zur Realität – zu einer realen Destruktion, und zwar zu einer Destruktion der Darstellungsmittel selbst. Dieser Tradition steht Luries NO!art nahe.

Diese Phase bildet die eigentliche Krise der Repräsentation: die Zerstörung der Repräsentationsmittel selbst. Fortan werden in der Kunst nicht mehr nur zerstörte Städte und Menschen sichtbar, sondern auch zerstörte Darstellungsmittel. Der erfahrene Zivilisationsbruch spiegelt sich im Bruch mit den klassischen Mitteln der Repräsentation: Leinwände, Filme, Bücher werden zerschlitzt, verbrannt und zerstört, Klaviere zertrümmert. Von der Autodestruktion einer Skulptur im MoMA, New York (*Homage to New York*), durch Jean Tinguely 1960 bis zum *Destruction in Art Symposium* (DIAS) 1966 in London oder Gustav Metzgers *South Bank Demonstration,* 1961, seine erste Performance auto-destruktiver Kunst, ist die Kunst gezeichnet von Selbst-Amputation, Auto-Aggression und Autodestruktion. Die reale Selbst- und Fremddestruktion Europas wiederholt und spiegelt sich in der Selbstdestruktion der Kunst. Die künstlerischen Gesten der Zerstörung und Selbstzerstörung wiederholen als Reaktionsbildung im Gefolge des Traumas die vorangegangenen Zerstörungen von Gebäuden, Werten und Menschen. Man erinnere sich nur an die Schießbilder von Niki de Saint-Phalle *Tirs* in der Ausstellung *Feu à volonté,* 1961. Die Erfahrung, dass auf Menschen geschossen wird, findet keine figurative Darstellung mehr wie in dem Gemälde *Execution IV*, 1948, von Andrzej Wróblewski, sondern wird auf das Darstellungsmedium selbst übertragen: Es wird auf eine Leinwand geschossen. Die Destruktion der Barbarei wird durch die Autodestruktion der Darstellungsmittel wiederholt. Die Reaktionsbildung der Inversion findet statt: Es wird wiederholt, was das Ich zerstört.

Die Nachkriegskunst offenbart sich in wesentlichen Teilen als therapeutische Reaktionsbildung (siehe die Installation *Zeige deine Wunde* von Joseph Beuys, 1974/75) und somit als Gefangene des Traumas. So wie in der Ära der Zivilisationsbrüche die Kunst verbrannt wurde und der Destruktionswut zum Opfer fiel, so setzen die Nachkriegskünstler diese Arbeit der Zerstörung als inverse Reaktionsbildung fort. Am Beispiel von Arman ist dies klar erkennbar. Seine Akkumulationen von realen Gegenständen verweisen auf die fotografischen Dokumente der Anhäufungen von Brillen, Schuhen, Kleidern in den Vernichtungslagern. Sein Objekt *Papierkorb* (Recycle Bin) von 1964 illustriert die These von Adorno,

Another example is Yves Klein's *Anthropométries*. In 1952, Klein went to Japan to further his training in the art of judo. There, he discovered photographs showing shadows of people that had been burned into the walls of houses or onto the ground by the heatwave of the atom bomb. The imprint of real naked bodies on his canvases repeats the picture of mere traces of people who have long since been annihilated. Klein experienced annihilation as the destruction of man, only surviving as a trace, recalling the proclamation at the end of Michel Foucault's *The Order of Things* (French original 1966; first English edition 1970): "that man would be erased, like a face drawn in sand at the edge of the sea."[20] As a reaction to this trauma, Klein sprayed the outlines of naked women onto canvases and burned them with a flamethrower. With the body prints of his *Anthropométries*, he invoked and repeated the shadows of the burned bodies he had seen in the photographs.

Yves Klein, *Hiroshima (ANT 79)*, ca. / ca 1961

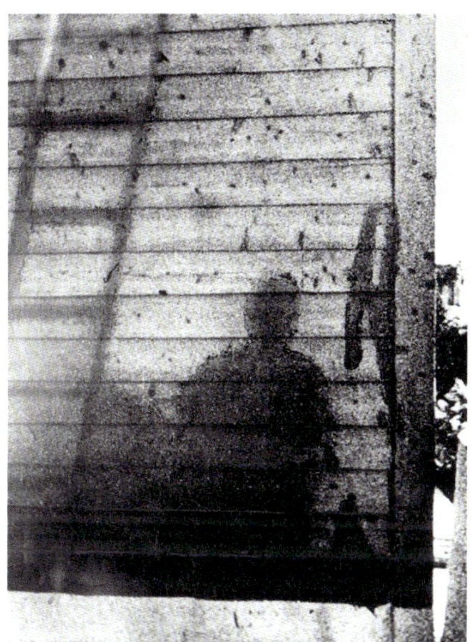

Eingebrannte Schatten von Opfern in Nagasaki, 1945

The theory that Klein's art was a reaction formation in response to the horror of Hiroshima is proved by the title he gave to one of the *Anthropométries*: *Hiroshima* (1961). In a witness statement captured on video, Klein's father-in-law confirms this interpretation, claiming to have discussed the matter with the artist.[21] In 1960, Klein himself wrote: "The shadows of Hiroshima in the wastes of the nuclear catastrophe, terrifying evidence without doubt, but nevertheless evidence of the hope of survival and the endurance of the body, even if only immaterial."[22] The real heat of the atomic bomb touched the means of representation of painting.

The example of Viennese Actionism, with its rituals and self-mutilations, its "befoulings" (Hermann Nitsch) with urine and feces, blood and guts, displayed an unconscious reaction formation against the conscious "cleansing" of postwar Austria from its crimes, its participation in Nazi fascism and the Holocaust. Because Austria officially washed itself clean, art did exactly the opposite, bathing in impurity, dirt, and filth. One could criticize Viennese Actionism, and thus part of the neo-avant-garde, on the grounds that reaction formation is an unconscious response from art, not a conscious elucidation. As a prisoner of trauma, reaction formation runs the risk of becoming part of the repression, or even of collusion. But even art as a mere symptom is nevertheless a truth, although it is a masked truth. Future generations will critically ask themselves how intimately the breaks with tradition perpetrated by the avant-gardes and neo-avant-gardes are linked with the barbaric breakdown of civilization, to what extent the unbridled subjective forms of expression and the abolition of forms of representation were inverting responses to the dehumanization of society, even serving it. What answers and information do the crises of art provide about the crises of society?

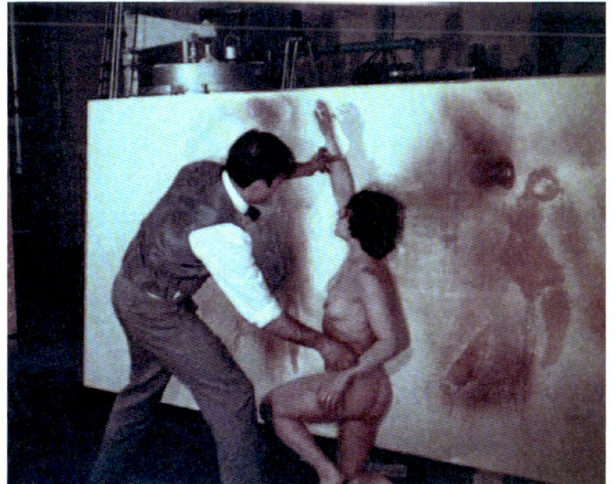

Yves Klein positioniert ein Modell vor der Leinwand / directs a model in front of the canvas, 1926

Phase 5: New Realism or: from Representation to Reality

As a prisoner of trauma, art after 1945 reacted with refusal and prohibition of representation in the form of abstraction, but also by processing the real injuries by injuring the means of representation, a total destruction of representation.

dass alle Kultur Müll sei. Künstler wie Alberto Burri, Joseph Beuys und andere verwenden Materialien, die auf den Krieg rückweisen, wie Filz, Zeltplanen und Brennstoffe. Die Sprache der Künste ist geprägt von den Spuren der erfahrenen Verwerfungen und Verwüstungen. Diese Selbstzerstörung der Darstellungsmittel zeigt die Kunst als Gefangene des Traumas.

Ein weiteres Beispiel bilden die *Anthropometrien* von Yves Klein. 1952 ging Klein nach Japan, um sich in der Kunst des Judo weiterzubilden. Dort entdeckte er Fotografien, die Schatten von Menschen zeigten, die durch die Hitzewelle der Atombombe in Häuserwände oder auf den Erdboden eingebrannt wurden. Der Abdruck der realen nackten Körper auf seinen Leinwänden wiederholt das Bild der bloßen Spuren von Menschen, die längst verlöscht sind. Die Erfahrung der Annihilation hat Klein als Vernichtung des Menschen erfahren, der nur mehr als Spur überlebt, ähnlich wie es der Schlusssatz des Buches *Les mots et les choses*, 1966, von Michel Foucault verkündet: „daß der Mensch verschwindet wie am Meeresufer ein Gesicht im Sand“[20]. Traumatisiert hat Yves Klein als Reaktionsbildung Umrisse von nackten Frauen auf die Leinwände gesprüht und mit einem Flammenwerfer angebrannt. Mit dem Körperabdruck seiner Anthropometrien hat er die Schatten der verbrannten Körper, wie er sie auf den Fotos gesehen hatte, beschworen und wieder hervorgeholt.

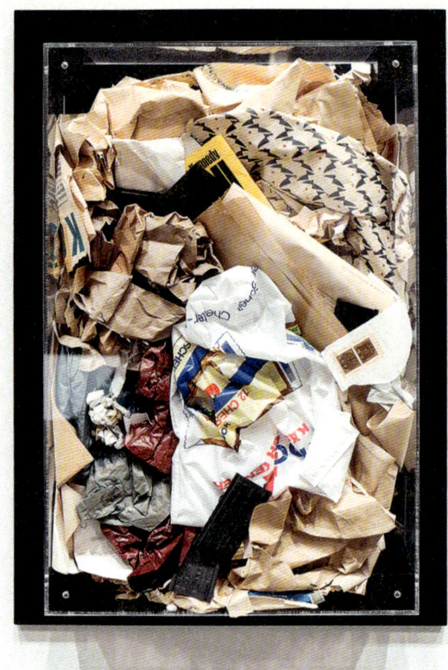

Arman, *Papierkorb (Recycle Bin)*, 1964
ZKM | Zentrum für Kunst und Medien, Karlsruhe

Als Beleg der These, die Kunst von Yves Klein sei eine Reaktionsbildung auf den Horror von Hiroshima, dient der Titel einer seiner Anthropometrien: *Hiroshima*, 1961. Sein Schwiegervater bestätigt in einer videografisch festgehaltenen Zeugenaussage[21] diese Interpretation, weil er sich mit Yves Klein zu diesem Thema ausgetauscht hatte. 1960 schrieb Klein selbst: „The shadows of Hiroshima in the wastes of the nuclear catastrophe, terrifying evidence without doubt, but nevertheless evidence of the hope of survival and the endurance of the body, even if only immaterial.“[22] Das reale Feuer der Atombombe erreichte auch das Repräsentationsmittel der Malerei.

Am Beispiel des Wiener Aktionismus, seiner Rituale und Selbstverstümmelungen, seiner „Besudelungen“ (Hermann Nitsch) durch Urin und Fäkalien, Blut und Gedärme zeigen sich unbewusste Reaktionsbildungen gegen die bewusste „Reinigung“ Nachkriegsösterreichs von seinen Verbrechen, seiner Beteiligung am Nationalsozialismus und Holocaust. Da sich Österreich offiziell reinwusch, machte die Kunst genau das Gegenteil: Sie badete in Unreinheit, Dreck und Schmutz. Man könnte dem Aktionismus und damit auch einem Teil der Neo-Avantgarden vorwerfen, dass Reaktionsbildung eine unbewusste Antwort der Kunst ist und noch keine bewusste Aufklärung darstellt. Es besteht die Gefahr, dass Reaktionsbildung als Gefangene des Traumas Teil der Verdrängung oder sogar Komplizenschaft wird. Doch auch eine Kunst als bloßes Symptom ist immerhin eine Wahrheit, wenn auch eine maskierte. Künftige Generationen werden sich kritisch die Frage stellen, wie weit die Traditionsbrüche der Avantgarden und Neo-Avantgarden mit den barbarischen Zivilisationsbrüchen verschränkt sind, wie weit die Enthemmungen der subjektiven Ausdrucksformen und die Abschaffungen der Repräsentationsformen einer Entmenschlichung der Gesellschaft spiegelbildlich geantwortet haben oder ihr dienten. Welche

Around 1960, however, the turn from subject-centered representation towards object-oriented reality set in. Raul Hilberg, the founder of Holocaust research, answered Adorno with an insistence on reality. The art of the neo-avant-gardes after 1945 moved between the poles of these opposing positions (Adorno's ban on representation, Hilberg's replacement of representation with reality). Two quotations illustrate these positions. Adorno writes:

"Auschwitz demonstrated irrefutably that culture has failed. That this could happen in the midst of the traditions of philosophy, of art, and of the enlightening sciences says more than that these traditions and their spirit lacked the power to take hold of men and work a change in them. [...] All post-Auschwitz culture, including its urgent critique, is garbage. [...] Whoever pleads for the maintenance of this radically culpable and shabby culture becomes its accomplice, while the man who says no to culture is directly furthering the barbarism which our culture showed itself to be."[23]

In response to the question of whether or how the Holocaust could be represented, Hilberg suggested

"a can of Zyklon B gas, with which the Jews were killed in Auschwitz and Maydanek. I would have liked to see a *single* can mounted on a pedestal in a small room, with no other objects between the walls, as the epitome of Adolf Hitler's Germany, just as a vase of Euphronios was shown [...] all by itself at the Metropolitan Museum of Art as one of the supreme artifacts of Greek antiquity."[24]

These quotations reflect two opposite reactions of art to the horror of the Holocaust: on the one hand, a ban on representation, on the other, an insistence on reality.

Reality Art and NO!art

Witnesses of the death camps testify to the inconceivability and unrepresentability of inhuman barbarism. Boris Lurie, born in 1924 in Leningrad, moved with his family to Riga, Latvia, in 1925/26. In 1941, Riga was occupied by the German army and 30,000 Jews, including Lurie's family, were confined to a ghetto. On December 8, 1941, a massacre occurred in the Rumbula forests near Riga. In three days, the SS killed roughly 25,000 Jews and Slavs, mostly women, children, and the elderly, including Lurie's mother, maternal grandmother, sister, and girlfriend. Between 1941 and 1945, father and son were interned in various concentration camps including Magdeburg (Polte-Werke), a sub-camp or satellite camp of Buchenwald. They survived the Holocaust and emigrated to the United States in 1946.

The violence, barbarism, and dehumanization experienced in the concentration camps shaped Lurie's art. Reaction formation in response to war, the traumas of the Holocaust, and the atom bomb defined his art, as it did that of the best artists of the European neo-avant-gardes after 1945. Like them, he began by attempting to respond figuratively to the tragedy of his family in his artistic works (*3 Women*, 1958/59). With the *Dismembered Women* series, that he worked on from 1947 to about 1959, he attempted a semi-abstract approach. In 1959 he founded what would come to be known as the NO!art movement,[25] a total rejection of the prevailing cultural consensus. Like Adorno and the neo-avant-gardes in Europe, Lurie negated art as a strategy of representation. For him, too, trauma and remembrance became the theme of his art. For a long time the fate of his

Antworten und welche Auskunft geben die Krisen der Kunst auf bzw. über die Krisen der Gesellschaft?

Phase 5: Neuer Realismus oder von der Repräsentation zur Realität

Als Gefangene des Traumas reagiert die Kunst nach 1945 mit einer Verweigerung und einem Verbot der Repräsentation durch Abstraktion, andererseits mit der Verarbeitung der realen Verletzungen durch die Verletzungen der Repräsentationsmittel, einer totalen Vernichtung der Repräsentation. Doch um 1960 setzt die Wende von der subjektzentrierten Repräsentation zur objektorientierten Realität ein. Raul Hilberg, der Begründer der Holocaust-Forschung, antwortete Adorno mit der Insistenz auf Realität. Zwischen den Klammern der gegensätzlichen Positionen, Verbot der Repräsentation (Adorno) und Substitution der Repräsentation durch Realität (Hilberg), bewegt sich die Kunst der Neo-Avantgarden nach 1945. Zwei Zitate von Adorno und Hilberg belegen diese konträren Pole.
Adorno schreibt, Auschwitz habe „[...] das Mißlingen der Kultur unwiderleglich bewiesen. Daß es geschehen konnte inmitten aller Tradition der Philosophie, der Kunst und der aufklärenden Wissenschaften, sagt mehr als nur, daß diese, der Geist, es nicht vermochte, die Menschen zu ergreifen und zu verändern. In jenen Sparten selber, im emphatischen Anspruch ihrer Autarkie, haust die Unwahrheit. Alle Kultur nach Auschwitz, samt der dringlichen Kritik daran, ist Müll. [...] Wer für Erhaltung der radikal schuldigen und schäbigen Kultur plädiert, macht sich zum Helfershelfer, während, wer der Kultur sich verweigert, unmittelbar die Barbarei befördert, als welche die Kultur sich enthüllte."[23]
Auf die Frage, ob und wie man den Holocaust darstellen könne, verweist Hilberg auf „[...] eine Dose Zyklon-B-Gas [...], mit dem die Juden in Auschwitz und Majdanek getötet wurden. Ich wollte, daß eine einzige Dose in einem kleinen, sonst leeren Raum auf einem Podest stand – als das Symbol für Adolf Hitlers Deutschland, so wie einst die im Metropolitan Museum of Art isoliert ausgestellte Vase des Euphronios als Inbegriff der griechischen Antike erschien."[24]
Diese beiden Zitate spiegeln zwei einander entgegengesetzte Kunstreaktionen auf den Horror des Holocaust: auf der einen Seite das Verbot der Repräsentation, auf der anderen Seite die Insistenz auf Realität.

Realitätskunst und NO!art

Zeugen der Vernichtungslager belegen die Unvorstellbarkeit und Undarstellbarkeit der inhumanen Barbarei. Boris Lurie, 1924 in Leningrad geboren, kam 1925/26 mit seiner Familie nach Riga, Lettland. 1941 wurde Riga von der deutschen Wehrmacht besetzt. 30 000 Juden, darunter Luries Familie, wurden in ein Ghetto verbannt. Am 8. Dezember 1941 kam es im Wald von Rumbula, nahe Riga, zu einem Massaker. Die SS tötete an drei Tagen ca. 25 000 Juden und Slaven, meistens Frauen, Kinder, Senioren, darunter Mutter, Großmutter, Schwester und Freundin von Boris Lurie. Vater und Sohn wurden in den Jahren 1941–45 in verschiedene Konzentrationslager, u.a. in Magdeburg (Polte-Werke), einem Außenlager von Buchenwald, interniert. Sie überlebten den Holocaust und wanderten 1946 in die USA aus.
Die im KZ erfahrene Gewalt, Barbarei und Entmenschlichung wurden prägend für Luries Kunst. Reaktionsbildungen auf Krieg, auf Traumata des Holocaust,

family was a taboo in his art, only depictable in what he called his "private paintings." The family did not speak of the Shoah. But the traumatic memories of the ghetto and the camps did return.

Probably between 1960 and 1963, he began using swastikas and then, maybe as early as the end of 1961, he began using the concentration camp photos. This was where his true art began, his rejection of western culture and the art market, his NO to Abstract Expressionism and the affirmations of Pop Art. What was repressed in the United States became the subject of his work: lynch mobs, serial killers, atomic bombs, racism, wars. In a way that scandalized the art world, Lurie combined images of concentration camps with pin-ups cut out of magazines. His collages looked like trash, affirming Adorno's declaration that culture was garbage. If culture is actually unculture, then NO!art can become the true art.

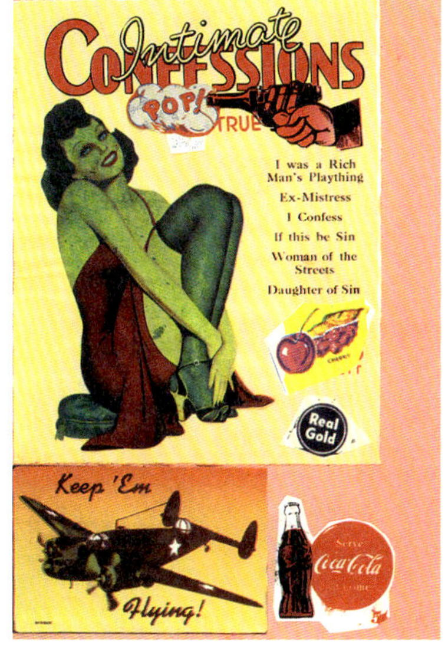

Eduardo Paolozzi, *I was a Rich Man's Plaything,* 1947. The Estate of Eduardo Paolozzi, Tate, London

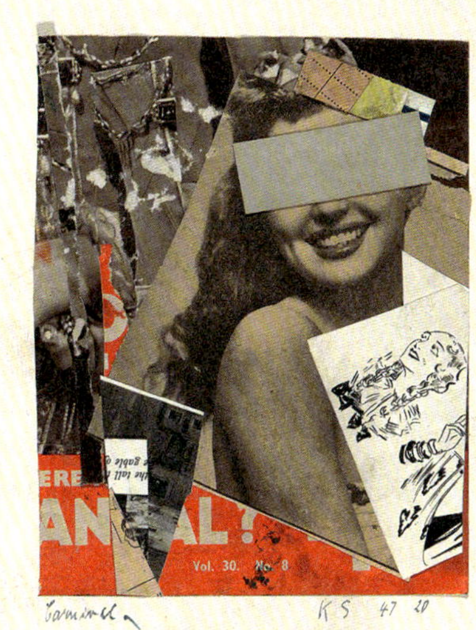

Kurt Schwitters, *Carnival,* 1947. Yale University Art Gallery, New Haven. Gift of the Estate of Katherine S. Dreier

Unlike Kurt Schwitters (*Carnival*, 1947) or Eduardo Paolozzi (*I was a Rich Man's Plaything*, 1947), with their ironic but ultimately affirmative commentaries on mass and consumer culture (an approach shared with Pop Art as a whole), Lurie wanted to transfer the humiliation he had experienced in the camps onto the material itself. Base materials, abased materials, pictures of humiliated women were intended to illustrate the debasement of humanity and the demeaning of culture beginning with the barbaric Nazi era. With his NO!art and the exhibitions *Vulgar Show* (1960), *Doom Show* (1961), and *NO!Show* (1963), Lurie wanted to point to a "shabby culture" that had rendered itself "culpable."

"Being caught up in a historic tragedy."[26] This is how gallerist Gertrude Stein formulated the origin of Lurie's artistic motivation: the fact that in Germany, in the "land of poets and philosophers," in highly civilized Europe, inhuman atrocities and total dehumanization were possible, prompted Lurie to reject "art" and to show that art itself is "garbage."

From the *Shit Sculptures* (1964) by Sam Goodman and Boris Lurie that picked up where Piero Manzoni left off with his *Merda d'artista* in 1961 (also a reaction to the traumas of World War II) to Lurie's collage *Hard Writings: PISS* (ca 1972–73), NO!art was the desperate cry of a prisoner of trauma for salvation. *PISS* is a continuation of the *Piss Action* (1968) by Viennese Actionist Otto Muehl, a former German soldier also imprisoned by the trauma of the war.

Otto Muehl, *Piss Aktion,* 1968

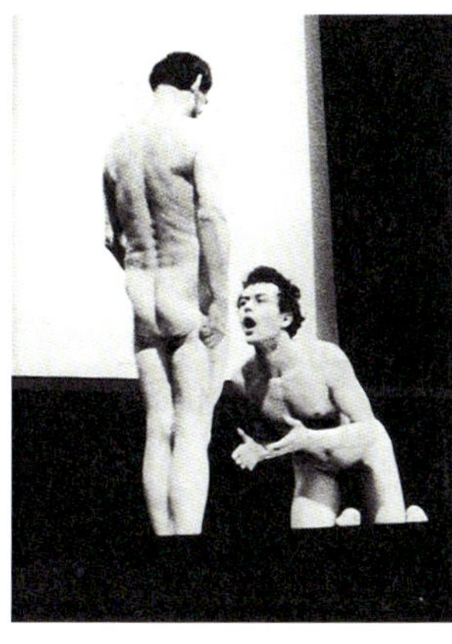

Boris Lurie, *Hard Writings: PISS,* ca. / ca 1972–73

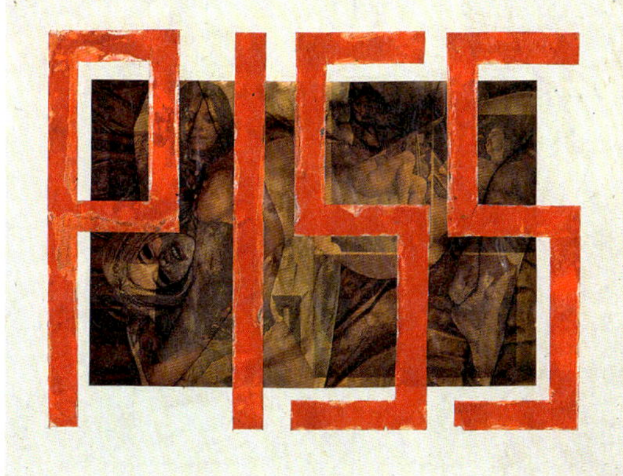

If only representation-based art is art (from figurative to abstract painting), then turning away from representation-based art means turning away from art as such. Anti-art or NO!art is thus nothing other than an attempt to overcome the antinomies of the classic art program, which is a program of representation. With his NO!art movement, Lurie pursued Adorno's argument, but by turning towards reality in the tradition of Duchamp he took anti-art a step further, in part adopting the position advocated by Hilberg. One achievement of the neo-avant-garde after 1945 thus consists in replacing the art of representation with the art of reality. By supplying the philosophy for an

die Atombombe bestimmen seine Kunst wie die der besten Künstler der europäischen Neo-Avantgarden nach 1945. Wie diese hat er zuerst versucht, in seinen künstlerischen Arbeiten figurativ auf die Tragödien seiner Familie zu reagieren (*3 Women*, 1958/59), mit der Serie *Dismembered Women*, an der Lurie von 1947 bis 1959 arbeitete, versuchte er einen semi-abstrakten Zugang. 1959 gründete er das NO!art-Movement[25], die totale Ablehnung der herrschenden kulturellen Übereinkünfte. Wie Adorno und die Neo-Avantgarden Europas hat auch Lurie die Kunst als Repräsentationsstrategie verneint. Trauma und Erinnerung wurden auch für ihn zum Thema seiner Kunst. Lange Zeit war das Schicksal seiner Familie für seine Kunst tabu, nur in *Private paintings*, wie er sie nannte, darstellbar. Die Familie sprach nicht über die Shoa. Doch die traumatischen Erinnerungen an das Ghetto, das KZ kamen zurück.

Etwa seit 1961 inkorporierte Lurie Fotografien von KZs in seine Arbeiten. Hiermit beginnt die eigentliche Kunst von Boris Lurie, sein Dissens mit der westlichen Kultur und dem Kunstmarkt, sein Nein gegen den Abstrakten Expressionismus und die Affirmationen der Pop-Art. Das, was die USA verdrängten, bildete den Gegenstand seiner Werke: Lynchjustiz, Serien-Morde, Atombombe, Rassismus, Kriege. Auf eine für die Kunstwelt skandalöse Weise kombinierte Lurie Abbildungen von Konzentrationslagern mit Ausschnitten aus Pin-up-Magazinen. Seine Collagen wirkten wie „trash", was Theodor W. Adornos Aussage bekräftigt, dass alle Kultur nach Auschwitz Müll sei. Mit seinen Pin-up-Collagen enthüllt Lurie im Sinne Adornos die Kultur als Unkultur. Wenn Kultur eigentlich Unkultur ist, dann kann nur NO!art zur eigentlichen Kunst werden.

Anders als Kurt Schwitters (*Carnival*, 1947) oder Eduardo Paolozzi (*I was a Rich Man's Plaything*, 1947), beides ironische, aber letztlich affirmative Kommentare zur Massen- und Konsumkultur wie die Pop-Art insgesamt, will Lurie die im KZ erfahrene Erniedrigung auf das Material selbst übertragen. Niedriges Material, erniedrigtes Material, Bilder von erniedrigten Frauen sollen die menschliche Erniedrigung und die Erniedrigung der Kultur seit der Nazi-Barbarei veranschaulichen. Lurie will mit seiner NO!art, 1959, und den Ausstellungen *Vulgar Show*, 1960, *Doom Show*, 1961, und *NO!Show*, 1963, auf die „schäbige Kultur" zeigen, die sich „schuldig" gemacht hat.

„Being caught up in a historic tragedy"[26] – so formuliert Gertrude Stein den Ursprung von Luries künstlerischer Motivation –, nämlich dass im Land der „Dichter und Denker", in Deutschland, im hochzivilisierten Europa, die inhumane Grausamkeit und die totale Entmenschlichung möglich waren, hat Lurie veranlasst, die „Kunst" abzulehnen und zu zeigen, dass sie selbst „trash" sei.

Seine NO!art – von der Collage *Hard Writings: PISS*, ca. 1972–73, bis zu den *Shit Sculptures*, 1964, von Sam Goodman und Boris Lurie, welche die Dosen *Merda d'artista*, 1961, von Piero Manzoni fortsetzten, der ähnlich wie Lurie auf die traumatisierenden „Erfolge" des Zweiten Weltkrieges reagierte – war der verzweifelte Schrei eines Gefangenen des Traumas nach Erlösung. Die Collage *PISS* ist eine Fortsetzung der *Pissaktion*, 1968, des Wiener Aktionisten Otto Muehl, ebenfalls als ehemaliger Wehrmachtssoldat ein Gefangener des Traumas des Zweiten Weltkrieges.

Wenn nur Repräsentationskunst, von der figurativen bis zur abstrakten Malerei, Kunst ist, so bedeutet Abkehr von Repräsentationskunst auch Abkehr von Kunst. Anti-Kunst bzw. NO!art ist daher nichts anderes als der Versuch, die Antinomien des klassischen Kunstprogramms, das ein Repräsentationsprogramm ist,

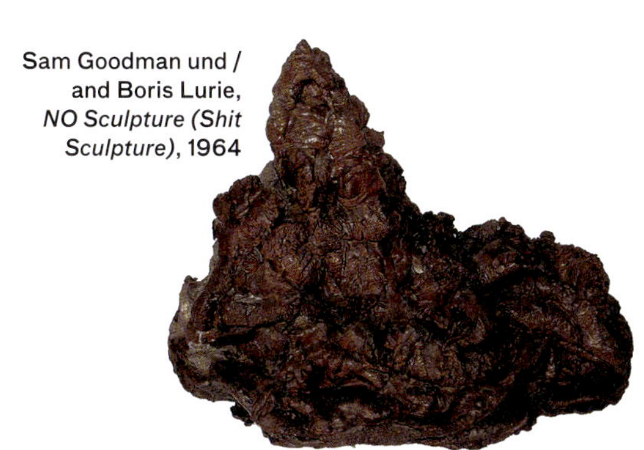

Sam Goodman und / and Boris Lurie, *NO Sculpture (Shit Sculpture)*, 1964

aesthetics of trauma (no representation is possible after Auschwitz; after the Holocaust, culture is garbage), Adorno proved himself to be a prisoner of trauma. Hilberg pointed a way out of trauma: reality instead of representation. Withdrawal from the picture also offers a way out of and withdrawal from the trauma. Boris Lurie's oeuvre should be seen in precisely this tradition.

After World War II, art proclaimed the death of art via the destruction of its means of production. Lurie's concept of NO!art corresponds to the Dadaists declaration that "art is dead." Both were reactions to the madness of world wars.

Boris Lurie, who was imprisoned in a concentration camp himself and whose family did not survive the Holocaust, dealt more radically than any other artist with the problem of representing the Holocaust. In art's trial against the crimes of the twentieth century, Lurie's chief witnesses were Kant and Adorno and their critique of representation and of art. Turning away from art because it had proved to be an affirmation of barbarism[27] meant NO!art.

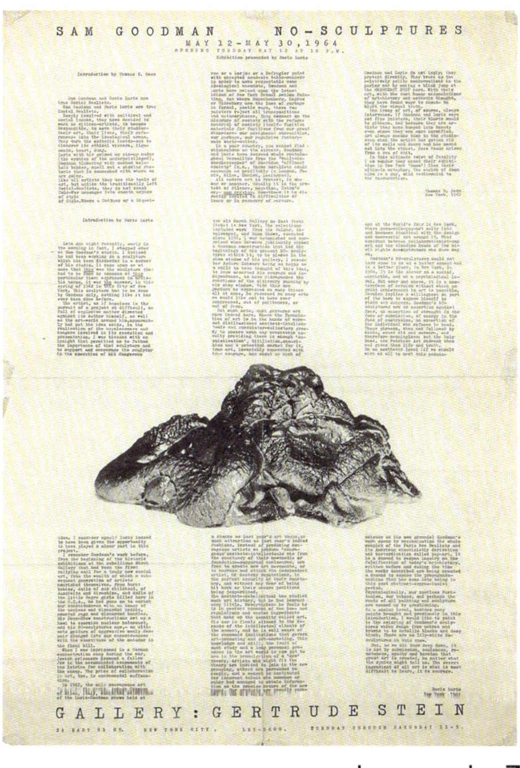

Gallery Gertrude Stein: *NO Sculptures (Shit) Show Poster*, 1964

At the same time as Lurie, German artists like Wolf Vostell also addressed the theme of the Holocaust (*Black Room Cycle*, 1958/59: *German View*, *Auschwitz Spotlight, Treblinka*), using real objects for reality-based art in the form of three-dimensional collages (assemblages), installations, and environments. In different ways, the artists worked against the tendency within society towards forgetting, responding to this repression of trauma with work of remembrance.

In their writings, those who witnessed the camps testify to their inconceivable barbarism. As members of the so-called Sonderkommando at Auschwitz-Birkenau, Jewish prisoners were forced to lead their own companions into the gas chambers, to salvage hair and gold teeth, then take the bodies of those who had been gassed to the ovens to be burned. Not long after, they, too, were murdered. With three other members of the Sonderkommando, Zelman Lewenthal and Zelman Landowski secretly documented what went on in the gas chambers as an act of resistance, burying their report in the camp grounds on November 26, 1944, shortly before they were murdered.[28] Lewenthal's excerpt, dated August 15, 1944, states: "No one can imagine exactly how things happened, for it is unimaginable that a precise account of our experiences could be given."[29] These words were written by a first-hand witness, not by someone born later. Which brings us back to Kant's problem: What can be imagined and represented, and what can not? How can art represent ugly things?

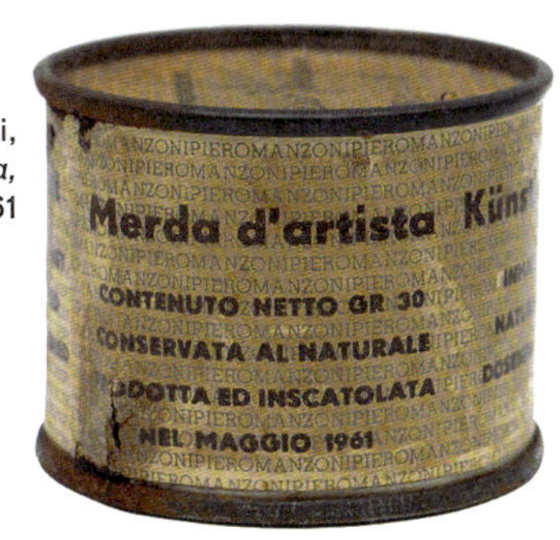

Piero Manzoni, *Merda d'artista*, 1961

The Horror of the Holocaust

The experience of the Holocaust took us to the limits of what can be imagined and of what can be represented. But this does not mean that certain artists did not continue to make art based on representation. Many great artists like Gerhard Frankl (*Die Sandgrube*, 1964) continued to try to portray the experiences of the Holocaust representatively. Is the horror of the Holocaust unrepresentable? – Unutterable? Unimaginable? Unportrayable? Is it possible or acceptable that the Holocaust is not suitable for representation even though it is or was a reality?

aufzuheben. Mit seiner Bewegung NO!art hat Boris Lurie einerseits die Argumentation von Adorno weitergeführt, aber mit seiner Hinwendung zur Realität in der Tradition Duchamps hat er die Anti-Art weitergeführt, und damit die Position von Raul Hilberg teilweise eingenommen.

Eine Leistung der Neo-Avantgarde nach 1945 besteht also in der Ablösung der Repräsentationskunst durch die Realitätskunst. Indem Adorno die Philosophie für die Ästhetik des Traumas liefert – Keine Repräsentation ist nach Auschwitz möglich und Kultur ist nach dem Holocaust Müll! –, erweist er sich als Gefangener des Traumas. Hilberg weist einen Weg aus dem Trauma: Realität statt Repräsentation. Der Ausstieg aus dem Bild bedeutet auch einen Ausstieg aus dem Trauma. Das Œuvre von Boris Lurie ist genau in dieser Tradition zu sehen.

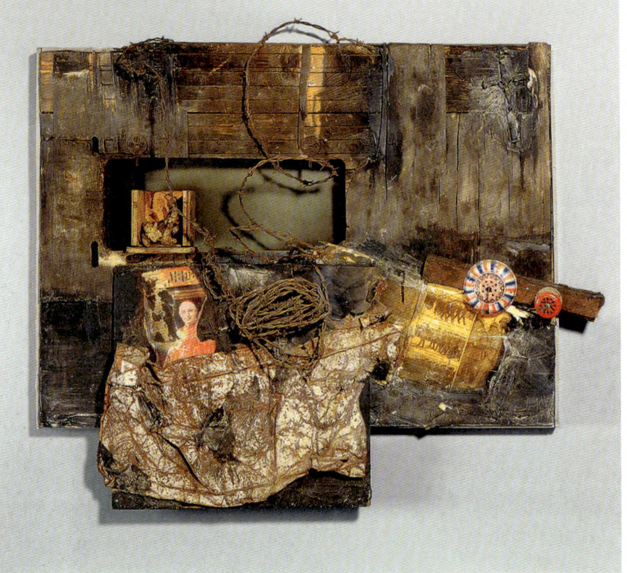

Nach dem Zweiten Weltkrieg erklärte die Kunst durch die Zerstörung der künstlerischen Mittel selbst noch einmal die Kunst für tot. Wenn Lurie von NO!art spricht, so entspricht das dem Ausspruch der Dadaisten: „Die Kunst ist tot." Beides sind Reaktionen auf den Wahnsinn der Weltkriege.

Boris Lurie, der selbst im KZ inhaftiert war und dessen Familie den Holocaust nicht überlebte, stellt sich radikal wie kein anderer Künstler dem Problem der Repräsentation des Holocaust. Im künstlerischen Prozess gegen die Verbrechen des 20. Jahrhunderts sind Luries Kronzeugen Kant und Adorno und deren Kritik an der Repräsentation und an der Kunst. Abwendung von der Kunst, weil diese sich als Affirmation der Barbarei erwiesen hat,[27] bedeutet als Konsequenz: NO!art.

Zeitgleich mit Boris Lurie wandten sich auch deutsche Künstler wie Wolf Vostell (dreiteilige Arbeit *Schwarzes Zimmer*, 1958/59, mit *Deutscher Ausblick*, *Auschwitzscheinwerfer*, *Treblinka*) dem Holocaust-Thema zu, nutzten reale Gegenstände für Realitätskunst in Form von dreidimensionalen Collagen, d. h. Assemblagen, von Installationen und Environments. Gegen die Tendenz der Gesellschaft, die vergessen wollte, arbeiteten die Künstler in verschiedener Form an und entgegneten der gesellschaftlichen Verdrängung der Traumata mit Erinnerungsarbeit.

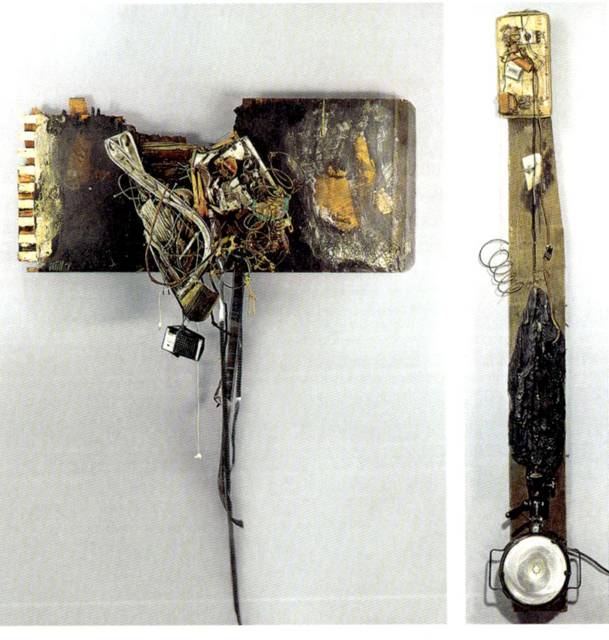

Wolf Vostell, *Deutscher Ausblick, Treblinka, Auschwitz-Scheinwerfer (aus dem Environment Schwarzes Zimmer)*, 1958/59
Berlinische Galerie – Landesmuseum für Moderne Kunst, Fotografie und Architektur

Zeugen der Vernichtungslager belegen in ihren Schriften die Unvorstellbarkeit und Undarstellbarkeit der inhumanen Barbarei. Als Mitglieder des sogenannten Sonderkommandos des KZs Auschwitz-Birkenau wurden jüdische Häftlinge gezwungen, ihre eigenen Gefährten in die Gaskammern zu führen, Haare und Zahngold zu bergen, ehe sie die vergasten Körper den Verbrennungsöfen zuführen und den Flammen überlassen mussten. Nach einiger Zeit wurden sie dann selbst auch ermordet. Zusammen mit drei weiteren Mitgliedern des Sonderkommandos dokumentierten Zelman Lewenthal und Zelman Landowski in einer Widerstandsaktion die Vorgänge in den Vergasungskammern heimlich und vergruben diese Schriften am 26. November 1944 kurz vor ihrer eigenen Ermordung auf dem Lagergelände.[28] In Lewenthals Auszug, datiert auf den 15. 8. 1944, heißt es: „So genau, wie die Geschehnisse selbst verliefen, kann sie kein Mensch sich vorstellen, denn es ist unvorstellbar, daß man so genau unsere Erlebnisse wiedergeben kann."[29] Zeugen der Ereig-

The camps are the zero point of meaning and existence. In the camp, there is no God. Nothing more exists for the people, who experience a totally exceptional state, in which nothing functions according to the rules they are familiar with. The camp is the world beyond normality. Here, lawlessness is the only law. The camp is the zero point of the human condition. Camps are sites of extermination created for the people by the people. How is this possible?

"What happened in the camps exceeds the juridical concept of crime to such an extent that the specific political-juridical structure within which those events took place has often been left simply unexamined. The camp is the place in which the most absolute *conditio inhumana* ever to appear on Earth was realized."[30]

For many people in many places around the world, the world resembles a Gulag archipelago, a camp of the *conditio inhumana*. How can this *conditio inhumana* be imagined and represented? That is the question. One answer, in the words of Zelman Lewenthal, is that it is simply impossible to get an idea of it. In his book *Remnants of Auschwitz: The Witness and the Archive* (2000), Giorgio Agamben points out that the usual task of the witness is to represent something, to testify to something, to say: This is how it was. With Lewenthal, we see that there are no witnesses. Even he, who was there, writes that "it is unimaginable," and thus unrepresentable. With Agamben, we must abandon the notion of a witness to this extreme event. The witness is nothing other than a symptom of unrepresentability, a symptom of the impossibility of representation. For certain theorists, then, the truth about the camps is unimaginable. Lewenthal also wrote: "The whole truth is much more tragic, much more horrible."[31] In this light, representation would even be untrue. Which brings us back to the problem identified by Kant in his discussion of the program of representation: the disgusting and the horrific cannot be represented.

For Agamben, the camp embodies the biopolitical paradigm of modernity.[32] In this sense, Boris Lurie is a key artist of modernity because he dealt intensively with the camps, a central motif of modernity. Lurie was a witness and he saw his artistic task in making the unimaginable true – to represent what is true, what is atrocious, what is terrifying. For this he chose the radical means of the collages in his NO!art program.

In his seminal book *The Society of the Spectacle* (1967), Guy Debord points to Dada and Surrealism as the two movements that marked the end of modern art.[33] But he accused Dadaism of seeking "to abolish art without realizing it" while Surrealism "sought to realize art without abolishing it."[34] Boris Lurie wanted to abolish art, but also to realize it, as NO!art. In his art, he demonstrated a possible path to the abolition of representation in art – how art could be abolished while art is realized nonetheless.

What does Boris Lurie's art teach us? The defense mechanisms of reaction formation must be broken through in order to arrive at a new art via NO!art. Lurie's art shows us that we must change our concept of representation in order to work through the crisis and the Adornian ban on representation. The greatest taboo and trauma of modern times is the Holocaust, because it contradicts everything that modernity stands for: equality, justice, freedom, universal human rights, inviolable human dignity, thou shalt not kill, and so forth. For the modern intellect – the Cartesian subject of the Enlightenment – it is totally unacceptable that the Holocaust was possible in a highly civilized Europe. How is it possible to portray such an "impossible" event?

nisse, nicht Nachgeborene, haben das geschrieben. Diese Aussagen führen uns zu Kants Problem zurück: Was ist vorstellbar, darstellbar und was nicht? Wie kann Kunst dann hässliche Dinge darstellen?

Der Horror des Holocaust

Die Erfahrung des Holocaust hat uns an die Grenze dessen geführt, was vorstellbar bzw. repräsentierbar ist. Das heißt nicht, dass manche Künstler nicht weiterhin Repräsentationskunst betrieben hätten. Viele große Künstler wie Gerhard Frankl (*Die Sandgrube*, 1964) haben versucht, die Erfahrungen des Holocaust noch repräsentativ darzustellen. Ist der Horror des Holocaust unrepräsentierbar? – unaussprechbar? unvorstellbar? undarstellbar? Darf es und kann es sein, dass er nicht für Repräsentation geeignet ist, obwohl er Realität ist oder war?
Aber das Lager war der Nullpunkt des Sinns und des Seins. Im Lager gibt es keinen Gott. Nichts mehr existiert für die Menschen. Dort erfahren sie den totalen Ausnahmezustand, in dem nichts mehr nach Regeln, die sie bisher kannten, funktioniert. Das Lager ist die Welt jenseits der Normalität. Hier ist Rechtlosigkeit das einzige Gesetz. Im Lager herrscht der Nullpunkt der conditio humana. Lager sind Vernichtungslager von Menschen für Menschen. Wie ist das möglich?
„Was in den Lagern geschehen ist, übersteigt den juristischen Begriff von Verbrechen in einem solchen Maße, dass man es häufig einfach unterlassen hat, die spezifische rechtlich-politische Struktur zu untersuchen, aus der jene Ereignisse hervorgegangen sind. Das Lager ist lediglich der Ort, an dem sich die absoluteste *conditio inhumana* realisiert hat, die es auf Erden je gegeben hat.“[30]
Für viele Menschen an vielen Orten der Erde gleicht die Welt einem Archipel Gulag, einem Lager der conditio inhumana. Wie kann man sich diese conditio inhumana vorstellen und wie sie darstellen? – das ist die Frage. Eine Antwort lautet mit Zelman Lewenthal: Sich eine Vorstellung zu machen, ist schier unmöglich. Agamben verwies in seinem Buch *Was von Auschwitz bleibt. Das Archiv und der Zeuge* 2003 darauf, dass der Zeuge normalerweise die Aufgabe hat, etwas zu repräsentieren, zu bezeugen: So ist es gewesen. Mit Lewenthal sehen wir, es gibt keine Zeugen, sogar er, der dabei war, schreibt, „es ist unvorstellbar“, folglich nicht darstellbar. Die Vorstellung, wir könnten für dieses extreme Ereignis einen Zeugen haben, muss man mit Agamben aufgeben. Der Zeuge ist nichts anderes als ein Symptom der Undarstellbarkeit, ein Symptom der Repräsentationsunmöglichkeit. Die Wahrheit über das Lager ist für bestimmte theoretische Positionen also unvorstellbar. Lewenthal schrieb ferner: „Die ganze Wahrheit ist viel tragischer, noch viel entsetzlicher ...“[31] Die Repräsentation wäre also sogar unwahr. Hier klingt wieder das Problem an, das bereits Kant in der Auseinandersetzung mit dem Repräsentationsprogramm erkannte: Der Ekel und das Schreckliche lassen sich nicht darstellen.
Für Agamben stellt das Lager das biopolitische Paradigma der Moderne dar.[32] Insofern ist Boris Lurie ein zentraler Künstler der Moderne, weil er sich intensiv mit dem Lager beschäftigte, mit einem zentralen Motiv der Moderne. Lurie war Zeuge und sah seine künstlerische Aufgabe darin, das Unvorstellbare wahr zu machen, d. h. das Wahre, das Entsetzliche, das Schreckliche darzustellen. Dafür wählte er die radikalen Mittel seiner Collagen in seinem NO!art-Programm.
In seinem Jahrhundertbuch *Die Gesellschaft des Spektakels*, 1967, verwies Guy Debord auf den Dadaismus und den Surrealismus als die beiden Kunstströmungen,

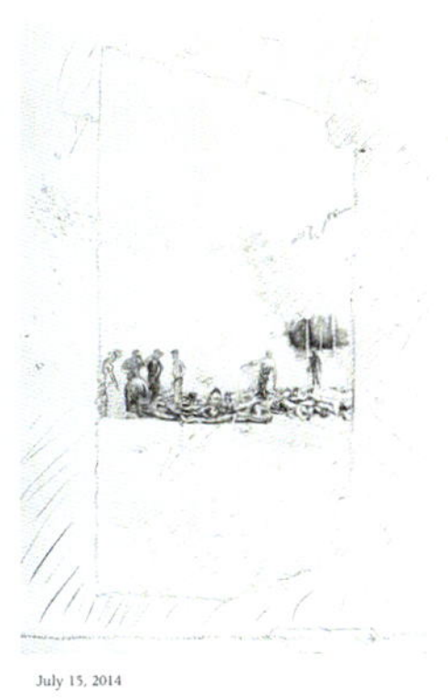

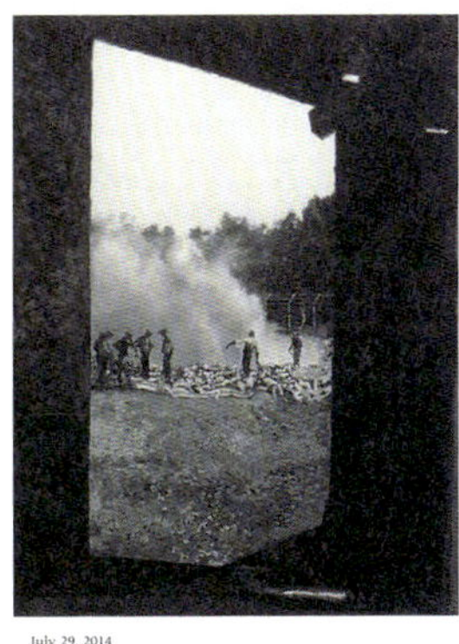

Gerhard Richter, *Birkenau*, 937–2, 2014

Adorno's answer was complete refusal and a total ban on representation. The iconoclastic impulse of modernism after two world wars, the destruction and self-destruction of the means of representation, was due to reaction formation in response to trauma. A second answer came from Hilberg, advocating a turn from abstraction to the object, from representation to reality, a passion for the real. These two contrary positions still apply today. On the one side there is Claude Lanzmann, whose 9.5-hour film *Shoah* (1985)[35] shows no images of the Holocaust, only the talking heads of witnesses. Lanzmann follows Adorno in acknowledging the collapse of Kantian aesthetics in the face of disaster. Where social catastrophes are concerned, a positive presentation, a "beautiful presentation" is not only inappropriate, but actually a falsification, a lie. Photographs of mountains of corpses, crematoria, and deportation trains do not make Auschwitz understandable, do not show the truth about Auschwitz. On the other side stands Georges Didi-Huberman. In his essay "Images malgré tout" (2001)[36] he shows four photographs taken in 1944 by prisoners at the Auschwitz-Birkenau camp showing Jewish victims participating in the genocide of the Sonderkommando. Richter used these photographs, which had been brought to his attention by an article in *Der Spiegel,* as the inspiration for his Auschwitz-Birkenau paintings. Didi-Huberman's essay triggered a major discussion in France about how far photography can be trusted as a medium of truth. Lanzmann accused Didi-Huberman of fetishizing the photographs in a Christian manner, while others endorsed a total prohibition of such images (*Bilderverbot*).[37]

Boris Lurie, *Saturation Painting (Buchenwald),* 1960–63

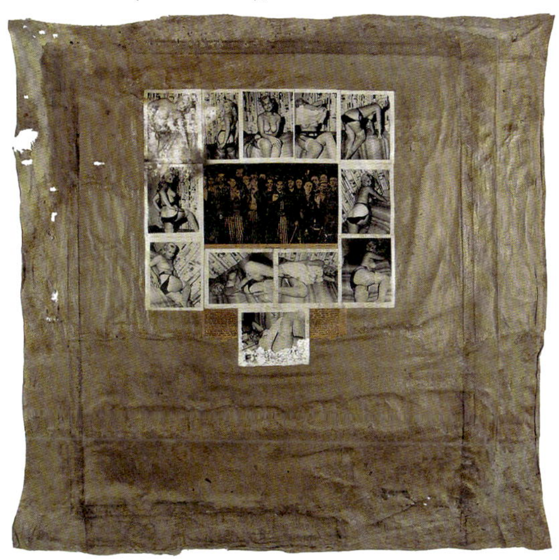

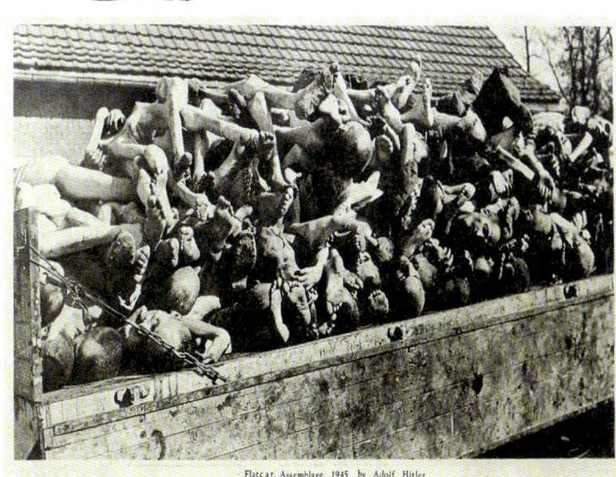

Boris Lurie, *Flatcar, Assemblage,* 1945 by Adolf Hitler, ca. / ca 1962

Unlike Hollywood, Lurie avoided the "beautiful illusion"; his provocative collages show a truth free of illusion in the manner of Adorno's dismissal of culture. As Adorno points out, not even those artists who focus in their work on the zero point of culture and on silence (John Cage, *Silence* 1939–61) escape the circle. Without knowledge of the history of critical engagement with the problem of the representability of the Holocaust, an artist like Boris Lurie cannot be properly understood.

Adorno's essay "Cultural Criticism and Society" (1949) contains a now famous passage criticizing representation and culture:

die das Ende der modernen Kunst kennzeichneten.[33] Dem Dadaismus warf er aber vor, dass er die „Kunst wegschaffen" wollte, „ohne diese zu verwirklichen". Der Surrealismus hingegen, so Debord, „wollte die Kunst verwirklichen, ohne sie wegzuschaffen".[34] Boris Lurie will die Kunst wegschaffen, aber auch verwirklichen, nämlich als NO!art. Er hat in seiner Kunst eine Möglichkeit aufgezeigt, wie der Weg zur Abschaffung der Repräsentation in der Kunst aussehen könnte, wie Kunst weggeschafft werden kann und trotzdem Kunst verwirklicht wird.
Was lehrt uns die Kunst von Boris Lurie? Die Abwehrmechanismen der Reaktionsbildung müssen durchbrochen werden, um durch NO!art zu einer neuen Kunst zu gelangen. Die Kunst von Lurie zeigt uns, wir müssen unser Konzept der Repräsentation verändern, um die Krise und das Verbot der Repräsentation à la Adorno zu verarbeiten. Das größte Tabu und Trauma der Moderne ist der Holocaust. Denn er widerspricht all dem, wofür die Moderne steht: Gleichheit, Gerechtigkeit, Freiheit, Universalität der Menschenrechte, die Würde des Menschen ist unantastbar, Du sollst nicht töten etc. Es ist für den modernen Geist – das cartesianische Subjekt der Aufklärung – vollkommen inakzeptabel, dass im hochzivilisierten Europa der Holocaust überhaupt möglich war. Wie kann man ein „unmögliches Ereignis" möglicherweise darstellen?
Die Antwort von Adorno war: Komplette Verweigerung und komplettes Verbot der Repräsentation. Der ikonoklastische Impuls der Moderne nach zwei Weltkriegen, die Zerstörung und Selbstzerstörung der Darstellungsmittel, verdankt sich der Reaktionsbildung auf Traumata. Eine zweite Antwort war die des Holocaustforschers Raul Hilberg, die Wende von der Abstraktion zum Gegenstand, von der Repräsentation zur Realität, eine Passion für das Reale. Diese zwei konträren Positionen gelten noch heute. Auf der einen Seite Claude Lanzmann, dessen 9½-stündiger Film *Shoa*, 1985,[35] in der Tradition Adornos keine Bilder des Holocaust zeigt, sondern nur die „talking heads" von Zeugen. Lanzmann folgt Adorno im Wissen um den Kollaps der Kant'schen Ästhetik angesichts einer Katastrophe. Eine positive Präsentation, „eine schöne Vorstellung", ist sozialen Katastrophen gegenüber nicht nur unangemessen, sondern sogar falsifizierend, lügenhaft. Fotografien von Leichenbergen, Verbrennungsöfen, Deportationszügen machen Auschwitz nicht verständlich, zeigen die Wahrheit über Auschwitz nicht. Auf der konträren Seite zu Lanzmann steht Georges Didi-Huberman. In seinem Essay „Images malgré tout"[36], 2001, zeigt er vier Fotografien, die 1944 von Gefangenen des Lagers Auschwitz-Birkenau aufgenommen wurden. Diese jüdischen Opfer wurden vom Sonderkommando gezwungen, sich am Genozid zu beteiligen. Gerhard Richter verwendete diese Fotos, auf die ihn ein *Spiegel*-Artikel aufmerksam gemacht hatte, als Inspiration für seine Auschwitz-Birkenau-Gemälde. Diese Publikation hat in Frankreich eine große Diskussion ausgelöst zur Frage, inwieweit der Fotografie als Medium der Wahrheit vertraut werden kann. Claude Lanzmann warf Georges Didi-Huberman vor, diese Fotos in einer christlichen Manier zu fetischisieren, und andere sprachen ein komplettes Bildverbot aus.[37]
Im Gegensatz zu Hollywood vermeidet Boris Lurie den „schönen Schein" und zeigt eine illusionslose, scheinlose Wahrheit mit seinen provokanten Collagen. Er folgt dabei der Absage an die Kultur im Sinne Adornos. Wie Adorno verdeutlicht, entkommen nicht einmal diejenigen Künstler, die sich für den Nullpunkt der Kultur stark machen und für das Schweigen (John Cage, *Silence*, 1939–61) plädieren, dem Zirkel. Ohne Kenntnis der Geschichte der kritischen Auseinan-

"Cultural criticism finds itself faced with the final stage of the dialectic of culture and barbarism. To write poetry after Auschwitz is barbaric. And this corrodes even the knowledge of why it has become impossible to write poetry today."[38]

He states his case more clearly still when he writes of culture:

"It abhors stench because it stinks – because, as Brecht put it in a magnificent line, its mansion is built of dogshit. Years after that line was written, Auschwitz demonstrated irrefutably that culture has failed."[39]

This is the horizon for Boris Lurie's work. The shit sculptures he and Sam Goodman made in 1963 are precisely the "mansions of dogshit" of which Adorno speaks. In this light, Lurie is the most radical adept of the Frankfurt School of critical theory. It is regrettable that an art magazine like *October,* that understands itself as left-wing and Marxist (as suggested even by its name), and whose critique of the culture industry owes a great deal to the critical method of the Frankfurt School, should have failed to acknowledge the position of Boris Lurie, voting instead for Pop Art, Andy Warhol, and Abstract Expressionism.

In the 1960s, Lurie's pairing of concentration camp and eroticism, of naked corpses and living nudes, under the umbrella of their shared degradation, was a shock and a scandal. But it was clearly the only artistic means of pointing to the shock and to the inhuman scandal of the Holocaust and to deal with the trauma. Interestingly, other artists had considered this method because it is clearly based on objective preconditions. The obscenity of inhuman sociality was portrayed by many protagonists of the neo-avant-gardes – on the one hand the Viennese Actionists and members of the NO!art movement like Erro, Yayoi Kusama, Jean-Jacques Lebel, Wolf Vostell, but also by painters from whom it was less expected. In 1967, Gerhard Richter discussed an exhibition with Konrad Lueg in which he planned to combine photographs from concentration camps with pornographic images. Although Richter eventually abandoned this plan, his project reveals an affinity with Lurie's ideas. In their day, most of Lurie's pin-up girls would have been considered pornographic; he began to use S&M pictures as early as 1962, but he almost never shows women being penetrated or handling a man's genitals without violence; from about 1969–75, the women are often highly sexualized, even aggressively so.

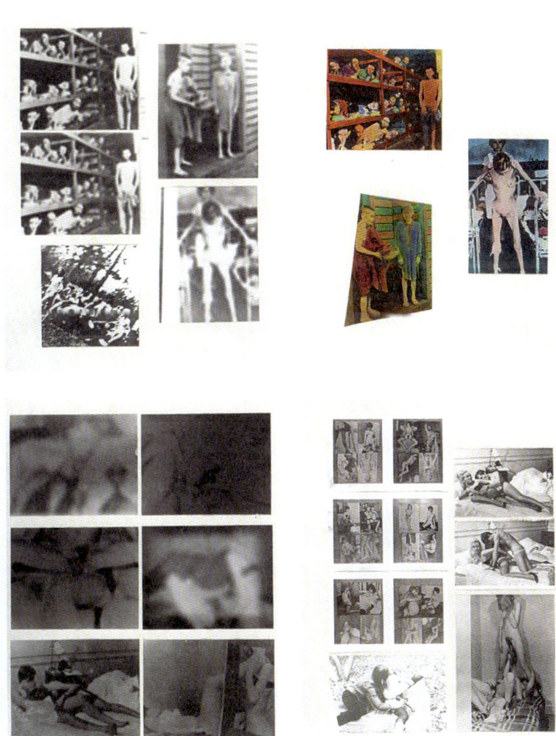

Gerhard Richter, *Atlas,* Fotos aus Büchern, Blatt 19–22, 1967

Writing about Richter, Benjamin Buchloh states that "the inclusion of these images [photographs of those murdered in the camps] within an artistic project was rather astonishing at the time, not to say scandalous. Richter exacerbated the scandal further, pushing it to a threshold of tolerability by juxtaposing these photographs with pornographic images on the opposite side of the panels. Worse yet, he eventually colored a set of these images with the garish colors of felt pen markers, at that moment one of the most innovative bureaucratic marking devices (comparable in many ways to the initially shocking deployment of ballpoint pens in drawings by Andy Warhol or Sigmar Polke thereafter),"[40] an approach described in the German version of Buchloh's essay as "extremely anti-aesthetic."

So how revolutionary and unusual is the art of Boris Lurie, who dared to do precisely what Richter decided not to do, and who did it much earlier? If Richter's

dersetzung mit der Darstellbarkeitsproblematik des Holocaust sind Künstler wie Boris Lurie nicht wirklich zu verstehen.
Dem Essay „Kulturkritik und Gesellschaft" von 1949 entstammt Theodor W. Adornos berühmt gewordenes Zitat, mit dem er Kritik an der Repräsentation und Kritik an der Kultur übt: „Kulturkritik findet sich der letzten Stufe der Dialektik von Kultur und Barbarei gegenüber: Nach Auschwitz ein Gedicht zu schreiben, ist barbarisch, und das frisst auch die Erkenntnis an, die ausspricht, warum es unmöglich ward, heute Gedichte zu schreiben."[38]
Noch einmal deutlicher wird Adorno, wenn er der Kultur attestiert: „Sie perhorresziert den Gestank, weil sie stinkt; weil ihr Palast [...] gebaut ist aus Hundsscheiße. Jahre später als jene Stelle geschrieben ward, hat Auschwitz das Mißlingen der Kultur unwiderleglich bewiesen."[39]
In diesem Horizont Adornos bewegt sich Boris Lurie. Seine und Sam Goodmans Shit-Skulpturen von 1963 sind genau diese „Paläste aus Hundsscheiße", von denen Adorno spricht. Lurie ist also der radikalste Adept der Frankfurter Schule der kritischen Theorie. Es ist bedauerlich, dass ein Kunstmagazin, das sich schon vom Titel her, nämlich *October*, als links und marxistisch versteht und in seiner Kritik der Kulturindustrie viel der kritischen Methode der Frankfurter Schule verdankt, die Position von Boris Lurie nicht zur Kenntnis genommen hat, aber stattdessen für Pop-Art bzw. Andy Warhol und den Abstrakten Expressionismus votierte.
Boris Lurie hat in den 1960er Jahren Holocaust-Bilder mit Pin-up-Girls collagiert. Die Paarung von KZ und Erotik, von nackten Toten und lebenden Nackten, unter dem Dach der gemeinsamen Degradierung war ein Schock und ein Skandal. Aber offensichtlich das einzige bildnerische Mittel, um auf den Schock und den unmenschlichen Skandal des Holocaust hinzuweisen und das Trauma zu bewältigen. Interessanterweise hatten auch andere Künstler diese Methode in Betracht gezogen, weil sie offensichtlich auf objektiven Voraussetzungen beruht. Die Obszönität des inhumanen Sozialen wurde von vielen Vertretern der Neo-Avantgarden dargestellt – zum einen von den Wiener Aktionisten und Mitgliedern der NO!art-Bewegung wie Erro, Yayoi Kusama, Jean-Jacques Lebel, Wolf Vostell, aber auch von Malern, von denen dies kaum erwartet wurde. 1967 plante Gerhard Richter eine Ausstellung mit Konrad Lueg, in der er Fotografien aus den Konzentrationslagern mit pornografischen Aufnahmen mischen wollte. Hier zeigt sich also eine gedankliche Nähe zu Lurie, dessen Pin-up-Girls in der damaligen Zeit als pornografisch galten. Nach klassischer Definition dienen pornografische Bilder dem finanziellen Profit und zeigen den sexuellen Akt, bei dem Frauen mitunter Gewalt zugefügt wird. Lurie zeigt nicht direkt den sexuellen Akt, sondern Akt-Fotografien. Festzuhalten bleibt, dass Gerhard Richter diese Ausstellungsidee verworfen hat.
Autoren wie Benjamin Buchloh schreiben über Richter, die „Verwendung fotografischer Abbildungen von Opfern der Konzentrationslager durch einen Künstler war zu dieser von extremer kollektiver Verdrängung geprägten Zeit noch sehr ungewöhnlich und rührt eigentlich schon an die Grenze eines künstlerischen Skandals. Aber Richter steigerte diesen Skandal noch, indem er den Abbildungen aus den Konzentrationslagern auf den gegenüberliegenden Panels eine Gruppe pornografischer Fotos gegenüberstellte. Was die Sache vielleicht noch unerträglicher machte, war die zusätzliche Provokation, einige dieser Fotos mit Filzstiften in leuchtenden Farben zu kolorieren, jenem Utensil eben, das damals

work with felt tip markers is praised as "extremely anti-aesthetic," why the lack of acknowledgment for Lurie's far more strongly anti-aesthetic NO!art? Who, if not Lurie, engaged for decades with the question of the representability of the Holocaust? And doing so using the same means that Richter later considered using, but then abandoned? No artist reflected more profoundly or more radially on the necessity and the impossibility of representing the Holocaust than Boris Lurie.

In this sense, Buchloh's description of Richter's work reads like a commentary on Boris Lurie's oeuvre,[41] as when he describes the "the question of a necessary, yet impossible mnemonic representation of the Holocaust" as "one of the central challenges" in his work:

"After extensive preparatory studies, now fully documented in the *Atlas* as well, Richter rejected this initial version of the project altogether. One could almost describe the editing process as a literal erasure, since Richter eventually decided to cancel these images. In a proposal which might have appeared comparatively bland at first sight, he replaced the photographs with three large-scale panels of enameled colored glass, black, red, and yellow, positioned vertically on top of each other to form a billboard-type structure twenty-one meters high. This tripartite glass wall now simulated a rigid vertical version of the German flag – the very flag that had been originally conceived at the moment of the foundation of the Weimar Republic, and that was then re-adopted when the Federal Republic of West Germany was declared in 1949 after the end of Nazi Fascism. The decision to chose erasure of traumatic images over representation was in fact already rather striking on this occasion, even though the traumatic images would have posed once again the question of a necessary, yet impossible mnemonic representation of the Holocaust. This would remain one of the central challenges to Richter's artistic projects over five decades, guiding his third attempt in the preparation of the Birkenau paintings as well: the question of whether and how iconic representations of Holocaust memory could possibly correspond to the social and the subjective desire for commemoration and representation. Or, by contrast, whether it was precisely one of the tasks of the artist to problematize any form of an iconically mediated reception of the unrepresentable, and therefore to delegitimize any of these attempts. Both criteria, the perpetual repetition of a necessary reflection on the necessity of reconstructing a mnemonic and the simultaneous insight that such an image cannot be produced, could possibly even be recognized as being among the foundational conditions of Richter's painterly production at large. Perhaps we could even advance our argument to suggest that this dialectic of an individual subjective desire for a mnemonic representation and the objective necessity to erase, if not prohibit, these images might be one of the structural conditions that have governed his work, evident from the very beginning after his arrival in West Germany in the most notorious example of *Tisch* (1962). And in spite of all inevitable formal differences and all intended changes in ambition and execution of the projects (i.e., photomontage for the Atlas in Düsseldorf in 1965 to 1967, the design for an architectural and monumental design for Berlin, and now, finally, the easel paintings of the Birkenau series), Richter's reflections and responses to these questions have remained constant. The artist returned to the question repeatedly over five decades, and his response remained equally constant in eras-

wohl noch als eines der avanciertesten Werkzeuge moderner Verwaltungsarbeit galt und damit (wie etwa auch Warhols oder Polkes Kugelschreiberzeichnungen) als extrem anti-ästhetisch angesehen werden musste."[40]

Wie revolutionär und ungewöhnlich ist dann die Kunst von Boris Lurie, der genau das gemacht und gewagt hat, und zwar schon viel früher, was Richter unterließ? Wenn die Arbeit mit Filzstiften als „extrem anti-ästhetisch" gelobt wird, warum wird dann nicht Luries noch viel stärkere anti-ästhetische NO!art zur Kenntnis genommen? Wer sonst, wenn nicht Lurie, hat sich mit der Frage der Darstellbarkeit des Holocaust jahrzehntelang auseinandergesetzt? Und zwar genau mit den Mitteln, die Richter später ergreifen wollte, aber dann schließlich doch wieder verwarf. Über die Notwendigkeit der Darstellung des Holocaust und dessen Unmöglichkeit gleichermaßen hat wohl kein Künstler tiefer und radikaler reflektiert als Boris Lurie.

In diesem Sinne liest sich Benjamin H. D. Buchlohs Beschreibung der Arbeit von Gerhard Richter stellenweise wie ein Kommentar zu Boris Luries Werk[41], z. B. wenn er die „(Un-)Möglichkeit der abbildenden Erinnerung des Holocaust als zentralste Frage innerhalb seines Schaffens" beschreibt:

„In der letzten Phase der Projektplanung jedoch verwarf der Künstler die ursprünglichen Entwürfe, die sich nun ebenfalls alle im *Atlas* dokumentiert finden. Man könnte fast sagen, diese Abbildungen wurden im Wortsinne gelöscht, als Richter sich schließlich entschied, den Auftrag anders, in Form eines 21 Meter hohen Glasreliefs auszuführen, bestehend aus sechs gleich großen, übereinander montierten monochromen Glasscheiben in den Farben Schwarz, Rot und Gold. Sie bilden ein starres monumentales Surrogat der deutschen Nationalflagge, jener Flagge, die erstmals von der Weimarer Republik offiziell eingeführt worden war und die 1949, vier Jahre nach dem Ende der Naziherrschaft, mit der Gründung der Bundesrepublik Deutschland wieder die Nationalflagge zumindest Westdeutschlands wurde. Obwohl die somit ‚gelöschten' Abbildungen die Notwendigkeit und (Un-)Möglichkeit der abbildenden Erinnerung des Holocaust selbst als vielleicht zentralste Frage innerhalb seines Schaffens über fünf Jahrzehnte aufgeworfen hätten, kam das Prinzip des vollständigen Löschens einer traumatischen fotografischen Darstellung auch bei Richters dritter großer künstlerischer Auseinandersetzung mit dem Thema zur Anwendung, dem Projekt der *Birkenau*-Bilder, begonnen 2014.

Mit der geschichtlich zentralen Fragestellung, ob und in welcher Weise das Abbilden des Holocaust dem individuellen und gesellschaftlichen Verlangen nach Darstellung und Erinnerung entsprechen könnte beziehungsweise ob er als Künstler diese Versuche einer ikonisch vermittelten Rezeption des Unvorstellbaren, des letztlich Unvermittelbaren, nicht gerade delegitimieren müsse, hat sich Richter über fünf Jahrzehnte hinweg wiederholt auseinandergesetzt. Trotz aller unvermeidlichen formalen Unterschiede und aller intendierten inhaltlichen Entwicklungen hinsichtlich Anspruch und Ausführung der Projekte (das heißt, der *Atlas*-Fotomontage aus Düsseldorf, des Entwurfs für das Wandbild in Berlin und zuletzt der *Birkenau*-Bilder) haben sich Richters Überlegungen und die von ihm gezogenen Schlüsse nicht verändert: weder dass der Künstler immer wieder zu dieser Frage der Darstellbarkeit des Holocaust (oder ihrer Unmöglichkeit) zurückgekehrt ist, noch dass er – obwohl immer wieder auf diese Fragen zurückkommend – auch immer wieder mit einer vergleichbaren Strategie der Auslöschung und Verneinung einer darstellenden Abbildung geantwor-

ing the possibility and negating the credibility of any iconic representation."[42]

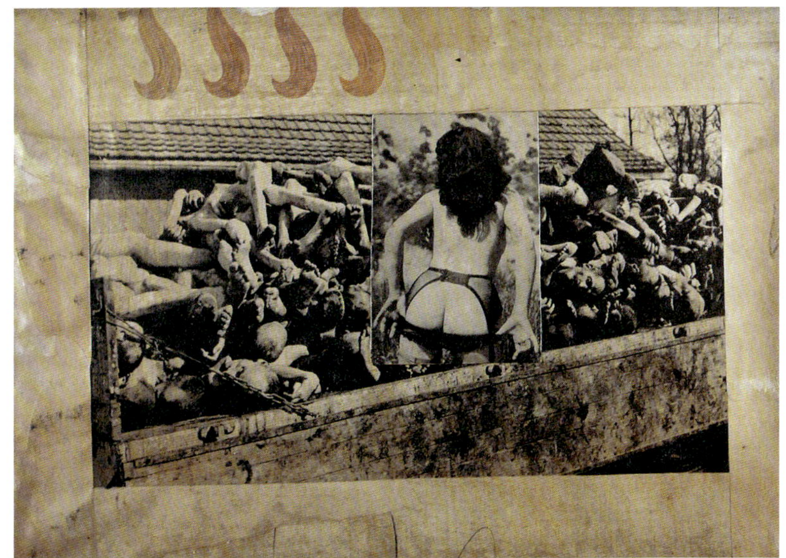

Boris Lurie, *Railroad to America (Railroad Collage)*, 1963

Against the backdrop of Lurie's works, Richter's withdrawal into abstraction appears as an act of resignation in the face of the problem of the representability of the Holocaust. Which is also why, as far as I am aware, Richter's work also contains no reference to shame. Lurie's pin-up collages like *Lolita* (1962) and *Railroad to America* (1963) appear shameless and that is how they must be. One painting with a photograph addresses this explicitly in its title: *Shame!* (1963). Who should be ashamed? The viewer? The artist? Everyone? In concentrated form, these collages show the shamelessness with which everything is presented side-by-side in the American mass-circulation press: a picture of a pin-up girl is printed next to a picture of a corpse. Lurie's art shows us that anyone who speaks about fascism must not remain silent on capitalism, where everything has its price but where nothing is of value. His works represent shame and disgust after the *conditio inhumana*. They are visual echoes of the Holocaust.

In the postwar years, art did not know how to work through the traumas of the Holocaust. One of the few artists who tried to do so before Wolf Vostell, Josef Beuys, Gerhard Richter, Christian Boltanski, and Anselm Kiefer was Boris Lurie. It is all the more tragic, then, that even today, his artistic achievements are still not really understood or acknowledged. Lurie was trying to work his way out of mere reaction formation. He realized that he had to free himself from art as a reaction formation in response to trauma. Hence NO!art – because reaction formation is a repetition of that which one actually abhors. Reaction formation is a mechanism that inverts the unacceptable impulse into its opposite, into recognition. Defense mechanisms of the ego are thus cultural processes that adapt themselves to the reality principle, acknowledging reality in a perverse and inverse manner. In order to expose this perversity, Lurie made "perverse" collages. The perversity of Auschwitz consists in the triumph of the pleasure principle over the reality principle. Culture as resistance to the real failed because, according to Jacques Lacan, the real is not accessible to the symbolic order, to culture. In our case, this means that the real concentration camp is not accessible to symbolic processing. Nonetheless, such a symbolic processing must be attempted; otherwise the camps will repeat themselves endlessly. If we do not try to retrieve the experience of the camps from reaction formation, it is certain that the experience will be repeated in real terms. This is what Boris Lurie's works teach us. In our society there exists knowledge that is repressed by society itself. Only in the mask of art-as-symptom can this social unconscious return. If the experience of atrocity came back directly as knowledge and certainty, we would not accept it as truth. Our society only accepts truth as a mask, and the mask is called symptom. If nothing else, this masked return has been achieved, as Lurie's art painfully shows.

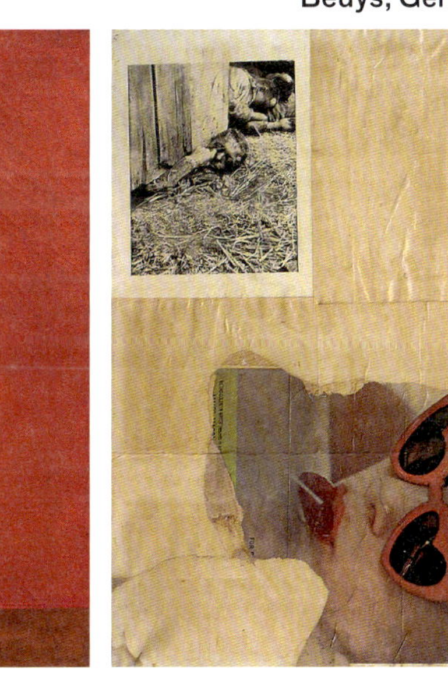

Boris Lurie, *Altered Photos: Shame!*, 1963

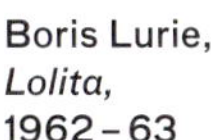

Boris Lurie, *Lolita*, 1962–63

tet hat. Beide Charakteristika, das stets wiederholte Nachdenken über die Notwendigkeit, der Erinnerung ein Bild zu verschaffen, und die gleichzeitige unmittelbare Erkenntnis, dass sich ein solches Bild nicht herstellen lässt, könnten somit als fundamentale Voraussetzungen der malerischen Arbeit Richters definiert werden. Vielleicht könnte man sogar behaupten, dass diese Dialektik von subjektivem Verlangen nach Darstellung und objektiver Notwendigkeit des Löschens eine der grundlegenden Bedingungen seines Œuvres im Allgemeinen ausmacht, die seiner Arbeit von Anfang an, seit dem Werk *Tisch* aus dem Jahr 1962, eingeschrieben war."[42]

Vor dem Hintergrund der Arbeiten von Lurie erscheint Richters Rückzug in die Abstraktion wie ein Resignieren am Problem der Darstellbarkeit des Holocaust. Deswegen fehlt in Richters Arbeit, soweit ich weiß, auch der Bezug zur Scham. Die Pin-up-Collagen wie *Lolita*, 1962, oder *Railroad to America*, 1963, von Lurie erscheinen schamlos und müssen schamlos sein. Ein Gemälde mit Foto von 1963 trägt die Scham nachdrücklich im Titel *Shame!*. Wer soll sich schämen? Der Betrachter? Der Künstler? Alle? Diese Collagen verdichten die Schamlosigkeit, mit der in der amerikanischen Massenpresse alles gleichwertig nebeneinander gezeigt wird: Das Bild eines Pin-up-Girls wird neben dem Bild einer Leiche abgedruckt. Luries Kunst zeigt uns, wer über Faschismus redet, darf über Kapitalismus nicht schweigen, wo alles seinen Preis, aber nichts einen Wert hat. Seine Werke zeigen die Scham und den Ekel nach der conditio inhumana. Sie sind visuelle Echos des Holocaust.

Die Kunst hat es in den Nachkriegsjahren nicht verstanden, die Traumata des Holocaust durchzuarbeiten. Einer der wenigen Künstler, der das vor Wolf Vostell, Josef Beuys, Gerhard Richter, Christian Boltanski und Anselm Kiefer versuchte, ist Boris Lurie. Es ist umso tragischer, dass seine künstlerische Leistung bis heute nicht wirklich verstanden oder anerkannt wird. Lurie versuchte, sich aus der bloßen Reaktionsbildung herauszuarbeiten. Lurie hatte erkannt, dass er sich aus der Kunst als traumatischer Reaktionsbildung befreien musste. Deswegen: NO!art, denn Reaktionsbildung ist die Wiederholung dessen, was man eigentlich verabscheut. Reaktionsbildung ist ein Mechanismus, der den nicht zu akzeptierenden Impuls in sein Gegenteil verkehrt, in die Anerkennung. Abwehrmechanismen des Ich sind also kulturelle Prozesse, die sich gewissermaßen dem Realitätsprinzip anpassen, die Realität auf perverse bzw. inverse Weise anerkennen. Um diese Perversität aufzudecken, machte Lurie „perverse" Collagen. Die Perversität von Auschwitz besteht gerade im Sieg des Lustprinzips über das Realitätsprinzip. Kultur als Widerstand des Realen hat versagt, weil das Reale gemäß Jacques Lacan dem Symbolischen, der Kultur, gar nicht zugänglich ist. Übertragen heißt das: Das reale KZ ist der symbolischen Verarbeitung nicht zugänglich. Dennoch gilt es aber, diese symbolische Verarbeitung zu versuchen, ansonsten wird sich das Lager endlos wiederholen. Wenn wir nicht versuchen, diese Lagererfahrung aus der Reaktionsbildung herauszuholen, ist garantiert, dass sich die Erfahrung real wiederholen wird. Diese Lehre können wir aus den Arbeiten Boris Luries ziehen. Es gibt in unserer Gesellschaft ein Wissen, das von der Gesellschaft selbst unterdrückt wird. Nur in der Maskierung der Kunst als Symptom kann dieses soziale Unbewusste zurückkehren. Wenn die Erfahrung des Schrecklichen direkt als Wissen und Wahrheit zurückkäme, würden wir die Erfahrung als Wahrheit nicht akzeptieren. Unsere Gesellschaft akzeptiert die Wahrheit nur als Maske, und die Maske heißt Symptom. Immerhin ist

The systematic annihilation of human beings in gas chambers and crematoria between 1942 and 1945 constituted the fundamental trauma for the reaction formations of the European neo-avant-gardes – and for Boris Lurie. The inconceivability and unrepresentability of the camps described by theorists like Adorno and Lanzmann and in the statements of witnesses like Lewenthal and Landowski is a traumatic reaction. Because trauma is the reaction of a subject to an event about which that subject is able to neither speak nor hear. Culture not having been capable of preventing the Holocaust, the second traumatic reaction was to mistrust culture and to call for an end to culture as a culture of representation. The final reaction formation was the destruction of the means of representation by the artists themselves as prisoners of the trauma. With his NO!art movement, Lurie stands in this tradition of the European neo-avant-garde. As the title of the program says: No art! No classical art of representation! No positive presentation! Techniques of collage from Pablo Picasso to Pop Art, screen-printing techniques from Robert Rauschenberg to Andy Warhol, material art from Alberto Burri to Joseph Beuys, the entire poor vocabulary of the neo-avant-gardes – all this was accumulated by Lurie, using relics as markers of traumatic events to make possible a negative presentation of these "unrepresentable" events. Particularly important in this context is Lurie's deliberate handling of the differences between trauma and the representation of trauma. Lurie shows that traumas point to the limits of representation. To paraphrase Lacan, trauma is a settlement with failure. As a consequence, Lurie chooses negativity, which admits that what is to be shown cannot be shown. Lurie's method of negative presentation is a process of deciphering traces, of ellipses, of omissions, of lack and failure.

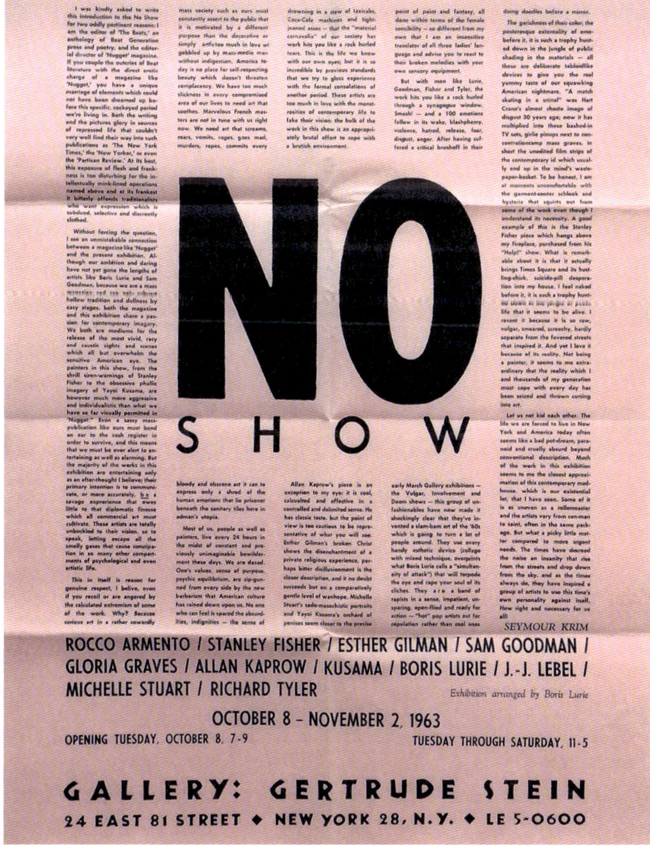

Gallery Gertrude Stein: *NO show poster*, 1963

The best comment on Boris Lurie's artistic approach is given by Georg Wilhelm Friedrich Hegel in his *Phenomenology of Mind* in 1807: "[Spirit] wins its truth only when, in utter dismemberment, it finds itself."[43] In *Railroad to America* (1963) and similar works, Lurie shows us the conflict between Eros and Thanatos, sensual desire and murderous desire, pleasure principle and reality principle. The notion of murderous desire (*Mordlust*) unites both sides of the drive in a single concept. The Spirit possesses power not as the positive that ignores the negative. That is the view embodied by the art of Gerhard Richter, whose overpaintings try to turn the negative into a positive in order to be able to overlook the negative. For Hegel also writes: "[Spirit] is this power, not as something positive, which closes its eyes to the negative, as when we say of something that it is nothing or is false, and then, having done with it, turn away and pass on to something else; on the contrary, Spirit is this power only by looking the negative in the face, and tarrying with it."[44] This is Lurie's position: tarrying with the negative, tarrying in the face of the camps, in the face of the Holocaust. There is no possibility to escape. Negative presentation, negative art, negative exhibition are strategies for representing the unrepresentable, for representing Auschwitz. Only when the subject faces up to the trauma can it free itself from the prison of trauma and from the bondage of both fascism and capitalism.

es gelungen, dass diese maskierte Wiederkehr gelingt, wie Luries Kunst schmerzlich zeigt.
Die systematische Vernichtung von Menschen in Gaskammern und Krematorien zwischen 1942 und 1945 bildete das grundlegende Trauma für die Reaktionsbildungen der europäischen Neo-Avantgarden und auch für Boris Lurie. Die von Theoretikern wie Adorno, Lanzmann und den Aussagen von Zeugen wie Lewenthal und Landowski beschriebene Unvorstellbarkeit und Undarstellbarkeit des Lagers ist eine traumatische Reaktion. Denn Trauma ist die Reaktion auf ein Ereignis, worüber das Subjekt weder selbst sprechen kann noch in der Lage ist, darüber zu hören. Nachdem die Kultur nicht imstande war, den Holocaust zu verhindern, war die zweite traumatische Reaktion, der Kultur zu misstrauen und ihr Ende als Repräsentationskultur zu fordern. Die letzte Reaktionsbildung war schließlich die Zerstörung der Darstellungsmittel durch die Künstler selbst als Gefangene des Traumas. Lurie steht mit seiner NO!art-Bewegung in dieser Tradition der europäischen Neo-Avantgarde. Wie der Titel des Programms schon sagt: Keine Kunst! Keine klassische Kunst der Repräsentation! Keine positive Präsentation! Die Collage-Techniken von Pablo Picasso bis Pop-Art, die Siebdruck-Verfahren von Robert Rauschenberg bis Andy Warhol, die Materialien von Alberto Burri bis Joseph Beuys, das gesamte arme Vokabular der Neo-Avantgarden hat Lurie akkumuliert, um durch Relikte als Markierungen von traumatischen Ereignissen eine negative Präsentation dieser „unrepräsentierbaren" Ereignisse zu ermöglichen. Besonders wichtig ist dabei Luries bewusste Handhabung der Differenzen zwischen Trauma und Repräsentation von Trauma. Lurie zeigt, Traumata verweisen auf die Grenzen von Repräsentation. Trauma ist mit Jacques Lacan eine Verabredung mit der Verfehlung. Daher wählt Lurie die Negativität, die zugibt, dass das, was gezeigt werden soll, nicht gezeigt werden kann. Die Lurie'sche Methode der negativen Präsentation ist ein Prozess der Entzifferung der Spuren, der Ellipsen, der Unter- und Auslassungen, des Fehlenden und Verfehlten.
Die beste Antwort auf die Werktechnik von Boris Lurie bietet Georg Wilhelm Friedrich Hegel in seiner *Phänomenologie des Geistes,* 1807: „Er [der Geist] gewinnt seine Wahrheit nur, indem er in der absoluten Zerrissenheit sich selbst findet."[43] Boris Lurie zeigt uns in *Railroad to America*, 1963, und ähnlichen Werken die Zerrissenheit zwischen Eros und Tanatos, Sinneslust und Mordlust, Lustprinzip und Realitätsprinzip. In dem Wort *Mordlust* zeigen sich beide Seiten eines Triebes vereint. Der Geist hat seine Macht nicht als das Positive, welches vom Negativen absieht. Diese Perspektive verkörpert die Kunst Gerhard Richters. Richters Übermalungen versuchen, das Negative ins Positive zu wenden, um über das Negative hinwegsehen zu können. Denn Hegel schreibt weiter: „Diese Macht ist er [der Geist] nicht als das Positive, welches von dem Negativen wegsieht, wie wenn wir von etwas sagen, dies ist nichts oder falsch, und nun, damit fertig, davon weg zu irgend etwas anderem übergehen; sondern er ist diese Macht nur, indem er dem Negativen ins Angesicht schaut, bei ihm verweilt."[44] – Das ist die Position von Lurie: verweilen im Negativen, verweilen im Angesicht des Lagers, des Holocaust. Er gibt uns keine Möglichkeit, zu entrinnen. Negative Präsentation, negative Kunst, negative Ausstellung sind Strategien, um das Nicht-Repräsentierbare wie Auschwitz darzustellen. Nur wenn sich das Subjekt dem Trauma stellt, kann es sich vom Gefängnis des Traumas und von der Knechtschaft des Faschismus wie des Kapitalismus befreien.

The fact that tarrying with the negative generates shame in the viewer is something we learn not only from Lurie, but also from Franz Kafka. His unfinished novel *The Trial* (1914/15) ends with the murder of the protagonist Josef K. and the seemingly enigmatic remark: “It was as if the shame of it would outlive him.”[45] Kafka’s novel anticipates what was to become the reality of the twentieth century: millions of innocents murdered by state terror with no trial and with no defense. People were deported to camps and killed with no legal process. The shame of this lives on in the twenty-first century. It has outlived those who were murdered. Boris Lurie’s pictures are shameless in order – as a negative presence, via a negative dialectic – to give an infamous and inhuman humankind back the shame it has lost. Boris Lurie’s NO!art succeeds in making the central violations and upheavals of the twentieth century visually experienceable.

1 Leonardo Da Vinci, *Notebooks,* selected by Irma A. Richter (New York, 2008), p. 119.
2 Immanuel Kant, “§41. On Empirical Interest in the Beautiful,” “§42. On Intellectual Interest in the Beautiful,” in: *Critique of the Power of Judgement* [1790] trans. Werner S. Pluhar (Indianapolis/Cambridge 1987), pp. 163–170.
3 This distinction is also reflected in the names of our art academies: we have the “Akademie der Schönen Künste” (literally: Academy of Beautiful Arts), but no “Academy of Beautiful Nature.”
4 Immanuel Kant, *Critique of the Power of Judgement,* p. 179.
5 Ibid., p. 180.
6 Ibid., p. 180.
7 Ibid., p. 180.
8 Ibid., p. 180.
9 Karl Rosenkranz, *Aesthetics of Ugliness* [1853] (London 2015), p. 25.
10 Ibid., p. 33.
11 See Georg Wilhelm Friedrich Hegel, *Phenomenology of Spirit* [1807], (Oxford 1977), p. 19.
12 The title of Baudelaire’s collection of poems was coined by the critic Hippolyte Babou.
13 The aesthetic revolution of modernism around 1900 was prepared by the industrial revolution. Whereas previously the arts had been devoted to beauty and the sublime – think of Romanticism – their extension to include the evil and the ugly laid the foundations for modernism. Since the mid-nineteenth century, then, beautiful/fine arts in the original sense no longer exist. Since then, it is the no-longer-fine/beautiful arts that dominate, even though the museums are still called *Palais des Beaux Arts,* as in Brussels. Beauty now became something for fashion, no longer for art. Which is why, in the twentieth century, art schools were no longer called Academies of Fine Art but Universities of Art.
14 See George Grosz and John Heartfield with the demonstration placard “Art is dead. Long live Tatlin’s new machine art” at the Dada exhibition in June 1920.
15 See Arthur C. Danto, *The Transfiguration of the Commonplace: A Philosophy of Art* (Cambridge, Mass. 1981).
16 Jean-Paul Sartre’s *Nausea* was published in 1938.
17 The personal fate of scriptwriter Marguerite Duras during the German occupation in Paris would need a lengthy analysis, but it supports my interpretation.
18 Clement Greenberg, “The Crisis of the Easel Picture,” in: *Partisan Review*, 15 (1948), pp. 481–485.
19 Mangelos also called his art “no art” and presented his manifesto *Shid Theory* (the title being an allusion to “shit”) in Zagreb in 1978.
20 Michel Foucault, *The Order of Things. An Archeology of the Human Sciences* [1966] (London 2002), p. 422.
21 The video is held in the archive of ZKM | Zentrum für Kunst und Medien, Karlsruhe.
22 Yves Klein, “Truth Becomes Reality,” in: *Overcoming the Problematics of Art. The Writings of Yves Klein*, trans. Klaus Ottman (Putnam, CT. 2007), p. 186.
23 Theodor W Adorno, *Negative Dialectics*, trans. E. B. Ashton, (New York 1973), p. 366f.
24 Raul Hilberg, *The Politics of Memory. The Journey of a Holocaust Historian* (Chicago 1996), pp. 130–131.
25 Until about 1962, Lurie and his fellow artists were known as the March Group; they started to be called the NO!artists in about 1963/64.
26 Gertrude Stein in: *Boris Lurie 1924–2008. Life After Death* (New York 2017), p. 122.
27 See Herbert Marcuse’s essay “The Affirmative Character of Culture” (1937).
28 The manuscript by Zelman (also referred to in the literature as Zalman or Salmen) Lewenthal, written in Yiddish and buried in the courtyard of the crematorium, was discovered in October 1962. See “Des voix sous la cendre, Manuscrits des Sonderkommandos d’Auschwitz-Birkenau” (Voices under the ashes. Manuscripts by the Sonderkommando at Auschwitz-Birkenau), *Revue d’histoire de la Shoah*, 171/2001.
29 Quoted from Hermann Langbein, *People in Auschwitz* [1972] (Chapel Hill 2000), p. 192.
30 Giorgio Agamben, “What Is a Camp?” in *Means Without End: Notes on Politics* [1996], (Minneapolis 2000), p. 36.
31 Quoted from Hermann Langbein, *People in Auschwitz*, p. 202.
32 See Giorgio Agamben, “The Camp as the ‘Nomos’ of the Modern” in: *Homo Sacer. Sovereign Power and Bare Life* [1995] (Stanford 1998), pp. 166–180. The concept of the camp is extended here to include that of the Gulag. See Angela Rohr’s autobiographical Gulag novel *Lager* (2015).
33 See Guy Debord, *Society of the Spectacle* [1967], trans. Donald Nicholson-Smith (London 1994), p. 191.
34 Ibid.
35 In the French version, the film ran for 613 minutes; it was edited for the American, British and Swedish releases.
36 Georges Didi-Huberman, “Images malgré tout” (Images in Spite of All), in: Clément Chéroux (ed.), *Mémoire des Camps. Photographies des camps de concentration et d’extermination nazis* (1933–1999) (Paris 2001), pp. 219–241.
37 See Gérard Wajcman, “De la croyance photographique,” in: *Les Temps Modernes*, no. 613 (2001), pp. 47–83; and Élisabeth Pagnoux, “Reporter photographe à Auschwitz,” in: ibid., pp. 84–108.
38 Theodor W. Adorno, “Cultural Criticism and Society” [1951], in: *Prisms* (Cambridge Mass. 1983), pp. 17–34: 34.
39 Theodor W. Adorno, *Negative Dialectics*, pp. 366–367.
40 Benjamin H. D. Buchloh, *Gerhard Richters „Birkenau Bilder“* (Cologne 2016), p. 6.
41 In a catalogue essay for the 1988 MoMA Warhol retrospective, which also appears in the *October Files* Warhol edition, Buchloh refers to a Lurie show in 1960 as giving a detailed account of the images that Warhol subsequently chose as the key figures of his iconography. See Benjamin Buchloh, “Andy Warhol’s One-Dimensional Art: 1956–1966”, in: *October Files 2: Andy Warhol* (Cambridge 2001), pp. 1–46, here 25.
42 Ibid., pp. 7–8.
43 Georg Wilhelm Friedrich Hegel, *Phenomenology of Spirit* [1807], (Oxford 1977), p. 19.
44 Ibid.
45 Franz Kafka, *The Trial* (1925). “Es war, als sollte die Scham ihn überleben.”

Dass beim Verweilen im Negativen auch notwendigerweise Scham beim Betrachter erzeugt wird, lehrt uns nicht nur Lurie, sondern auch Franz Kafka. Sein 1914/15 entstandenes Romanfragment *Der Prozess* endet mit der Ermordung des Protagonisten Josef K. durch zwei Messerstiche und die scheinbar rätselhafte Bemerkung: „[E]s war, als sollte die Scham ihn überleben."[45] Kafkas Roman nimmt vorweg, was für das 20. Jahrhundert Realität wurde: Millionenfache Ermordungen von Unschuldigen durch Staatsterror ohne Verhandlung und ohne Verteidigung. Menschen wurden in Lager deportiert, ermordet ohne Prozess, ohne Verhandlung. Die Scham darüber lebt im 21. Jahrhundert weiter. Sie überlebt die Ermordeten. Boris Luries Bilder sind schamlos, um als negative Präsenz, als negative Dialektik den infamen und inhumanen Menschen die Scham zurückzugeben, die sie verloren haben. Boris Luries NO!art gelingt es, die zentralen Verfehlungen und Verwerfungen des 20. Jahrhunderts visuell erfahrbar zu machen.

1 Lionardo da Vinci: *Das Buch von der Malerei. Nach dem Codex Vaticanus 1270*, übers. von Heinrich Ludwig, Bd. 1: *Text und Übersetzung des 1.–4. Theiles*, Wien 1882.
2 Immanuel Kant: „§ 41. Von dem empirischen Interesse am Schönen", „§ 42. Von dem intellektuellen Interesse am Schönen", in: ders., *Kritik der Urteilskraft* [1790], Leipzig: Meiner, 1922, S. 147–155.
3 Eine Trennung, die sich auch in der Benennung unserer Kunstakademien abzeichnet. Wir haben Akademien der Schönen Künste. Hingegen haben wir keine Akademien der schönen Natur.
4 Kant: *Kritik der Urteilskraft*, vgl. Anm. 2, S. 165.
5 Ebd., S. 165–166.
6 Ebd., S. 166.
7 Ebd., S. 166.
8 Ebd., S. 166.
9 Karl Rosenkranz: *Ästhetik des Häßlichen* [1853], Stuttgart: Reclam, 2007, S. 5.
10 Ebd., S. 15.
11 Vgl. Georg Wilhelm Friedrich Hegel: *Phänomenologie des Geistes* [1807], Frankfurt am Main: Suhrkamp, 1989, S. 36.
12 Der Titel von Baudelaires Gedichtsammlung wurde von dem Kritiker Hippolyte Babou geprägt.
13 Die ästhetische Revolution der Moderne um 1900 wurde durch die industrielle Revolution vorbereitet. Nachdem zuvor die Künste nur dem Schönen und Sublimen gewidmet waren – man denke an die Romantik –, wurde nun mit der Erweiterung der Künste um das Böse und Hässliche das Fundament der Moderne gelegt. Seit Mitte des 19. Jahrhunderts gibt es die schönen Künste im eigentlichen Sinne also nicht mehr. Es herrschen seitdem die nicht mehr schönen Künste, obwohl sich die Museen noch *Palais des Beaux Arts* nennen, z. B. in Brüssel. Schönheit wurde stattdessen etwas für die Mode, nicht mehr für die Kunst. Deswegen heißen die Kunstschulen im 20. Jahrhundert auch nicht mehr Akademien der schönen Künste, sondern Hochschulen für Gestaltung.
14 Siehe George Grosz und John Heartfield mit dem Demonstrationsschild „Die Kunst ist tot. Es lebe die neue Maschinenkunst Tatlins" anlässlich der Dada-Ausstellung im Juni 1920.
15 Vgl. hierzu Arthur C. Danto: *Die Verklärung des Gewöhnlichen. Eine Philosophie der Kunst* [1981], Frankfurt am Main: Suhrkamp, 1984.
16 Jean-Paul Sartres *La nausée* [*Der Ekel*] erschien 1938.
17 Das persönliche Schicksal der Drehbuchautorin Marguerite Duras zur Zeit der deutschen Okkupation von Paris bedürfte einer längeren Analyse, unterstriche aber meine Interpretation.
18 Clement Greenberg: „The Crisis of the Easel Picture", in: *Partisan Review*, 15 (1948), 4, S. 481–485.
19 Mangelos bezeichnete seine Kunst ebenfalls als „no art" und präsentierte sein Manifest *Shid Theory* (eine Anspielung auf „Shit") 1978 in Zagreb.
20 Michel Foucault: *Die Ordnung der Dinge. Eine Archäologie der Humanwissenschaften* [1966], Frankfurt am Main: Suhrkamp, 1974, S. 462.
21 Das Video befindet sich im Archiv des ZKM | Zentrum für Kunst und Medien Karlsruhe.
22 Yves Klein: „Truth Becomes Reality", in: *Overcoming the Problematics of Art. The Writings of Yves Klein*, trans. Klaus Ottman, Putnam, CT: Spring Publications, 2007, S. 186.
23 Theodor W. Adorno: „Negative Dialektik" [1966], in: ders., *Negative Dialektik. Jargon der Eigentlichkeit.* Gesammelte Schriften, Bd. 6, hrsg. von Rolf Tiedemann, Frankfurt am Main: Suhrkamp, 1997, S. 359.
24 Raul Hilberg: *Unerbetene Erinnerung. Der Weg eines Holocaust-Forschers*, Frankfurt am Main: Fischer, 1994, S. 113.
25 Boris Lurie und gleichgesinnte Künstler wurden zunächst als March Group bekannt, ehe sie ab 1962 als NO!artists bezeichnet wurden.
26 Gertrude Stein in: *Boris Lurie 1924–2008. Life After Death*, New York City: Westwood Gallery, 2017, S. 122.
27 Siehe den Essay von Herbert Marcuse: „Über den affirmativen Charakter der Kultur" (1937).
28 Das in Jiddisch verfasste und im Hof des Krematoriums vergrabene Manuskript von Zelman (in der Literatur auch Zalman oder Salmen) Lewenthal wurde im Oktober 1962 entdeckt. Siehe *Des voix sous la cendre, Manuscrits des Sonderkommandos d'Auschwitz-Birkenau* (Stimmen aus der Asche, Manuskripte der Sonderkommandos von Auschwitz-Birkenau), *Revue d'histoire de la Shoah*, 171/2001.
29 Zitiert nach Hermann Langbein: *Menschen in Auschwitz*, Wien: Europa-Verlag, 1972, S. 222.
30 Giorgio Agamben: „Was ist ein Lager?", in: ders., *Mittel ohne Zweck. Noten zur Politik* [1996], Freiburg, Berlin: Diaphanes, 2001, S. 43.
31 Zitiert nach Langbein 1972, vgl. Anm. 29, S. 234.
32 Vgl. Giorgio Agamben: „Das Lager als biopolitisches Paradigma der Moderne", in: ders., *Homo sacer. Die souveräne Macht und das nackte Leben* [1995], Frankfurt am Main: Suhrkamp, 2002, S. 127–198.
In Erweiterung des Lagerbegriffs ist hier auch der Gulag zu nennen. Vgl. Angela Rohrs autobiografischen Gulag-Roman *Lager*, Berlin: Aufbau, 2015.
33 Vgl. Guy Debord: *Die Gesellschaft des Spektakels*, Berlin: Edition Tiamat, 1996, S. 164.
34 Ebd., S. 164–165.
35 In der französischen Fassung hat der Film die Länge von 613 Minuten, für die amerikanische, britische und schwedische Fassung wurde er gekürzt.
36 Georges Didi-Huberman: „Images malgré tout" (Bilder trotz allem / Images in Spite of All), in: Clément Chéroux (Hg.), *Mémoire des Camps. Photographies des camps de concentration et d'extermination nazis* (1933–1999), Paris: Marval, 2001, S. 219–241.

37 Siehe Gérard Wajcman: „De la croyance photographique", in: *Les Temps Modernes*, no. 613 (2001), S. 47–83; Élisabeth Pagnoux: „Reporter photographe à Auschwitz", in: ebd., S. 84–108.

38 Theodor W. Adorno: „Kulturkritik und Gesellschaft" [1951], in: ders., *Prismen. Kulturkritik und Gesellschaft*, Frankfurt am Main: Suhrkamp 1976, S. 7–31, hier S. 31.

39 Theodor W. Adorno: „Negative Dialektik" [1966], in: ders., *Negative Dialektik*, vgl. Anm. 23, S. 359.

40 Benjamin H. D. Buchloh: *Gerhard Richters „Birkenau Bilder"*, Köln: Walther König, 2016, S. 6.

41 Buchloh beschreibt in seinem Essay über Warhol, den er 1988 anlässlich einer Warhol-Retrospektive im MoMA verfasste und der erneut in den *October Files* 2001 publiziert wurde, eine Lurie-Show von 1960 als detaillierte Darstellung von Bildern, die später zu Schlüsselfiguren in Warhols Ikonografie werden sollten. Siehe Benjamin Buchloh „Andy Warhol's One-Dimensional Art. 1956–1966", in: *October Files 2: Andy Warhol*, Cambridge, 2001, S. 1–46, hier S. 25.

42 Buchloh 2016, vgl. Anm. 40, S. 7–8.

43 Hegel: *Phänomenologie des Geistes*, vgl. Anm. 11, S. 36.

44 Ebd., S. 36.

45 Franz Kafka: *Der Prozess* [1925], Frankfurt am Main: Fischer, 1994, S. 241.

Around Lurie

Thomas Heyden

„Ich würde gern zugeben, dass man so gut wie ich gesagt habe, dass man nach Auschwitz *kein* Gedicht mehr schreiben kann – womit ich das Hohle der auferstandenen Kultur habe bezeichnen wollen –, andererseits *doch* Gedichte schreiben *muss,* im Sinne des Satzes von Hegel aus der ‚Ästhetik', dass es solange, wie es ein Bewusstsein von Leiden unter den Menschen gibt, eben auch Kunst als die objektive Gestalt dieses Bewusstseins geben müsse."[1]

Theodor W. Adorno, *Metaphysik. Begriffe und Probleme,* 1965

Around Picasso hieß 1980 eine Ausstellung im Museum of Modern Art in New York. Diesen Titel im Zusammenhang mit Boris Lurie anklingen zu lassen, soll nicht als anmaßend verstanden werden. Vielmehr geht es um die Prägnanz der Formulierung, die sowohl vom Umkreis eines Künstlers spricht als auch von dessen Ausstrahlung auf bzw. Beeinflussung durch andere. Im Falle von Boris Lurie liegt es besonders nahe, den Künstler nicht als isoliertes Phänomen zu behandeln. Allein seine Zugehörigkeit zur March Group (zusammen mit Sam Goodman und Stanley Fisher) verbietet eine solche Sicht.[2] Und die NO!art-Bewegung, als deren Kristallisationspunkt und Motor die March Group fungierte, weitet den Kreis um Lurie, Goodman und Fisher um weitere Namen. Diese umfassendere Perspektive kennzeichnete beispielsweise die erste große historische Bestandsaufnahme der NO!art in Deutschland, welche die Neue Gesellschaft für Bildende Kunst (NGBK) 1995 in Berlin leistete. Es dauerte mehr als zwei Jahrzehnte, bis Boris Lurie wieder in einer großen Ausstellung in Berlin gezeigt wurde. Die monografische Ausstellung im Jüdischen Museum Berlin (2016) konzentrierte sich zwar ausschließlich auf Lurie, doch kam der Katalogbeitrag von Mirjam Wenzel, Direktorin des Jüdischen Museums Frankfurt, auch auf Wolf Vostell und Gerhard Richter zu sprechen.[3]

Diesen Ansatz zu einer kunsthistorischen Kontextualisierung greift die Ausstellung im Neuen Museum Nürnberg auf und setzt ihn fort. Ohne die Bedeutung von Boris Luries Biografie für sein Werk schmälern zu wollen, legt sie den Akzent auf die Kunst von Boris Lurie, die in ein Netz von Bezügen und Fragestellungen gestellt wird. *Around Lurie* bedeutet in diesem Zusammenhang auch einen Hinweis auf die räumliche Struktur der Ausstellung: Auf den vier, vielfach gebrochenen, frei stehenden Wänden in der Mitte entfaltet sich Boris Luries Kunst, gegliedert in verschiedene Kapitel, die allerdings keiner Chronologie folgen. Rundherum, an und vor den Außenwänden des quadratischen Ausstellungssaals, also *around Lurie*, werden 20 Werke anderer Künstler präsentiert. Sie werfen Schlaglichter auf die Kunst von Boris Lurie, beleuchten unterschiedliche Aspekte und unterstreichen die Tatsache, dass Lurie nicht allein stand in seinem lebenslangen Kampf gegen eine selbstverliebte und vom Kapital gehätschelte Kunst, gegen Imperialismus und Militarismus und gegen das Verschweigen des beispiellosen Verbrechens des Holocausts. Dabei gliedert sich der Kontext in drei konzentrische gedankliche Kreise: die engsten Weggefährten der March Group (Sam Goodman, Stanley Fisher), die NO!art-Mitstreiter (stellvertretend für viele andere Jean-Jacques Lebel) bzw. Freunde (Wolf Vostell) und schließlich als äußerster Kreis jene Künstler, die in bestimmten Aspekten aufschlussreiche Vergleiche ermöglichen (H. P. Alvermann, Piero Manzoni, Gustav Metzger und Gerhard Richter). Auch wenn Boris Lurie im Folgenden nicht im Mittelpunkt steht,

Around Lurie

Thomas Heyden

Around Picasso was the title of an exhibition held in 1980 at the Museum of Modern Art in New York City – hopefully it will not be considered presumptuous to adapt this phrase for an essay on Boris Lurie. The title was in fact chosen because it concisely describes not only an artist's surroundings, but also his influence on or by others. In the case of Boris Lurie, it seems particularly worthwhile not to view him in isolation. The very fact that he was a founding member of the March Group (along with Sam Goodman and Stanley Fisher) should discourage us from taking a narrow view.[2] And if we consider how the March Group became the focal point and driving force of the NO!art movement, the circle around Lurie, Goodman, and Fisher immediately expands to include other names. One example of a wider historical perspective was the first large-scale presentation of NO!art in Germany, which was organized by the Neue Gesellschaft für Bildende Kunst (NGBK) in Berlin in 1995. More than 20 years then went by before Boris Lurie's work was included in another major exhibition in Berlin, this time at the Jewish Museum (2016). While the solo show was devoted to Boris Lurie, Mirjam Wenzel, Director of the Jewish Museum Frankfurt, also discussed the work of Wolf Vostell and Gerhard Richter in her essay in the accompanying catalogue.[3]

"I would readily concede that, just as I said that after Auschwitz one *could not* write poems – by which I meant to point to the hollowness of the resurrected culture of that time – it could equally well be said, on the other hand, that one *must* write poems, in keeping with Hegel's statement in his *Aesthetics* that as long as there is an awareness of suffering among human beings, there must also be art as the objective form of that awareness."[1]

Theodor W. Adorno, *Metaphysics: Concept and Problems* (1965)

The Boris Lurie exhibition at Neues Museum in Nuremberg takes up and extends this curatorial approach based on art-historical contextualization. While it does not in any way wish to play down the significance of Lurie's biography for his work, this exhibition places the main emphasis on his art, situating his practice within a network of references and related issues. In this regard, *Around Lurie* also refers to the layout of the display: Works by Boris Lurie himself are shown on four freestanding, zigzagging walls in the center of the space. Although the presentation of his artworks is divided into different chapters, it is not chronological. The 20 works by other artists that are presented literally "around Lurie" – on and in front of the outer walls of the square exhibition space – shed light on his art and illuminate different aspects of his practice. They also underline the fact that he was not alone in his lifelong battle, among other things against self-centered art that was indulged by the capitalist system, against imperialism and militarism, and against the deafening silence with regard to the unprecedented crime of the Holocaust. The context is thereby notionally divided into three concentric circles: the first includes Lurie's closest associates in the March Group (Sam Goodman and Stanley Fisher); the second consists of other artists linked to the NO!art movement (Jean-Jacques Lebel here represents many others) as well as friends (Wolf Vostell); and the third, outer circle is made up of artists whose work in one way

laufen die Fluchtlinien der Argumentation doch immer wieder in seiner Person und Kunst zusammen.

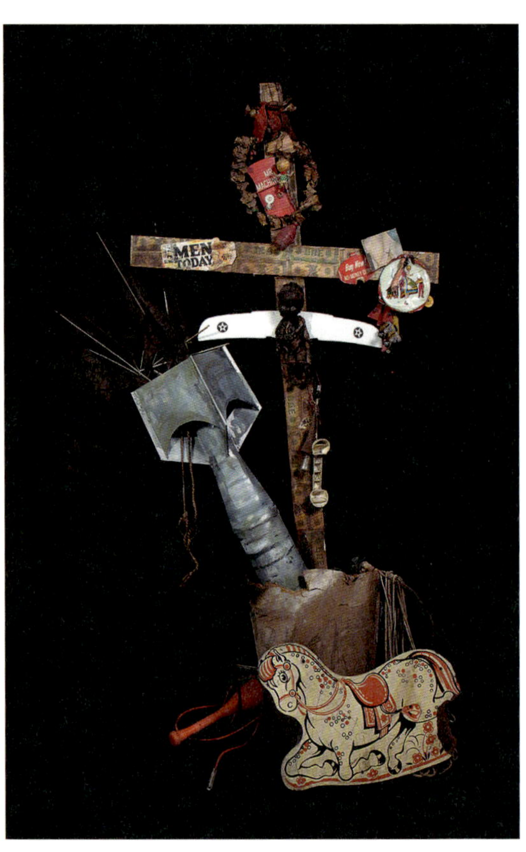

Sam Goodman, *The Bomb*, 1960/61
Boris Lurie Art Foundation

Sam Goodman (1919–1967) war neben Boris Lurie und Stanley Fisher einer der drei Köpfe der March Group, benannt nach der gleichnamigen Galerie in der East Tenth Street, einer Künstler-Selbsthilfe-Galerie. Der aus Toronto stammende Künstler, der 1947 nach New York gekommen war, malte noch in den späten fünfziger Jahren abstrakt-expressionistische Bilder. Als Mitglied der March Group trat Goodman dann mit teils kruden Assemblagen hervor. Wie die Werke von Lurie und Fisher waren sie „weder geistreich, brillant, noch kritisch im Sinne der Tradition der politischen Kunst [...]. Ihre einzigartigen Ausdrucksmittel wurden aber von einer zunehmenden Zahl Andersdenkender verstanden. Sie waren aus tiefster Seele ekelhaft."[4]
Seine wohl bekannteste Arbeit ist *The Bomb*, auch genannt *The Cross*, die in Lucy Lippards einflussreichem Buch *Pop Art* (1966) abgebildet wurde. Das Kunstwerk thematisiert die Angst vor der totalen Vernichtung der menschlichen Zivilisation durch einen Atomkrieg und erklärt das Waffenarsenal der Militärs zum Spielzeug von Verrückten. Ein bekanntes Foto zeigt Goodman mit einem Gewehr in der Hand, stehend, auf einem Schaukelpferd vor seinem Objektkunstwerk, als wolle er damit den Krieg als Steckenpferd der Generäle entlarven. *The Bomb* stellte einen Beitrag Goodmans zur *Doom Show* (1961) dar, die schon in ihrem Titel die nukleare Apokalypse an die Wand malte. Wie realistisch diese Befürchtung war, bewies 1962 die Kuba-Krise. In einem Statement zur „Untergangsausstellung" betonte Goodman die aus der drohenden Katastrophe erwachsende Verantwortung: „Der Mensch muss jetzt seine ganze Macht zur Kenntnis nehmen."[5] Wie das geht, illustrierte Goodman ausgesprochen simpel, indem er eine Bombe in den Mülleimer steckte. Ursprünglich war die Assemblage von Zeichnungen flankiert, die politische Parolen wie „Stop Testing" transportierten.
Die Profanierung eines Kreuzes in *The Bomb* findet in *Eichmann Remember* eine Parallele: Hier ist es die sakrale Form des Triptychons, die durch ihren zentralen Bildgegenstand, ein Foto des ehemaligen SS-Obersturmbannführers Adolf Eichmann, konterkariert wird. 1961, als Goodman diese Assemblage schuf, stand Eichmann als Hauptverantwortlicher des Holocausts in Jerusalem vor Gericht. In Luries *Lumumba is Dead (Adieu Amérique)* taucht das gezeichnete Porträt des Nazi-Verbrechers inmitten der zentralen Hakenkreuzfahne ebenfalls auf.[6] Der Prozess markierte den Beginn einer neuen weltweiten Aufmerksamkeit für den Holocaust. „Der Eichmannprozess brachte nämlich bisher gewaltig unterdrücktes Material zutage, das die meisten wohl lieber verdrängt hätten", erinnerte sich Boris Lurie 1970: „Jetzt endlich müsste doch mit dem tödlichen Schweigen, der Angst und Konformität des Kalten Krieges gebrochen werden; jetzt endlich müsste Schluss sein mit dem Verheimlichen der Nachkriegszeit!"[7] Neun Jahre zuvor hatte Lurie noch sein Erstaunen darüber zum Ausdruck gebracht, dass es „nur eines einzigen Menschen bedurft" habe – gemeint ist der Generalstaatsanwalt Fritz Bauer –, „um die Welt aufzuwecken".[8] Boris Lurie schätzte Goodmans Eichmann-Altar, der in der *Involvement Show* (1961) präsen-

or another provides an interesting comparison to Lurie's (H. P. Alvermann, Piero Manzoni, Gustav Metzger, and Gerhard Richter). Boris Lurie may not be the primary focus in what follows, but the lines of perspective and argument all lead back to this man and his art.

Sam Goodman (1919–1967) was a founding member of the March Group, along with Boris Lurie and Stanley Fisher. The group took its name from the March Gallery, an artist-run space on East 10th Street in New York City. Originally from Toronto, Sam Goodman came to New York in 1947, where he continued to paint in an Abstract Expressionist style long into the 1950s. After he joined the March Group, however, he began producing assemblages. These sometimes rather crude works, like those of Lurie and Fisher, were "not witty, brilliant, or even scathing in the great tradition of political art, [but] they were the only terms in which an increasing number of dissidents could see their predicament! Nauseating to the seat of their soul."[4]

Goodman's best-known work is *The Bomb* (1960–61), also known as *The Cross*. This sculptural object, which was reproduced in Lucy Lippard's seminal book on *Pop Art* (1966), addresses the fear that nuclear war could wipe out human civilization, and compares the weapons stockpiled by the armed forces to the toys of madmen. A well-known photograph shows Goodman with a gun in his hand, standing on a rocking horse in front of this artwork, as if to imply that war is the hobbyhorse of army generals. *The Bomb* was one of Goodman's contributions to the *Doom Show* (1961), the title of which indicated the possibility of a nuclear apocalypse. The Cuban Missile Crisis in 1962 proved just how realistic this fear was. In a statement on the *Doom Show*, Goodman stressed the responsibility accruing from the impending disaster: "Man must face his Full Potential! NOW!"[5] His demonstration of how this should be done was extremely simple – he stuck a bomb into a garbage can. The assemblage was originally flanked by drawings with political slogans such as "Stop Testing".

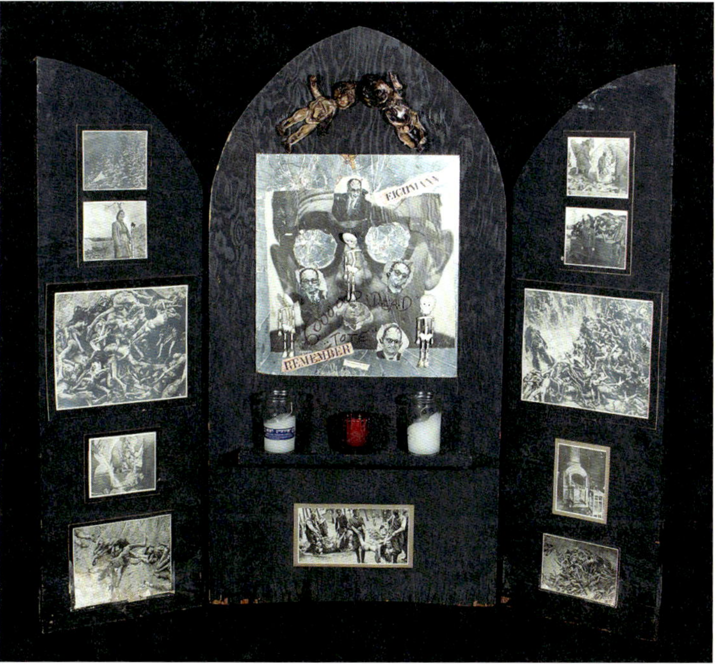

Sam Goodman, *Eichmann Remember (Eichmann Triptych)*, 1961
Boris Lurie Art Foundation

The desecration of a cross in *The Bomb* finds a parallel in *Eichmann Remember* (1961). Here, it is the religious format of the triptych which is countered by the central motif, a photograph of the former SS Obersturmbannführer Adolf Eichmann. In 1961, when Goodman created this assemblage, Eichmann was standing trial in Jerusalem as one of the key individuals responsible for the Holocaust. In Boris Lurie's *Lumumba is Dead (Adieu Amérique)* (1959 – 61), a drawn portrait of this Nazi criminal also appears inside the centrally placed swastika flag.[6] The Eichmann trial marked the beginning of a new global interest in and awareness of the Holocaust. "[T]he Eichmann trial powerfully revived suppressed material preferred to be forgotten by most, had also ruptured the death of silence and fear and conformity of the Cold War and postwar period of suppression," Boris Lurie recalled in 1970.[7] Nine years previously, he had expressed his astonishment that it "only took one man" – he is referring to Chief State Prosecutor Fritz Bauer – "to awaken the world".[8] For Lurie, Goodman's "Eichmann altarpiece", which was exhibited in the *Involvement Show* in 1961, was the first work of art to truly address the Holocaust.[9] The harrowing photographs of the atrocities mounted on the side

tiert wurde, als erstes Kunstwerk, das sich wirklich mit dem Holocaust beschäftige.[9] Die drastischen Fotos des Grauens auf den Seitenflügeln und der „Predella“ bedeuteten für Lurie sicherlich auch Impulse für sein eigenes Werk. Es war auch Sam Goodman gewesen, der seinem Freund Boris Lurie Ende 1956 oder Anfang 1957 Fotos aus den Konzentrationslagern gegeben hatte. „Lurie legte sie weg und ertrug es lange nicht, sie sich anzusehen.“[10]
Sam Goodman und Boris Lurie verschafften sich mit der letzten Manifestation der NO!art-Bewegung im engeren Sinne einen denkwürdigen Abgang. Die Ausstellung *NO-Sculptures* in der Gallery Gertrude Stein im Mai 1964 übertraf alle vorangegangenen Provokationen: „Wir hatten jetzt alle Brücken hinter uns in die Luft gesprengt. Scheiterte diese Offensive, so würden wir mit ihr untergehen“, erinnerte sich Lurie.[11] Scheiße und nichts als Scheiße – radikaler konnten Erwartungen an eine Kunstausstellung nicht enttäuscht werden. Die Scheißehaufen aus Gips waren Gemeinschaftswerke von Sam Goodman und Boris Lurie, der die „Exkremente“ naturalistisch bemalte. Die Botschaft war unmissverständlich: Die übliche Ware auf dem Kunstmarkt – auch und gerade die Pop Art – war in ihren Augen schlichtweg Scheiße. Lediglich ein „großes Geschäft“ im doppelten Sinne des Wortes. Schon Sigmund Freud hatte auf den Zusammenhang von Geld und Kot aufmerksam gemacht.

Piero Manzoni (1933–1963), der 1961 seine *Merda d'artista* (Künstlerscheiße) 30-grammweise zum aktuellen Goldpreis verkaufte, griff diese Identifizierung auf. Damit lieferte der italienische Künstler einen ironischen Kommentar zum Mythos des Künstlers, der nach Johannes Meinhardt „mit spirituellen Riten und auratischem Anspruch eine Produktion verteidigt, die die wirkliche gesellschaftliche Welt überhaupt nicht mehr erreicht.“[12] Das auf einem Sockel präsentierte Döschen fungiert in der Ausstellung als konzeptuelles Aperçu zu den naturalistischen Provokationen von Goodman und Lurie.

Stanley Fisher, *Empire*,
ca. / ca 1961 – 63
Boris Lurie Art Foundation

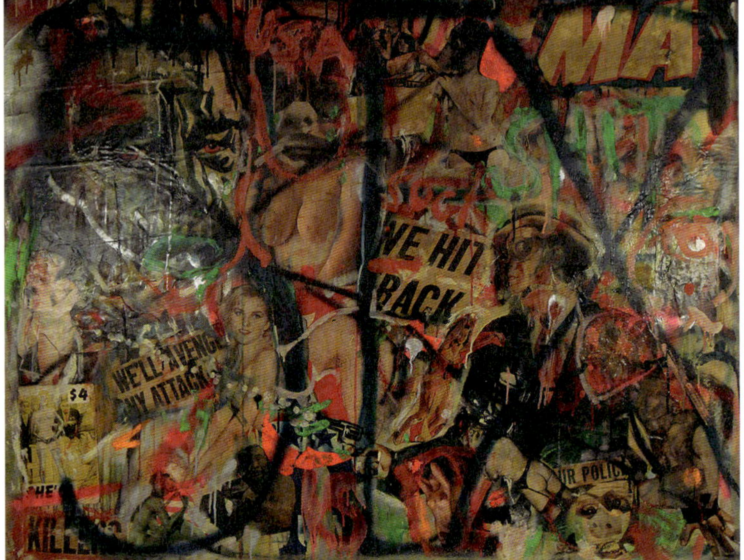

Stanley Fisher (1926–1980) war der Dritte im Bunde der March Group. Boris Lurie wurde auf den Künstler als Schriftsteller aufmerksam, als dieser 1959 an seiner Anthologie *Beat Coast East* arbeitete. Neben Fisher selbst waren auch Allen Ginsberg, Jack Kerouac und andere Beat-Poeten mit Gedichten darin vertreten. Der „Brooklyn-Lehrer aus der Lower-Middle-Class und liebevolle Familienvater“, als den ihn Lurie in seinem Nachruf charakterisierte, war andererseits ein wahrer Sex Maniac: „Sein Geschlechtstrieb und sein Anliegen waren ein und dasselbe.“[13] In *Empire* nimmt das Wort SEX das gesamte Bildfeld ein. Stanley Fisher kam zwar vom Wort, doch steuerte er zu seiner Publikation auch Zeichnungen bei. Als NO!art-Künstler wusste er sich in seinen Collagen schnell die visuelle Ausdrucksweise Luries anzueignen.
Dennoch besitzen seine Arbeiten durch die Anlehnung an die Collage-Tradition eine Eigenheit: „Fishers Collagen [...] erinnern an die Fotomontagen John Heartfields, Raoul Hausmanns und besonders an die von Hannah Höch, obgleich die NO!art-Künstler erst viel später vom Berliner Dada erfuhren“,[14] stellt Simon Taylor fest. In der Ausstellung im Neuen Museum lässt sich diese unbewusste Nähe zu Dada an *Spectre* beobachten. Boris

panels and the predella must surely have given Lurie inspiration for his own work. And it was also Sam Goodman who, at some point in late 1956 or early 1957, gave his friend Lurie some photographs of the concentration camps, "which the latter put aside, unable to bear to look at them for some time."[10]

Sam Goodman and Boris Lurie made a memorable exit with the final manifestation of the NO!art movement in a narrower sense. The *NO-Sculptures* exhibition at Gallery Gertrude Stein in May 1964 outdid all of their previous provocations: "We knew that now all but all the bridges had been burned definitively, if this offensive failed we would fall with it," Lurie later recalled.[11] An exhibition of shit and nothing but shit – viewers' expectations could not have been more radically disappointed. The heaps of shit on display were made by Sam Goodman in collaboration with Boris Lurie, who painted the plaster "excrement" to make it appear realistic. The message was loud and clear: In their view, the products that were generally available on the art market – also and above all the works of Pop Art – were simply shit, and expensive heaps of shit at that! The connection between feces and money had already been established by Sigmund Freud.

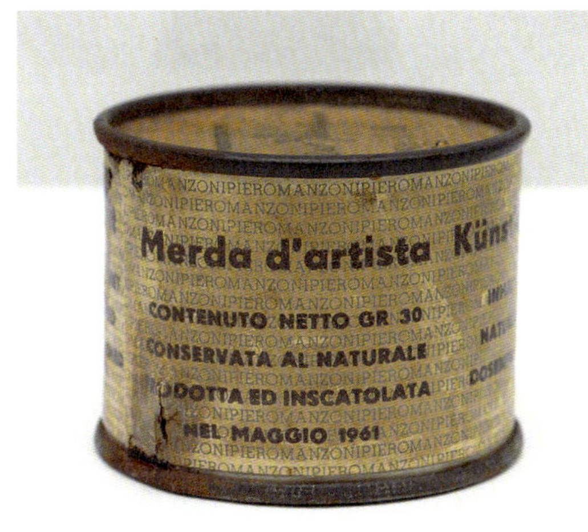

Piero Manzoni,
La Merda d'artista, 1961
Sammlung Block

Piero Manzoni (1933–1963), who in 1961 sold 30-gram portions of *Merda d'artista* [Artist's Shit] for the market price of the equivalent weight in gold, highlighted the same linkage. The Italian artist's work was an ironic commentary on the myth of the artist who, according to Johannes Meinhardt, "uses spiritual rituals and auratic claims to defend an output that that no longer reaches the real world of contemporary society at all."[12] Manzoni's little can, presented on a pedestal in the current exhibition, serves as a conceptual aperçu to complement the naturalistic provocations of Goodman and Lurie.

Stanley Fisher (1926–1980) was the third founding member of the March Group. Boris Lurie first encountered Fisher as a writer in 1959, when he was editing a poetry anthology entitled *Beat Coast East*. It included some of his own poems alongside works by Allen Ginsberg, Jack Kerouac, and other Beat poets. The "Brooklyn lower middle-class schoolteacher and devoted family man," as Fisher was described by Lurie in his obituary, was also a veritable sex maniac: "His sex drive was one with his cause."[13] In *Empire* (ca 1961–63), for example, the word "SEX" fills the entire picture plane. Although Fisher came from the world of text, *Beat Coast East* also included drawings by him. As a NO!artist, he soon began to adopt Lurie's visual language in his own collages.

Fisher's works nevertheless have a distinctive quality on account of their connections to the collage tradition: "Fisher's collages (…) recall the photomontages of John Heartfield, Raoul Hausmann, and especially Hannah Höch, although the NO!artists were unaware of Berlin Dada until much later,"[14] Simon Taylor has noted. In the exhibition at the Neues Museum, this unintended proximity to Dada can be seen in *Spectre* (ca 1961–63). Boris Lurie, on the other hand, regarded Fisher's collages as a reflection of his wartime experiences: "[H]e had been to Normandy in the War, with the Medics. He must have seen seen many injured bodies, for his later NO!art collages were based on the grafting of photo faces onto faces and bodies onto bodies."[15]

Lurie dagegen führte Fishers Collagen auf dessen Kriegserfahrungen zurück: „Während des Krieges hatte er in der Normandie bei den Sanitätern gedient. Er muss viele zerschmetterte Körper gesehen haben, da seine späteren NO!art-Collagen darauf basierten. Er pfropfte Fotos von Gesichtern auf Gesichter und von Körpern auf Körper."[15]

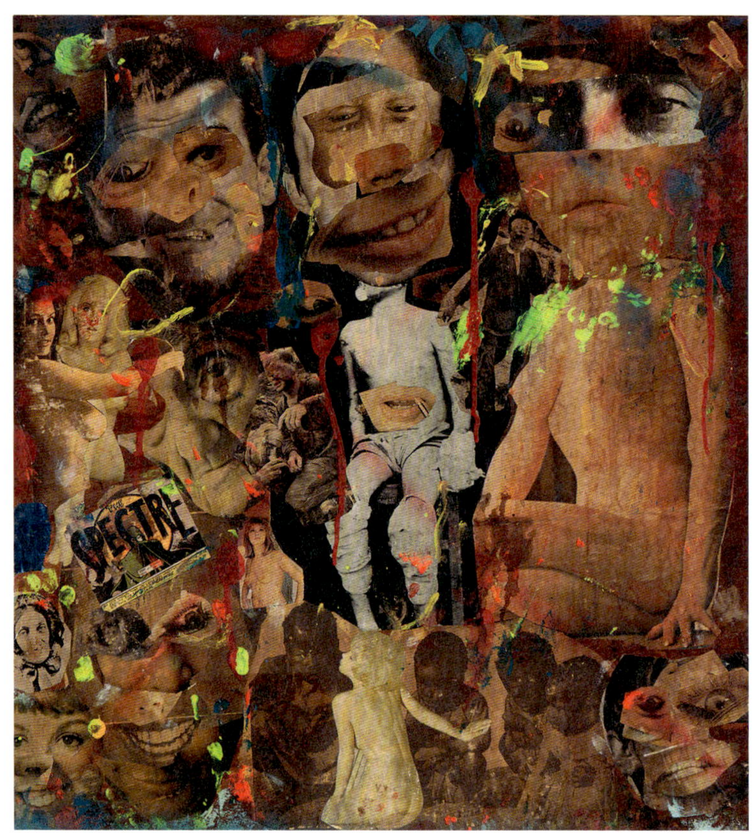
Stanley Fisher, *Spectre*, ca. / ca 1961–63
Boris Lurie Art Foundation

Jean-Jacques Lebel (geb. 1936) ist ein durch und durch politisches Temperament. Er produziert Kunst nicht um ihrer selbst willen, sondern um damit Gesellschaft zu verändern. Der Sohn eines bekannten französischen Kunst- und Literaturkritikers kam schon als Kind nach New York, wohin die Familie 1940 vor den deutschen Besatzern geflüchtet war. New York sollte auch später für den Künstler, der vor allem durch seine Happenings, Performances und Aktionen bekannt wurde, eine wichtige Rolle spielen. 1961 kehrte Lebel von Frankreich kurzzeitig nach New York zurück, das sich gerade anschickte, Paris den Rang als Weltkunsthauptstadt abzulaufen. In der March Group fand Lebel wahlverwandte Künstler, die widerständige Kunst produzierten. Jean-Jacques Lebel war 1961 an der *Involvement Show* sowie an der *Doom Show* beteiligt und nahm 1963 auch an der *NO!Show* in der Gallery Gertrude Stein teil.
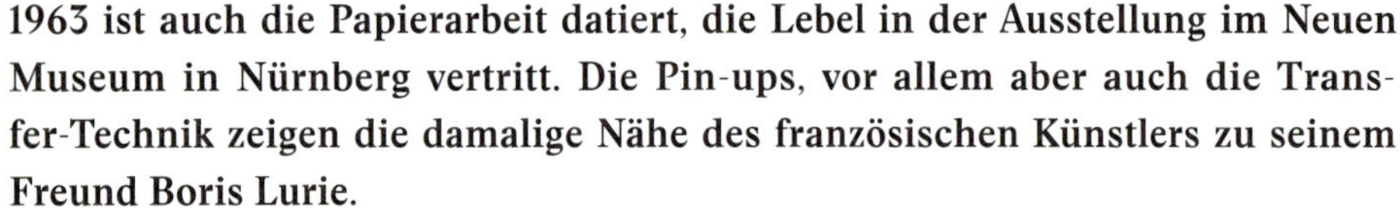
1963 ist auch die Papierarbeit datiert, die Lebel in der Ausstellung im Neuen Museum in Nürnberg vertritt. Die Pin-ups, vor allem aber auch die Transfer-Technik zeigen die damalige Nähe des französischen Künstlers zu seinem Freund Boris Lurie.
Jean-Jacques Lebel wies den Weg aus der Malerei hin zur Aktion: „Es war unser Wunsch", schrieb Lebel 1967, „tiefer in die besondere Erfahrung der Malerei einzutauchen. [...] Alles was von Action Painting übrig blieb, war die AKTION."[16] Die Grenzen zwischen Kunst und Politik wurden im Mai 1968 in beide Richtungen durchlässig. So erlebte Lebel die Studentenunruhen als „theatralisch": „Der Mai-Aufstand war insofern theatralisch als er ein riesiges Fest war, eine Offenbarung und eine Explosion des Sinnlichen jenseits der ‚normalen' Regeln der Politik."[17] Ein Foto wie jenes, das Lebel bei einer Demonstration im Mai 1968 in Paris zeigt, die schöne Caroline de Bendern auf den Schultern, die wie eine neue Marianne die Fahne Vietnams schwenkt, ein solches Foto gibt es von Boris Lurie oder seinen NO!art-Mitkämpfern nicht.

NO!art bedeutet nicht „no art", also „keine Kunst", sondern Kunst, die „NEIN" sagt. Nein zu Rassismus, nein zu Militarismus und Imperialismus, nein zu L'art pour l'art und Ästhetizismus. „Nein heißt Engagement", auf diese einfache Formel brachte es die Künstlerin Michelle Stuart.[18] Doch hätte diese Selbstverpflichtung zu politisch-sozialem Engagement nicht ebenfalls den Weg aus den Ateliers auf die Straße weisen müssen? Den Weg von der künstlerischen Produktion zur politischen Aktion? Boris Lurie hatte in seinem Statement zur *Involvement Show* 1961 davon gesprochen, dass „lebendiges Engagement" im „Elfenbeinturm" nicht möglich sei.[19] Mit dem „Elfenbeinturm" meinte er allerdings nicht die Kunst an sich, sondern lediglich „ästhetische Turnübungen" um ihrer selbst willen.[20] Kunst hatte weiterhin eine Existenzberechtigung, wenn sie nur

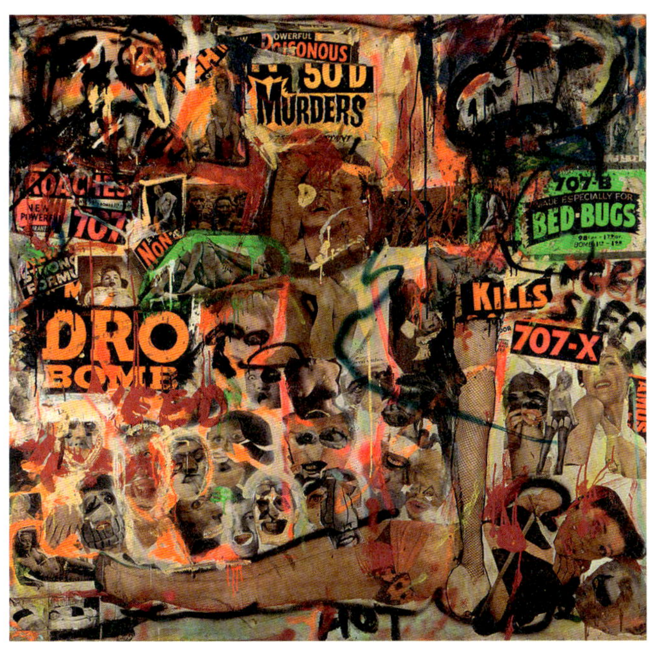

Stanley Fisher, *DRO Bomb*, ca. / ca 1961–63
Boris Lurie Art Foundation

Jean-Jacques Lebel (b. 1936) is a truly political spirit. He produces art not for its own sake, but in order to change society. The son of a well-known French art and literary critic, Lebel first came to New York as a child in 1940, when his family fled the German occupation. The city was also to play an important part in his later career, when he became known above all for his Happenings, performances, and actions. In 1961, Lebel returned briefly to New York, which was then in the process of replacing Paris as the world's art capital. In the March Group, Lebel found kindred spirits whose aim was to produce an art of resistance. He exhibited with them in 1961 in the *Involvement Show* and the *Doom Show*, and in 1963 he also took part in the *NO!Show* at Gallery Gertrude Stein. The work on paper by Lebel in the current exhibition is also from 1963. The incorporation of pin-ups, but above all the transfer technique, shows how close the French artist's practice was to that of his friend Boris Lurie at this time.

Jean-Jacques Lebel showed other artists the path away from painting and into action: "We wish to delve more deeply into the very experience of painting," he wrote in 1967. "All that was left of 'action painting' was action."[16] In May 1968, the borders between art and politics were being crossed in both directions, prompting Lebel to describe the student protests as "theatrical": "The May uprising was theatrical in that it was a gigantic fiesta, a revelatory and sensory explosion outside the 'normal' pattern of politics."[17] There is no photograph of Boris Lurie or any of his NO!art colleagues to match that of Lebel at a demonstration in Paris in May 1968; the iconic image shows the beautiful Caroline de Bendern sitting on the artist's shoulders, waving a Vietnam flag like a modern Marianne.

Jean-Jacques Lebel, *Untitled*, 1963
Boris Lurie Art Foundation

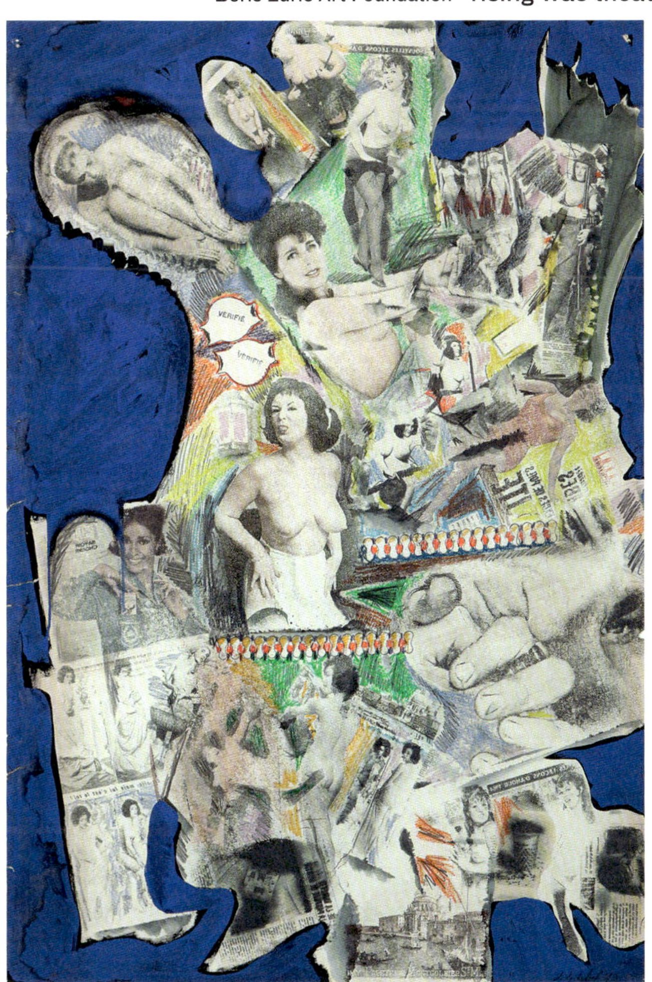

NO!art does not mean "no art" in the sense of rejecting art in its entirety; it refers instead to art that says no: no to racism; no to militarism and imperialism; no to *l'art pour l'art* and aestheticism. "No is an involvement," was how artist Michelle Stuart summed it up.[18] But should this commitment to political and social involvement not also have shown the way out of the studios and into the streets? From artistic production to political action? In his statement on the *Involvement Show* in 1961, Boris Lurie had argued that the "ivory tower is no substitute for Involvement in life."[19] By "ivory tower" he did not mean art per se, but rather the kind of "aesthetic exercises" that were performed only for their own sake.[20] In his view, art would still have a raison d'être if it would only state its intention loudly enough, or indeed what it was about at all. Flouting conventions and good manners was guaranteed to attract attention. "We want to talk, to shout, so that everybody can understand."[21] It is anyone's guess whether the shouting from the basement on East 10th Street, where the March Group gathered, could actually be heard on the street. In this context, Brian O'Doherty has ob-

laut genug verkündete, worum es ihr ging oder, besser gesagt, worum es überhaupt ging. Die Verletzung der guten Manieren garantierte für Aufmerksamkeit. „Wir wollen reden, schreien, damit uns jeder verstehen kann."[21] Ob allerdings der Schrei aus dem Kellerraum in der East Tenth Street, in dem die March Group ihr Domizil hatte, überhaupt auf der Straße zu vernehmen war, sei dahingestellt. Brian O'Doherty macht in diesem Zusammenhang darauf aufmerksam, dass die Ziele der NO!art-Gruppe „meist allgemeiner Natur" waren: „Amerika, die Atombombe, die Gaskammer [...] Ziele also, die keine Möglichkeit fanden, den Protest in Aktionen zu verwandeln. Niemand erkannte damals die Wege, die in den späten sechziger Jahren offen da lagen: nämlich die Universitäten und die Massenproteste auf der Straße."[22] Als die March Group mit der *Vulgar Show*, der *Involvement Show* oder der *Doom Show* auf sich aufmerksam machte, gingen die Afro-Amerikaner auf die Straße, um ihre Bürgerrechte einzufordern. Das Civil Rights Movement erlebte genau in dieser Zeit seinen Höhepunkt: Der Marsch auf Washington im August 1963 mobilisierte 250 000 Schwarze und Weiße, die Zeugen von Martin Luther Kings Rede *I Have a Dream* wurden. Ein Jahr später unterzeichnete Lyndon B. Johnson das Bürgerrechtsgesetz und King erhielt den Friedensnobelpreis. In der NO!art-Bewegung, angeführt von drei weißen, jüdischen Künstlern, spielte das Thema dagegen kaum eine Rolle. In einem rückblickenden Text von Boris Lurie aus dem Jahre 1970 ordnet es der Künstler jenen „ernsthafteren Intellektuellen, Studenten und Bohemiens" zu, welche die „Kunstszene völlig mieden".[23] Entsprechend gab es auch keine Kontakte zur sich formierenden Studentenbewegung, etwa zur SDS, der „Students for a Democratic Society", die 1960 gegründet wurde. Sie unterstützte die Bürgerrechtsbewegung und wurde später zum Sammelbecken des studentischen Protests gegen den Vietnamkrieg. Der Widerstand gegen den sinnlosen Krieg in Fernost vereinte Hippies, Neue Linke und Studenten. Die Friedensbewegung nahm jedoch erst im Herbst 1964 an Fahrt auf, als die March Group bereits Geschichte war.

Wolf Vostell (1932–1998) war langjähriger Freund Boris Luries und vor allem in den siebziger Jahren sein Wegbereiter in Europa. In den sechziger Jahren kam der Fluxus-Künstler jüdischer Abstammung dreimal nach New York. Schon bei seinem ersten Aufenthalt 1963, als er eine Einzelausstellung in der Smolin Gallery hatte, traf er Lurie: „Es war allzu natürlich, dass sich eine Begegnung ergab", erinnerte sich Vostell 1977, „weil wir am selben Thema, an der gleichen Ausdrucksweise arbeiteten."[24] Die offensive Auseinandersetzung mit dem verdrängten Thema des Holocausts verband die beiden Künstler. Vostells Art, sich zu kleiden, bedeutete in diesem Zusammenhang eine öffentliche Demonstration: „Deshalb schlüpfte Wolf Vostell in die Haut eines altfromm gekleideten Juden, trug Streimel und Pejes zu einer Zeit, als es Mode war, Palästinensertücher zu tragen."[25] Von einer Provokation spricht Vostells Witwe: „Auch seine Art sich anzuziehen war eine Provokation. Er hat sich nicht so angezogen, um zu sagen: ‚Ich bin Jude.' Es war eher, um die Deutschen daran zu erinnern: ‚Wir sind immer noch da!'"[26] Wolf Vostells Schaffen ist von seinen Anfängen bis zu seinem Ende ein einziger Kampf gegen das Vergessen und Verdrängen. Drei Werke seien stellvertretend für diese lebenslange Auseinandersetzung mit dem Massenmord genannt. 1958/59 schuf Wolf Vostell mit dem Environment *Schwarzes Zimmer* eine der Inkunabeln der deutschen Kunst nach Auschwitz. Die drei Teile dieses Kunstwerks, das heute der Berlinischen Galerie gehört, heißen: *Treblinka, Deut-*

served that the targets of the NO!art group were "mostly general": "America, the Bomb, the Gas-chamber. (...) But with no way of channeling their protest into action, no way of discovering the routes that the late sixties found were open and vulnerable – the universities and mass protests in the streets."[22] While the March Group was attracting attention with the *Vulgar Show*, the *Involvement Show* or the *Doom Show*, African-Americans were taking to the streets to demand their civil rights. The Civil Rights Movement reached its peak in this period: In August 1963, the March on Washington mobilized 250,000 black and white demonstrators, who were able to witness Martin Luther King's famous "I have a dream" speech. A year later, Lyndon B. Johnson signed the Civil Rights Act and King was awarded the Nobel Peace Prize. In the NO!art movement, by contrast, which was led by three white Jewish artists, civil rights were not a major concern. In a text written by Boris Lurie in 1970, he attributes activism on this issue to the "more seriously inclined intellectuals, students and bohemians" who "were quitting the art scene altogether."[23] Accordingly, there was no direct contact between the NO!artists and the emerging student activist movement, for example the Students for a Democratic Society (SDS), which was founded in 1960. The SDS supported the Civil Rights Movement and later became a hotbed of student protest against the Vietnam War. Opposition to the senseless war in the Far East was uniting hippies, students, and the New Left, but the peace movement did not really begin to pick up speed until fall 1964, by which time the March Group was already history.

Wolf Vostell (1932–1998) was a long-time friend of Boris Lurie's and helped to introduce him to European audiences in the 1970s. Vostell, a Fluxus artist of Jewish descent, had come to New York three times during the 1960s. It was on the first of these visits, for a solo show at the Smolin Gallery in 1963, that he met Lurie. Vostell recalled in 1977 how it was "all too natural that this meeting materialized – we had been working on the same theme and in the same mode of expression."[24] Both artists wanted to directly confront the subject of the Holocaust and its repression. In this context, Vostell's way of dressing was also intended as a public demonstration: "That is why Wolf Vostell slipped into the skin of a traditionally dressed Jew, wore a shtreimel (fur hat) and sidelocks at a time when it was fashionable to wear Palestinian scarves."[25] Vostell's widow described it as deliberately provocative: "His way of dressing was also a provocation. He didn't dress that way in order to say: 'I'm Jewish.' It was more to remind the Germans: 'We're still here!'"[26] Wolf Vostell's entire oeuvre is devoted to the fight against forgetting and repressing; three artworks are outlined here as examples of his lifelong preoccupation with the mass murder of the Jews. In 1958 – 9 Vostell created the environment *Schwarzes Zimmer* [Black Room], one of the key works of German art after Auschwitz. The three parts of *Schwarzes Zimmer*, which is now in the collection of the Berlinische Galerie, are entitled *Treblinka*, *Deutscher Ausblick* [German Outlook] and *Auschwitz-Scheinwerfer* [Auschwitz Searchlight]. "The title *Black Room* relates both to the dark and sinister Nazi period as as to the black hole of forgetting, blackouts in regard to the crimes of the Nazi period," writes Peter Weibel. "Vostell crams repressed consciousness into the path of the searchlight of attention. The objects used here are exclusively finds like the searchlight from Auschwitz."[27] In Vostell's Happening Room *Thermo-Elektronischer Kaugummi* [Thermo-Electronic Chewing Gum] (1970), visi-

scher Ausblick und *Auschwitz-Scheinwerfer*. „Der Titel *Schwarzes Zimmer* bezieht sich sowohl auf die dunkle und finstere Zeit des Nationalsozialismus wie auch auf das schwarze Loch des Vergessens, des blackouts hinsichtlich der Verbrechen der Nazi-Zeit", schreibt Peter Weibel. „Vostell zerrt das Verdrängte in das Scheinwerferlicht der Aufmerksamkeit. Die dabei verwendeten Objekte sind ausschließlich Fundstücke, wie der aus Auschwitz stammende Scheinwerfer."[27]
Im Happening-Raum *Thermo-Elektronischer Kaugummi* von 1970 laufen die Besucher zwischen Stacheldrahtzäunen über 12 000 Löffel und Gabeln, welche die Habseligkeiten der in Auschwitz ermordeten Menschen ebenso andeuten wie die am Boden stehenden Koffer. 1997 schließlich, ein Jahr vor seinem frühen Tod, präsentierte Wolf Vostell in Berlin sein Vermächtnis zu diesem Themenkomplex: das monumentale, 270 × 660 cm messende Gemälde *Shoah 1492–1945*.
Alle sechs Werke Wolf Vostells in der Boris-Lurie-Ausstellung des Neuen Museums handeln vom Nationalsozialismus und vom Massenmord an den europäischen Juden. Die Farbserigrafie *Treblinka* (1967) und die Objektgrafik *Kämme* (1968) zeigen weitgehend unverändert Fotodokumente der Tötung jüdischer Frauen in Babi Jar und Ivangorod. Die Vorlagen entnahm der Künstler einer polnischen Publikation.[28] Das Motiv der Erschießung einer Frau mit Kind auf dem Arm (Ivangorod, Ukraine, 1942) zählt zu den Ikonen der Holocaust-Rezeption in den 1960er Jahren.[29] Unter dem Titel *We have not forgotten – Nous n'avons pas oublié – Wir haben es nicht vergessen* findet es sich zum Beispiel auf dem Cover der gleichnamigen Publikation mit 277 Abbildungen, die erstmals 1959 im Warschauer Polonia-Verlag erschienen war. Der amerikanische Künstler R. B. Kitaj reproduzierte dieses Cover in seiner Siebdruckfolge *In unserer Zeit* (1969).[30] Die Kämme, die Vostell in Höhe der Horizontlinie auf seine Grafik montierte, lassen an jene materiellen Hinterlassenschaften von ermordeten Menschen denken, die in Auschwitz in Form makabrer Akkumulationen aufbewahrt und präsentiert werden. Gleichzeitig antworten die acht braunen Schildpatt-Kämme auf die Szene grotesker Gewalt mit einem alltäglichen Instrument der Schönheitspflege – eine Geste ganz aus dem Geist von Fluxus, wie sie auch Vostells berühmten *Lippenstiftbomber* charakterisiert. Die Kämme bei Vostell spielen in gewisser Hinsicht eine ähnliche Rolle wie jene stilisierten Haarlocken in unterschiedlichen Farbtönen, die Boris Lurie am oberen Bildrand von *Railroad to America* zeigt. Auch in einer von Luries Kofferarbeiten von 1963 sowie in *Hard Writings: PLEASE* taucht dieses Bildmotiv auf. Es geht gewiss nicht zu weit, in diesem Zusammenhang auf das Scheren der Haare in den Lagern hinzuweisen, das vor allem Frauen entwürdigte. In Vostells Blatt *Treblinka,* das jedoch abweichend vom Titel nackte Frauen in der Schlucht von Babi Jar bei Kiew vor der Erschießung zeigt (1941), wird die grausige Szene von einer Wetterkarte überlagert. Die Konfrontation des Belanglosen mit dem Verdrängten ist verstörend, da die beiden Bildebenen eine sehr unterschiedliche Wahrnehmung bedingen. Dieselbe Strategie kennzeichnet Vostells Blatt *Mylai* von 1970. Auch hier wird das Massaker der US-Amerikaner in Vietnam von einer Wetterkarte überblendet. Vostell schuf visuelle Bestandsaufnahmen des zeitgenössischen, medieninfiltrierten Bewusstseins, in dem sofort wieder unterzugehen droht, was kurzzeitig nach oben gespült wird. „Für Vostell sind es die von den Medien übermittelten Bilder, aus denen wir unsere Lebenswirklichkeit aufbauen."[31]
Die beiden Bildvorlagen aus dem Holocaust finden sich wieder in einem Objektbuch Wolf Vostells aus dem Jahr 1974, das ihm als Skizzenbuch diente. Die

tors walking between the barbed-wire fences also have to walk over 12,000 spoons and forks; these items, along with the suitcases standing on the floor, bring to mind the belongings of people who were murdered in Auschwitz. In 1997, a year before his untimely death, Vostell presented his definitive work on this theme in Berlin: *Shoah 1492–1945*, a monumental painting measuring 270 x 660 cm.

The six works by Wolf Vostell in the Boris Lurie exhibition at Neues Museum all address the theme of the Third Reich and the mass murder of European Jews. The color screenprint *Treblinka* (1967) and the print *Kämme* [Combs] (1968) both incorporate largely unaltered photographs that document the killing of Jewish women in Babi Yar and Ivangorod. Vostell found the source images in a Polish publication.[28] The photograph of a woman with a child in her arms being shot (Ivangorod, Ukraine, 1942) is an iconic image with regard to the reception of the Holocaust in the 1960s.[29] Under the heading *We have not forgotten – Nous n'avons pas oublié – Wir haben es nicht vergessen*, for example, it was the titular image of a publication featuring 277 images that was first issued in 1959 by the Warsaw-based Polonia publishing company. This cover was later reproduced by the American artist R. B. Kitaj in a series of screenprints entitled *In Our Time* (1969).[30] The combs Vostell has mounted along the horizon in his printed image bring to mind the material goods left behind by people who were murdered, which were preserved and displayed in Auschwitz in the form of macabre collections. At the same time, the nine brown tortoiseshell combs respond to the scene of grotesque violence with an everyday object used in beauty care – a gesture that is very much in the spirit of Fluxus and also characterizes Vostell's famous *Lippenstiftbomber* [Lipstick Bomber] (1968). To some extent, these combs have a similar function in Vostell's work as do the stylized, variously colored locks of hair at the top of Lurie's *Railroad to America (Railroad Collage)* (1963). This motif also appears in one of Lurie's suitcase-based works from 1963 and in *Hard Writings: PLEASE* (ca 1963–72). It is certainly not going too far to draw a parallel here to the act of cutting inmates' hair in the concentration camps, which served to humiliate women above all. Although the title suggests otherwise, Vostell's screenprint *Treblinka* (1967) shows a group of naked women just before they were murdered in the Babi Yar ravine near Kiev in 1941. A weather map has been superimposed over the harrowing scene. This confrontation between something banal and something horrific that has been repressed is highly disturbing, as the two layers of the composition demand to be perceived in very different ways. The same strategy is employed in Vostell's screenprint *Mylai* (1970). Here, too, the image of a massacre (in this case committed by U.S. Army soldiers in Vietnam) is overlaid with a weather map. Vostell took visual stock of the media-infiltrated consciousness of the day, where anything that briefly rises to the surface is in danger of immediately being submerged again. "For Vostell, the images conveyed by the media are the basis upon which we construct our everyday reality."[31]

Wolf Vostell, *Kämme,* 1968
Boris Lurie Art Foundation

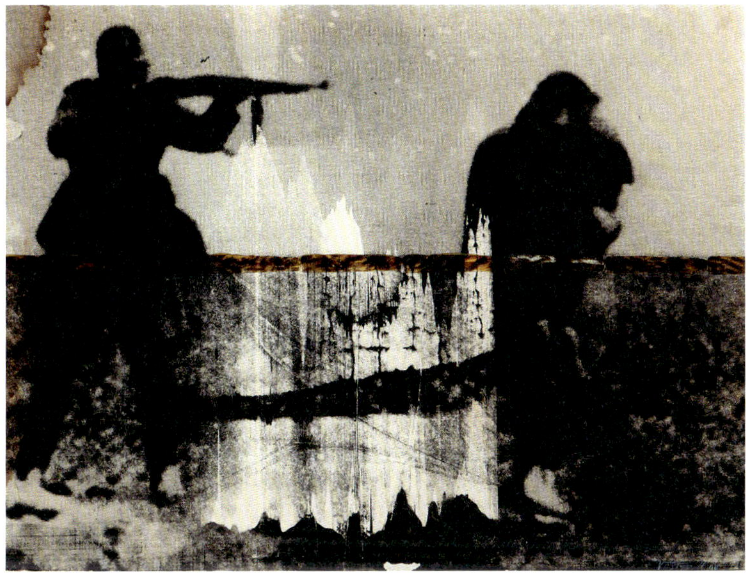

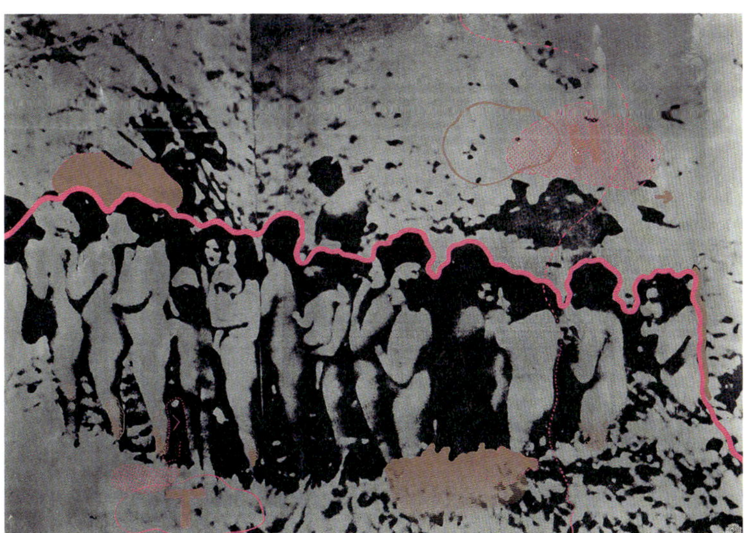

Wolf Vostell, *Treblinka,* 1967
The Wolf Vostell Estate

Erschießung der Mutter mit ihrem Kind auf dem Arm wird darin kombiniert mit einer Wasserski fahrenden Bikinischönheit und mit pornografischem Bildmaterial. Es handelt sich offensichtlich um die Vorarbeit zum Schichtenbild *Für die Dauer des Mittag- und Abendessens ist das Rauchen im Speisewagen unerwünscht* von 1968. Die Kombination von pornografischen Fotos mit Bildern des Holocausts in den ursprünglichen Überlegungen des Künstlers erinnert an Boris Lurie, aber auch an Gerhard Richters nicht realisiertes Ausstellungsprojekt von 1966. Das Buch aus dem Museum Morsbroich in Leverkusen trägt den schönen Titel *Leben gleich Kunst* – die umgedrehte Formel für das avantgardistische Projekt der Aufhebung der Autonomie der Kunst und der „Rückführung der Kunst in die Lebenspraxis", wie es Peter Bürger formuliert hat.[32] Den zynischsten Kommentar zum historischen Scheitern der Avantgarde und zu Vostells Titel lieferte Wolf Vostells Freund Boris Lurie mit *Flatcar, Assemblage, 1945 by Adolf Hitler*. Denn dieses Readymade beantwortet Luries Frage, wer der größte Künstler des Jahrhunderts sei: „Ist es Duchamp (!!), ist es Picasso (!!!), Boris Lurie (!!!!) oder ist es doch Adolf Hitler? Letzterer scheint mir der wahrscheinlichste Kandidat für diesen erlauchten Titel zu sein: Der Große Künstler der Zerstörung, der lebende (ja, lebende) Spuren seiner Meisterwerke hinterlassen hat. [...] Zwar erklärte Duchamp, dass sein ganzes Leben Kunst sei, Hitler jedoch nahm das wirkliche Leben und formte es nach seinen Vorstellungen."[33]

Das große Leinwandbild *Eine Autofahrt Köln–Frankfurt auf überfüllter Autobahn kostet mehr Nerven als eine Woche angestrengt arbeiten* von 1964 reflektiert die mediale Bilderflut, die das Grauen von Auschwitz nivelliert. Das Holocaust-Foto am rechten Bildrand trifft völlig unzusammenhängend auf einen Bericht über die Nagold-Prozesse (Misshandlung Untergebener in einer Fallschirmjäger-Ausbildungs-Kompanie), ein Foto der auf einem Arne-Jacobsen-Stuhl nackt posierenden Christine Keeler (Profumo-Affäre) und andere Fundstücke aus der bundesrepublikanischen Presselandschaft. 1961 hatte Vostell für kurze Zeit als Layouter für die Zeitschrift *Neue Illustrierte* gearbeitet: „Er kam jetzt täglich in Kontakt mit Hunderten von Agenturfotos zeitgeschichtlicher Ereignisse, wie Kriege, Unfälle, Katastrophen", schrieb Eckhart Gillen. „Im Fotoarchiv der Illustrierten wurde er zum erstenmal mit Bildern über KZ, Folter, Massenmord konfrontiert, die damals noch für eine Veröffentlichung tabu waren."[34] Dies sollte sich spätestens durch den Auschwitz-Prozess (1963–65) ändern. In dem Bild *Wir waren so eine Art Museumsstück*, das im selben Jahr wie *Eine Autofahrt* ... entstand und genauso groß ist, bildete Vostell einen Bericht aus der *Frankfurter Allgemeinen Zeitung* ab, in dem es um die Zeugenaussage des russischen Soldaten Pjotr Mischin im Auschwitz-Prozess am 29. Oktober 1964 geht. In *Eine Autofahrt* ... dokumentiert

Wolf Vostell, *Eine Autofahrt Köln – Frankfurt auf überfüllter Autobahn kostet mehr Nerven als eine Woche angestrengt arbeiten*, 1964
Sammlung Ludwig – Ludwig Forum für Internationale Kunst, Aachen

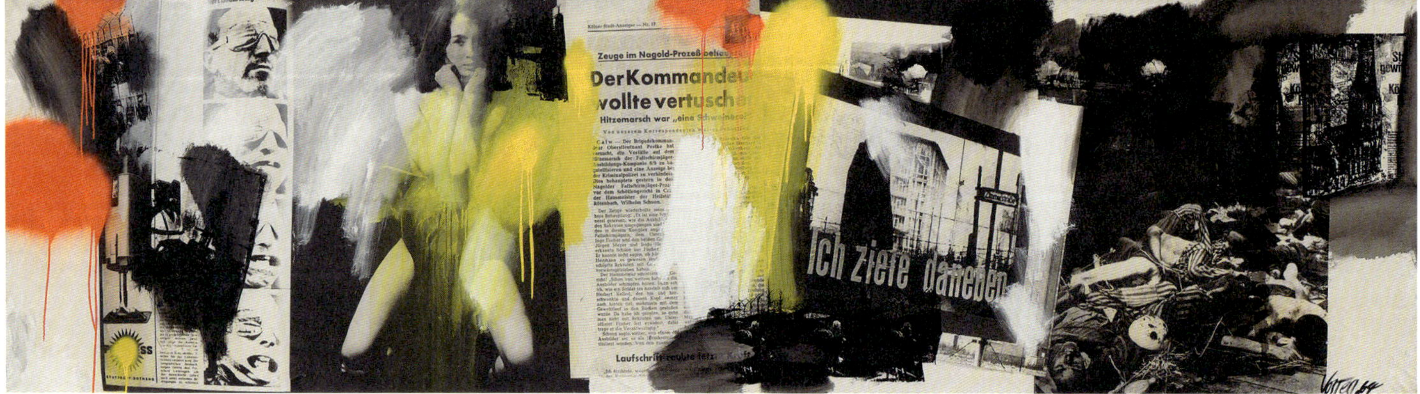

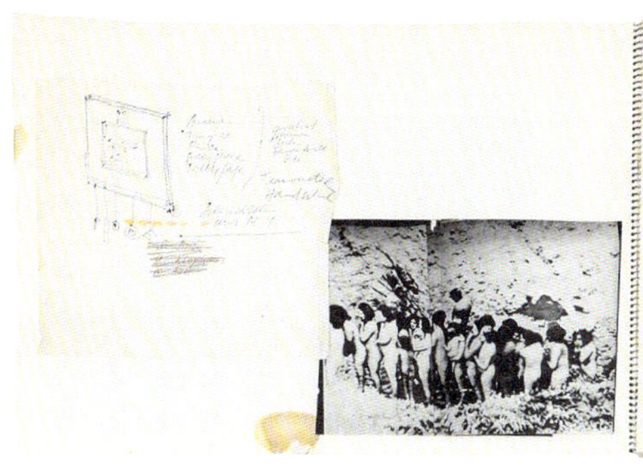
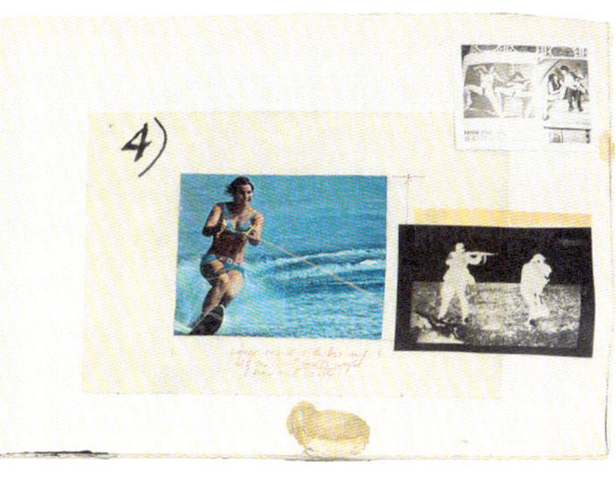

Wolf Vostell, *Leben gleich Kunst*, 1974
Museum Morsbroich, Leverkusen; Dauerleihgabe des Landes Nordrhein-Westfalen

The same two source images from the Holocaust are also included in Vostell's book object from 1974, which he used as a sketchbook. Here, the theme of the mother and child being shot is combined with a beautiful bikini-clad woman on waterskis and some pornographic imagery. This is evidently a preliminary study for his layered picture *Für die Dauer des Mittag- und Abendessens ist das Rauchen im Speisewagen unerwünscht* [No smoking in the dining car during lunch and dinner] (1968). The idea of combining pornographic photographs with images of the Holocaust not only recalls Boris Lurie, but can also be linked to an unrealized exhibition project by Gerhard Richter from 1966, as I will go on to discuss. Vostell's book object, which is now in the collection of Museum Morsbroich in Leverkusen, is entitled *Leben gleich Kunst* [Life Equals Art] – reversing the formula for the avant-garde project that involved the sublation of the autonomy of art and the "reintegration of art into the praxis of life," as Peter Bürger put it.[32] The most cynical commentary on the historical failure of the avant-garde, and on Vostell's title, was provided by his friend Boris Lurie with the work *Flatcar, Assemblage, 1945 by Adolf Hitler* (ca 1962). This readymade answers Lurie's question as to who the great artist of the century was: "Is it Duchamp (!!), is it Picasso (!!!), Boris Lurie (!!!!), or is it Adolf Hitler? The last one seems to me the most likely candidate to this august title: The Great Artist of Destruction who left living (yes, living) traces of his masterpieces. (...) So then Duchamp said all life was art, but Hitler took real life and molded it to his liking."[33]

The large-format canvas *Eine Autofahrt Köln–Frankfurt auf überfüllter Autobahn kostet mehr Nerven als eine Woche angestrengt arbeiten* [Driving from Cologne to Frankfurt on an overcrowded autobahn costs more nerves than a week's hard work] (1964) reflects the flood of media images that ultimately trivializes the horrors of Auschwitz. Here, a Holocaust photograph at the right edge of the picture has been juxtaposed to an entirely unrelated report on the Nagold trials (concerning the abuse of paratroop recruits by training officers), a photo of Christine Keeler (Profumo affair) posing naked on an Arne Jacobsen chair, and other items culled from the West German press. In 1961, Vostell worked for a short time as a layout artist for the magazine *Neue Illustrierte*: "He now came into daily contact with hundreds of agency photos of current events, such as wars, accidents, and catastrophes," Eckhart Gillen wrote. "In the magazine's photo archive, he was confronted for the first time by pictures of concentration camps, torture, and mass murder, which at that time were still taboo for publication."[34] This situation had changed, however, at the latest by the time of the Frankfurt Auschwitz trials (1963–5). Vostell's *Wir waren so eine Art Museumsstück* [We Were a Kind of Museum Piece] (1964), which is the same size and was produced in the same year as *Eine Autofahrt ...*, includes a clipping from the *Frankfurter Allgemeine Zeitung*. It is a report on the testimony given by a Russian soldier, Pyotr Mishin, at the Auschwitz trial on October 29, 1964. The photograph on the right edge of *Eine Autofahrt ...* documents the "death train" that left the Buchenwald concentration camp on April 7, 1945, carrying hundreds of prisoners. Although its original destination was Flossenbürg, the train eventually arrived in Dachau after a 21-day odyssey – shortly before this camp was liberat-

das Foto am rechten Bildrand den sogenannten Todeszug von Buchenwald, der am 7. April 1945 in Buchenwald mit Hunderten von KZ-Häftlingen losgefahren war. Nach einer Odyssee von 21 Tagen erreichte der ursprünglich für Flossenbürg bestimmte Zug Dachau – kurz vor der Befreiung durch die Amerikaner. Vermutlich waren etwa 2 300 Menschen an Hunger gestorben oder auf der Fahrt erschossen worden. Vostells zeitgeschichtliche Panoramen warfen einen ausgesprochen skeptischen Blick auf die Aufarbeitung des Holocausts, indem sie den Untergang des Themas in der Nachrichtenflut fürchten ließen. Martin Walser, der den Auschwitz-Prozess beobachtet hatte, sah die Gefahr aus entgegengesetzter Richtung kommen. Er beklagte 1965 ein Zuviel an Einzelheiten des Grauens, die auf Distanz gehen ließen.[35] Boris Lurie teilte dreißig Jahre später Walsers Sorge. Mittlerweile war aus dem verdrängten Thema ein medial inflationiertes geworden. Die vielen Fernsehberichte über Hitler ließen diesen schon wie einen „Onkel" erscheinen: „Das alles rührt her vom Überfluss an Informationen. Die Details von allem verdrängen das Fühlen. Es ist viel wirksamer, alles in einer Stille, von einem Geheimnis umgeben, schweben zu lassen. Die Überbelichtung tötet die Wirklichkeit. Und das gilt auch für den Holocaust."[36]

Wolf Vostells Umgang mit den Bildern der Medien ist durchaus ambivalent. Sie geben Zeugnis, werden jedoch zugleich entwertet und zerstört. Sogenannte Verwischungen zählen zu den typischen Techniken Vostells in den sechziger Jahren. Mit einer Mischung aus Terpentin und Tetrachlorkohlenstoff bearbeitete er Fotografien aus Zeitschriften. Was *Nürnberg* (1968) ursprünglich zeigte, bleibt im Unklaren, da es kaum noch Anhaltspunkte zur Identifizierung des Fotos gibt. Es könnte sich um eine Aufnahme vom Nürnberger Hauptkriegsverbrecherprozess oder um ein Foto vom Reichsparteitagsgelände handeln. Das unsichtbare Bild gewinnt an Aufmerksamkeit zurück, was es an Sichtbarkeit eingebüßt hat. „Verwischen, um klar zu sehen!" So erklärte Vostell die Intention, die er mit der Technik der Verwischung verfolgte: „Die Imagination des Betrachters kann das Fehlende durch Vermutungen über das Vorher-Dagewesene ergänzen, so entsteht ein andauernder Spannungszustand."[37] Im Rahmen der Ausstellung im Neuen Museum Nürnberg dient das Bild auch dazu, gemeinsam mit H.P. Alvermanns Figur eine Brücke zum Ort der Ausstellung zu schlagen und Nürnbergs besondere Verantwortung gegenüber der Geschichte zu unterstreichen.

Für die Galerie René Block veranstaltete Wolf Vostell am 10. November 1965 das Dé-coll/age-Happening *Berlin, 100 Ereignisse – 100 Minuten – 100 Stellen für Zufallspublikum*. Die Serigrafie von 1966, die eines der „Ereignisse" zeigt, ist eine der frühesten Dokumentationsgrafiken Vostells. Das Blatt zeigt das Ereignis 21: „Nackte Frau mit Gasmaske liegt in leerem Zimmer in die Ecke gekauert". Mercedes Guardado Olivenza Vostell, Wolf Vostells spanische Ehefrau, sitzt unter einem Sicherungskasten mit seitlich abgewinkelten Beinen und aufgestützten Armen auf dem Boden. Diese Körperhaltung, vor allem jedoch die Nacktheit in Verbindung mit der Gasmaske genügen, um die Gaskammern der Vernichtungslager zu evozieren. Wolf Vostell hat wiederholt bei Happenings auf den Holocaust angespielt, ohne dabei explizit zu werden. In diesem Zusammenhang ist das Happening *You* wichtig, das am 19. April 1964 in Great Neck, Long Island, auf dem Grundstück von Bob und Rhett Brown stattfand. Schon im Konzept war von „Greuelscenen"

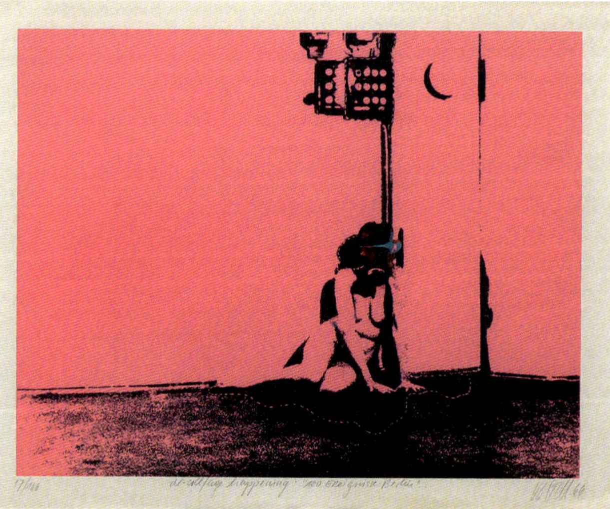

Wolf Vostell, *100 Ereignisse Berlin. Frau mit Gasmaske*, 1966
The Wolf Vostell Estate

ed by US Army forces. It is estimated that around 2,300 people died of starvation or were shot during this journey. Vostell's contemporary panoramas presented a highly skeptical view of attempts to come to terms with the Holocaust, highlighting the danger of this issue being drowned in the flood of news. The German writer Martin Walser, having observed the Auschwitz trials, perceived a threat from the opposite direction. In 1965, he criticized the surfeit of detail with regard to the atrocities, pointing out that this fostered detachment.[35] Walser's concern was shared by Boris Lurie 30 years later, by which time the previously repressed theme had been hugely inflated by the mass media. Due to the large number of TV reports and features, Hitler had now acquired the familiarity of an "uncle": "This all stems from the abundance of information. The details of it all suppress feeling. It's much more effective to let everything float in silence, surrounded by mystery. Overexposure kills reality. And that also applies to the Holocaust."[36]

Wolf Vostell's use of media images was highly ambivalent. While the pictures he incorporated provided testimony, they were simultaneously stripped of any value and destroyed. One of the techniques Vostell frequently employed in the 1960s was "blurring", which involved treating photographs taken from magazines with a mixture of turpentine and carbon tetrachloride. There is no way of knowing what the source image was for *Nürnberg* (1968), as there is little visual information left to identify it. The photograph may have shown the Major War Criminals Trial in Nuremberg or the Nazi Party Rally Grounds. But what the image has lost in terms of legibility, it has gained in terms of impact. "Blur, in order to see clearly!" was the reason Vostell gave for using this technique: "The observer's imagination can elaborate the absence with assumptions about the what-had-been-there-before; thus, a constant state of tension arises."[37] In the current exhibition at Neues Museum, this work, along with H. P. Altermann's sculptural figure, also forges a link to the show's location in Nuremberg and underlines the particular historical responsibility borne by this city.

Wolf Vostell, *Nürnberg*, 1968
The Wolf Vostell Estate

On November 10, 1965, Wolf Vostell staged the dé-coll/age-Happening *Berlin, 100 Ereignisse – 100 Minuten – 100 Stellen für Zufallspublikum* [100 Events – 100 Minutes – 100 Places for a Random Audience] at Galerie René Block in Berlin. A screenprint from 1966 is among Vostell's earliest documentary prints, and depicts Event no. 21: "Naked woman with a gas mask lies cowering in the corner of an empty room." Mercedes Guardado Olivenza Vostell, Wolf Vostell's Spanish wife, sits on the floor beneath a fuse box with her legs twisted to one side, propping herself up with her hands. The position of her body, but above all the combination of her nakedness and the gas mask is enough to evoke the gas chambers in the death camps. Vostell's Happenings frequently alluded to the Holocaust without making explicit reference to it. An important work in this context is the Happening *You*, which took place on April 19, 1964, on a property in Great Neck, Long Island, that belonged to Bob and Rhett Brown. The concept for this work already contained a reference to "Greuelscenen" [horror scenes]. Participants were asked to crawl into an empty swimming pool, where they were expected to "lie down and try to form a mound

die Rede. Das Publikum wurde aufgefordert, in den Swimmingpool zu kriechen: „Legen Sie sich hin und versuchen Sie einen Menschenberg zu bilden wie in einem Massengrab".[38] Der Fluxus-Künstler Al Hansen erinnerte sich: „Ich hatte den Eindruck, dass alles, was darin war, eine schwere Bedrohung war, die auf jenem gesamten Ort lastete, als ob man mich gegen meinen Willen geschnappt hätte, um ein KZ zu besuchen, als ob man mich sehen lassen wollte, wie Menschen tyrannisiert werden, und das war noch nicht alles: Ich ging mit dem merkwürdigen Verdacht weg, dass man entdeckt hatte, dass ich Jude war."[39] Das Motiv des Massengrabs klang auch in der vierten Aktion des Happenings *Rasten und Tanken* (1969) an. Vostell forderte das Publikum auf, sich in eine „Erd-Vertiefung" zu begeben, die ein Bulldozer ausgehoben hatte. „Stellen und pressen Sie sich so dicht wie möglich zusammen."[40] Auch das Dé-coll/age-Happening *Regen* (1976), das ursprünglich ebenfalls für New York geplant war, dann aber in Berlin stattfand, lieferte mit dem Motiv eines Güterwagens einen unmissverständlichen Hinweis auf den Holocaust. In die vorbereitende „1. Partitur" von 1975 collagierte der Künstler in der linken oberen Ecke ein Foto, von dem er annehmen musste, dass es einen offenen Deportationszug mit Tausenden von Menschen zeigt.[41] Rainer Wick, der 1977 dem Happening im *Kunstforum* eine ausführliche Interpretation widmete, identifizierte das Foto ebenfalls in diesem Sinne. In der Verknüpfung mit anderen zeichenhaften Objekten (Brausegriff, Kleiderberg, Brikett, Blechdose und Tierknochen) ergibt sich eine geschlossene Ikonografie, nämlich eine „Todessymbolik, die in allen genannten Motiven als KZ-spezifisch identifizierbar ist ...".[42] Als Beweis für die Verständlichkeit dieser Zeichen zitierte Wick einen Happening-Teilnehmer mit den Worten: „Bei dem Anblick der Duschen ... hat es bei mir geklickt; ich erinnerte mich sofort an ein Konzentrationslager, was ich früher einmal besichtigt habe."[43] Für Wolf Vostell war das Happening das geeignete Medium, um sein Publikum durch physischen wie psychischen Nachvollzug, also ein Durchleben von archetypischen Situationen, mit dem verdrängten Thema des Holocausts zu konfrontieren.

Gerhard Richter (geb. 1932) entzieht sich in vielerlei Hinsicht einem Vergleich mit Boris Lurie. Die Instrumentalisierung von Kunst für außerkünstlerische Zwecke – und seien sie noch so ehrenwert – ist ihm zuwider: „Ich gehöre nicht zu denen, die sich als Antifaschist darstellen, denn das bin ich nicht. Ich bin auch kein Faschist. Ich hatte nie die Neigung, mir allzu viele Dinge bewusst zu machen, das wäre schlecht fürs Malen", sagte Richter 2002.[44] Dennoch hat gerade dieser Maler mit Gemälden wie *Onkel Rudi* (1965), *Tante Marianne* (1965) oder *Herr Heyde* (1965) die einprägsamsten Bilder für die „bleierne Zeit" in der Bundesrepublik gefunden, in welcher der Horror von Nationalsozialismus, „Endlösung" und Euthanasie noch in den Familienalben auf die Entdeckung durch die Generation der Söhne und Töchter wartete.
Gerhard Richter ist in der Boris-Lurie-Ausstellung mit einem Bild vertreten, das ein Projekt vertritt, das nie realisiert wurde. Richter malte 1967 *Olympia* als letztes Bild einer kleinen Werkgruppe mit zehn, teilweise pornografischen Aktdarstellungen. Ein Jahr zuvor hatte der Künstler zusammen mit Konrad Lueg an einer Ausstellung für die Düsseldorfer Galerie Niepel gearbeitet, die den Titel *Sex und Massenmord* tragen sollte. Diese Zusammenführung des Inkompatiblen ist wie auch bei Boris Lurie nur denkbar vor dem Hintergrund einer radikalen Infragestellung des Obszönitätsbegriffs. Was wirklich obszön ist, wurde in den

of bodies as if in a mass grave."[38] The Fluxus artist Al Hansen later recalled: "For me, a feeling of evil pervaded the entire piece – something ominous, as if I had been asked out to a concentration camp to see people bullied, and went with the sneaking suspicion that they'd found out I was Jewish."[39] The theme of the mass grave was also evoked in the fourth action of Vostell's Happening *Rasten und Tanken* [Rest and Refuel] (1969). Here, Vostell asked participants to climb down into a pit that had been dug out by a bulldozer, and then to "Stand and press yourselves together as closely as possible."[40] The dé-coll/age-Happening *Regen* [Rain] (1976), which had originally been planned for New York but was actually staged in Berlin, also unmistakably referenced the Holocaust with the incorporation of a railway freight car. In the top left corner of his preparatory "1st score" for this piece, dating from 1975, Vostell collaged a photograph of what he assumed was a deportation train carrying thousands of people in open wagons.[41] Rainer Wick, who wrote an in-depth analysis of this Happening for the magazine *Kunstforum* in 1977, also interpreted the image in this way. The combination of the freight car with other symbolic objects (shower heads, piles of clothes, briquettes, tin cans, animal bones) creates a cohesive iconography, namely a "symbolism of death that can be identified in all of the elements named above as specific to concentration camps ...".[42] As proof of the comprehensibility of these symbols, Wick quotes a participant in the Happening who said: "When I saw the showers ... I suddenly realized; I immediately recalled a concentration camp I had once visited."[43] For Wolf Vostell, the Happening was the ideal medium in which to confront his audience with the repressed theme of the Holocaust, as it involved a process of physical and mental reenactment, in other words, the personal experience of archetypical situations.

Gerhard Richter, *Olympia*, 1967
Sammlung Böckmann

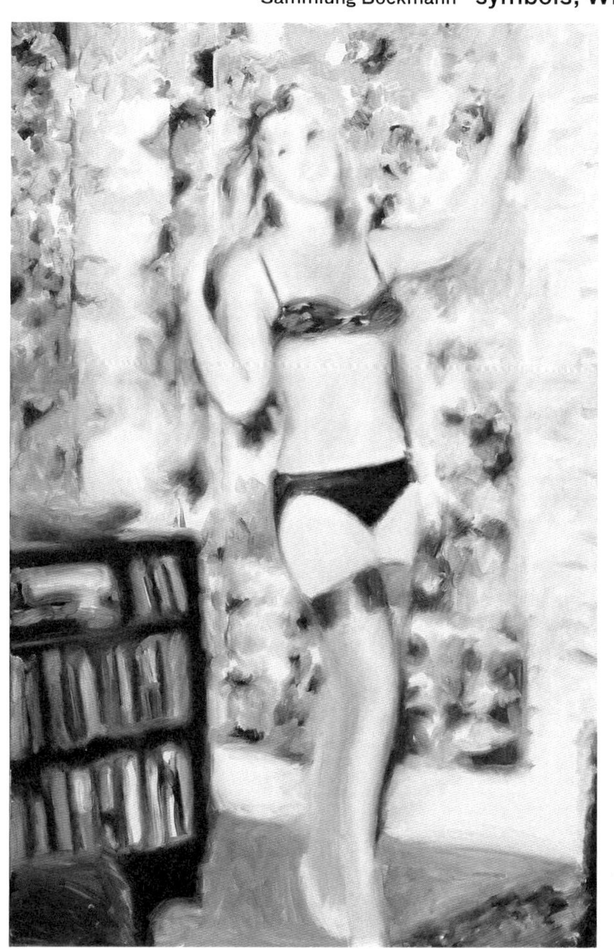

Gerhard Richter (b. 1932). In many respects, it is impossible to draw a comparison between Boris Lurie and Gerhard Richter. For one thing, Richter is opposed to the instrumentalization of art for non-artistic purposes – however honorable the intentions: "I do not belong to those who present themselves as anti-fascists, because I am not. I am also not a fascist. I was disinclined to be conscious of too many things," he said in 2002.[44] Nevertheless, with paintings such as *Onkel Rudi* [Uncle Rudi], *Tante Marianne* [Aunt Marianne] or *Herr Heyde* [Mr. Heyde] (all from 1965), it was Richter who created the most memorable images of the 'leaden times' in West Germany, when the unspeakable horrors of the Third Reich, the Final Solution, and euthanasia were still waiting in family photo albums to be discovered by the generation of sons and daughters.

The Richter painting on show in the exhibition at the Neues Museum represents a project that was never realized. Painted in 1967, *Olympia* was the last in a small group of 10 nudes, some of them pornographic. A year before that, Gerhard Richter and Konrad Lueg had been preparing an exhibition for Galerie Niepel in Düsseldorf that was to be titled *Sex und Massenmord* [Sex and Mass Murder]. As in Boris Lurie's artistic practice, this kind of juxtaposition of incompatible elements can only be conceived in relation to a radical questioning of the notion of obscenity. In the 1950s and 1960s, what was truly obscene was being redefined by a criti-

fünfziger und sechziger Jahren von der kritischen Gegenkultur neu definiert: „Diese Gesellschaft ist insofern obszön, als sie einen erstickenden Überfluss an Waren produziert und schamlos zur Schau stellt, während sie draußen ihre Opfer der Lebenschancen beraubt; obszön, weil sie sich und ihre Mülleimer vollstopft, während sie die kärglichen Lebensmittel in den Gebieten ihrer Aggression vergiftet und niederbrennt; obszön in den Worten und dem Lächeln der Politiker und Unterhalter; in ihren Gebeten, ihrer Ignoranz und in der Weisheit ihrer gehüteten Intellektuellen. [...] Nicht das Bild einer nackten Frau, die ihre Schamhaare entblößt, ist obszön, sondern das eines Generals in vollem Wichs, der seine in einem Aggressionskrieg verdienten Orden zur Schau stellt", schrieb Herbert Marcuse 1969 in seinem *Versuch über die Befreiung*.[45] Ein Zitat, das auch mitten hinein in die Kunst von Boris Lurie führt.
Im Zusammenhang der geplanten Düsseldorfer Ausstellung sammelte Richter sowohl Aufnahmen aus Konzentrationslagern als auch pornografische Fotos aus Magazinen. Doch Richter und Lueg mussten erkennen, dass sich die KZ-Fotos gegen eine künstlerische Inanspruchnahme verweigerten: „Ich habe keine moralische oder formale Lösung gesehen, wie man die KZ- und die Pornobilder hätte ausstellen können, so wie es Konrad Lueg und ich geplant hatten. [...] Wir hätten Aufsehen erregt, aber es wäre unergiebig, unangemessen – mindestens unangemessen gewesen."[46] Doch das Thema Holocaust blieb weiterhin präsent, wenn auch losgelöst aus der Allianz mit dem Pornografischen. 1997 beschäftigte sich Gerhard Richter erneut mit Fotos aus den Vernichtungslagern, als er an seinem Beitrag zur Ausgestaltung des Bundestages im Reichstagsgebäude arbeitete. Wieder verwarf der Künstler seine Überlegungen. Erst mit dem vierteiligen Gemälde *Birkenau* (2014) gelang ihm eine Formulierung des Unaussprechlichen. Die Bilder aus dem Lager sind dem Blick unter einer abstrakten, mehrschichtigen Übermalung entzogen. Sie sind – wie Helmut Friedel zutreffend schreibt – im dreifachen Sinne Hegels „aufgehoben".[47]
Die Fotos, die Gerhard Richter Mitte der sechziger Jahre gesammelt hatte, gingen zum Teil in den *Atlas* ein, das chronologische Bildvorlagenarchiv Richters. Leider findet sich zu *Olympia* keine entsprechende Vorlage. Doch auf der Rückseite des Gemäldes vermerkte der Künstler hinter dem Bildtitel in Klammern: „Roxi Hamburg". Da das „Roxi" ein Hamburger Transvestitenlokal war, liegt der Verdacht nahe, dass es sich bei der jungen Frau um einen jungen Mann in Frauenunterwäsche handelt. Diese Form der Obszönität besitzt utopische Züge, worauf Peter Gorsen 1969 aufmerksam machte: „In der obszönen Vermengung klassengesellschaftlich vermittelter Geschlechtsmerkmale und in der sexualästhetischen Intention auf einen hermaphroditischen Menschentypus ist ein unüberhörbarer Hinweis enthalten auf die Utopie der Versöhnung von Mann und Frau in einer Gesellschaft, die den Unterschied von geschlechtlich Herrschenden und Beherrschten nicht mehr kennt."[48] Die sexuelle Revolution holte die Sexualität aus dem Reservat des Privaten und zog sie auf das Feld des Politisch-Gesellschaftlichen. Obszönität wurde zum Instrument der Aufklärung.

Hans Peter Alvermann (1931–2006) zählte zu jenen gesellschaftskritischen deutschen Künstlern, die Boris Lurie schätzte, ohne dass er mit ihnen je zusammen ausstellte. Angesprochen auf „NO!artists", die mehr Aufmerksamkeit verdient hätten, nannte Lurie in einem 2003 veröffentlichten Interview den Düsseldorfer Künstler an erster Stelle. Max Liljefors wollte wissen: „Which NO!artists

cal counterculture: “This society is obscene in producing and indecently exposing a stifling abundance of wares while depriving its victims abroad of the necessities of life; obscene in stuffing itself and its garbage cans while poisoning and burning the scarce foodstuffs in the fields of its aggression; obscene in the words and smiles of its politicians and entertainers; in its prayers, in its ignorance, and in the wisdom of its kept intellectuals. [...] Obscene is not the picture of a naked woman who exposes her pubic hair but that of a fully clad general who exposes his medals rewarded in a war of aggression,” Herbert Marcuse wrote in his *Essay on Liberation* (1969).[45] This statement also brings us to the very core of Boris Lurie’s art.

In preparation for the planned gallery exhibition in Düsseldorf, Gerhard Richter had collected photographs of concentration camps as well as pornographic images from magazines. In the end, however, he and Konrad Lueg had to acknowledge that the concentration camp photographs eluded artistic appropriation: “I saw no possible moral or formal solution to how to exhibit the camp and the porno pictures as Konrad [Lueg] and I had planned. (...) We would have gotten a lot of attention, but it would have been unproductive and inadequate – at least inadequate.”[46] The theme of the Holocaust stayed with Richter, but it was no longer associated with pornography. In 1997, he returned to photographs of the death camps when he was preparing an artwork for the Reichstag building in Berlin, where the Bundestag [the lower house of the German Parliament] meets. Again, he ended up rejecting his original concept. It was only when he created the four-part painting *Birkenau* (2014) that he found a way to express the unspeakable. The images of the concentration camp in this overpainted work are hidden from view behind multiple layers of abstraction. They are – as Helmut Friedel accurately notes – “sublated” in Hegel’s threefold sense.[47]

Some of the photographs Gerhard Richter collected in the mid-1960s did find their way into the *Atlas*, his chronological archive of source images. Unfortunately, the corresponding image for *Olympia* is not among them. On the back of the painting, however, Richter wrote the words “Roxi Hamburg” in brackets after the title. As the “Roxi” was a transvestite club in Hamburg, the young woman may in fact be a young man wearing women’s underwear. This form of obscenity has utopian traits, as Peter Gorsen pointed out in 1969: “In the obscene merging of sex characteristics mediated by class society, and in the sexual-aesthetic intention towards a hermaphroditic human type, there is an unmistakable reference to the utopia of reconciliation between man and woman in a society where the sexually determined distinction between the rulers and the ruled no longer exists.”[48] The sexual revolution hauled sexuality out of the private realm and into the field of the political/social. Obscenity thus became a tool of enlightenment.

Hans Peter Alvermann (1931–2006) was one of the critical German artists whom Boris Lurie admired, even though they never exhibited together. In an interview with Max Liljefors from 2003, when Lurie is asked: “Which NO!artists do you think should receive more attention today?”, the Düsseldorf-based Alvermann is the first person he mentions: “I’d prefer to extend that question to several other artists who didn’t participate in NO!art exhibitions and yet worked in a similar (and sometimes different) spirit: Peter Alvermann, in Germany, who did very early strictly political [art like] NO!art ...”[49]

do you think should receive more attention today?" Und Boris Lurie antwortete: „I'd prefer to extend that question to several artists as well, who didn't participate in NO!art exhibitions; yet working in a similar (and sometimes different) spirit: Peter Alvermann, in Germany, who did very early strictly political [art like] NO!art [...]".[49]
Es liegt auf der Hand, warum Boris Lurie auf H. P. Alvermann aufmerksam wurde. Es war dessen „Einsicht in die Überflüssigkeit der etablierten Kunst" und in die „Überflüssigkeit des Establishments".[50] Als weitere Parallele kam die Technik der Assemblage hinzu, wie sie in der March Group vor allem von Sam Goodman praktiziert wurde. In den Jahren von 1959 bis 1966 schuf Alvermann rund 130 Objektkunstwerke in der Nachfolge von Dada und Surrealismus. Dabei unterschied der Künstler zwei Werkphasen: „magische Objekte" (1960 – 62) und „soziografische Modelle" (1963 – 66).[51] Jürgen Morschel erklärte den Griff zum vorgefundenen Objekt mit dem höheren Realitätsgehalt im Vergleich zum gemalten Bild. „Es geht nicht, wie bei den ready-mades von Duchamp oder zumeist bei der Pop-art, um den Gegenstand an sich, um seine Faktizität, sondern um den Gegenstand als Attribut von sozialen, politischen Verhaltensweisen und Befindlichkeiten."[52] Die Zielscheiben von Alvermanns Attacken mit seinen „politischen Objekten" waren nach Morschel „die verschiedenen Formen von Ausbeutung, frömmelnder Heuchelei, Nationalismus, Wohlstandseuphorie".[53] Und Willy Rotzler führte einen ganzen „Katalog ungelöster Probleme" auf, die Alvermann verhandelte: „Mechanismen und Exzesse der Wirtschaft, der Mief des Kleinbürgertums, die Bundeswehr als Ausdruck neuen Säbelgerassels, Zivilschutz, Wohlstandskomfort und unbewältigte Vergangenheit, daneben ungelöste Probleme der Vereinigten Staaten, Rassismus, Prosperität und Elend, Vietnam-Krieg, aber auch der Hunger in der Welt, Kosmetik, Sex-Kult und Priapismus".[54] Diese Gemengelage entsprach weitgehend der Sicht Boris Luries auf die herrschenden Verhältnisse. Alvermann war ein Bruder im Geiste, lediglich dessen Marxismus trennte die beiden Künstler. Besonders gefallen hätte Lurie gewiss auch das QUIBB-Manifest, das Alvermann gemeinsam mit Winfred Gaul im Januar 1963 veröffentlichte: „QUIBB-Kunst ist keine deutsche Version von Pop-Art", hieß es darin.[55] Und die beiden so unterschiedlichen Künstler, die denn auch bald wieder getrennte Wege gingen, betonten, dass sie es ablehnten, „eine gesinnungshomogene Clique von Snobs und Spekulanten mit Sensationen und Gags zu füttern".[56] War das nicht reinster „Anti-Pop", made in Germany?
Immer mehr begann Alvermann zu begreifen, dass es zunächst einmal galt, ein Publikum für jene Kunst zu schaffen, die er machen wollte: „Das kann aber die Kunst für sich allein nicht. Das war und ist eine soziale Fragestellung, die etwas mit den Eigentumsverhältnissen in unserer Gesellschaft zu tun hat."[57] In letzter Konsequenz seines politischen Selbstverständnisses stellte er 1966 die künstlerische Produktion für einige Jahre ein, um sich ganz der politischen Aktion in der außerparlamentarischen Opposition widmen zu können. „Er organisierte das ‚Republikanische Centrum' in Düsseldorf und engagierte sich in der Bewegung gegen die Notstandsgesetze und den Vietnam-Krieg", heißt es auf der Website der Stiftung Kunstfonds, die seit 2009 den Nachlass verwaltet.[58] Solange der Sozialismus noch nicht erreicht war, hatte sich Kunst der Politik dienend unterzuordnen: „Politische Kunst ist eine alberne Farce ohne das gleichzeitige politische Handeln. Sie entsteht und formuliert sich in der politischen Praxis",

It is easy to see why Boris Lurie became interested in H. P. Alvermann, whose "insight into the superfluousness of established art" and into the "superfluousness of the establishment"[50] doubtless struck a chord with him. Other parallels include the technique of assemblage, as practiced in the March Group above all by Sam Goodman. Between 1959 and 1966, Alvermann created around 130 sculptural objects in the tradition of Dada and Surrealism, whereby he made a distinction between two bodies of work: "magic objects" (1960 – 2) and "sociographic models" (1963 – 6).[51] Jürgen Morschel attributed Alvermann's use of found objects to the fact that these contained more truth than a painted picture: "Here it is not about the object per se, its facticity, as it is with Duchamp's readymades or, for the most part, with Pop Art, but rather about the object as an attribute of social, political modes of behavior and sensitivities."[52] The targets of Alvermann's attacks with his "political objects" were, according to Morschel, "the various forms of exploitation, bigoted hypocrisy, nationalism, [and] the euphoria of prosperity".[53] Willy Rotzler, meanwhile, presented a whole "catalogue of unsolved problems" that Alvermann was addressing: "economic mechanisms and excesses, the stuffiness of the petty bourgeoisie, the Bundeswehr [German Armed Forces] as a new expression of saber rattling, civil defense, comfortable affluence and the failure to come to terms with the past, as well as unresolved issues in the United States, racism, prosperity and misery, the Vietnam War, not to mention global starvation, cosmetics, the cult of sex, and priapism."[54] This hodgepodge of themes largely corresponded to Boris Lurie's view of the current situation. Alvermann was a kindred spirit; the only thing that separated the two artists was Alvermann's Marxist leanings. Lurie would no doubt have liked the "QUIBB" manifesto, published by Alvermann and Winfred Gaul in January 1963, which contained the statement that: "QUIBB art is not a German version of Pop Art."[55] And both Gaul and Alvermann – two very different artists who soon went their separate ways again – firmly rejected the idea of "feeding a like-minded clique of snobs and speculators with sensations and gags."[56] Was this not the purist form of "Anti Pop" – made in Germany?

Alvermann became increasingly aware that his primary concern must be to create an audience for the art he wanted to make. "But that cannot be done by art alone. That was and is a social issue that has something to do with the ownership structure in our society."[57] In 1966, as the logical consequence of his political stance, Alvermann stopped producing art for a number of years in order to devote himself entirely to political activism. "He organized the 'Republikanisches Centrum' in Düsseldorf and was active in the movement against the Emergency Laws act and the Vietnam War," one reads the entry on the website of Stiftung Kunstfonds, a foundation that has managed the artist's estate since 2009.[58] Alvermann believed that as long as socialism had not been realized, art had to take on the subordinate role of serving politics. "Political art is a ridiculous farce without simultaneous political action. It emerges and is expressed through political practice," he asserted in 1970, citing the posters from the May 1968 uprising in Paris as an example.[59]

Alvermann's assemblage *Warten auf Nürnberg II* [Waiting for Nuremberg II] (1966) is a prominent example of political art that touches on the subject of how German crimes committed during World War II were hushed up and forgotten. The artist's skillful use of a few found objects makes this sculpture stand out from the rest of his oeuvre. Alvermann frequently incorporated parts of dress-

postulierte der Künstler 1970 und verwies als Beispiel auf die Plakate im Pariser Mai.[59]

Alvermanns Assemblage *Warten auf Nürnberg II* von 1966 ist ein prominentes Beispiel für politische Kunst, die am Totschweigen und Vergessen der deutschen Verbrechen im Zweiten Weltkrieg rührt. Durch den präzisen Einsatz weniger Fundstücke ragt die Plastik aus dem Werk des Künstlers hervor. Alvermann arbeitete in den sechziger Jahren wiederholt mit Teilen von Schaufensterpuppen. Die untere Hälfte einer weiblichen Puppe schließt oben etwa in Höhe der Taille mit der Andeutung einer rot geschminkten Unterlippe ab. Zum Mund ergänzt, wird die Lippe durch die leicht nach vorne gezogene Unterkante eines Stahlhelms, der die Figur sexuell zwiespältig in Erscheinung treten lässt. Eine gekrümmte Schneide, deren ursprünglicher Zweck im Dunkel bleibt, dringt wie ein Säbel durch das behaarte weibliche Geschlecht und wirkt wie ein bedrohlicher Phallus. Solcherart gelingt es dem Künstler, Opfer und Täter in eins fallen zu lassen.

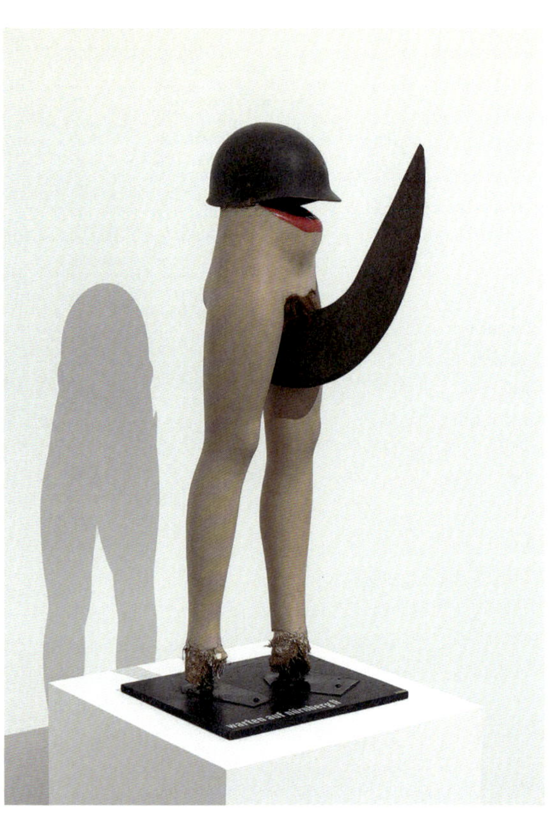
H.P. Alvermann,
Warten auf Nürnberg II, 1966
Památník Lidice /
Gedenkstätte Lidice /
Lidice Memorial

Das eindrückliche Bild für Folter und Krieg will auch als Mahnung an die Zeitgenossen verstanden werden. Zu seinem Titel „Nürnberg II", der eine Neuauflage der Nürnberger Prozesse meint, merkte der Künstler an: „Wenn die Opfer von gestern nicht umsonst gewesen sein sollen, kann es nur in ihrem – und in unser allereigenstem Interesse sein – die Mörder von heute zu denunzieren. Jede Illusion über die Brutalität und die Methoden des Terrors der Herrschenden heute illustriert, wie sehr wir es verstanden haben, die Vergangenheit zu bewältigen – eine Bewältigung, die hauptsächlich darin bestand, das Leiden der Opfer und die Ursachen, die sie zu Opfern machten und jene zu Mördern, recht gründlich zu verdrängen. Und dann zum Titel des Objekts: wir werden nicht zulassen, dass unsere mörderische Gegenwart, wenn sie erst einmal Vergangenheit geworden sein wird, ebenso tatenlos bewältigt werden wird, wie unsere Väter und ihre Kumpane die ihrige seit zwanzig Jahren bewältigen. Wir werden uns die Namen derer, die heute am Werk sind, gut merken."[60]

Bei diesem „Monstrum"[61], von dem der Künstler selbst sprach, handelte es sich um Alvermanns Beitrag zu einer Ausstellung des Berliner Galeristen René Block, der 1967 an das 25 Jahre zurückliegende Massaker im tschechischen Lidice (1942) erinnerte. Viele wichtige Künstler beteiligten sich daran: u.a. Joseph Beuys, K. P. Brehmer, Gotthard Graubner, Sigmar Polke, Gerhard Richter und Wolf Vostell. Dieser repräsentative Querschnitt deutscher Avantgardekunst in Form von 21 Beiträgen wurde im Frühjahr 1968 von René Block persönlich in die Tschechoslowakei gebracht, um in Prag kurz vor dem Einmarsch der Truppen des Warschauer Paktes noch ausgestellt zu werden. Erst 1996 wurden die Kunstwerke im Schloss Nelahozeves bei Prag wiederentdeckt, wo sie versteckt worden waren. Heute bilden diese Werke den Grundstock der Sammlung der Gedenkstätte Lidice. Es zeichnet René Block aus, dass er fortsetzte, was er 1967 mit der *Hommage à Lidice* begonnen hatte. 1997 führte er sein Projekt mit *Pro Lidice* fort, und Anfang Juni 2017 wird die Gedenkstätte anlässlich des 75. Jahrestags der Vernichtung von Lidice die zweite, diesmal internationale Erweiterung unter dem Titel *Remember Lidice* in Empfang nehmen. Diese Form eines

maker's dummies into the works he produced in the 1960s. Here, the bottom half of a female dummy is topped off at roughly waist height by the suggestion of a lower lip with red lipstick. This lip forms the shape of a mouth in combination with the rim of a steel helmet that has been pulled forward slightly, making the figure appear sexually ambiguous. A curved blade, its original use unclear, cuts into the mannequin's hairy crotch like a sabre, invoking a threatening phallus. In this way, Alvermann brings victim and perpetrator together as one.

This striking image of torture and war is also intended as a warning to people in the present day. On the title of his work – "Nürnberg II" – referring to a restaging of the Nuremberg trials, Alvermann wrote: "If the victims of yesterday are not to have suffered in vain, it can only be in their – and our – best interests to denounce the murderers of today. Every illusion about the brutality and terror methods employed by today's rulers forces illustrates how well we have been able to come to terms with the past – a process that has mainly consisted in thoroughly repressing the victims' suffering and the causal circumstances that turned them into victims and others into murderers. And as far as the title of the object is concerned: we will not allow our murderous present, once it has become the past, to be dealt with in the way our fathers and their pals have dealt with theirs for the last 20 years – by remaining silent and failing to act. We will be sure to remember the names of those who are at work today."[60]

The "monster,"[61] as the artist himself called it, was Alvermann's contribution to the exhibition *Hommage à Lidice*, organized by the Berlin gallerist René Block in 1967 to commemorate the massacre in the Czech village of Lidice 25 years earlier, in June 1942. Many leading artists took part in the show, including Joseph Beuys, K. P. Brehmer, Gotthard Graubner, Sigmar Polke, Gerhard Richter, and Wolf Vostell. In spring 1968, Block himself transported this representative cross-section of German avant-garde art (21 works) to Czechoslovakia, where it was presented in Prague just before the country was invaded by Warsaw Pact troops. The artworks were not rediscovered until 1996, having been hidden away in Nelahozeves Castle, near Prague, in the intervening period. Today, these works form the core of the art collection at the Lidice Memorial. Credit is due to René Block for continuing what he began in 1967 with *Hommage à Lidice*. The second stage of the project was *Pro Lidice* (1997), and in early June 2017, the Lidice Memorial will host *Remember Lidice*, a third exhibition featuring works by many international artists, to mark the 75th anniversary of the massacre. This kind of living, growing monument made up of numerous donated artworks may well be the only one of its kind in the world.

Gustav Metzger (1926–2017) belonged to the same generation as Boris Lurie, with whom he also shared the experience of suffering in the Holocaust. Witnessing at first hand the fragility and vulnerability of human civilization was formative for Metzger, who was born in Nuremberg but later lived and worked in London. He was the son of Orthodox Jews who were murdered in the Holocaust, and survived by being sent to England under the auspices of the Refugee Children's Movement. In the late 1950s, Metzger developed the concept of auto-destructive art; from then on, destructive and transformative processes were central to his explicitly political art, which denounced capitalism, rejected the art market to the point of calling on artists to strike, and drew attention to the fact that mankind was destroying the ecological basis of its own existence.

lebendigen, wachsenden Denkmals, das aus vielen Kunstwerken besteht, dürfte weltweit einzigartig sein.

Gustav Metzger (1926–2017) entstammte derselben Generation wie Boris Lurie. Darüber hinaus teilte er mit Lurie das Leid des Holocausts. Die Brüchigkeit und Gefährdung menschlicher Zivilisation bildeten die Urerfahrung des in Nürnberg geborenen Künstlers, der in London lebte. Der Sohn orthodoxer Juden, die im Holocaust ermordet wurden, überlebte dank des „Refugee Children's Movement" in England. Ende der 1950er Jahre trat Metzger mit dem Konzept der „Autodestruktiven Kunst" hervor. Seitdem standen Prozesse der Zerstörung und Transformation im Mittelpunkt seiner explizit politischen Kunst, die sich kritisch mit dem Kapitalismus auseinandersetzte, sich dem Kunstmarkt bis hin zum Streikaufruf verweigerte und die Vernichtung unserer ökologischen Existenzgrundlagen bewusst machte.
Das ausgestellte Kunstwerk setzt einen aktiven Betrachter voraus: *Historic Photographs: To Crawl Into – Anschluss, Vienna, March 1938*. „To crawl into" heißt „hineinkriechen". Wer der Aufforderung des Künstlers folgt und unter das gelbe Tuch kriecht, entdeckt ein historisches Foto, das eine sogenannte Reibpartie nach dem „Anschluss" Österreichs im März 1938 zeigt, bei der jüdische Frauen und Männer von der Hitlerjugend gezwungen wurden, missliebige politische Parolen vom Straßenpflaster zu waschen. Der Schriftsteller Carl Zuckmayer beschrieb diese antisemitischen Erniedrigungen als „Alptraumgemälde des Hieronymus Bosch [...]. Die Luft war von einem unablässig gellenden, wüsten, hysterischen Gekreische erfüllt, aus Männer- und Weiberkehlen, das tage- und nächtelang weiterschrillte. Und alle Menschen verloren ihr Gesicht, glichen verzerrten Fratzen: die einen in Angst, die andren in Lüge, die andren in wildem, haßerfülltem Triumph. [...] Ich erlebte die ersten Tage der Naziherrschaft in Berlin. Nichts davon war mit diesen Tagen in Wien zu vergleichen. [...] Was hier entfesselt wurde, war der Aufstand des Neids, der Mißgunst, der Verbitterung, der blinden, böswilligen Rachsucht – und alle anderen Stimmen waren zum Schweigen verurteilt."[62]
Unter dem Tuch, dessen gelbe Farbe für die Stigmatisierung der Juden durch den „Judenstern" steht, ist der kriechende Besucher in der Position der gedemütigten Menschen auf dem Foto. Es kommt zu einer Vergegenwärtigung der historischen Szene: „Wenn die Besucher vorher schon wüssten, was unter dem Tuch ist, würden sie lieber nicht hineingehen [...]. Es gibt Reaktionen wie ‚Ich bin erschüttert'. Das ist der Zweck meiner Arbeiten. Dieser Effekt würde nicht erreicht, wenn sie an der Wand hängen würden", erklärte Gustav Metzger.[63] Wer erst einmal unter das Tuch gekrochen ist, kann sich der Darstellung nicht mehr entziehen. Gleichzeitig ermöglicht der körperliche Nachvollzug eine Einfühlung in die Szene. Dies unterscheidet Metzgers Konzept grundsätzlich von Luries Strategie der Konfrontation und des Schocks, die in Kauf nimmt, den Betrachter auf Abstand zu halten.

„Reproduzierte Tragik": Gustav Metzger und Boris Lurie – und dies gilt für auch für Gerhard Richter und Wolf Vostell – vertrauen sich dem historischen Foto an. Sigmar Polke schuf 1982 das Bild *Lager* ebenfalls nach einem Foto. Es zeigt den Todesstreifen eines Konzentrationslagers zwischen Stacheldrahtzäunen. Polke betonte, dass es sich um keine Malerei handle: „Es ist eine Reproduk-

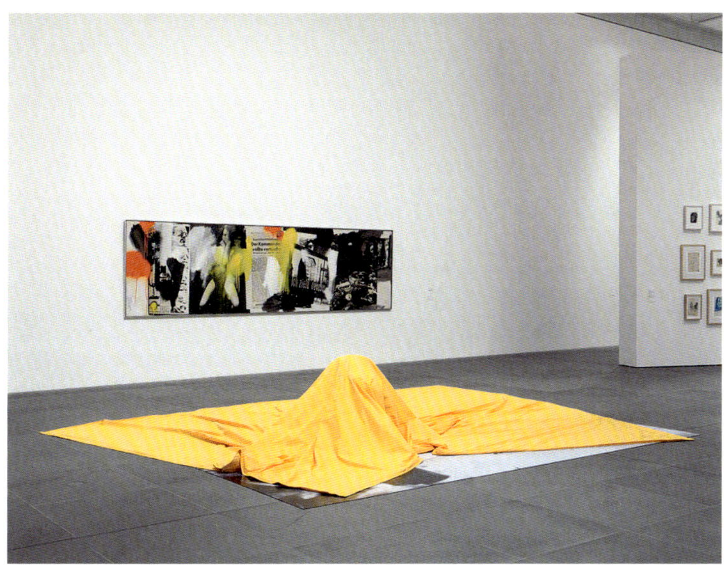

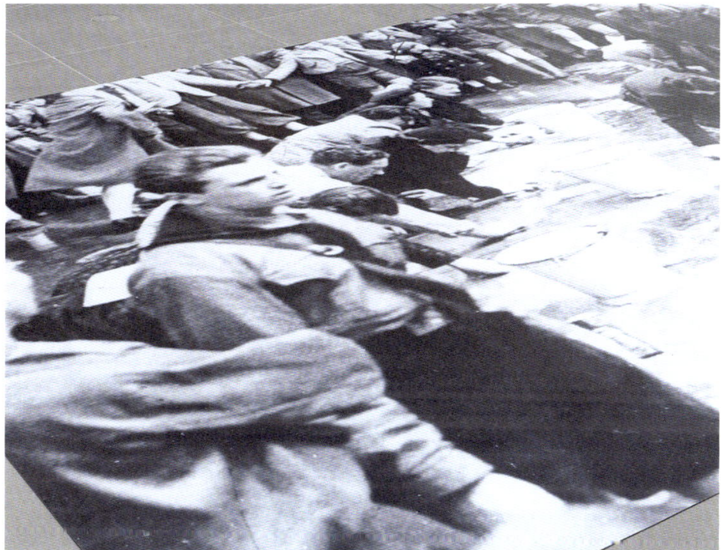

Gustav Metzger, *Historic Photographs: To Crawl Into – Anschluss, Vienna, March 1938*, 1996/2017
Collection of the artist

Metzger's work in the current exhibition demands active participation on the part of the viewer: *Historic Photographs: To Crawl Into – Anschluss, Vienna, March 1938* (1996/2017). When they crawl beneath the yellow cloth according to the artist's instructions, they will discover a historical photograph of a "Reibpartie" [scrubbing party]; following the annexation of Austria into Nazi Germany in March 1938, members of the Hitler Youth forced Jewish women and men to scrub off the political protest slogans that had been scrawled over paving stones. The writer Carl Zuckmayer compared these humiliating, anti-Semitic actions to "a nightmare painting by Hieronymus Bosch (...) The air was filled with incessant screeching, horrible, piercing, hysterical cries from the throats of men and women who continued screaming day and night. People's faces vanished, were replaced by contorted masks: some of fear, some of cunning, some of wild, hate-filled triumph. (...) I saw the early period of Nazi rule in Berlin. But none of it was comparable to those days in Vienna. (...) What was unleashed upon Vienna was a torrent of envy, jealousy, bitterness, blind, malignant craving for revenge. All better instincts were silenced."[62]

Crawling under the yellow cloth – its color symbolizing the stigmatization of Jews by making them wear yellow stars – exhibition visitors find themselves in the same position as the humiliated people in the photograph. The historical scene is visualized in the present. "If the visitors knew in advance what was under the cloth, they would rather not go in there (...). There are reactions like 'I'm devastated'. That's the purpose of my artworks. This effect would not be achieved if they were hung on the wall," Metzger explained.[63] Once you have crawled under the cloth, you can no longer avoid the image. At the same time, the physical reenactment enables you to empathize with the people shown in the photograph. This highlights a fundamental distinction between Metzger's concept and Lurie's strategy based on confrontation and shock, which runs the risk of distancing the viewer.

The reproduction of tragedy: Gustav Metzger and Boris Lurie put their faith in historical photographs, and the same applies to Gerhard Richter and Wolf Vostell. Sigmar Polke's painting *Lager* [Camp] (1982), which shows a death strip between barbed-wire fences in a concentration camp, was also based on a photograph. Polke stressed that for him, "the painting in *Camp* is not painting. It's a reproduction. (...) [I]t would be impossible to paint (...). I used the narrative form and the assumed objectivity of a photograph to reproduce tragedy."[64] Photographs offer a way out of the dilemma resulting from the fact that any allegorization of the Holocaust would require appropriation by the artist, which is impossible. Only reproduction can guarantee the "adequacy" referred to by Gerhard Richter, which any attempt at authentic production would be unable to achieve. That is why photographs are so important as far as artistic responses to the mass murder of the European Jews are concerned. One of the most impressive and earliest of these responses is a series of collaged drawings made by the

tion. Man könnte das gar nicht malen. [...] Ich habe die narrative Form und das Objektive eines Photos benutzt als reproduzierte Tragik."[64] Das Foto bietet einen Ausweg aus dem Dilemma, dass jede Form von Allegorisierung des Holocausts eine Aneignung durch den Künstler zur Voraussetzung hätte, die nicht möglich ist. Erst die Reproduktion garantiert jene Angemessenheit, von der Gerhard Richter spricht, die jeder Versuch authentischer Produktion verfehlen müsste. Deshalb kommt dem Foto bei der künstlerischen Auseinandersetzung mit dem Massenmord an den europäischen Juden diese Bedeutung zu. Eines der eindrücklichsten und frühesten Beispiele dafür sind die collagierten und gezeichneten Blätter *Meinen Freunden, den Juden,* die der polnische Künstler Władysław Strzemiński bereits 1945 schuf. Zeichnungen, die eine in Auflösung befindliche Figuration zeigen, sind durch Aufnahmen aus dem Ghetto und den Konzentrationslagern ergänzt.

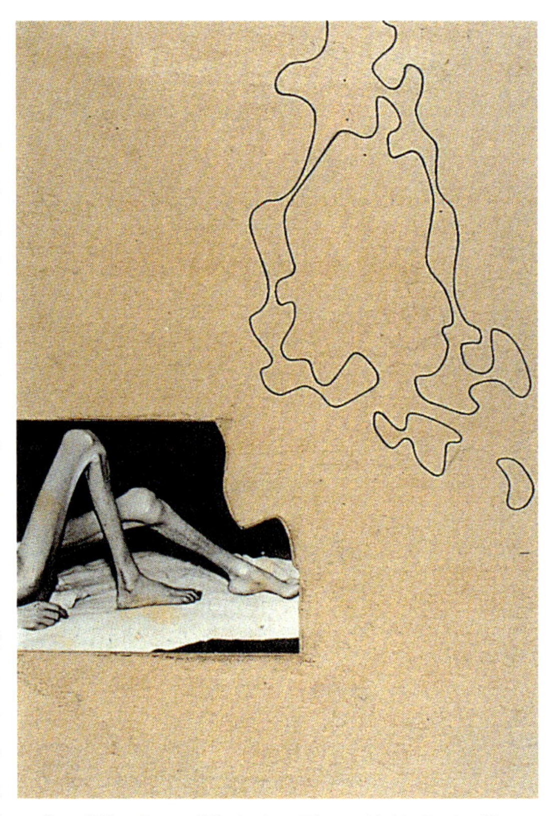

Władysław Strzemiński: *Gestrafft von den Saiten der Beine,* aus dem Zyklus *Meinen Freunden, den Juden,* 1945
Yad Vashem Art Museum, Jerusalem

Ein anderer Versuch, sich dem Holocaust anzunähern, kommt dagegen weitgehend ohne Fotos aus. Er baut auf Materialmetaphorik und eine Fülle von Verweisen und Beziehungen. Es handelt sich um die 1968 eingerichtete Vitrine *Auschwitz Demonstration* von Joseph Beuys. Sie enthält Objekte aus den Jahren 1956 bis 1964. Der Künstler hatte sich 1958 an einem internationalen Wettbewerb für ein Denkmal in Auschwitz-Birkenau beteiligt. „Ich maße mir nicht an, dass ich dadurch – durch diese Sachen – etwas wiedergegeben habe von dem Schrecklichen", antwortete Beuys 1982 auf die Frage nach der Darstellbarkeit von Auschwitz.[65]

Nach Auschwitz ein Gedicht zu schreiben oder ein anderes Kunstwerk zu schaffen, ist ebenso barbarisch, wie es im „Bewusstsein von Leiden unter den Menschen" zu unterlassen. Joseph Beuys erkannte in Auschwitz das „Prinzip Auschwitz", das in der „Delegation von Verantwortung an Spezialisten und im Schweigen der Intellektuellen und Künstler fortgeführt" werde.[66] Boris Lurie hätte dem gewiss zugestimmt.

1 Theodor W. Adorno: *Metaphysik. Begriffe und Probleme,* 1965, zit. nach: Georges Didi-Huberman: „Die Malerei in ihrem aporetischen Moment", in: Helmut Friedel (Hrsg.): *Gerhard Richter. Birkenau,* Ausstellungskatalog, Museum Frieder Burda, Baden-Baden, 6. 2. – 29. 5. 2016, Köln 2016, S. 40.

2 Unter dem Titel *The Three Prophets* wurden die drei New Yorker Künstler 2013 in der Galerie The Box in Los Angeles gemeinsam vorgestellt.

3 Vgl. Mirjam Wenzel: „Von der Schau zur Lust. Zur Dekonstruktion der Fotografie in den Collagen von Boris Lurie", in: *Keine Kompromisse! Die Kunst des Boris Lurie,* Ausstellungskatalog, Jüdisches Museum Berlin, 26. 2. –31. 7. 2016, S. 144 ff., insbesondere S. 150 – 152.

4 Dore Ashton: „Merdre, Alors!", 1969, in: Boris Lurie und Seymour Krim: *NO!art. Pin-ups, Excrement, Protest, Jew-Art,* Köln/Berlin 1988, S. 62.

5 Sam Goodman: „Statement zur Untergangsausstellung", 1961, in: Lurie und Krim 1988, vgl. Anm. 4, S. 45.

6 Es handelt sich um den Artikel „Eichmann Confesses", in: *Life,* 21. November 1960.

7 Boris Lurie: „Scheiß Nein!", 1970, in: Lurie und Krim 1988, vgl. Anm. 4, S. 66 f.

8 Boris Lurie: „Involvement Show Statement", 1961, in: Lurie und Krim 1988, vgl. Anm. 4, S. 43.

9 Vgl. John Wronoski: „Boris Lurie: Ein Leben im Lager", in: *KZ – Kampf – Kunst. Boris Lurie: NO!art,* Ausstellungskatalog, NS-Dokumentationszentrum der Stadt Köln, 27. 8. – 2. 11. 2014, hrsg. von der Boris Lurie Art Foundation,, New York 2014, S. 176.

10 Ebd., S. 139.

11 Boris Lurie: „Scheiß Nein!", 1970, in: Lurie und Krim 1988, vgl. Anm. 4, S. 72.

12 Johannes Meinhardt: *Ende der Malerei und Malerei nach dem Ende der Malerei,* Ostfildern-Ruit 1997, S. 130.

13 Boris Lurie: „Stanley Fisher (1926 – 1980). Geheimnisvoll bis zum Ende", 1980, in: Lurie und Krim 1988, vgl. Anm. 4, S. 115 f.

14 Simon Taylor: „Die NO!art-Bewegung in New York, 1960 bis 1964", in: *NO!art,* Ausstellungskatalog, Neue Gesellschaft für Bildende Kunst, Berlin, 21. 10. – 26. 11. 1995, S. 16.

15 Boris Lurie: „Stanley Fisher (1926 – 1980). Geheimnisvoll bis zum Ende", 1980, in: Lurie und Krim 1988, vgl. Anm. 4, S. 116.

16 Jean-Jacques Lebel: „Theory and Practice", 1967, zit. nach: Alyce Mahon: „Rückgeburt und Wiedergeburt: Das Festival de la Libre Expression, 1964 – 1967", in: Axel Heil, Robert Fleck, Alyce Mahon: *Jean-Jacques Lebel. Barrikaden,* Sonderausgabe zur Ausstellung *Jean-Jacques Lebel. Die höchste Kunst ist der Aufstand,* ZKM | Zentrum für Kunst und Medientechnologie Karlsruhe, 26. 7. – 9. 11. 2014, Köln 2014, S. 64 f.

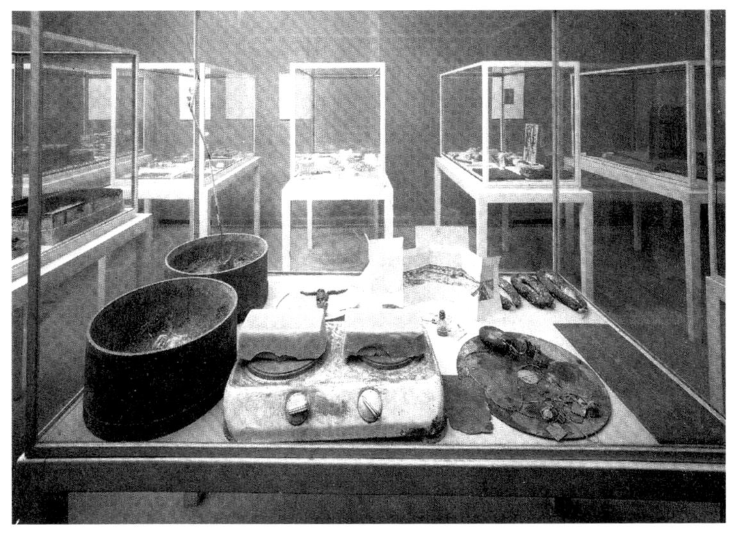

Joseph Beuys: *Auschwitz Demonstration*, 1956 – 64
Hessisches Landesmuseum Darmstadt

Polish artist Władysław Strzemiński in 1945, entitled *Meinen Freunden, den Juden*, [To My Friends, the Jews]. Here, drawings of figures in the process of dissolving are combined with photographic images of the ghetto and the concentration camps.

Another artistic approach to the theme of the Holocaust does largely without photographs, relying instead on material metaphors and a wealth of references and associations. It is Joseph Beuys' vitrine *Auschwitz Demonstration*, which he installed in 1968. The objects in the vitrine date from the period 1956 – 64. In 1958, Beuys had taken part in an international competition to create a monument for Auschwitz-Birkenau. "I do not presume to have reproduced any of the horror through this – through these things," Beuys said in 1982, when asked about the possibility of depicting Auschwitz.[65]

Writing poetry or creating any other kind of artwork after Auschwitz is just as barbaric as not doing so on account of an "awareness of suffering among human beings." In the context of his reflections on Auschwitz, Joseph Beuys perceived what he called the "principle of Auschwitz" that "finds its perpetuation (...) in the delegation of responsibility to groups of specialists, and in the silence of intellectuals and artists."[66] It is an observation that Boris Lurie would no doubt have agreed with.

1 Theodor W. Adorno, *Metaphysics: Concept and Problems*, ed. Rolf Tiedemann, trans. Edmund Jephcott (Stanford, CA: Stanford University Press, 2000), p. 110.
2 In 2013, the three New York artists were the subject of a joint exhibition at The Box gallery in Los Angeles entitled *The Three Prophets*.
3 Cf. Mirjam Wenzel, 'From Display to Lust: The Deconstruction of Photographs in Boris Lurie's Collages,' in *No Compromises! The Art of Boris Lurie*, exh. cat. Jewish Museum Berlin, February 26–July 31, 2016 (Bielefeld & Berlin, Kerber Verlag, 2016), pp. 144 – 52, especially pp. 150 – 2.
4 Dore Ashton, 'Merde, Alors!' (1960), in Boris Lurie and Seymour Krim (eds.), *NO!art. Pin-ups, Excrement, Protest, Jew-Art* (Berlin/Cologne: Edition Hundertmark, 1988), pp. 54 – 6, here p. 55.
5 Sam Goodman, 'Doom Show Statement' (1961), in Lurie and Krim 1988, see note 4, p. 41.
6 The portrait illustrated the article 'Eichmann Confesses' that appeared in *Life* magazine on November 21, 1960.
7 Boris Lurie, 'Shit No! (1970), in Lurie and Krim 1988, see note 4, pp. 56 – 64, here p. 59.
8 Boris Lurie, 'Involvement Show Statement' (1961), in Lurie and Krim 1988, see note 4, pp. 39f, here p. 39.
9 Cf. John Wronoski, 'Boris Lurie: A Life in the Camps,' in *KZ – Kampf – Kunst. Boris Lurie: NO!art*, exh. cat., NS-Dokumentationszentrum der Stadt Köln, August 27 – November 2, 2014 (New York, 2014), pp. 25 – 292, here p. 174.
10 Ibid., p. 137.
11 Boris Lurie, 'Shit No!' in Lurie and Krim 1988, see note 4, p. 63.
12 Johannes Meinhardt, *Ende der Malerei und Malerei nach dem Ende der Malerei* (Ostfildern-Ruit: Cantz, 1997), p. 130.
13 Boris Lurie, 'Stanley Fisher (1926 – 1980), Mysterious to the End' (1980), in Lurie and Krim 1988, see note 4, pp. 99 – 101, here pp. 99f.
14 Simon Taylor, 'Die NO!art-Bewegung in New York, 1960 bis 1964,' in *NO!art*, exh. cat., Neue Gesellschaft für Bildende Kunst, Berlin, October 21 – November 26, 1995 (Berlin: Neue Gesellschaft für Bildende Kunst, 1995). English version: 'The NO!art Movement in New York, 1960 – 1964', available online at <<http://text.no-art.info/en/taylor_%20no-art-movement.pdf>>; accessed April 12, 2017.
15 Boris Lurie, 'Stanley Fisher (1926–1980), Mysterious to the End' (1980), in Lurie and Krim 1988, see note 4, p. 99.
16 Jean-Jacques Lebel, 'Theory and Practice' (1967), quoted in Alyce Mahon, 'Unbirth and Rebirth: The Festival of Free Expression, 1964 – 1967,' in Axel Heil, Robert Fleck, and Alyce Mahon, *Jean-Jacques Lebel. Barricades*, special issue for the exhibition *Jean-Jacques Lebel. Die höchste Kunst ist der Aufstand. The Highest of All the Arts is Insurrection. Il n'est d'art qu'insurrection*, ZKM – Zentrum für Kunst und Medientechnologie Karlsruhe, July 26 – November 9, 2014 (Cologne: Verlag der Buchhandlung Walther König, 2014), pp. 40 – 69, here pp. 64f.
17 Jean-Jacques Lebel, 'Notes on Political Street Theatre, Paris: 1968, 1969' (1969), *TDR/The Drama Review* 13, no. 4 (Summer 1969), pp. 111 – 8, here p. 112.
18 Michelle Stuart, 'NO is an Involvement' (1969), in Lurie and Krim 1988, see note 4, pp. 44f, here p. 44.
19 Boris Lurie, 'Involvement Show Statement' (1961), in Lurie and Krim 1988, see note 4, p. 39.
20 Ibid.
21 Ibid.
22 Brian O'Doherty, 'Introduction' (1971), in Lurie and Krim 1988, see note 4, p. 17.
23 Boris Lurie, 'Shit No! (1970), in Lurie and Krim 1988, see note 4, p. 61.
24 Wolf Vostell, 'No Blood ... Please ...' (1977), in Lurie and Krim 1988, see note 4, pp. 18f, here p. 18.
25 Andreas Nachama, 'Holocaust Memorial,' in *Wolf Vostell, Meine Kunst ist der ewige Widerstand gegen den Tod; My Art is the Eternal Resistance to Death*, exh. cat., Rheinisches Landesmuseum Bonn, August 15 – November 25, 2007; Carré d'art/Musée d'Art Contemporain de Nîmes, February 12 – May 12, 2008 (Cologne: Landschaftsverband Rheinland, 2007), pp. 79 – 83, here p. 82.
26 Fritz Emslander, '"Für mich waren die Happenings das Wichtigste". Ein Gespräch mit Mercedes Guardado Olivenza Vostell,' in *Wolf Vostell. Die Druckgrafik*, exh. cat., Städtische Galerie Villa Zanders, Bergisch Gladbach, September 4 – November 27, 2005; Kunsthalle Bremen, September 5 – November 5, 2006; Museo Vostell, Malpartida, 2007 (Bergisch Gladbach: Städtische Galerie Villa Zanders, 2005), p. 33.
27 Peter Weibel, 'The German View,' in Vostell, exh. cat. 2007, see note 25, pp. 12 – 15, here p. 13.

17 Jean-Jacques Lebel: „Notes on Political Street Theatre, Paris: 1968, 1969“, 1969, zit. nach: Mahon 2014, vgl. Anm. 16, S. 67.
18 Michelle Stuart: „Nein heißt Engagement“, 1961, in: Lurie und Krim 1988, vgl. Anm. 4, S. 48.
19 Boris Lurie: „Involvement Show Statement“, 1961, in: Lurie und Krim 1988, vgl. Anm. 4, S. 42.
20 Ebd.
21 Ebd., S. 43.
22 Brian O'Doherty: „Einleitung“, 1971, in: Lurie und Krim 1988, vgl. Anm. 4, S. 17.
23 Boris Lurie: „Scheiß Nein!“, 1970, in: Lurie und Krim 1988, vgl. Anm. 4, S. 69.
24 Wolf Vostell: „Zuviel Blut auf den Bildern“, 1977, in: Lurie und Krim 1988, vgl. Anm. 4, S. 18.
25 Andreas Nachama: „Holocaust Memorial“, in: *Wolf Vostell. Meine Kunst ist der ewige Widerstand gegen den Tod,* Ausstellungskatalog, Rheinisches Landesmuseum Bonn, 15. 8. – 25. 11. 2007, S. 82.
26 Fritz Emslander: „‚Für mich waren die Happenings das Wichtigste'. Ein Gespräch mit Mercedes Guardado Olivenza Vostell“, in: *Wolf Vostell. Die Druckgrafik,* Ausstellungskatalog, Städtische Galerie Villa Zanders, Bergisch Gladbach, 4. 9. – 27. 11. 2005, Kunsthalle Bremen, 5. 9. – 5. 11. 2006, Museo Vostell, Malpartida, 2007, S. 33.
27 Peter Weibel: „Der deutsche Ausblick“, in: Vostell, Ausstellungskatalog 2007, vgl. Anm. 25, S. 13.
28 Vgl. René Block: *Grafik des Kapitalistischen Realismus,* Berlin 1971, S. 172 (V 10) und S. 175 (V 20): „Foto aus dem polnischen Bildband ‚Nie wieder – never – jamais'.“ Ein Buch dieses Titels konnte allerdings nicht nachgewiesen werden. „Nie wieder – never – jamais“ war der Titel von Vostells Dé-coll/age-Happening am 20.7.1964 in Aachen.
29 Ivangorod, Ukraine, A German policemen aims a rifle at a woman and a child, 1942; Yad Vashem, Photos Archive, Archival Signature: 1878 (Detail), Archival Signature: 143DO5 (gesamt).
30 Vgl. Abb. in: *Kunst und Politik,* Ausstellungskatalog, Badischer Kunstverein, Karlsruhe, 31. 5. – 16. 8. 1970, o. S.; vgl. auch: *Kitaj. Neue Alchimie,* in: Der Spiegel, Nr. 7, 1970, S. 135 ff.
31 Wolfgang Vomm: „Zur Druckgrafik Wolf Vostells“, in: Vostell. Druckgrafik, Ausstellungskatalog 2005, vgl. Anm. 26, S. 13.
32 Peter Bürger: *Theorie der Avantgarde,* Frankfurt am Main 1982, S. 80.
33 Boris Lurie: Autobiografische Aufzeichnungen, nicht veröffentlicht, zit. nach: Wronoski 2014, vgl. Anm. 9, S. 29.
34 Eckhart Gillen: „Wolf Vostell: ‚Deutscher Ausblick'“, in: ders. (Hrsg.): *Deutschlandbilder. Kunst aus einem geteilten Land,* Ausstellungskatalog, Martin-Gropius-Bau, Berlin, 7. 9. 1997 – 11. 1. 1998, Köln 1997, S. 240 f.
35 Vgl. Martin Walser: „Unser Auschwitz“, in: Hans Magnus Enzensberger (Hrsg.): *Kursbuch Nr. 1,* 1965, S. 189 – 200.
36 Boris Lurie: „Anmerkungen zu Kunst, Leben und Politik“, in: *NO!art,* 1995, vgl. Anm. 14, S. 125.
37 Wolf Vostell, zit. nach: Gillen 1997, vgl. Anm. 34, S. 244.
38 Konzept zum Happening *You,* zit. nach: *Das Theater ist auf der Straße. Die Happenings von Wolf Vostell,* Ausstellungskatalog, Museum Morsbroich Leverkusen, 6. 6. – 15. 8. 2010, Museo Vostell Malpartida, Oktober 2010 bis Februar 2011, Bielefeld, Leipzig, Berlin 2010, S. 163.
39 Al Hansen zit. nach: José Antonio Agúndez Garcia: „Eine Reise in die Utopie. Das Neuartige in den Happenings von Wolf Vostell“, in: *Happenings von Wolf Vostell,* Ausstellungskatalog 2010, vgl. Anm. 38, S. 57.
40 Aktionsanleitungen zu *Rasten und Tanken:* zit. nach: *Happenings von Wolf Vostell,* Ausstellungskatalog 2010, vgl. Anm. 38, S. 239.
41 Das Foto stammt vermutlich aus dem Buch von Helmut Eschwege: *Kennzeichen J. Bilder, Dokumente, Berichte,* Berlin 1966. Auf rechtsradikalen und neonazistischen Websites wird das Foto als Beispiel für Geschichtsfälschung angeführt. Es handle sich nicht um einen Deportationszug, sondern um einen Güterzug mit Flüchtlingen 1946. Als Quelle wird die Bundesbahndirektion Hamburg genannt.
42 Rainer Wick: „Zur Symbolik in Vostells Happening Regen“, in: *Kunstforum International,* Bd. 24, 6/77, S. 154.
43 Ebd., S. 156.
44 Gerhard Richter: „MoMA-Interview mit Robert Storr, 2002“, in: Dietmar Elger und Hans Ulrich Obrist (Hrsg.): *Gerhard Richter. Text 1961 bis 2007. Schriften, Interviews, Briefe,* Köln 2008, S. 416.
45 Herbert Marcuse: *Versuch über die Befreiung,* Frankfurt am Main 1969, S. 21 f.
46 Gerhard Richter in: Elger und Obrist 2008, vgl. Anm. 44, S. 416.
47 Helmut Friedel: „Gerhard Richter. Aufgehoben im Bild – Zum Birkenau-Bild“, in: Friedel 2016, vgl. Anm. 1, S. 15.
48 Peter Gorsen: *Das Prinzip Obszön. Kunst, Pornographie und Gesellschaft,* Reinbek bei Hamburg 1969, S. 88.
49 Max Liljefors: „Boris Lurie and NO!art“, in: *Heterogénesis, Revista de Artes Visuales – Tidskrift för visuell konst,* Nr. 44, Juli 2003 (www.heterogenesis.com/H-44/Liljefors.htm).
50 H. P. Alvermann zit. nach: Willy Rotzler: *Objektkunst. Von Duchamp bis zur Gegenwart,* Köln 1975, S. 103.
51 Vgl. zum Beispiel die Biografie in: *H. P. Alvermann. Denkmale 65,* Ausstellungskatalog, Haus am Lützowplatz, Berlin, 21.3.–27.4.1965, o. S.
52 Jürgen Morschel: *Deutsche Kunst der 60er Jahre. Teil II: Plastik, Objekte, Aktionen,* München 1972, S. 110.
53 Ebd.
54 Rotzler 1975, vgl. Anm. 50, S. 103.
55 Zit. nach: Dietmar Rübel: „‚Do anything that you want to do, but uh-uh ...'. German Pop und das Ende des Dingzeugs“, in: *German Pop,* Ausstellungskatalog, Schirn Kunsthalle Frankfurt, 6. 11. 2014 – 8. 2. 2015, Köln 2014, S. 74.
56 Zit. nach: Lea Schleiffenbaum: „QUIBB-Manifest“, in: *German Pop,* Ausstellungskatalog, vgl. Anm. 55, S. 67.
57 H. P. Alvermann zit. nach: Rotzler 1975, vgl. Anm. 50, S. 103.
58 http://www.kunstfonds.de/kuenstlernachlaesse/kuenstler/hp-alvermann/. Vgl. zum „Republikanischen Centrum“ Peter Brügge: „Auf dem Wartebänkchen der Revolution“, in: *Der Spiegel,* Nr. 52, 1968, S. 69 ff.
59 H. P. Alvermann, April 1970, in: *Kunst und Politik,* Ausstellungskatalog 1970, vgl. Anm. 30, o. S.
60 H. P. Alvermann zit. nach: René Block: „Auf einer Reise nach Prag am 19. Januar 1997“, in: *Pro Lidice. 52 Künstler aus Deutschland,* Ausstellungskatalog, České Muzeum Výtvarných Umění, 9. 3. – 6. 4. 1997, o. S.
61 Ebd.
62 Carl Zuckmayer: *Als wär's ein Stück von mir. Horen der Freundschaft,* Frankfurt am Main 1966, S. 71 f., zit. nach: https://de.wikipedia.org/wiki/Reibpartie.
63 „‚Form ist das wichtigste' oder ‚Ich würde niemals meine Arbeiten nur als Kunst betrachten'. Ein Gespräch von Michaela Unterdörfer mit Gustav Metzger, 16. und 17. Januar 1999 in der Kunsthalle Nürnberg“, in: *Gustav Metzger. Ein Schnitt entlang der Zeit,* Ausstellungskatalog, Kunsthalle Nürnberg, 24. 6. – 12. 9. 1999, S. 41 f.
64 Sigmar Polke: Gespräch mit Bice Curiger, zit. nach: Anne Erfle: „Sigmar Polkes Deutschlandbilder“, in: Gillen 1997, vgl. Anm. 34, S. 272.
65 Joseph Beuys: Interview mit Max Reithmann, 1982, zit. nach: Mario Kramer: „Joseph Beuys: ‚Auschwitz Demonstration' 1956 – 1964“, in: Gillen 1997, vgl. Anm. 34, S. 303.
66 Joseph Beuys: Gespräch mit Caroline Tisdall, zit. nach: Gillen 1997, S. 302

28 Cf. René Block, *Grafik des Kapitalistischen Realismus* (Berlin: Edition René Block, 1971), p. 172 (V 10) and p. 175 (V 20): "Foto aus dem polnischen Bildband 'Nie wieder – never – jamais'." A book by this title could not be found, however. *Nie wieder – never – jamais* was the title of Vostell's dé-coll/age-Happening on July 20, 1964 in Aachen.

29 Ivangorod, Ukraine. A German policeman aims his rifle at a woman and a child, 1942. Yad Vashem, Photos Archive, archival signatures: 1878 (detail); 143DO5 (full image).

30 Cf. illustration in *Kunst und Politik*, exh. cat., Badischer Kunstverein, Karlsruhe, May 31 – August 16, 1970 (Karlsruhe: Badischer Kunstverein, 1970), unpaginated; see also 'Kitaj. Neue Alchimie,' *Der Spiegel* 7/1970 (February 9, 1970), pp. 135ff.

31 Wolfgang Vomm, 'Zur Druckgrafik Wolf Vostells,' in Vostell. Druckgrafik, exh. cat. 2005, see note 26, p. 13.

32 Peter Bürger, *Theory of the Avant-Garde*, trans. Michael Shaw (Minneapolis, MN: University of Minnesota Press, 1984), p. 99.

33 From Boris Lurie's unpublished autobiographical notes, quoted in Wronoski 2014, see note 9, p. 29.

34 Eckhart Gillen, 'Wolf Vostell: *German View*,' in idem (ed.), *German Art from Beckmann to Richter: Images of a Divided Country*, exh. cat., Martin-Gropius-Bau, Berlin, September 7, 1997 – January 11, 1998 (Cologne: DuMont, 1997), pp. 208 – 13, here p. 208.

35 Cf. Martin Walser, 'Unser Auschwitz,' in Hans Magnus Enzensberger (ed.), *Kursbuch Nr. 1* (Frankfurt am Main: Zweitausendeins, 1965), pp. 189 – 200.

36 Boris Lurie, 'Anmerkungen zu Kunst, Leben und Politik,' in *NO!art,* 1995, see note 14, p. 125.

37 Wolf Vostell, quoted in Gillen 1997, see note 34, p. 212.

38 Concept for the dé-coll/age-Happening *You*, quoted in *Das Theater ist auf der Straße. Die Happenings von Wolf Vostell*, exh. cat., Museum Morsbroich Leverkusen, June 6 – August 15, 2010; Museo Vostell Malpartida, October 2010 – February 2011 (Bielefeld: Kerber, 2010), p. 163.

39 Al Hansen, quoted in José Antonio Agúndez Garcia, 'Eine Reise in die Utopie. Das Neuartige in den Happenings von Wolf Vostell,' in *Happenings von Wolf Vostell*, exh. cat. 2010, see note 38, p. 57.

40 Instructions for the action *Rasten und Tanken*, quoted in *Happenings von Wolf Vostell*, exh. cat. 2010, see note 38, p. 239.

41 The photograph is probably taken from Helmut Eschwege's book *Kennzeichen J. Bilder, Dokumente, Berichte* (Berlin: Deutscher Verlag der Wissenschaften, 1966). This image has been presented on extreme right-wing and neo-Nazi websites as an example of the falsification of history. The allegation made is that the depicted train is not a deportation train but a freight train carrying refugees in 1946. The source provided is the Bundesbahndirektion Hamburg.

42 Rainer Wick, 'Zur Symbolik in Vostells Happening "Regen",' *Kunstforum International* 24 (June 77), p. 154.

43 Ibid., p. 156.

44 Gerhard Richter, quoted in 'Robert Storr. Interview with Gerhard Richter,' in Robert Storr, *Gerhard Richter: Forty Years of Painting*, exh. cat., Museum of Modern Art, New York, February 14–May 21, 2002; The Art Institute of Chicago, June 22 – September 15, 2002; San Francisco Museum of Modern Art, October 11, 2002 – January 14, 2003; Hirshhorn Museum and Sculpture Garden, Washington D.C., February 20 – May 18, 2003 (New York: Museum of Modern Art, 2002), pp. 287 – 309, here p. 290.

45 Herbert Marcuse, *An Essay on Liberation* (Boston, MA: Beacon Press, 1971), pp. 7f.

46 Gerhard Richter, quoted in *Forty Years of Painting*, exh. cat. 2002, see note 44, p. 290.

47 Helmut Friedel, 'Gerhard Richter. Aufgehoben im Bild – Zum Birkenau-Bild,' in idem (ed.), *Gerhard Richter. Birkenau*, exh. cat., Museum Frieder Burda, Baden-Baden, February 6 – May 29, 2016 (Cologne: Verlag der Buchhandlung Walther König, 2016), p. 15.

48 Peter Gorsen, *Das Prinzip Obszön. Kunst, Pornographie und Gesellschaft* (Reinbek bei Hamburg: Rowohlt, 1969), p. 88.

49 Max Liljefors, 'Boris Lurie and NO!art,' *Heterogénesis. Revista de Artes Visuales – Tidskrift för visuell konst* 44 (July 2003), pp. 32 – 41. Available online at <<www.heterogenesis.com/H-44/Liljefors.htm>>; accessed April 12, 2017.

50 H. P. Alvermannn, quoted in Willy Rotzler, *Objektkunst. Von Duchamp bis zur Gegenwart* (Cologne: DuMont, 1975), p. 103.

51 See, for example, the biography in *H. P. Alvermann. Denkmale 65*, exh. cat., Haus am Lützowplatz, Berlin, March 21 – April 27, 1965 (Berlin: Petersen Press, 1965), unpaginated.

52 Jürgen Morschel, *Deutsche Kunst der 60er Jahre. Teil II; Plastik, Objekte, Aktionen* (Munich: Bruckmann, 1972), p. 110.

53 Ibid.

54 Rotzler 1975, see note 50, p. 103.

55 Quoted in Dietmar Rübel, '"Do Anything That You Wanna Do, but Uh-uh …" German Pop and the End of the Thingamajig,' in *German Pop*, exh. cat., Schirn Kunsthalle Frankfurt, November 6, 2014 – February 8, 2015 (Cologne: Verlag der Buchhandlung Walther König, 2014), pp. 236 – 7, here p. 236.

56 Quoted in Lea Schleiffenbaum, 'QUIBB Manifesto,' in *German Pop*, exh. cat. 2014, see note 55, p. 245.

57 H. P. Alvermann, quoted in Rotzler 1975, see note 50, p. 103.

58 <<www.kunstfonds.de/kuenstlernachlaesse/kuenstler/hp-alvermann/>>; accessed April 12, 2017. On the 'Republikanisches Centrum', see Peter Brügge, 'Auf dem Wartebänkchen der Revolution', *Der Spiegel* 52/1968 (December 23, 1968), pp. 69ff.

59 H. P. Alvermann, April 1970, in *Kunst und Politik*, exh. cat. 1970, see note 30, unpaginated.

60 H. P. Alvermann, quoted in René Block, 'Auf einer Reise nach Prag am 19. Januar 1997,' in Pro Lidice. 52 Künstler aus Deutschland, exh. cat., České Muzeum Výtvarných Umění, March 9 – April 6, 1997 (Prague: České Muzeum Výtvarných Umění, 1997), unpaginated.

61 Ibid.

62 Carl Zuckmayer, *A Part of Myself. Portrait of an Epoch*, trans. Richard and Clara Winston (New York, NY: Harcourt, Brace, Jovanovich, 1970), p. 50.

63 '"Form ist das wichtigste" oder "Ich würde niemals meine Arbeiten nur als Kunst betrachten". Ein Gespräch von Michaela Unterdörfer mit Gustav Metzger, 16. und 17. Januar 1999 in der Kunsthalle Nürnberg,' in *Gustav Metzger. Ein Schnitt entlang der Zeit*, exh. cat., Kunsthalle Nürnberg, June 24 – September 12, 1999 (Nuremberg: Kunsthalle Nürnberg, 1999), pp. 41f.

64 Sigmar Polke, quoted in 'Poison is Effective; Painting is Not. Bice Curiger in Conversation with Sigmar Polke,' *Parkett* 26 (December 1990), pp. 18 – 27, here p. 26.

65 Joseph Beuys in an interview with Max Reithmann (1982), quoted in Mario Kramer, 'Joseph Beuys: *Auschwitz Demonstration*, 1956 – 1964,' in Gillen 1997, see note 34, pp. 261 – 75, here p. 270.

66 Joseph Beuys in conversation with Caroline Tisdall, quoted ibid.

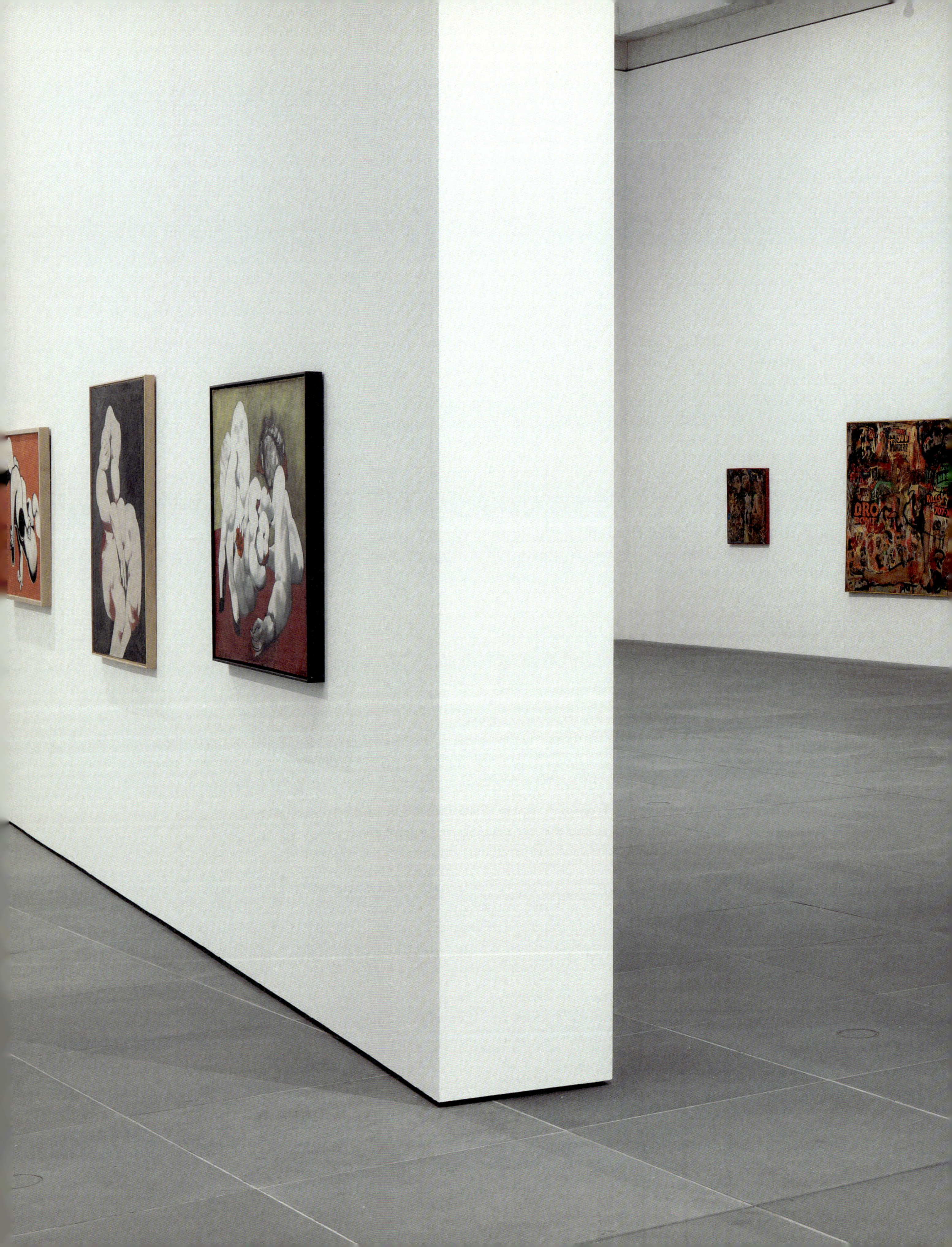
MURDERS
DRO
KILLS

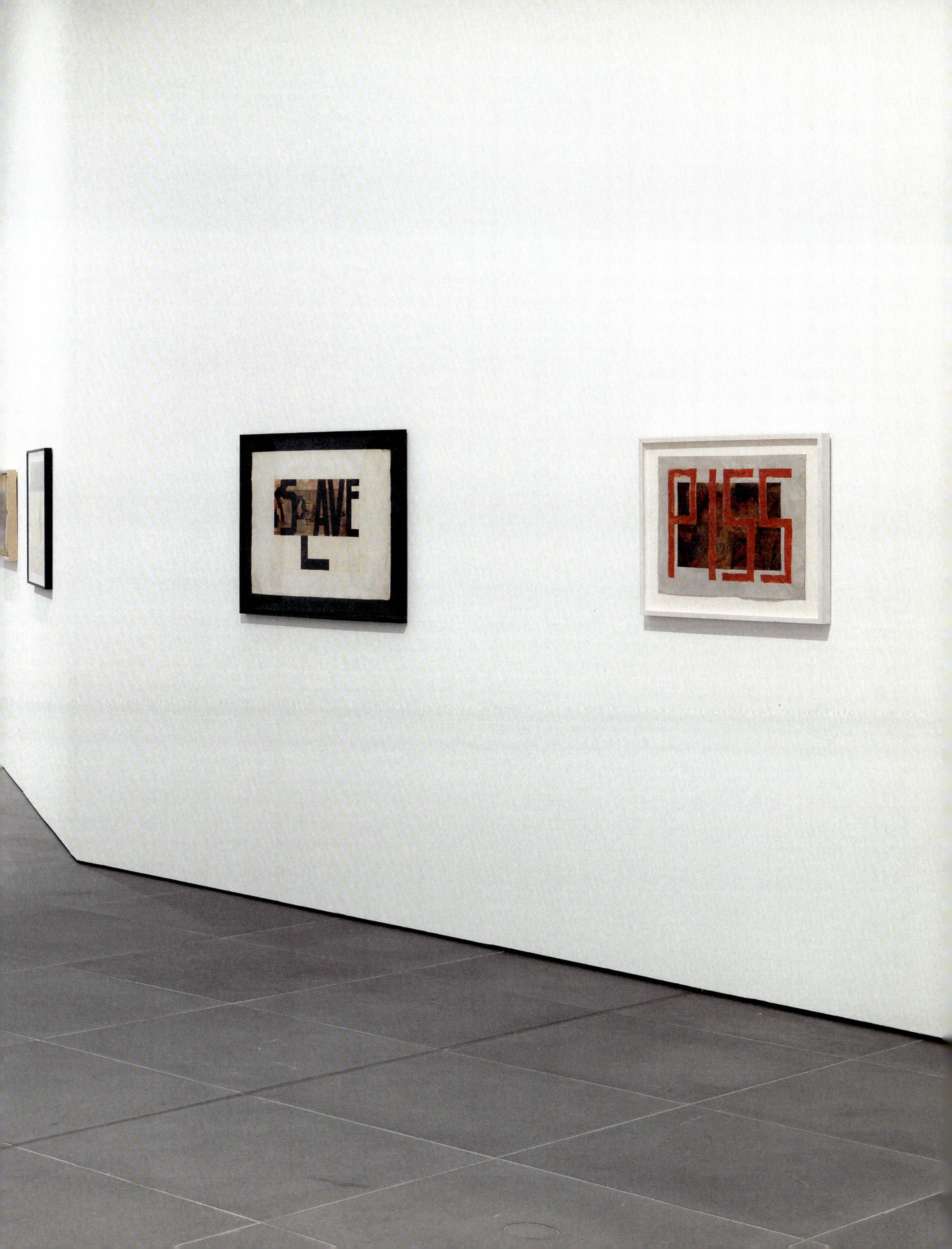
S AVE
L
PISS

Liste der ausgestellten Werke
List of exhibited works

Boris Lurie

Untitled, ca. / ca 1946
Tusche auf Papier / Ink on paper
22,8 x 14 cm
Abb. S. / Ill. p. 54

Untitled, ca. / ca 1946
Tusche auf Papier / Ink on paper
13,3 x 13 cm
Abb. S. / Ill. p. 55

Untitled, ca. / ca 1946
Feder, Tusche, Gouache auf Papier / Pen, ink, gouache paint on paper
24,1 x 20,3 cm
Abb. S. / Ill. p. 54

Untitled, ca. / ca 1946
Bleistift auf Papier / Pencil on paper
29,6 x 20,9 cm
Abb. S. / Ill. p. 55

Untitled, ca. / ca 1946
Blauer Buntstift auf liniertem Papier / Blue crayon on ruled paper
29,8 x 20,9 cm
Abb. S. / Ill. p. 55

Untitled, ca. / ca 1946
Tusche, Buntstift und Estompe auf Papier / Ink, conté crayon and estompe on paper
24,8 x 20,3 cm
Abb. S. / Ill. p. 55

Untitled, ca. / ca 1946
Conté-Buntstift und Estompe auf Papier / Conté crayon and estompe on paper
25,7 x 20,6 cm
Abb. S. / Ill. p. 55

Untitled, ca. / ca 1946
Kohle und Bleistift auf Papier / Charcoal and pencil on paper
29,5 x 20,9 cm
Abb. S. / Ill. p. 55

Untitled, ca. / ca 1946
Bleistift und Estompe auf Papier / Pencil and estompe on paper
27,3 x 18,6 cm
Abb. S. / Ill. p. 54

Untitled, ca. / ca 1946
Tusche und Gouache auf Papier / Ink and gouache paint on paper
27,9 x 21,3 cm
Abb. S. / Ill. p. 54

Untitled, ca. / ca 1946
Tusche auf Papier auf Papier / Ink on paper mounted on paper
13,3 x 17,1 cm
Abb. S. / Ill. p. 54

Untitled, ca. / ca 1946
Bleistift, Farbstift und Estompe auf Papier / Pencil, color conté crayon and estompe on paper
63,5 x 29,2 cm
Abb. S. / Ill. p. 53

Portrait of My Mother Before Shooting, 1947
Ölfarbe auf Leinwand / Oil paint on canvas
93 x 65 cm
Abb. S. / Ill. p. 52

Combat, 1951
Ölfarbe auf Hartfaser / Oil paint on masonite
76,8 x 92,1 cm
Abb. S. / Ill. p. 32

Dismembered Woman, ca. / ca 1955
Ölfarbe auf Leinwand / Oil paint on canvas
145 x 135 cm
Abb. S. / Ill. p. 34

Dismembered Woman: Nude, Stepping, 1955
Ölfarbe auf Baumwollgewebe / Oil paint on cotton twill fabric
155 x 119 cm
Abb. S. / Ill. p. 35

Dismembered Woman: The Stripper, 1955
Ölfarbe auf Leinwand / Oil paint on canvas
165 x 109 cm
Abb. S. / Ill. p. 36

Dismembered Woman, 1955
Ölfarbe auf Leinwand / Oil paint on canvas
89 x 112 cm
Abb. S. / Ill. p. 37

Dismembered Stripper, 1956
Ölfarbe auf Leinwand / Oil paint on canvas
109 x 102 cm
Abb. S. / Ill. p. 33

Lumumba is Dead (Adieu Amérique), 1959 – 61
Öl, Collage, Spielkarten, Fotos und NO-Plakate auf Leinwand / Oil, paper collage, playing cards, photos and NO posters on canvas
181 x 197 cm
Abb. S. / Ill. p. 59

Saturation Painting (Buchenwald), 1960 – 63
Fotografien und Papier auf Leinwand / Photographs and paper mounted on canvas
91 x 91 cm
Abb. S. / Ill. p. 41

Black Susan, 1962
Papier, Transfertechnik und Farbe auf Leinwand / Paper, transfer and paint on canvas
136 x 132 cm
Abb. S. / Ill. p. 70

Flatcar, Assemblage, 1945 by Adolf Hitler, ca. / ca 1962
Lithographie auf Papier / Lithograph on paper
40,5 x 61 cm
Abb. S. / Ill. p. 43

NO in Orange, ca. / ca 1962
Ölfarbe auf Leinwand / Oil paint on canvas
25,4 x 28 cm
Abb. S. / Ill. p. 118

NO-ON, 1962
Ölfarbe auf Leinwand / Oil paint on canvas
65 x 72 cm
Abb. S. / Ill. p. 122

NO Record, 1962
Assemblage, Vinyl, Ölfarbe auf Holzplatte / Assemblage, vinyl with oil paint mounted on board
35,5 x 35,5 cm
Abb. S. / Ill. p. 118

NO with Linoleum, 1962
Ölfarbe und Linoleum auf Platte / Oil paint and linoleum on board
62 x 47 cm
Abb. S. / Ill. p. 119

Quench Your Thirst, 1962
Farbe, Papier-Collage und Transfertechnik auf Leinwand / Paint, paper collage and transfer on canvas
174 x 107 cm
Abb. S. / Ill. p. 71

Salad, 1962
Farbe, Transfertechnik, Papier-Collage auf Leinwand / Paint, transfer and paper collage on canvas
115 x 99 cm
Abb. S. / Ill. p. 75

Yellow NO Cutouts, 1962
Farbe und Tusche auf Karton / Paint and ink on cardboard
94 x 76,2 x 7,6 cm
Abb. S. / Ill. p. 123

Lolita, 1962 – 63
Collage, Papier auf Leinwand / Paper collage mounted on canvas
142 x 103 cm
Abb. S. / Ill. p. 47

Torn Pinups, ca. / ca 1962-63
Collage, Papier, Farbe und Kleber auf Stoff / Paper collage, paint and glue on fabric
119 x 118 cm
Abb. S. / Ill. p. 77

Altered Photos: Shame!, 1963
Ölfarbe und Photo auf Leinwand / Oil paint and photo on canvas
81 x 57 cm
Abb. S. / Ill. p. 93

Altered Photos: Pinup (Body), ca. / ca 1963
Photoemulsion und Acrylfarbe auf Leinwand / Photo emulsion and acrylic paint on canvas
127 x 117 cm
Abb. S. / Ill. p. 95

Altered Photos: Pinup (Dismembered Figure), ca. / ca 1963
Photoemulsion und Acrylfarbe auf Leinwand / Photo emulsion and acrylic paint on canvas
116 x 142,3 cm
Abb. S. / Ill. p. 94

Amérique Amer (Pleasure), ca. / ca 1963
Collage, Zeitschriften-, Zeitungspapier auf Papier / Collage, magazine, newspaper on paper
33 x 19 cm
Abb. S. / Ill. p. 65

Feel Painting NO with Red and Black, 1963
Farbe auf Kunststoff auf Leinwand / Paint on plastic mounted on canvas
56 x 89 cm
Abb. S. / Ill. p. 121

Love Series, ca. / ca 1963
Farbe auf SW-Fotografie / Paint on black and white photograph
15 x 17 cm
Abb. S. / Ill. p. 107

Love Series: Bound and Gagged, ca. / ca 1963
Photoemulsion und Farbe auf Leinwand auf Karton / Photo emulsion and paint on canvas mounted on cardboard
58 x 39 cm
Abb. S. / Ill. p. 107

Love Series: Bound on Red, ca. / ca 1963
Photoemulsion und Farbe auf Leinwand / Photo emulsion and paint on canvas
196 x 138 cm
Abb. S. / Ill. p. 99

Love Series: Fighting Females, ca. / ca 1963
Collage, Ölfarbe auf Leinwand auf Karton / Collage, oil paint on canvas mounted on cardboard
49 x 32 cm
Abb. S. / Ill. p. 104

Love Series: Posed, ca. / ca 1963
Collage, Ölfarbe auf Leinwand auf Karton / Collage, oil paint on canvas, mounted on cardboard
38 x 27 cm
Abb. S. / Ill. p. 107

Gallery Gertrude Stein: NO Posters Show Poster, 1963
Plakat / Poster
55,5 x 34,3 cm

Gallery Gertrude Stein: NO Show Poster, 1963
Plakat / Poster
55,5 x 43 cm
Abb. S. / Ill. p. 165

NO Sprayed, 1963
Sprayfarbe auf Hartfaserplatte / Spray paint on Masonite
56 x 52 cm
Abb. S. / Ill. p. 120

NO with Mrs. Kennedy, 1963
Collage, Ölfarbe und Collage auf Hartfaserplatte / Collage, oil paint and collage on Masonite
36 x 27 cm
Abb. S. / Ill. p. 117

Oswald, 1963
Collage, Papier und Farbe auf Karton / Paper collage and paint on cardboard
58 x 38 cm
Abb. S. / Ill. p. 64

Railroad to America (Railroad Collage), 1963
Collage, Papier auf Leinwand / Paper collage mounted on canvas
37 x 54 cm
Abb. S. / Ill. p. 45

Suzy Sweet, 1963
Farbe, Papier und Fotos auf Leinwand / Paint, paper and photos on canvas
130 x 109 cm
Abb. S. / Ill. p. 81

Untitled (On Stomach), ca. / ca 1963
Ölfarbe auf Leinwand / Oil paint on canvas
91,5 x 84 cm
Abb. S. / Ill. p. 105

Untitled (Saturation Painting), ca. / ca 1963
Collage, Papier und Lack auf Baumwolltuch / Paper collage and varnish on cotton towel
52 x 71 cm
Abb. S. / Ill. p. 49

Untitled, ca. / ca 1963
Papier und Farbe auf Kartondeckel / Paper and paint on cardboard box top
35,6 x 28 cm
Abb. S. / Ill. p. 88

Hard Writings: PLEASE, ca. / ca 1963–72
Collage, Papierbilder, Klebeband und Graphit auf Karton / Collage, pictures, tape and charcoal on cardboard
46 x 91 cm
Abb. S. / Ill. p. 111

Anti-Pop Stencil, 1964
Collage, Ölfarbe und Papier auf ungrundierter Leinwand / Collage, oil paint and paper on unprimed canvas
53 x 61 cm
Abb. S. / Ill. p. 128

Gallery Gertrude Stein: NO Sculptures (Shit) Show Poster, 1964
Plakat / Poster
60,5 x 43 cm
Abb. S. / Ill. p. 126

Large Pinup: Why Long Roads?, ca. / ca 1964
Collage, Zeitschriftenbilder auf Leinwand / Collage, magazine pictures on canvas
121,9 x 121,9 cm
Abb. S. / Ill. p. 87

Sam Goodman und / and Boris Lurie, NO Sculpture (Shit Sculpture), 1964
Ölfarbe auf Gips und Papier / Oil paint on plaster and paper
43,2 x 66 x 63,5 cm
Abb. S. / Ill. p. 127

Sam Goodman und / and Boris Lurie, NO Sculpture (Shit Sculpture), 1964
Gips und Farbe / Plaster and paint
38 x 68,6 x 61 cm
Abb. S. / Ill. p. 127

Sam Goodman und / and Boris Lurie, NO Sculpture (Shit Sculpture), 1964
Gips, Zeitung und Farbe / Plaster, newspaper and paint
40,5 x 61 x 46 cm
Abb. S. / Ill. p. 127

Sam Goodman und / and Boris Lurie, NO Sculpture (Shit Sculpture), 1964
Gips und Farbe / Plaster and paint
21,6 x 31,7 x 30,5 cm
Abb. S. / Ill. p. 127

Stenciled NOs, 1969
Ölfarbe auf ungrundierter Leinwand / Oil paint on unprimed canvas
34 x 76 cm
Abb. S. / Ill. p. 124

Untitled (Deliberate Pinup), ca. / ca 1971 – 73
Collage, Ölfarbe und Papierbilder auf Leinwand / Collage, oil paint and pictures on canvas
61 x 46 cm
Abb. S. / Ill. p. 103

Hard Writings: LICK, ca. / ca 1972
Collage, Papier und Lack auf Papier / Paper collage and varnish mounted on paper
55,9 x 76,2 cm
Abb. S. / Ill. p. 110

Hard Writings: LOAD, 1972
Papier und Klebeband auf Papier auf Leinwand / Paper and tape on paper, mounted on canvas
60 x 88 cm
Abb. S. / Ill. p. 112

Hard Writings: NO on Pinup, ca. / ca 1972
Ölfarbe auf Papier auf Leinwand / Oil paint on paper mounted on canvas
53 x 39 cm
Abb. S. / Ill. p. 125

Hard Writings: SLAVE, ca. / ca 1972
Collage, Papier, Farbe und Lack auf Papier / Paper collage, paint and varnish on paper
56 x 79 cm
Abb. S. / Ill. p. 111

Postart, ca. / ca 1972
Ölfarbe und Klebeband auf Holzplatte / Oil paint and tape on board
106,5 x 43 cm

Sold, 1972
Ölfarbe auf Leinwand / Oil paint on canvas
78 x 67 cm
Abb. S. / Ill. p. 129

Hard Writings: IN, ca. / ca 1972 – 73
Collage, Papier, Farbe und Lack auf Papier / Paper collage, paint and varnish on paper
55 x 81 cm
Abb. S. / Ill. p. 110

Hard Writings: PISS, ca. / ca 1972 – 73
Collage, Papier, Farbe und Lack auf Papier / Paper collage, paint and varnish on paper
43 x 58 cm
Abb. S. / Ill. p. 113

Untitled, Mitte der 1970er Jahre / mid-1970s
Collage, Papier und Farbe auf Papier / Paper collage and paint on paper
28 x 22 cm
Abb. S. / Ill. p. 91

Untitled, Mitte der 1970er Jahre / mid-1970s
Collage, Papier / Paper collage
25 x 20 cm
Abb. S. / Ill. p. 91

Untitled (Deliberate Pinup), ca. / ca 1975
Collage, Ölfarbe und Papier auf Leinwand auf Holzplatte / Collage, oil paint and paper mounted on canvas board
61 x 50 cm
Abb. S. / Ill. p. 89

Untitled (Deliberate Pinup), ca. / ca 1975
Collage, Papier, Farbe auf Karton / Collage, pictures, paint on cardboard
50,8 x 38,1 cm
Abb. S. / Ill. p. 90

Alle Werke Leihgaben der Boris Lurie Art Foundation / All works on loan from the Boris Lurie Art Foundation

Around Lurie

H.P. Alvermann, *Warten auf Nürnberg II*, 1966
Objekt, Assemblage / Object, Assemblage
90 x 35 x 35 cm
Památník Lidice / Gedenkstätte Lidice / Lidice Memorial
Abb. S. / Ill. p. 192

Stanley Fisher, *DRO Bomb*, ca. / ca 1961 – 63
Collage, Ölfarbe und Sprayfarbe auf Papier auf Leinwand / Collage, oil paint and spray paint over paper mounted on canvas
165 x 177,8 cm
Boris Lurie Art Foundation
Abb. S. / Ill. p. 177

Stanley Fisher, *Empire*,
ca. / ca 1961–63
Collage, Ölfarbe und Papier auf Leinwand / Collage, oil paint and paper on canvas
167 x 182 cm
Boris Lurie Art Foundation
Abb. S. / Ill. p. 174

Stanley Fisher, *Spectre*,
ca. / ca 1961–63
Collage, Ölfarbe und Papier auf Leinwand / Collage, oil paint and paper on canvas
78,7 x 73,7 cm
Boris Lurie Art Foundation
Abb. S. / Ill. p. 176

Sam Goodman, *The Bomb*, 1960/61
Skulptur aus Fundstücken / Found objects sculpture
193 x 121,9 x 58,4 cm
Boris Lurie Art Foundation
Abb. S. / Ill. p. 172

Sam Goodman, *Eichmann Remember (Eichmann Triptych)*, 1961
Holzkonstruktion mit Collage und Objekten / Wood construction with collage and objects
99 x 91,4 x 20,3 cm
Boris Lurie Art Foundation
Abb. S. / Ill. p. 173

Jean-Jacques Lebel, *Untitled*, 1963
Farbe, Buntstift und Transfertechnik auf Papier / Paint, crayon and transfer collage on paper
107 x 74 cm
Boris Lurie Art Foundation
Abb. S. / Ill. p. 177

Piero Manzoni, *La Merda d'artista*, 1961
Blechdose, Exkremente (Multiple) / Can, excrements (multiple)
4,8 x 6,5 x 6,5 cm
Sammlung Block
Abb. S. / Ill. p. 175

Gustav Metzger, *Historic Photographs: To Crawl Into – Anschluss, Vienna, March 1938*, 1996/2017
SW-Fotografie auf PVC, Baumwollabdeckung / Black-and-White photography, cotton cover on PVC
315 x 425 cm
Ausstellungskopie / Exhibition copy
Collection of the artist
Abb. S. / Ill. p. 195

Gerhard Richter, *Olympia*, 1967
Öl auf Leinwand / Oil on canvas
200 x 130 cm
Sammlung Böckmann
Abb. S. / Ill. p. 187

Wolf Vostell, *Eine Autofahrt Köln–Frankfurt auf überfüllter Autobahn kostet mehr Nerven als eine Woche angestrengt arbeiten*, 1964
Siebdruck, Sprayfarbe, Verwischung auf Fotoleinwand / Screen printing, spray paint, blurring on photo canvas
123 x 450 cm
Sammlung Ludwig – Ludwig Forum für Internationale Kunst, Aachen
Abb. S. / Ill. p. 182

Wolf Vostell, *100 Ereignisse Berlin. Frau mit Gasmaske*, 1966
Serigrafie auf Bütten / Serigraphy on Bütten paper
45 x 56 cm
The Wolf Vostell Estate
Abb. S. / Ill. p. 184

Wolf Vostell, *Treblinka*, 1967
Farbserigrafie auf Karton / Color serigraphy on cardboard
70,8 x 100,5 cm
The Wolf Vostell Estate
Abb. S. / Ill. p. 181

Wolf Vostell, *Kämme*, 1968
Offsetdruck mit Objekten / Offset print with objects
61 x 95 cm
Boris Lurie Art Foundation
Abb. S. / Ill. p. 181

Wolf Vostell, *Nürnberg*, 1968
Verwischung auf SW-Foto / Blurring on black-and-white photography
100 x 100 cm
The Wolf Vostell Estate
Abb. S. / Ill. p. 185

Wolf Vostell, *Leben gleich Kunst*, 1974
Objektbuch, Skizzenbuch, Papier / Sketchbook, paper
36 x 50 x 40 cm
Museum Morsbroich, Leverkusen; Dauerleihgabe des Landes Nordrhein-Westfalen
Abb. S. / Ill. p. 183

Biography

18 July 1924
Born in Leningrad, the youngest of three children of the Jewish couple Ilja and Schaina Lurje

1925
Moves to Riga and attends the German high school there

October/November 1941
Thirty thousand Jewish residents of Riga are forced to live in a ghetto

8 December 1941
Boris Lurie's mother, Schaina, and his sister, Jeanna, are murdered in the massacre of Rumbula. His childhood sweetheart, Ljuba, and his grandmother are also among the dead.

1941–45
Imprisoned in the Lenta and Salaspils labour camps, Stutthof and Buchenwald concentration camps

11 April 1945
Liberated from Magdeburg-Polte, a Buchenwald satellite camp

1946
Emigrates with his father, Ilja to New York, United States

1950
First individual exhibition in the Barbizon Gallery, New York

1958–61
Takes part in various exhibitions at the March Gallery, an artists' co-operative on 10th Street in New York

1959
Lurie founds the March Group together with Sam Goodman and Stanley Fisher

1964
Death of his father, Ilja Lurje

1988
Publication of the NO!art anthology *PIN-UPS, EXCREMENT, PROTEST, JEW-ART*

1980s–1990s
Works on his memoirs, which have never been published, as well as on the novel *House of Anita,* which was published in 2010

2003
Publication of his poetry collection Boris Lurie: *Geschriebigtes / Gedichtigtes* for the exhibition held at the Buchenwald memorial site near Weimar in 1999

7 January 2008
Boris Lurie dies in New York

2010
Establishment of the Boris Lurie Art Foundation, dedicated to preserving Lurie's artistic legacy

Biografie

18. Juli 1924
Geburt in Leningrad als jüngstes von drei Kindern des jüdischen Ehepaars Ilja und Schaina Lurje

1925
Übersiedlung nach Riga, Besuch des deutschsprachigen Gymnasiums

Oktober/November 1941
Ghettoisierung von 30.000 jüdischen Bürgern Rigas

8. Dezember 1941
Ermordung von Mutter Schaina, Schwester Jeanna, Jugendliebe Ljuba und der Großmutter beim Massaker von Rumbula

1941–45
Arbeitslager Lenta und Salaspils sowie Konzentrationslager Stutthof und Buchenwald

11. April 1945
Befreiung aus dem Buchenwald-Außenlager Magdeburg Polte

1946
Auswanderung mit Vater Ilja nach New York, USA

1950
Erste Einzelausstellung in der Barbizon Gallery, New York

1958–61
Diverse Ausstellungen in der New Yorker March Gallery, einer Künstlerkooperative in der 10th Street.

1959
Gründung der NO!art-Bewegung, zusammen mit Sam Goodman und Stanley Fisher

1964
Tod des Vaters Ilja Lurje

1988
Publikation der NO!art-Anthologie *PIN-UPS – EXCREMENT-PROTEST – JEW-ART*

1990er Jahre
Arbeit an seinen bisher unveröffentlichten Memoiren sowie am Roman *House of Anita,* der 2010 erscheint

2003
Publikation des Gedichtbands Boris Lurie: *Geschriebigtes / Gedichtigtes,* entstanden zur Ausstellung in der Gedenkstätte Weimar-Buchenwald 1999

7. Januar 2008
Tod in New York

2010
Gründung der Boris Lurie Art Foundation, die sich seither um das künstlerische Vermächtnis Boris Luries kümmert

Boris Lurie in der / at the March Gallery, ca. / ca 1961

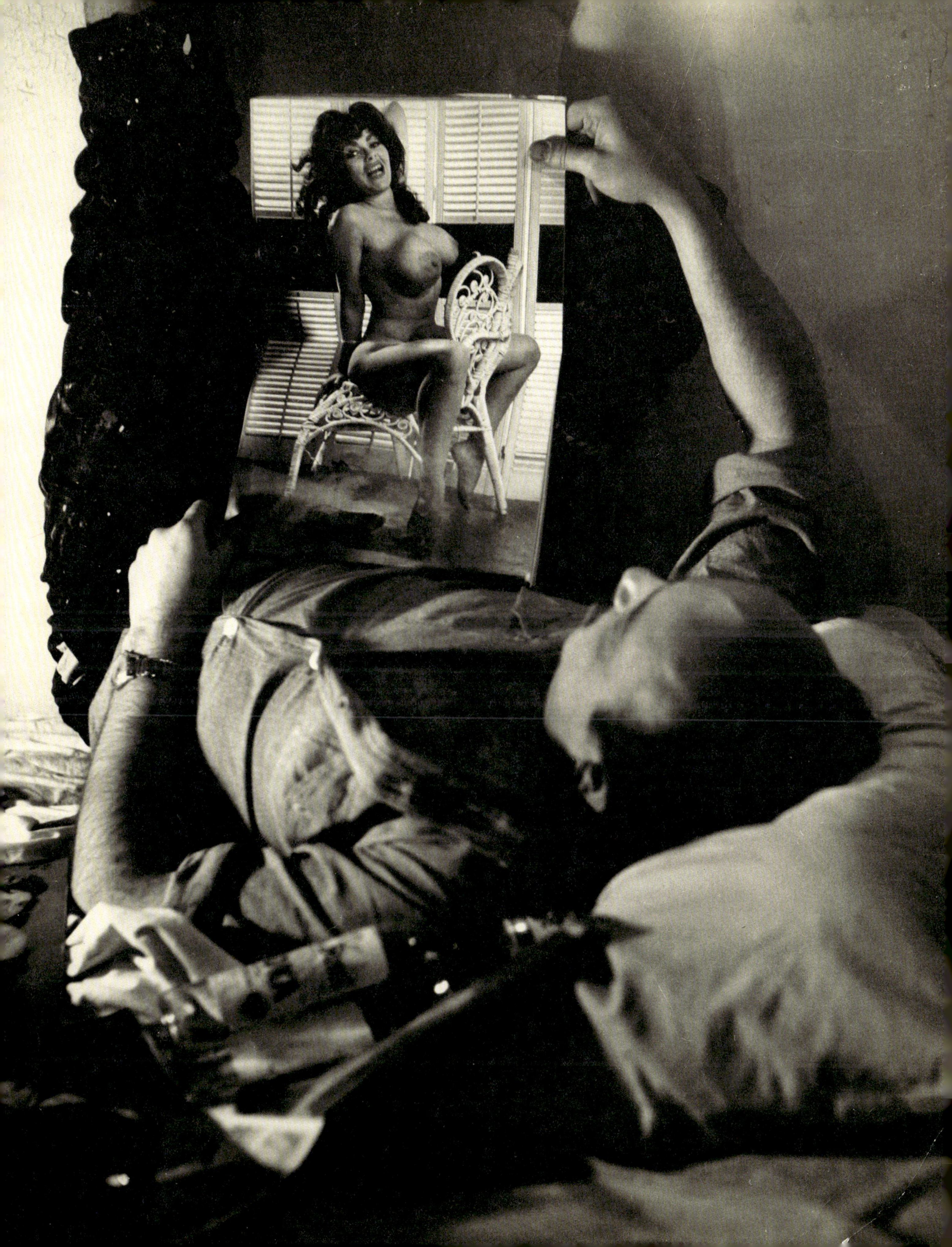

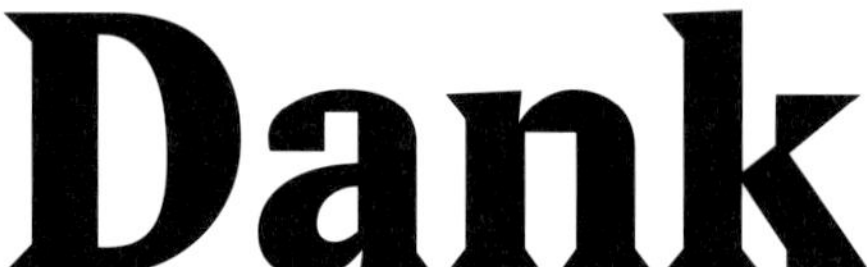

Die Ausstellung wäre nicht zustande gekommen ohne die Kooperation mit der Boris Lurie Art Foundation. Seit ihrer Gründung im Jahre 2009 setzt sich diese unermüdlich für Luries Legacy ein, ihrer Agilität verdankt Lurie posthum eine neue Sichtbarkeit, in naher Zukunft kann eine kleine Erfolgsgeschichte an weltweit stattfindenden Ausstellungsprojekten geschrieben werden. Auf ihr reichhaltig ausgestattetes und vorbildlich geführtes Archiv in New York konnten wir zurückgreifen, um die über 80 Werke von Boris Lurie auszuleihen. Ohne die große Professionalität der Mitarbeiter im Archiv der Stiftung, insbesondere Chris Shultz und Jessica Wallen, sowie des Anwalts Anthony Williams wäre ein solches Projekt nicht so reibungslos ermöglicht worden. Ihnen allen sei für ihre Hilfsbereitschaft und Großzügigkeit gedankt, insbesondere Gertrude Stein, Präsidentin der Stiftung. Sie war die damalige unerschrockene Galeristin, Tochter einer aktiven Anarchistin, die heute die Boris Lurie Art Foundation leitet und uns bei diesem Projekt mit großem Vertrauen generös unterstützt hat. Rafael und Miriam Vostell sind wir überaus verbunden, die als Ideenbringer auf uns zukamen und für ihre Vermittlung zwischen der Stiftung und unserem Haus sich überaus engagierten.
Für den Bereich „Around Lurie“ danken wir der Gedenkstätte in Lidice für ihre Leihgabe der wunderbaren Arbeit von Hans Peter Alvermann, *Warten auf Nürnberg II*. In diesem Zusammenhang soll auch René Block – langjähriger Mäzen unseres Hauses – erwähnt sein, der uns in unserem Vorhaben, Lurie auszustellen, sehr bekräftigte. In Lidice hat er mit herausragendem Engagement eine völlig neue Form des Gedenkens entwickelt.
Weiteren Leihgebern gebührt unser Dank – Herrn Markus Heinzelmann, Direktor des Museum Morsbroich in Leverkusen, wie auch dem Direktor des Ludwig-Forums Aachen, Andreas Beitin, für ihre unkomplizierte Abwicklung unserer kurzfristigen Anfragen. Dem Studio von Gustav Metzger sind wir dankbar für das wunderbare Werk des Künstlers, der auch aus Nürnberg stammte und dessen Familie, ähnlich der von Boris Lurie, Opfer des Holocausts wurde. Der Familie Vostell danken wir für ihre Leihgaben. Die *Olympia* von Gerhard Richter stammt aus der Sammlung des Ehepaars Böckmann, dem das Neue Museum zu großem Dank verpflichtet ist.
Dem gesamten Team im Neuen Museum Nürnberg danke ich für die stets kollegiale, zielorientierte Zusammenarbeit und die überaus große Einsatzbereitschaft – durch die mitunter selbst Unmögliches möglich wird. Herausheben möchte ich meinen Kollegen Thomas Heyden, Kurator der Ausstellung, der sich mit großer Empathie des Werkes von Boris Lurie angenommen hat. In diesem Zuge sei auch lobend das museumspädagogische Team unter Leitung von Claudia Marquardt genannt, das einen besonderen Beitrag in der Vermittlungsarbeit der Position Luries leistet. Unserer Kollegin, der Registrarin Susanne Teichmann, sei für ihren übermäßig großen Einsatz bei diesem Projekt sehr gedankt. Auch dem Grafiker des vorliegenden Buches, Timo Reger, möchte ich danken und seinen gewissenhaften wie auch gestalterisch feinfühligen Umgang mit den visuell herausfordernden Bildwelten wertschätzend anerkennen. Melitta Kliege sei sehr gedankt für ihre engagierte Unterstützung bei der Redaktion dieses Kataloges. Jedem einzelnen der Autoren – Eckhart Gillen, Peter Weibel, Thomas Heyden und Claudia Marquardt – danke ich für ihre ausgezeichneten Beiträge, sie sind eine große Bereicherung für den Katalog.

Acknowledgements

Without the partnership with the Boris Lurie Art Foundation, this exhibition would not have been possible. Since its foundation in 2009, the Foundation has worked tirelessly to promote Lurie's legacy, posthumously giving the artist a new visibility. In the near future, a small success story will be written, with exhibition projects taking place worldwide. We were able to draw on the riches of the Foundation's superbly managed archive in New York, from which we loaned more than 80 works for the exhibition. Without the professionalism of the archive's staff, especially Chris Shultz and Jessica Wallen, as well as lawyer Anthony Williams, such a project could never have run so smoothly. Our thanks to them for their helpfulness. We are especially grateful to Gertrude Stein. She was Lurie's dauntless gallerist, the daughter of an active anarchist, and in her current role as president of the Boris Lurie Art Foundation she gave us her trust and generously supported us in this project. We are much obliged to Rafael and Miriam Vostell who approached us with the idea for the show and established the contact between the museum and the Foundation.

For the "Around Lurie" section, we thank the Lidice Memorial for loaning us Hans Peter Alvermann's work, *Warten auf Nürnberg II*. In this context, we must also mention René Block – a longstanding patron of the museum – who strongly supported us in our plans for a Lurie exhibition. With his outstanding commitment in Lidice, he has developed an entirely new form of commemoration.

Our thanks also go to those who loaned other works – Markus Heinzelmann, director of Museum Morsbroich in Leverkusen, and Andreas Beitin, director of the Ludwig Forum in Aachen – for their uncomplicated processing of our requests at such short notice. We are grateful to the studio of Gustav Metzger for the wonderful work by the artist, who was originally from Nuremberg and whose family, like Boris Lurie's, also didn't survive the Holocaust. We thank the Vostell family for its loans. Gerhard Richter's *Olympia* is from the Böckmann Collection, to whom the Neues Museum owes an ongoing debt of gratitude.

I want to thank the entire team at Neues Museum Nürnberg for being such a pleasure to work with and for their commitment – which sometimes makes even the impossible possible. In particular, I thank my colleague Thomas Heyden, curator of this exhibition, who attended to Boris Lurie's work with great empathy. I would like to commend the educational team directed by Claudia Marquardt for its special contribution to communicating Lurie's position. For her major contribution to the project, I would like to thank our coordinator of loans, Susanne Teichmann. I would also like to thank the graphic designer Timo Reger and express my appreciation of his conscientious and sensitive treatment of these challenging visual materials. Many thanks to Melitta Kliege for her committed support during the editing process, and to the authors – Eckhart Gillen, Peter Weibel, Thomas Heyden, and Claudia Marquardt – for their outstanding contributions that have hugely enriched this catalogue.

Last, but not least, möchte ich der Künstlerpersönlichkeit meine große Verbundenheit aussprechen, insbesondere für ihre unbeugsame Haltung, die größten Respekt verdient. Mit Boris Lurie würdigen wir im Neuen Museum eine Position, die gegen das Vergessen sowie die Unterdrückung mit den Mitteln der Kunst ankämpfte. Er hat mit seinem künstlerischen Werk einen Beitrag zur Aufarbeitung der dunklen Geschichte hinterlassen, der seinesgleichen sucht. Wie kaum ein Zweiter hat sich der russisch-jüdische Künstler des visuellen Erbes des Holocausts angenommen, das schier unmöglich schien, in der bildenden Kunst behandelt werden zu können.

Eva Kraus, Direktorin Neues Museum Nürnberg

Last, but not least, I would like to express my attachment to the artist himself, in particular for an unbending stance that commands the greatest respect. With this exhibition, Neues Museum honors a man who fought against forgetting and oppression with the means of art. Boris Lurie's legacy is an unparalleled contribution to the process of coming to terms with history, dealing as it does with the visual legacy of the Holocaust, material it had previously seemed impossible to deal with in fine art.

Eva Kraus, Director, Neues Museum Nürnberg

Impressum
Imprint

Der vorliegende Band erscheint anlässlich der Ausstellung / The catalog is published on the occasion of the exhibition

Boris Lurie. Anti-Pop

Neues Museum – Staatliches Museum für Kunst und Design Nürnberg / State Museum for Art and Design Nuremberg

Eine Kooperation des Neuen Museums Nürnberg mit der / A cooperation of Neues Museum Nürnberg with Boris Lurie Art Foundation, New York

17. März – 18. Juni 2017 / 17 March – 18 June 2017

Katalog / Catalog

Redaktion / Editing
Thomas Heyden, Melitta Kliege, Eva Kraus

Übersetzung / Translation
Nicholas Grindell (Vorwort / Preface; Marquardt; Weibel; Biografie / Biography)
Jacqueline Todd (Gillen; Heyden)

Lektorat / Copy Editing
Martina Buder (deutsch)
Gaines Translations (English)

Konzept und Gestaltung / Concept and Design
Timo Reger

Fotografie / Photography
Annette Kradisch, Nürnberg (Neues Museum Nürnberg)

Bildbearbeitung / Image Editing
Alexander Kovacs, Nürnberg

Gesamtherstellung / Production
hofmann druck Nürnberg GmbH & Co. KG

Fotocredits / Photocredits
© Boris Lurie Art Foundation S./pp. 18, 21, 22, 25, 32, 33, 34, 36, 37, 41, 43, 45, 47, 49, 53, 54, 55, 64, 65, 70, 71, 75, 77, 81, 87, 88, 89, 90, 91, 94, 95, 103, 104, 105, 110, 111, 112, 113, 117, 118, 119, 120, 121, 122, 123, 124, 125, 126, 127, 128, 129, 151, 153, 157, 163, 165, 172, 173, 174, 176, 177, 181
Claudio Abate S./p. 197
Berlinische Galerie, Berlin S./p. 154
MOA I Museum oud Amelisweerd, Bunnik S./p. 143
Sam Goodman S./p. 209
© Betty Holiday S./p. 15
Ilija & Mangelos Foundation und / and Galerie Frank Elbaz S./p. 144
Yad Vashem Art Museum, Jerusalem S./p. 196
ZKM I Zentrum für Kunst und Medien, Karlsruhe S./p. 148
Otto Muehl-Archiv S./p. 151
Alexander Kovacs, Nürnberg S./pp. 35, 52, 59, 93, 121
Annette Kradisch, Nürnberg S./pp. 8–13, 28/29, 40, 46, 48, 60–63, 66, 67, 72, 73, 74, 78, 79, 80, 82, 83, 99, 101, 102, 106, 107, 116, 175, 181, 182, 183, 184, 185, 187, 192, 195, 200/201
© Yale University Art Gallery, New Heaven S./p. 151
© The Estate of Eduardo Paolozzi, Tate, London S./p. 151
Joseph Schneberg S./pp. 18, 22, 25
Süddeutsche Zeitung Photo S./p. 147
Polish Army Museum, Warsaw S./p. 145
© Photo-Graphik-Witting / Hundertwasser Archiv, Wien (mit freundlicher Genehmigung von Bazon Brock) S./p. 144

Bibliografische Information der Deutschen Nationalbibliothek
Die Deutsche Nationalbibliothek verzeichnet diese Publikation in der Deutschen Nationalbibliografie; detaillierte bibliografische Daten sind im Internet über http://dnb.de abrufbar.

Bibliographic information published by the Deutsche Nationalbibliothek
The Deutsche Nationalbibliothek lists this publication in the Deutsche Nationalbibliografie; detailed bibliographic data are available in the Internet at http://dnb.de.

ISBN 978-3-903153-52-3

www.vfmk.org
hello@vfmk.org

Printed in Germany

Ausstellung / Exhibition

Kuratoren / Curators
Thomas Heyden, Eva Kraus

Ausstellungsgestaltung / Exhibition Design
Kilian Fabich

Registrar
Susanne Teichmann

Ausstellungstechnik / Exhibition technicians
Werner Henne, Jutta Birle, Jürgen Schuster

Presse und Öffentlichkeitsarbeit / Press and PR
Eva Martin, Lioba Schroeder, Mario Rau, Csilla Wenczel

Kunstvermittlung / Education
Claudia Marquardt, Ulrike Rathjen

Restauratorische Betreuung / Conservation
Eva Pridöhl, Nürnberg

Dank an die Leihgeber der Ausstellung / Special thanks to the lenders who were so generous to loan the works for the exhibition.

Mitarbeiter / Staff

Direktorin / Director
Eva Kraus

Sekretariat – Assistenz der Direktorin / Secretariat – Assistant to the director
Andrea Kriegsch

Konservatoren / Curators
Thomas Heyden, Melitta Kliege

Registrar
Susanne Teichmann

Sammlungsdokumentation / Documentation and Collections Management
Birgit Suk

Presse und Öffentlichkeitsarbeit / Press and PR
Eva Martin, Lioba Schroeder, Mario Rau, Jennifer Kraus, Csilla Wenczel

Kunstvermittlung / Education
Claudia Marquardt, Ulrike Rathjen

Ausstellungstechnik / Exhibition technicians
Werner Henne, Jutta Birle, Jürgen Schuster

Verwaltung / Administration
Angela Götz, Lioba Schroeder

Kasse / Cash desk
Elisabeth Hager, Csilla Wenczel

Haustechnik / Facility Management
Alois Kaufmann, Erich Dietz

Neues Museum
Staatliches Museum für
Kunst und Design Nürnberg
Luitpoldstraße 5
90402 Nürnberg
Deutschland / Germany
Tel. +49-911-2402020
www.nmn.de

Boris Lurie Art Foundation, New York

Präsidentin / President
Gertrude Stein

Vorstandsvorsitzender / Chairman of the Board
Anthony Williams

Wissenschaftliche Mitarbeiter / Scientific staff
Chris Shultz, Jessica Wallen

Berater der Boris Lurie Art Foundation / Adviser
Rafael Vostell

BORIS LURIE
ART FOUNDATION